Gettysburg
An Alternate History

*This book is fondly dedicated to my father-in-law, Richard T. Foley, and his grand-
father, Private James T. Faulkner, 6th Virginia Cavalry*

Books by Peter G. Tsouras

Disaster at D-Day: The Germans Defeat the Allies, June 1944
Changing Orders: The Evolution of the World's Armies, 1945
to the Present
Gettysburg: An Alternate History
The Great Patriotic War: An Illustrated History of Total War
Warlords of the Ancient Americas: Mesoamerica

Editor
The Anvil of War
Fighting in Hell
The U.S. Army: A Dictionary
Warriors' Words: A Dictionary of Military Quotations

Contributor
The Hitler Options
Military Lessons of the Gulf War
Napoleon: The Final Verdict
The Soviet Navy: Strength and Liabilities
The Soviet Naval Threat to Europe: Military and
Political Dimensions

Gettysburg

AN ALTERNATE HISTORY

Peter G. Tsouras

Skyhorse Publishing

Visit our website at www.skyhorsepublishing.com.

10 9 8 7 6 5 4 3 2 1

Library of Congress Cataloging-in-Publication Data is available on file.

Cover design by Brian Peterson

Print ISBN: 978-1-63450-532-1

Printed in the United States of America

Contents

		Page
List of illustrations and maps		7
Acknowledgements		9
Prologue		11
Chapter 1	1st July 1863: 'The Devil's to pay'	13
Chapter 2	1st July 1863: 'It's my turn to take them now'	32
Chapter 3	1st–2nd July 1863: Marching through the moonbeams	47
Chapter 4	1st–2nd July 1863: 'General Lee wants that hill taken'	61
Chapter 5	2nd July 1863: 'They will soon stir up a fight'	84
Chapter 6	2nd July 1863: 'Remember, at all costs!'	108
Chapter 7	2nd July 1863: 'There is a price for leadership'	126
Chapter 8	2nd July 1863: Dominus noster Jesus Christus vos absolvat	165
Chapter 9	2nd July 1863: 'Ten G-d d——d minutes'	188
Chapter 10	2nd July 1863: 'I held you long enough'	215
Chapter 11	2nd–3rd July 1863: 'General, we have got them nicked'	234
Chapter 12	3rd July 1863: 'My men will stay!'	248
Chapter 13	3rd July 1863: Longstreet's Charge	273
Chapter 14	3rd July 1863: 'My men, follow me!'	302
Epilogue		314
Postscript	Battles and controversies	318
	A note on the footnotes	320

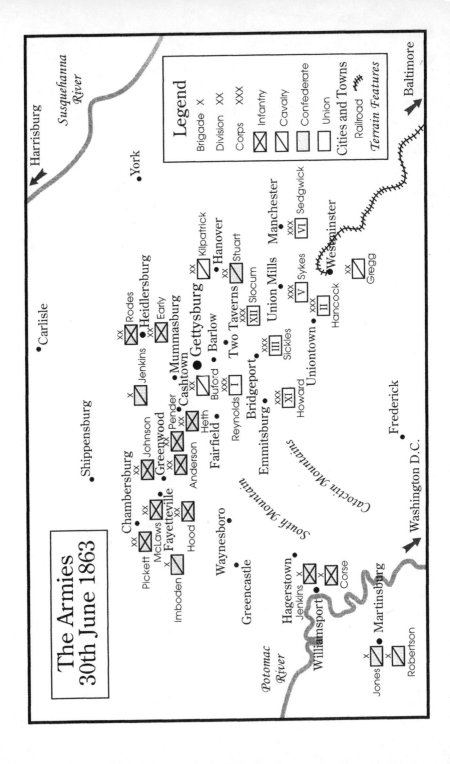

The Armies
30th June 1863

List of illustrations and maps

ILLUSTRATIONS: Pages 129–44

General Robert E. Lee.

Major General George Meade.

Lieutenant General James Longstreet.

Major General Winfield Scott Hancock.

Major General J.E.B. Stuart.

Brigadier General John Buford.

Brigadier General Henry J. Hunt.

Major General Daniel E. Sickles.

Buford's cavalry opposing the Confederate advance on Gettysburg.

I Corps' 2nd Maine Light Battery.

XI Corps' Battery G, 4th US Artillery.

The Union I Corps makes a stand on Seminary Ridge.

Brockenbrough's Brigade attacks the McPherson Farm.

Colonel Hiram Berdan's 1st US Sharpshooters in Pitzer's Woods.

Major-General Jubal Early.

Major-General Abner Doubleday.

Major-General Oliver P. Howard rallies XI Corps on Cemetery Hill.

Union dead of III Corps.

Captain John Bigelow's 9th Battery, Massachusetts Light Artillery.

Brigadier General Joseph B. Kershaw.

Major General John Sedgwick.

Major General John Bell Hood.

Colonel Joshua Lawrence Chamberlain.

Fourteen-year-old Willie Johnson.

Colonel Porter Alexander's artillery of 1st Corps goes into action.

The great cavalry fight at Barlow on 2nd July.

Union cavalry under Brigadier General Elon Farnsworth.

The 1st Minnesota charges.

Early's attack on Cemetery Hill almost washes over Rickett's Battery.

Brigadier General Montgomery D. Corse.

Brigadier General Micah Jenkins.

Major General George Pickett.

Captain Ulric Dahlgren.

Brigadier General Louis Armistead.

First Lieutenant Frank A. Haskell.

Widow Leister's house behind Cemetery Hill.

Confederate soldiers of Pickett's Division sheltering in Seminary Woods.

Stannard's 2nd Vermont Brigade of the Army of the Potomac's I Corps.

The arrival of Henry Hunt's 'Ghost Trains' of the Reserve Artillery.

Arnold's Battery A, 1st Rhode Island Light Artillery.

Armistead's breakthrough of II Corps' position on Cemetery Ridge.

Sedgwick's grand counter-attack with the entire Union center and reserve.

MAPS

1	The Armies, 30th June 1863	6
2	Stuart's ride around the Yankees, 28th June–1st July 1863	10
3	Johnson's night attack, 1st–2nd July 1863	71
4	The Longstreet–Lee plan of attack, 2nd July 1863	100
5	Holding the Taneytown Road, 2nd July 1863	145
6	Sickles turns the Confederate flank, 2nd July 1863	152
7	Longstreet unhinges the Union left, 2nd July 1863	218
8	The Armies, 3rd July 1863	263
9	Longstreet's Charge, 3rd July 1863	280
10	Final phase of the attack on the center, 3rd July 1863	306
11	Sedgwick's counter-attack, 3rd July 1863	311

Acknowledgements

This book on America's own greatest ever (and still controversial) battle could not have been written without the generous help and advice of a number of friends. Foremost among them is Lieutenant Colonel Jay Zollitsch who tramped with me along Plum Run between Big Round Top and Bushman's Woods and pulled me out of the marsh. Checking each other for ticks was male bonding at its best.

The book originated with an idea from my British publisher Lionel Leventhal, and his Greenhill Books publication of my alternate history *Disaster at D-Day*. Alternate history for Greenhill has to be entirely within the bounds of the genuinely possible, and therefore accurate in all technical details. To this end my British publisher arranged a team of American specialists to check through what this American, who has studied the battle of Gettysburg at length and walked the battlefield many times, had written.

As a result I owe a thousand thanks to David Martin, author of *Gettysburg July 1*, to Kenneth Gallagher, and to another military history publisher, Bob Pigeon, for their encouragement and numerous specific comments that added luster to the book. To Lieutenant Colonel (Ret) Wayne Wachsmuth, of the Gettysburg guides, my thanks are unbounded, for many invaluable observations. I especially appreciated his reminder of Gettysburg's particular version of the 'fog of war': the rolling clouds of black powder smoke that hung over the fighting in the hot, humid, mizzling weather of the three epic days at Gettysburg. Any errors or misinterpretations remains stubbornly my own.

I thank Edward Longacre for generously sharing his notes on the adventures of Captain Ulric Dahlgren, and Glenn Hicks whose captivating stage interpretation of James Longstreet was an inspiration. Special thanks are due to Dr Mary A. Wu and Dr Lynn V. Doering for their careful explanation, to this layman, of the nature and stages of a heart attack.

I am also grateful to Ian Heath, who edited the manuscript with skill and style.

Above all, my thanks go to my wife, Patty, for offering to spend our anniversary walking over the battlefield one last time – no greater love!

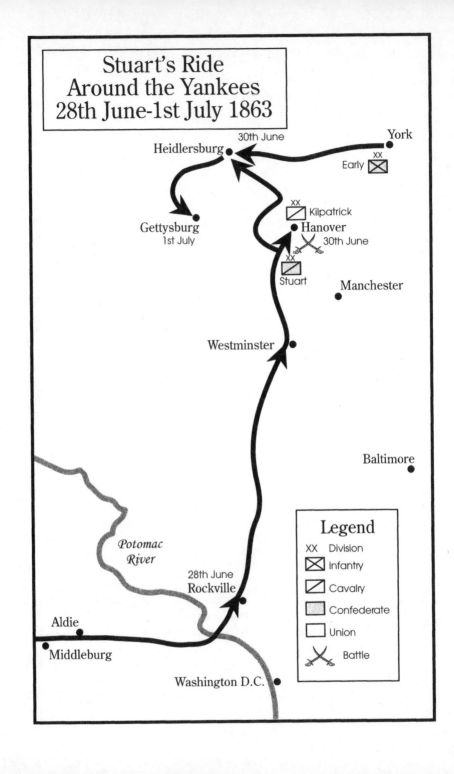

Stuart's Ride
Around the Yankees
28th June-1st July 1863

York

Early

30th June

Heidlersburg

Kilpatrick

Hanover
30th June

Gettysburg
1st July

Stuart

Manchester

Westminster

Baltimore

Potomac
River

Legend

XX   Division

Infantry

Cavalry

Confederate

Union

Battle

28th June
Rockville

Aldie

Middleburg

Washington D.C.

Prologue

'Rally them, Blackford!' J.E.B. Stuart laughed and waved his saber at his aide. The 2nd North Carolina Cavalry had just burst into Hanover, Pennsylvania, and had just burst back out with Union cavalry in hot pursuit, leaving Stuart and Blackford alone directly in the enemy's path. The Carolinians were long past rallying, but Stuart could not resist tweaking danger with a good-natured joke as he got his aide's attention. He pulled his mare, Virginia, towards a low gap in the rough hedge lining the road and took it at a gallop, with Blackford right behind.

They alighted in a field of tall timothy grass barely ten paces ahead of an enemy flanking party, who called out to them to surrender. The two raced their thoroughbreds across the field, with the pursuing Union cavalrymen firing their pistols as fast as they could cock them. The grass was so high that Stuart and Blackford did not see the fifteen-foot ravine until their horses were only a few strides away. The animals quickened their pace for a leap and were up, sailing through the air. Blackford turned at that moment to see Stuart and Virginia poised in mid-air, the indelible vision of a lifetime, the magnificent Southern war-horse and the beau saber of the Confederacy. Then the spell broke as both horses thudded down on the other side, with feet to spare. The Yankees pulled short so quickly that they barely avoided pitching into the ravine.

Stuart rode up a hill to direct a battery against the enemy, cavalrymen of Judson Kilpatrick's division. Standing there on horseback with his silk-lined cape and black-plumed hat, he was hard to miss, and it took only a few minutes for three mounted couriers to arrive with a dispatch for him. 'From General Early, Sir.' Stuart read the hastily scribbled note, from the commander of the lead division of Dick Ewell's 2nd Corps, the spearhead of the invasion of the North. Lee had informed Ewell that the enemy was moving north and directed him to concentrate the corps on the west side of South Mountain.[1] Then came the direct reference to Stuart. His heart quickened. He worshipped Lee, who had practically adopted him at West Point, and with whom he had ridden as an aide to seize John Brown by the scruff of the neck at Harper's Ferry. 'General Lee also instructs me to find you and

---

[1] Jubal A. Early, *Jubal Early's Memoirs: Autobiographical Sketch of the War Between the States* (J.B. Lippincott, Philadelphia, 1912) p. 263.

direct you to follow my division without delay.'[2] It was dated 29th June, at York. It was now late morning on the 30th.

Stuart chewed on the message only briefly. His anticipated rendezvous with Early at York was off; something must be brewing if Lee was ordering a concentration much further south in Pennsylvania than previously planned. Stuart's main concern was to break off this spreading battle and slip north-west around Hanover to follow Early. As he studied the map, the little town of Gettysburg drew his practised eye. Roads radiated from it in every direction. It was a natural strategic communications hub. Lee was concentrating around it to the north and west. He grinned. Lee knew what he was doing, of course. With any luck he could be in Gettysburg tomorrow, 1st July.[3]

---

[2]* H.B. McClellan, 'Stuart in the Gettysburg Campaign', *Military Annals of the Confederacy* (hereafter cited as *MAC*), vol.XIV (1879) p.37.
[3]* J.E.B. Stuart, *Riding Around the Yankees: the War Memoirs of a Southern Cavalryman* (D. Appleton, New York, 1877) p.332.

CHAPTER 1

1st July 1863
'The Devil's to pay'

Mid-morning, McPherson's Ridge

They arrived just in time. The 1st Brigade of the 1st Division of I Corps of the Army of the Potomac, the men of the famed Iron Brigade, heard the noise of battle west of Gettysburg and stretched out their marching stride behind the 2nd Brigade to hurry to the fight as the band struck up their war-song, *The Girl I Left Behind Me*.

Ahead of them, Brigadier General John Buford's 1st Cavalry Division had played itself out to breaking point holding off the Confederate infantry brigades of Henry Heth's division to the west of the town. All morning Buford had held them, sending messenger after messenger to speed up the arrival of I Corps. Now, as the enemy seemed ready to swamp him, he looked down from his observation point in the steeple of the Lutheran Seminary and saw the dapper Major General John Reynolds ride up with his staff, the long blue columns of I Corps in the not-too-far distance. Buford virtually flew down the steps. Almost teasingly, Reynolds asked, 'What is the matter, John?'

'The Devil's to pay,' he replied.

There was a quick handshake, and then Reynolds, with Buford behind him, raced up the stairs two at a time. From the steeple it took him only moments to survey the battlefield and make his decision. Reynolds turned to Captain Stephen W. Weld. 'Ride at once with utmost speed to General Meade. Tell him the enemy are advancing in strong force, and that I fear they will get to the heights beyond the town before I can. I will fight them inch by inch, and if driven into the town, I will barricade the streets and hold them as long as possible.'[1] Turning to Buford, he added, 'I hope you can hold on until my corps arrives.'

'I reckon I can.'

They did not have long to wait. Brigadier James Wadsworth's 1st Division was already passing through Gettysburg. In the lead was Brigadier General Lysander Cutler's 2nd Brigade, coming out of the town onto the Chambersburg or Cashtown Pike. Reynolds had seen the importance of this terrain and had

---

[1] Stephen M. Weld, *Diary and Letters of Stephen Minot Weld, 1861–1865* (Riverside Press, Cambridge, Massachusetts, 1913) p. 230.

already posted Captain James Hall's Battery B, 2nd Maine Light Artillery, just
south of the railroad cut which paralleled the Pike. Reynolds told Hall to
'damage the artillery to the greatest possible extent, and keep their fire from our
infantry until they are deployed.'[2] Cutler was just arriving when Wadsworth, at
Reynolds' direction, ordered him to send three of his five regiments north of the
railroad cutting and two south of it to support Hall's Battery.

The 2nd Brigade quickly took up its position on the northern extension of
the ridge. The 56th Pennsylvania fired a volley into the 55th North Carolina as
soon as it showed itself, the first shots fired by Union infantry in the battle. Two
of the 55th's color guard fell. The Carolinians fired in turn, bringing down
Cutler and two of his staff.

The 1st 'Iron' Brigade double-timed onto the field to the left of Cutler's two
regiments south of the railroad cut. The band of the 6th Wisconsin changed its
tune to *The Campbells are Coming*. They were an awesome sight that morning,
the 1,900 men of the brigade in their blue dress frock-coats and black Hardee
hats turned up on the side and adorned with blue ribbons, an elegant contrast
to the fatigue blouse and kepi worn by the rest of the army. But it was not for
their appearance that both armies respected them. They had earned their pride
of place with iron resolve and a lethal combativeness. They figured that if the
army was stretched in a single line they would have the place of honor on the
extreme right. Few could be found who would disagree. Such was their pride in
themselves that when Major General Abner Doubleday exhorted them to fight
to the last, they responded: 'If we can't hold it, where will you find men who
can?'[3]

Now they flowed onto the field, a powerful killing-machine of five veteran
western regiments – the 2nd and 7th Wisconsin, the 19th Indiana, the 24th
Michigan, and the 6th Wisconsin. The gallant Reynolds rode down to post the
2nd Wisconsin, then moved on to the next regiment. He had not been in the
line for ten minutes when, turning in the saddle, he fell with a bullet in the back
of the head – whether from a Confederate sniper or a stray friendly bullet has
never been ascertained. The Iron Brigade's commander, Brigadier General
Solomon Meredith, pressed on and took his men directly into battle against
Brigadier General James Archer's brigade in the woods along Willoughby Run.

Archer was about to pay the price for his superiors' cavalier approach to their
orders. Lee had specifically directed that no element of the army was to bring on
a battle until the whole army was up. But Archer's division commander, Major

---

[2] James A. Hall to John Bachelder, 27th February 1867, Bachelder Papers, New Hampshire
Historical Society, Concord, New Hampshire (hereafter cited as Bachelder Papers).
[3] *The War of the Rebellion, A Compilation of the Official Records of the Union and Confederate Armies*
(hereafter cited as *OR*), vol. XXVII, part I (Government Printing Office, Washington DC, 1889)
p.244.

General Henry Heth, and the 3rd Corps commander, Lieutenant General A.P. Hill, had done just that this morning. Hill's corps was concentrated between Cashtown and Gettysburg when Heth got it into his head that there was a large store of shoes in Gettysburg, sorely needed by his troops. He knew that Early had marched through the town already; how he could have expected even a single pair of shoes to have escaped Early's flinty thoroughness no-one knows. The skirmishers of Brigadier General James Pettigrew's brigade had brushed with Buford's cavalry the day before, but so powerful was the lure of shoes that Heth insisted on believing they were only militia, or, at Hill's suggestion, at best a small cavalry detachment of observation. When Heth asked if Hill had any objection to his advancing, the latter had replied airily, 'None whatsoever'. Pettigrew became almost desperate to convince Heth and Hill of the risk, and produced an officer who had served with Hill, Captain Louis Young, to explain that there was more than a detachment of observation in the town, and that they were trained troops, not militia. Young's warnings too were brushed aside. Pettigrew then tried to alert Archer, whose turn it was, in the rotation of brigades, to be first into Gettysburg, but he too was caught up in the mood of optimism. Young commented: 'This spirit of disbelief had taken such hold that I doubt if any of the commanders of brigades, except General Pettigrew, believed that we were marching into battle, a weakness on their part which rendered them unprepared for what was about to happen.'

At first the fighting was between Archer's light skirmish lines and Buford's pickets, an affair which seemed to confirm to Heth that he faced minimal opposition. By the time he leisurely approached McPherson's Ridge, he found a strong Union battle-line running along Willoughby Run, toward which the skirmishing was drawing his command. At this moment he should have broken off the fight pursuant to Lee's orders. He did not. Instead he deployed the rest of his division from column, a time-consuming evolution that ate up the clock as Reynolds rushed his corps to Buford's aid.

Archer's Brigade had crossed Willoughby Run and was moving up McPherson's Ridge with Brigadier General Joseph Davis' brigade on his left. Almost effortlessly, Buford's cavalry pulled back as Reynolds' two infantry brigades took their places. Almost immediately the Confederates felt the difference. The cry went up from Archer's ranks: 'Here are those damned black-hat fellers gain . . . 'Taint no militia – that's the Army of the Potomac.' Both sides fired together at forty yards with deadly impact, and it was here that Reynolds fell. But Meredith was quicker than Archer and outnumbered him three to two as well. He overlapped Archer's right with the 19th Indiana and 24th Michigan. Almost automatically they wrapped themselves around Archer's flank and seared it with enfilade fire. The 2nd and 7th Wisconsin drove the rest of Archer's men down through Willoughby Run and into the woods to the west. Although it was hurt itself, the Iron Brigade had wrecked Archer's Brigade and taken many prisoners, including Archer himself.

To the north of the railroad cut, Davis' Mississippi and North Carolina regiments were severely handling Cutler's men. Flanked by the 55th North Carolina, these three regiments broke and ran back to Seminary Ridge. The Confederates pursued as quickly and soon flanked Hall's Battery, which had to withdraw, leaving one gun behind. In response to a request for help, Doubleday sent the 6th Wisconsin forward at a run. It came up on the fence along the Pike and immediately fired into the flank of Davis' regiments. Instinctively seeking shelter from this enfilade, the nearest Confederates – the 2nd and part of the 42nd Mississippi – rushed into the railroad cut. Cutler's other two regiments, the 84th and 95th New York, immediately changed front, and rushed to the fence along the Pike on the left of the 6th Wisconsin. Davis ordered his men out of the cut under the 55th's covering fire, but it was too late. The cut was too deep to fire from, and the Mississippians did not control either approach into it. Their delay was fatal. The 6th's commander, Lieutenant Colonel Rufus R. Dawes, immediately saw the opportunity. Rushing over to the 95th's commander, he shouted, 'We must charge!' The major replied, 'Charge it is!' Together they shouted down the firing line, 'Forward, charge!'[4]

The North Carolinians on the other side of the cut fired into the oncoming Federals so furiously that their position could only be distinguished by their battle-flag, waving over a cloud of black powder smoke. The 6th lost over 160 men covering just 175 paces. When they reached the packed cutting, Dawes peered over into it and demanded a surrender, or he would fire. Incredibly he got it. Over 200 men surrendered. However, a significant number of the Mississippians would have nothing of it and fought their way out, and some vicious fighting took place for the colors of the 2nd Mississippi even after the mass surrender. A soldier of the 6th, Sergeant James 'Mickey' Sullivan, was in the middle of the confusion: 'Some of the Johnnies threw down their guns and surrendered. Some would fire and then throw down their guns and cry, I surrender, and some of them broke for the rear. I jumped into the railroad cut and a rebel officer handed me his sword and passed through the cut with the intention of stopping the Johnnies, who were limbering to the rear.'[5] The battle that Lee had not wanted had arrived with a crash, and first laurels had already gone to the enemy.

[4] Rufus Dawes, *Service with the Sixth Wisconsin Volunteers* (E.R. Alderman & Sons, Marietta, Ohio, 1890) pp.167–8.
[5] William J.K. Beaudot and Lance J. Herdegen, eds., *An Irishman in the Iron Brigade: The Civil War Memoirs of James P. Sullivan, Sergt., Company K, 6th Wisconsin Volunteers* (Fordham University Press, New York, 1993) pp.95–6.

'I cannot think what has become of Stuart'

11:00 AM, outside Cashtown

General Robert E. Lee struck his gloved fist into the palm of his other hand. 'I have been kept in the dark ever since crossing the Potomac. Stuart's disappearance has materially hampered the movements and disorganized the plans of this campaign.'[6]

Already he could hear the heavy thunder of artillery in the direction of Gettysburg. The members of his traveling party maintained an embarrassed silence. Lee's outburst of irritation was rare outside his immediate staff. For it to be directed at the young general whom Lee cherished almost like a son was even more menacing. 'I expected Stuart to have reported to me here in Pennsylvania. I am troubled that his cavalry forces were not between us and those people, as I expected them to be.'[7] An hour earlier he had summoned Major General R. H. Anderson, whose division was resting near Cashtown. Anderson was alarmed to see the army commander so 'depressed and disturbed'. He was even more surprised to hear Lee declare, 'I cannot think what has become of Stuart; I ought to have heard from him long before now. He may have met with disaster, but I hope not. In the absence of reports from him, I am in ignorance as to what we have in front of us here. It may be the whole Federal army, or it may be only a detachment. If it is the whole Federal force we must fight a battle here; if we do not gain a ... those defiles and gorges through which we passed this morning will shelter us from disaster.'[8]

Lee was still fuming from the shock of learning from one of Lieutenant General James Longstreet's spies on 28th June that the Army of the Potomac was fast approaching from the south-east. Prior to this, since the Army of Northern Virginia had begun its invasion of the North two weeks before, he had heard nothing of the enemy, and had presumed it was because they had not left Virginia. Surely the ever-vigilant Stuart, his favorite, would have informed him had they moved? But no word had come from the brilliant young commander of Lee's cavalry division, who had been practically a member of his family while he served as Superintendent at West Point. Young Stuart had been at his side as his aide when Lee commanded the marine battalion which had stormed Harper's Ferry in 1860 and captured the incendiary John Brown. Once war had come, Stuart's genius and dash as a cavalry commander had earned him respect and glory. It was his ability to screen Lee's army and keep him advised

[6] A.L. Long, *The Memoirs of Robert E. Lee: His Military and Personal History* (J.M. Stoddart & Co., New York, 1886) p.275.

[7] James P. Smith, 'With Stonewall Jackson', *Southern Historical Society Papers* (cited hereafter as *SHSP*), vol.XLIII (1920) p.56.

[8] James Longstreet, 'Lee in Pennsylvania', *The Annals of the War* (Morningside Press, Dayton, Ohio, 1988) p.420.

of the Army of the Potomac's movements that had played a large part in Lee's string of glittering victories.

Now something had gone terribly wrong. Though the meaning of the last conferences in Virginia as the invasion of the North began must have seemed clear enough to both Lee and Stuart, unspoken assumptions, and the inconvenience of the enemy's interference, had upset Lee's plans. Stuart, backed by James Longstreet, Lee's senior and most trusted corps commander, had recommended he ride around the Army of the Potomac. This would accomplish several vital tasks: it would disrupt the enemy's communications with Washington; it would threaten Washington itself, and so divert attention from Lee's army moving northward west of the Blue Ridge; and it would gather much-needed supplies. Lee was certain that the enemy would sooner or later realize he had slipped away north and begin to follow. What he did not appear to plan for was that the enemy might move fast enough to totally interpose himself between Stuart and Lieutenant General Richard Ewell's 2nd Corps, the lead element of the army already marching through Maryland. Lee subsequently notified Stuart that he was to make contact with Major General Jubal Early's lead division of 2nd Corps as far north as York, Pennsylvania. Stuart could only have concluded that York was the first concentration point of the army.

At the same time, Lee assumed that Stuart would be in constant communication with him after he rode around the lumbering Army of the Potomac. For Lee, Stuart himself rather than the cavalry of the Army of Northern Virginia embodied its intelligence gathering arm. For his part, Stuart was satisfied that Lee had adequate cavalry to screen the army and report on the enemy, having been directed by Lee to leave him with sufficient for the task. Although Stuart was riding with his three best brigades, totaling 5500 men, two brigades comprising over 2700 men were left under the command of the senior brigade commander, Brigadier General Beverly Robertson, to guard the southern gaps in the Blue Ridge as the army marched north, and then to guard the army's flank and rear. Although many, including Stuart, considered Robertson to be woefully lacking in the dash and character needed in such a command, the bane of seniority had left it in his hands; Stuart had hoped that Brigadier General William 'Grumble' Jones, who commanded the other brigade, and was considered the finest outpost officer in the army, would keep Robertson on the right path. Another brigade of 1300 men under Brigadier General Albert Jenkins screened Ewell's advance, and a fifth brigade (Brigadier General John Imboden's), 2200-strong, but not subordinate to Stuart, guarded the army's left flank. Stuart therefore concluded, not unnaturally, that the 6200 cavalry and more that he had left with Lee were surely enough to provide the army's eyes and ears until he rejoined it around York. In addition he had taken pains to ensure that Robertson would fulfil Lee's immediate needs for cavalry. Should the enemy in his front disappear, he was to ride north after the army, place himself under Longstreet's orders, and protect the right and rear of Longstreet's 1st Corps, the last in column, while Stuart himself was detached.

These plans started to go awry almost immediately. The Army of the Potomac began to move with unexpected energy, its commander, Major General Joseph Hooker, setting it in motion to move north and cross the Potomac. It was part of this vast, undulating blue column that blocked Stuart's easiest route north, forcing him to move considerably further eastward to cross the Potomac. Consequently he did not cross the river until 27th June, long after much of the enemy was already across. Instead of marching by way of Frederick and Emmitsburg, Maryland, which Lee had apparently expected, Stuart took a route at least twenty miles to the east, to more thoroughly frighten and threaten Washington and Baltimore. On the 27th, near Rockville, outside of the capital, he fell upon a rich prize, a train of 150 new wagons drawn by fine mule teams and stuffed with supplies for the Army of the Potomac. With a whoop his men fell upon the wagons and in a fox-hunt style chase netted all but twenty-five. Immensely pleased with himself, Stuart carefully shepherded this prize, the contents of which would feed 5000 men for a week. It was exactly the kind of trophy Lee had specifically asked for. And for his men, the raid seemed to be another page in the unfolding Stuart legend. Every day was a hard ride, but the countryside was rich, the girls pretty, and victory always waved her garland in Stuart's favor whenever the Yankees showed their faces.

Unbeknownst to either Stuart or Lee, however, the Army of the Potomac was stealing a march on them. On the day Stuart took his wagons, President Lincoln relieved Hooker, tarnished by defeat at Chancellorsville in May and distrusted for his politicking. He was replaced by the dour but decisive and able Major General George G. Meade, former V Corps commander. Almost immediately the army quickened its march north, along the very Frederick–Emmitsburg route Lee had outlined for Stuart. The couriers that Stuart began sending west to find Lee beyond the Blue Ridge never made it through the mass of blue moving north, which filled every parallel route.

By the 29th, Lee was becoming nervous. There was an increasingly disquieting silence instead of the normal flow of information he had come to expect from Stuart. Even the couriers that Stuart had dispatched to inform Lee of his longer than expected detour around the enemy had not arrived. He began asking every officer whom he met whether he had word of Stuart, exhibiting the lack of composure that so struck these men. Strangely, he had not thought to recall Robertson's two brigades to supply the want of intelligence of the enemy, and Robertson did not use his own initiative to rectify this oversight, instead clinging to his original orders after both armies had long-since passed his position.

Though Lee continued to hope that Stuart would appear at any moment, he prudently began to rein in his army, which was spread out in line of march all the way from Harper's Ferry, Virginia, to the outskirts of Harrisburg, Pennsylvania. Longstreet's scout had alerted him that all seven infantry corps of the Army of the Potomac were on the march north directly to his east, apparently in a far more compact body than his own army. But he still had time to draw it together. So orders went out to all commands to concentrate in the vicinity of Cashtown just east of South Mountain. Lee had remembered Robertson's cavalry brigades at last and directed him to join the army immediately. His couriers also found Early in York, and Early passed the word to find Stuart.

Stuart had kept his brigades moving through the night of the 30th; the continuous movement north was draining the last reserves of his command. The mules from the captured wagons were in the worst shape, in frantic agony from not having been fed or watered for days. Breaking contact with an unusually aggressive Kilpatrick had proved easier said than done, and before long Stuart had a full-blown battle on his hands as the Union cavalry struck hard at his flanks. He could have slipped away more easily but for the train of captured wagons, but a primary objective of the Army of Northern Virginia's invasion of the North had been to strip away enough supplies from Pennsylvania's bounty to supply the army for the rest of the year, in order to spare threadbare Virginia another year's support of two armies. A second objective had been to draw the Army of the Potomac away from Virginia, and Stuart was more than aware of their success on this score: he had just been fighting a healthy part of that army. His rearguard had also reported the approach of the enemy XII Corps, likewise drawn north by Lee's invasion. The direct route to Cashtown would take him through Gettysburg, but with XII Corps behind him they could easily be across that route already. Instead, as darkness fell, he had his three cavalry brigades and captured wagons safely out of contact with Kilpatrick and marching northwest to Heidlersberg behind Early's division. The route was almost thirty miles long, but it would still get him to Cashtown or Gettysburg by the morning of 1st July at the latest.

Had his optimistic calculations proved right, he would have run into exactly the same problem that now confronted Longstreet as he attempted to concentrate his 1st Corps near Cashtown as Lee had directed. Longstreet always planted his corps headquarters within walking distance of Lee's own. He had a particularly close, professional relationship with Lee, and in effect served as the army's second-in-command. On the morning of 1st July he accompanied Lee towards Cashtown as the 1st Corps marched in their wake. Unexpectedly, the division of Major General Edward Johnson of 2nd Corps suddenly marched onto the road from a side-road, on orders from Ewell to concentrate to the east of Cashtown. Lee gave right of way to Johnson's division, all fourteen miles of infantry, artillery, and trains. It was then that Longstreet left Lee to see to his own corps, now marking time. Whatever was going to happen that day, Longstreet's corps would not be a part of it.

Lee had not yet heard the guns from east of Cashtown. Unwittingly he had put forward 2nd Corps under its new, untried commander, Lieutenant General Dick Ewell. Ewell had been an excellent division commander under the great Jackson, and had lost a leg during the Second Manassas campaign. After Chancellorsville, Lee had reorganized the army from two corps into three. Ewell now commanded Jackson's old corps, a body of unsurpassed fighting-men who could work wonders under a man like Jackson. But the corps had a number of new units and commanders, none schooled in the Jacksonian style of war. For Ewell personally, that schooling had perhaps shaped him into too specialized a military tool. Jackson took counsel of no subordinate, much less informed any of them of his thoughts. He gave no more information than was required to exactly fulfil a particular order. He held his reins taut. Now Ewell worked directly for Lee, who held the reins with the lightest touch, depending more on a fusion of understanding than strict limits. This would be a time of testing for Ewell in his first battle as corps commander. If anything, too great a burden of expectation was placed on Ewell; he had to live up to the reputation of Jackson, the fallen demigod, called 'Old Blue Light' by his men from the other-worldly glow of his eyes in battle. The *Richmond Whig* expressed Ewell's dilemma neatly: 'The leader who succeeds [Jackson], be he who he may, will be impelled as by supernatural impulse, to emulate his matchless deeds. Jackson's men will demand to be led in "Stonewall Jackson's Way." The leader who will not or cannot comply with that demand, must drop the baton quickly. Jackson's corps will be led forever by the memory of its great chieftain.'[9] The very phrase 'Stonewall Jackson's Way' had come into usage as shorthand for Jackson's brilliant expression of both personal and operational initiative coupled with a remorseless determination to prevail. It had even been immortalized by the popular poem of the same name.

He's in the saddle now! Fall in!
Steady the whole Brigade!
Hill's at the Ford, cut off! – we'll win
His way out, ball and blade.
What matter if our shoes are worn?
What matter if our feet are torn?
Quick step! we're with him before morn!
That's Stonewall Jackson's way.[10]

---

[9] *Richmond Whig*, 9th May 1863, cited in Freeman, *Lee's Lieutenants: A Study in Command*, vol.2, *Cedar Mountain to Chancellorsville* (Charles Scribner's Sons, New York, 1946). p.689.
[10] Written by a member of the Stonewall Brigade, quoted in Mary Anna Jackson, *Life and Letters of General Thomas J. Jackson*, 1892, pp.285–7.

In the opening moves of the campaign, Ewell had, indeed, seemed to be Jackson's true successor. On 14th June, Lee had sent him to crush an overly-extended division of the Union's VIII Corps. Commanded by Major General Milroy, this division was 9000 men strong, the size of a corps in the Army of the Potomac. In two days, Ewell demolished it, inflicting 4443 casualties in a combination of surprise, ambush, and hard-fighting that led everyone to acclaim him as a true exemplar of 'Stonewall Jackson's Way'.

The 3rd Corps commander, A.P. Hill, was in a similar position. Another of Jackson's former division commanders, he now commanded the army's new corps. It included Major General R.H. Anderson's division from Longstreet's corps, and two divisions built from Hill's own large division and now commanded by Major Generals Henry Heth and W. Dorsey Pender, his former brigade commanders.

There had been much complaint when A.P. Hill had been chosen by Lee. Non-Virginians complained that the Army of Northern Virginia already reflected 'too much of Virginia' in its senior ranks, especially when South Carolinian Major General D.H. Hill seemed plainly the better man. But Lee had insisted that A.P. Hill was 'upon the whole ... the best soldier of his grade with me.' [11] He was also one of Jackson's successors. In his deathbed delirium, Jackson had cried out, 'Order A.P. Hill to prepare for action... Pass the infantry to the front.' These laurels were richly-deserved, for Hill was inseparable from Jackson's string of victories. He effected a system of command and discipline within his division which made it a model within the Army of Northern Virginia. His emphasis on speed led it to become known as the 'Light Division', despite its large size (six brigades). His light shone brightly in the Seven Days' Battle, and he was Jackson's right arm at Cedar Mountain and Second Manassas. At Sharpsburg, he came to the rescue of the army by a forced march when the enemy was on the point of victory. At Chancellorsville, where he was wounded, he also played a critical role in the victory. With a reputation as a hypochondriac, Hill genuinely suffered from prostatitis, a painful and debilitating infection of the prostate, that would flair up at moments of high stress.

By the morning of 1st July, therefore, Lee had his two most inexperienced corps commanders nearest the enemy. Longstreet, whom Lee had praised at Antietam as 'My Old Warhorse', was bringing up the rear. With Jackson dead, Longstreet no longer had a rival for the coveted position of Lee's right arm. Lee seemed to depend upon him more now as his senior corps commander and second-in-command. He, and not Ewell or Hill, had taken an active part in the planning of this campaign. He was under the firm impression that the campaign would be one of strategic offense and tactical defense, the winning combination of this war: maneuver the enemy into attacking you in an impregnable position and use the power of the rifled musket and massed artillery to slaughter him; then deliver a crushing blow to finish him off. Second Manassas had been the perfect example, and Longstreet had delivered the killing stroke. His fondness and respect for Lee did not prevent his growing reservations about Lee's fitness to command, however. Chancellorsville, hailed as a glorious, perfect victory, was, to Longstreet, simply useless sacrifice:

> The battle as pitched and as an independent affair was brilliant, and if the war was for glory could be called successful, but, besides putting the cause upon the hazard of a die, it was crippling in resources and of future progress, while the wait of a few days would have given time for a concentration and opportunities against Hooker more effective than we experienced with Brunside at Fredericksburg. This was one of the occasions where success was not a just criterion.[12]

The problem, he was to write, was that Lee's 'characteristic fault was headlong combativeness; when a blow was struck, he wished to return it on the spot. He chafed at inaction; always desired to beat up the enemy at once and have it out. He was too pugnacious.'[13] Longstreet had his own detractors as well. Many whispered that he was too slow. Even Lee, in a rare admission of frustration, had said it. Instead, Longstreet was careful to ensure that each finger was tightened into a hard fist before he struck. Then he led his brigades into the fight personally, making sure each blow was perfectly delivered and timed for maximum effect. He also had enough self-control and objectivity to calculate when the game was no longer worth the cost, and withdraw to fight another day on better terms. There was considerable danger in this personal style of his, as noted by an observer with the army, the British Coldstream Guards officer Lieutenant Colonel Arthur Lyons Freemantle: 'Everyone deplores that Longstreet *will* expose himself in such a reckless manner.'[14]

Longstreet was the Confederate Mars. A tall, broad-shouldered man with a full beard, he relished his pride of place in the estimation of the army and its commander. At Chancellorsville his only rival, the great Jackson, had perished. Never a great admirer of Jackson, he was contemptuous both of the high cost of his victories and his bizarre command style. Forty-two years old and in his prime, Longstreet's energy was inexhaustible. His determination

---

[12]* James Longstreet, *From Manassas to Gettysburg* (J.B. Lippincott, Philadelphia, 1896) p.330.

[13] Longstreet, *Washington Post*, 11th June 1893.

[14] Arthur Lyon Freemantle, *Three Months in the Southern States* (William Blackwood and Sons, Edinburgh and London, 1863) p.267.

had all the inevitability of an avalanche. The observation that cut to the heart of the warrior was made by Freemantle, the visiting British officer, on the field of Gettysburg itself: 'Difficulties seemed to make no other impression upon him than to make him a little more savage.'[15] The impression from the ranks was equally warlike. One of his infantrymen wrote long after the war: 'We soldiers on the firing line knew there was no greater fighter in the whole Confederate army than Longstreet. I am proud that I fought under him.'[16] His old friend in the Old Army, Ulysses S. Grant, wrote: 'He was brave, honest, intelligent, a very capable soldier, subordinate to his superiors, just and kind to his subordinates, but jealous of his own rights, which he had the courage to maintain. He was never on the lookout to detect a slight, but saw one as soon as anybody when intentionally given.'[17] John Bell Hood, who commanded one of Longstreet's divisions, said: 'Of all the men living, not excepting our incomparable Lee himself, I would rather follow James Longstreet in a forlorn hope or desperate encounter against heavy odds. He was our hardest hitter.'[18]

Once a hale fellow well met, the social heart had gone out of him when three of his children died in a scarlet fever epidemic in 1862; the loss burned something out of him. From that time he never again drank or smoked, and avoided the after-hours conviviality of the mess. Brigadier General George Pickett had earned his eternal gratitude at that cruel time, though there had already been a close bond. In the Mexican War, Longstreet had leaped over the parapet at Chapultepec carrying the colors, only to fall wounded, and it was to Pickett that he had passed the colors. Pickett had instantly become a national hero. That bond had deepened immeasurably when Pickett and his fiancé, the fifteen-year-old Sallie Corbell, quietly took over the details of the funerals and buried the three children while the Longstreets desperately tried to save their fourth. George and Sallie were at hand constantly, doing what they could. Sallie had adored the Longstreet boys, and her grief was that of an adoring sister. Longstreet never forgot. When Pickett was promoted to command one of Longstreet's divisions, Longstreet made certain his staff showed special care to ensure that things went well for his old friend. Pickett was an eternal adolescent, in his fine uniform and overly-perfumed, long oily locks, and none too bright, and, as Freemantle was to describe him at

---

[15] Freemantle, op.cit. p. 273.

[16] 'Survivor of Charge Defends Longstreet', Buffalo *Evening News*, 5th July 1938, cited in Jeffry Wert, *General James Longstreet: The Confederacy's Most Controversial General – A Biography* (Simon & Schuster, New York and London, 1993) p.297.

[17] Ulysses S. Grant, *Personal Memoirs of U.S. Grant: Selected Letters 1839–1865* (The Library of America, New York, 1990) p.450. Originally published in two volumes by Charles L. Webster, New York, 1888.

[18] Attributed to Major General James Bell Hood, CSA, cited in Wert, op.cit. p.163.

Gettysburg, 'altogether rather a desperate-looking character'.[19] Already it was evident that he had risen beyond his capacity. Yet Longstreet would protect him.

Pickett was on his mind as Longstreet rode back to his corps. Two of his divisions, those of Major Generals John Bell Hood and Lafayette McLaws, were stopped on the road outside of Chambersburg. But his third division, Pickett's, was still in camp. In the absence of his cavalry, Lee had directed that Pickett's division of over 5900 men guard the army's trains as they moved behind the fighting divisions. Only when Imboden's cavalry brigade arrived from the west would he be able to rejoin 1st Corps. Longstreet did not like to have Pickett that far off, since he caused more trouble than all the rest of 1st Corps put together. Jefferson Davis had intervened shortly before the invasion to detach two of Pickett's brigades, under Brigadier Generals Micah Jenkins and Montgomery Corse: Jenkins' Brigade had reinforced Major General D.H. Hill's small army blockading the Federal force in New Bern, North Carolina, while Corse's Brigade had been sent to guard the critical junction at Hanover, Virginia. The hero of Chapultepec had been furious, and did not hide it from his commander and friend or anyone else. 'I ask this in no spirit of complaint,' he had written on 21st June to the Adjutant and Inspector General of the Army of Northern Virginia, 'but merely as an act of justice to my division and myself, for it is well known that a small division will be expected to do the same amount of hard service as a large one, and, as the army is now divided, my division will be, I think, decidedly the weakest.' Longstreet had then traded more heavily on his relationship with Lee than he liked to, insisting, as far as he dared, that the brigades be returned. The old man had reluctantly agreed. Davis was amenable as long as appropriate substitutes could be provided; with a little difficulty Lee was able to recommend a North Carolina brigade, on garrison duty elsewhere, that would fill in for Jenkins. Pickett's brigades were consequently released and dispatched on the road north. The addition of their 3527 men would give Pickett the strongest division in the army, the size of a Union corps.[20] However, the episode had not done Pickett much good in Lee' eyes. Pickett was indifferent to the debt he owed the army commander and continued to act as if he had been slighted.

The almost semi-divine status Lee had already assumed in the eyes of the Confederacy was nowhere more apparent than in the Army of Northern Virginia. Its officers and men had unwavering faith in him after his string of shining victories. He was the great gentleman standing at the top of the

---

[19] Freemantle, op.cit. p.253.

[20] OR, series I, vol.XXVII, part 3, pp.893, 910, 947. On 15th June, Corse reported that he had an effective strength of 1200 men. Returns of 30th June showed Jenkins' strength at 2327, a very large brigade in either army.

Southern social hierarchy, and most Southerners expected to be led by gentlemen. Freemantle's prose sketch of the man is a wondrous likeness.

> General Lee is, almost without exception, the handsomest man of his age I ever saw. He is fifty-six years old, tall, broad-shouldered, very well made, well set up – a thorough soldier in appearance; and his manners are most courteous and full of dignity. He is a perfect gentleman in every respect. I imagine no man has so few enemies, or is so universally esteemed.[21]

What is more, he was all of that with an ease that stood above rank. Often a man would fall out of the ranks to talk to him informally. He never displayed the smallest sense of injured dignity. General John B. Gordon related that

> General Lee evidenced his appreciation of the privates when he said to one of them who was standing near his tent, 'Come in, captain, and take a seat.'
> 'I'm no captain, general; I'm nothing but a private,' said this modest soldier.
> 'Come in, sir,' said Lee; 'come in and take a seat. You ought to be a captain.' [22]

Lee's concept of self, found scribbled on a note in his briefcase after his death, is a more glorious epitaph than all the laurels of the battlefield:

> The forbearing use of power does not only form a touchstone, but the manner in which an individual enjoys certain advantages over others is a test of a true *gentleman*.
> The power which the strong have over the weak, the magistrate over the citizen, the employer over the employed, the educated over the unlettered, the experienced over the confiding, even the clever over the silly – the forbearing or inoffensive use of all this power or authority, or a total abstinence from it when the case admits it, will show the gentleman in a plain light. The gentleman does not needlessly and unnecessarily remind an offender of a wrong he may have committed against him. He cannot only forgive, he can forget; and he strives for the nobleness of self and mildness of character which impart sufficient strength to let the past be but the past. *A true gentleman of honor feels humbled himself when he cannot help humbling others.*[23]

Although he could be sharp with his staff, there is almost no record of his loss of composure around anyone else. If he valued one thing above others it was duty,

[21] Freemantle, op.cit. p.253.
[22] John B. Gordon, *Reminiscences of the Civil War* (Louisiana State University Press, Baton Rouge and London, 1993) p.136.
[23] J. William Jones, *Personal Reminiscences, Anecdotes, and Letters of Robert E. Lee* (D. Appleton and Co., New York, 1874) p.163.

which was to him the 'most sublime word in the English language.' His professional and personal lives had been in thrall to his duty to his country, as an
officer in the Old Army, and to his family.

As a soldier he was incomparable; victory perched on his shoulders. His
gentleman's demeanor hid one of the most aggressive soldiers in history.
According to Longstreet

> He seemed fresh from West Point, so trim was his figure and so elastic his step.
> Out of battle he was as gentle as a woman, but when the clash of arms came he
> loved fight, and urged his battle with wonderful determination. As a usual thing
> he was remarkably well-balanced – always so, except on one or two occasions of
> severe trial when he failed to maintain his exact equipoise. Lee's orders were
> always well considered and well chosen. He depended almost too much on his
> officers for their execution.[24]

His warrior's soul was caught up in battle, but he never fostered a cult of war.
He said at Fredericksburg that it was a good thing that war was so terrible lest
men come to enjoy it too much. His deep Christian spirit kept that demon in
check. It was this image of the Christian knight, fearless and without blame,
that ignited the admiration of others, even among Union troops. His standing
orders required that the wounded be picked up and cared for in the order in
which they were found regardless of uniform, and that prisoners receive the
same rations as his own men. But the warrior's body was exhausted by a hard
military life even before the war and the rigors of two years' active campaigning,
most of which he spent in the field, refusing to sleep in a house while his men
slept on the ground. A tent was his only roof. His diet was no better than his
men's, which was dreadful. He had fought his most perfect battle at Chancellorsville in May. Such triumphs had taken a toll, and now he was somehow
not his robust, razor-sharp self. It did not help that for days he had been
afflicted with a bad case of diarrhea, probably brought on by eating so much
semi-ripe fruit from the rich orchards of Maryland and Pennsylvania.

With Stuart absent, Lee was concentrating the army east of Cashtown. It was
the greatest army the Confederacy would ever put in the field after the Seven
Days' Battle. In all over 80,000 men had marched north with him. Out there,
to the east and south-east, he knew the Army of the Potomac was also moving,
towards him. Longstreet's spy had provided the vital intelligence which all of
Stuart's cavalry division had failed to provide. It was priceless. If he could
concentrate first, he could draw the enemy corps into battle piecemeal and

---

[24] James Longstreet, ' "The Seven Days" including Frayser's Farm', *Battles and Leaders of the Civil
War* (hereafter cited as *Battles and Leaders*), vol.II, Robert U. Johnson and Clarence C. Buel, eds.
(The Century Co., New York, 1887) p.405.

destroy them. The artillery rumble from beyond Cashtown now told him that this may already have begun. The problem was that this was neither the time nor place he had planned, and without Stuart, he could not tell whether it was only a few corps that had stumbled into contact with him, or the whole Army of the Potomac.

A man he knew and could trust

11:20 AM, Taneytown, Pennsylvania

Fourteen miles from Gettysburg at Taneytown, Captain Weld threw himself off his lathered horse and reported Reynolds' message to Meade at his head-quarters. Meade asked him to repeat the message. 'Good! That is just like Reynolds, he will hold on to the bitter end.' [25] No-one was yet aware that Reynolds had been dead for over an hour, but Meade now knew that the enemy had been found and engaged. Reynolds had been given overall command not only of his own corps but of XI Corps under Major General Oliver O. Howard and III Corps under Major General Daniel Sickles as well. That meant that almost one-half of his army would soon be engaged around Gettysburg.

It had been barely four days since Lincoln had fired Hooker and appointed Meade, commanding V Corps, to command the Army of the Potomac. Meade had tried to avoid the command, despising the politics that surrounded it, but Lincoln's orders had been mandatory. He shrugged and did his duty, saying, half in jest, 'Well, I've been tried and condemned without a hearing, and I suppose I shall have to go to execution.' [26] When Reynolds had come to wish him well, he had been immensely relieved. He and everyone else, including Lincoln, had believed Reynolds the best choice. Only Reynolds had disagreed, and the choice had then fallen on Meade, the solid and reliable engineer who had performed well as a brigade, division, and corps commander in turn. A somber man, he was stiff to outsiders who talked badly of him, while to those around him his irritability in moments of crisis rendered his sharp tongue wounding. Yet afterwards he was always eager to make amends, and he had many friends. He inspired trust and respect, for he knew what he was doing, took care of his men, and let nothing come between him and his duty. Just as importantly, he was known and respected by the men of the Army of the Potomac, who instinctively knew they were in good hands. Major Henry Livermore Abbott described him in much the same terms as did the rest of the army: 'In person, Meade is a tall, thin, lantern-jawed, respectable [man], wearing spectacles, looking a good sort of a family doctor... An extremely

---

[25] Weld, op.cit. p.230.

[26] C. Benjamin, 'Hooker's Appointment and Removal', *Battles and Leaders of the Civil War*, vol.III (1888) p.243.

good officer you see, with no vanity or nonsense of any kind, knowing just exactly what he could do & what he couldn't.'[27] Lee's opinion of his fellow engineer was probably the most astute: 'General Meade will commit no blunder in my front, and if I make one he will make haste to take advantage of it.'[28]

Since the morning of 28th June, when he assumed command, Meade's unsought responsibilities had reached almost crushing proportions, for Lee had slipped out of Virginia and again invaded the North. The crisis of the war had erupted with such clarity that even the simplest soldier knew that the survival or ruin of the Union was at hand. Washington was screaming over the telegraph wires that, above all, Meade must put himself between the enemy and both the capital and Baltimore. Should Washington fall, the war would be over and the Confederacy triumphant. Meade quickly grasped the strategic essentials, and with an energy rarely seen among his predecessors put the Army of the Potomac on a forced but efficiently planned march north. He was also quick to extract from Washington as much latitude as he could while fear gripped the capital. He demanded and received from Secretary of War Stanton the right to appoint and promote any man as he saw fit, regardless of rank or seniority. Stanton, an able and tyrannical man, had previously kept too tight a grip on such matters and thereby done much to limit Meade's predecessors. Now the emergency loosened his grasp, and Meade quickly seized the prize, immediately promoting three young but extremely able cavalry captains to the rank of brigadier-general and giving each of them a brigade in the reorganized cavalry corps.

When Meade assumed command, his army was scattered along the Potomac or facing the southernmost gaps in the South Mountain Range around Middletown, Maryland, when Lee had already concentrated most of his army between Carlisle and Chambersburg, Pennsylvania, several days' march to the north. Now the blue host surged north, almost drawn in the direction of Gettysburg by the attraction of the enemy hovering to the west of it. By the following morning, most of the Army of the Potomac was at or beyond Frederick. By the morning of 1st July, I, III, and XI Corps were in the area of Emmitsburg, Maryland, within easy march of Gettysburg. II Corps was reaching Taneytown; V and VI Corps were to the north at Union Mills and Manchester; and XII Corps had reached the army's northernmost point of advance, at Littletown, and had come so close to Stuart that he had shied northwest to stay out of its way rather than take the direct route to Gettysburg on

[27] Henry Livermore Abbott, *Fallen Leaves: The Civil War Letters of Major Henry Livermore Abbott* (The Kent State University Press, Kent, Ohio, and London, 1991) p.189.
[28] George Cary Eggleston, *A Rebel's Recollection* (Bloomington, Illinois, 1959) p.130; cited in Edwin B. Coddington, *The Gettysburg Campaign* (Charles Scribner's Sons, New York, 1968) p.196.

the evening of the 30th. Had he not done so, he would have run straight into Buford, who rode into Gettysburg late the same day.

Meade's dispositions had brought his army after Lee in such a fashion that each part of it would be within supporting distance of the rest. He had also flung his three cavalry divisions out to screen the army and find the enemy, and they had done just that, bringing him an increasingly clear picture of Lee's concentration to the east of Gettysburg. Indeed, they were doing for Meade what Stuart was not doing for Lee. One division had even flushed Stuart as he blindly continued his move north. Unfortunately, the sound of the guns had been a homing beacon for Early's couriers carrying Lee's message to rendezvous near Cashtown. Most importantly, Meade had pushed Buford's cavalry division to the east, gathering more and more information on the enemy, while behind him at Emmitsburg he had stationed Reynolds, his most trusted subordinate, with command of three corps. He was sending his best forward, with their eyes wide open and looking for a fight. The army was now resonating with its commander's own drive and eagerness to find and fight the enemy.

When Meade had received the first message from Reynolds he had just finished briefing his II Corps commander, Major General Winfield Scott Hancock, on the general situation. After Reynolds, Meade held Hancock in highest esteem. A tall, graceful, but imposing man who radiated bearing and command, Hancock's performance in the Peninsular Campaign in 1862 had so impressed the army's commander, Major General George B. McClellan, that he dubbed him 'Hancock the Superb'. His talents quickly elevated him first to the command of a division, and then to that of II Corps shortly after the debacle at Chancellorsville in May, when his corps commander had demanded a transfer, refusing to serve any longer under Hooker.

Meade now rode over to Hancock's headquarters to inform him of Reynolds' death. He then ordered Hancock to turn over his corps to Major General John Gibbon, one of his division commanders, and proceed immediately to take charge of the army's left wing at Gettysburg. He was to decide if Gettysburg was a suitable site for a battle, and if so to inform Meade, who, on Hancock's assessment, would order up the rest of the army. At first Hancock objected that he was junior to the commanders of III and XI Corps, Major Generals Dan Sickles and Oliver Howard. Meade waved that aside: he had secured the authority to put the right man in the right job, 'a man he knew and could trust', regardless of rank or seniority, and that man was Hancock. Still, Hancock knew enough of the power of seniority in the army to ask Meade for written orders confirming his authority. They were supplied immediately, and by 1:30 Hancock was on his way to Gettysburg with a small staff. While these rode around him he traveled in an ambulance in order that he could study maps of the Gettysburg area.

First Lieutenant Frank Haskell, on Gibbon's staff, watched him as he rode off. At thirty-one, Haskell was possessed of decisive good judgement which was never more accurate than in his description of Hancock:

> Upon horseback, I think he was the most magnificent looking general in the whole Army of the Potomac at that time. With a large, well-shaped person, always dressed with elegance, even upon that field of confusion, he would look as if he was the *'monarch of all he surveyed,'* and few of his subjects would dare to question his right to command or do aught else but to obey. His quick eye, in a flash, saw what was to be done; and his voice and his royal right hand at once commenced to do it...
>
> He always dresses remarkably well, and his manner is dignified, gentlemanly, and commanding. I think if he were in citizen's clothes and should give commands in the army to those who did not know him, he would be likely to be obeyed at once and without any question as to his right to command.[29]

---

[29] Frank A. Haskell, *The Battle of Gettysburg* (Wisconsin Historical Commission, Madison, Wisconsin, 1908).

CHAPTER 2

1st July 1863
'It's my turn to take them now'

2:30 PM, McPherson's Ridge

The Union troops on McPherson's Ridge could plainly see that the lull in the battle was about to end. Henry Heth had pushed two of his brigades forward and seen them savaged and flee to the rear. Now A.P. Hill was going to put in a second division, that of Major General William Pender; the Union I Corps men could see their multiple battle-lines fill the opposite ridge. During the lull the Federals had been reinforced by the rest of I Corps, the two divisions under Major General Abner Doubleday and Brigadier General John C. Robinson. Howard's XI Corps had rushed in to fill in the line to the north, and as senior officer Howard had assumed overall command of both corps at about 11:30. This was not necessarily comforting to the I Corps men. XI Corps, which was half made up of immigrant Germans, had a bad reputation – they had a habit of running away. It did not help that Howard was always blaming them for his own failures. Under their former commander, Franz Sigel, they used to announce proudly, 'I fights mit Sigel'. Now the rest of the army had begun to snicker, 'I runs mit Howard',[1] especially after Chancellorsville, when they had bolted spectacularly after Jackson had fallen on their flank like the wrath of God. Now these 'Half-Moon Men', as they were called (because of the shape of their corps badge), were about to receive the attentions of one of Ewell's divisions, that of Major General Robert Rodes, coming down from the north. Both Union corps would have taken even less comfort had they known that Lee himself had arrived on the field and was watching the unfolding attack.

For the Iron Brigade in McPherson's Woods, the sight was awesome. Opposite them was Pettigrew's Brigade, huge by the standards of either army, with almost 2600 men in four big regiments. The largest and most aggressive of these, the 26th North Carolina, with 843 men, was coming straight for them. The 26th had last seen combat a year before, at Seven Pines, but had been trained to a razor's sharpness by its twenty-one year old colonel, Harry Burgwyn, a young Mars who, as its lieutenant-colonel, had hammered the new regiment into shape with such vigor that his men wanted to kill him. But he led

---

[1] Edward J. Stackpole, *They Met at Gettysburg* (Stackpole Books, Harrisburg, Pennsylvania, 1969) p.146.

from the front and was the last man to leave the field, and in between he taught his men to soldier with the best of them. When the regiment's colonel had departed, the brigade commander stated he wanted no 'boy colonel'. Then the men of the regiment, who had earlier wanted to murder their drill-master, shouted that they would have no other. Now he led his regiment down the slope towards Willoughby Run and the Iron Brigade on the other side.

The Tar Heels marched in precise alignment behind their skirmishers, who pushed back the enemy's own skirmish line. Here and there gaps were made in their ranks, and then, as they rushed through the run's thickets and surged up into the woods, artillery enfiladed them, cleaving bloody furrows. They rushed right into the waiting sights of the 24th Michigan. Both sides fired a point-blank volley into each other, but the Carolinians just 'came on with rapid strides, yelling like demons.'[2] Colonel Henry Morrow of the 24th, an old Detroit judge and Mexican War veteran, had forged his unit of the same steel as his young opponent, and was not about to yield even in the face of irrepressible Southern valor. His men were deadly shots and fought back a step at a time through the smoke-filled oaks. But the Michiganders fell in heaps to match the enemy's dead and wounded. Morrow only pulled his regiment back as he saw the enemy flank the neighboring 19th Indiana.

The bullets on both sides seemed to eagerly seek out the color-bearers and their guards. As the Tar Heels grappled with the Michiganders on the ridge, they lost ten color-bearers and eight color guards. The colors of the 24th also saw much blood spilled in their honor that afternoon. But now the crisis of the fight had arrived, as the two sides exchanged titanic blows along the 24th's second line on the ridge. Burgwyn shouted Pettigrew's praise to the men, that the regiment had covered itself with glory. The latest color-bearer fell at his side; he seized the falling colors himself and ordered the men to dress on them. Private Frank Honeycutt rushed from the ranks to beg the honor of carrying the colors, and as he passed them over Burgwyn was shot through the side and both lungs, the force of the shot throwing him wildly to the ground, draping him in the colors. Honeycutt fell dead over him a moment later, shot through the head.

Lieutenant Colonel J.R. Lane immediately took command and organized the regiment for another lunge up the ridge. He found the colors on the ground and reached to pick them up. Another officer warned him that it was death to touch them. Lane raised the colors defiantly, saying, 'It's my turn to take them now. 26th North Carolina, follow me!'[3] The regiment surged forward into the fire of the 24th, which had now abandoned its third line and was doggedly retreating

[2] John Robertson, ed., *Michigan in the War* (Lansing, Michigan, 1882), p.441; cited by Tucker, *High Tide at Gettysburg*, p.147.
[3] George C. Underwood, 'Twenty-Sixth Regiment', *NC Regts*, vol.II, p.353.

towards the Seminary. One of the Michiganders turned to see Lane leading his shrunken band forward, flag in hand. 'As Colonel Lane turns to see if his regiment is following him, a ball is fired by this brave and resolute adversary, strikes him in the back of the neck just below the brain, which crashes through his jaw and mouth, and for the fourteenth and last time the colors are down.' [4]

The men of the 24th had died as freely for their colors as the men of the 26th. At one point Colonel Morrow himself had taken the flag from the fallen color-bearer, only to have Private William Kelley grab it from him saying, 'The colonel of the 24th shall never carry the colors while I am alive,' only to fall instantly himself. The 24th lost nine color-bearers that day. Colonel Morrow himself was the last man to carry them, and was felled by a bullet through the scalp just as he reached the safety of the Seminary barricade. Command had fallen to a captain, who retrieved the colors just as the battle was sweeping on towards Cemetery Hill. [5]

By now the battle had turned into a catastrophe for both Union corps. Although Howard had been in command on the field as the senior officer, he did little but direct his own corps. Buford's report to his cavalry corps commander during the battle underlined the problem: 'In my opinion there seems to be no directing person.' [6] Early had fallen on Howard's open right flank, in a replay of Chancellorsville, and shattered it; XI Corps collapsed and fled through Gettysburg in shambles. Doubleday's winnowed I Corps had no sooner retreated into the Seminary and its ridge than Major General Dorsey Pender's fresh division arrived. Dawes of the 6th Wisconsin described their approach. 'For a mile up and down the open fields in front, the splendid lines of the veterans of the Army of Northern Virginia swept down upon us. Their bearing was magnificent. They maintained their alignment with great precision.' [7]

Confederate J.F.J. Caldwell of Colonel Abner Perrin's Brigade remembered that I Corps still had plenty of fight left. 'Passing an open meadow and a small stream (Willoughby Run), we mounted the small hill beyond. Here we found and marched over the Pettigrew's Brigade of North Carolinians... The field was thick with wounded hurrying to the rear, and the ground was gray with dead and disabled. There was a general cheer for South Carolina as we moved past them... The artillery of the enemy now opened upon us with fatal accuracy. They had a perfectly clear, unobstructed fire upon us.' [8]

Three batteries of these guns were massed just to the north of the Seminary. They sent sheets of canister into the pursuing Confederates to cover the

---

[4] Underwood, ibid.
[5] Robertson, op.cit., pp.441–2; cited by Tucker, pp.148–9.
[6] *OR*, vol.XXVII, part I, p.925.
[7] Rufus Dawes, *Service with the Sixth Wisconsin Volunteers* (E.R. Alderman & Sons, Marietta, Ohio, 1890) p.175.
[8] Richard Wheeler, *Witness to Gettysburg* (Harper & Row Publishers, New York, 1987) p.149.

withdrawal of I Corps. Lieutenant James Stewart's Battery B, 4th US Artillery, straddled the railroad cutting, with three 12-pounder bronze Napoleons on either side. Just to the south, Captain Greenleaf T. Stevens' six 12-pounders of the 5th Maine Battery were aligned with the four 3 inch rifles of Cooper's Battery B, 1st Pennsylvania Artillery. Save for the 6th Wisconsin and the 11th Pennsylvania in support of the guns, all the infantry had filed onto Seminary Ridge or into Gettysburg itself. The artillery was the shield of the bleeding I Corps infantry.

Stewart's guns were advanced further than the others. Their fire had thrown to ground the Confederates advancing north of the railway cutting, but others south of it were racing forward to envelop the Seminary. Lieutenant Davison, who commanded the half-battery south of the cutting, was so badly wounded that one of his men had to hold him up, but he would not leave the field. He ordered his guns turned directly south, parallel to the Cashtown Pike.

Private Augustus Buell recounted:

> Well, this change of front gave us a clean rake along the rebel line for a whole brigade length, but it exposed our right flank to the raking volleys of their infantry near the pike, who at that moment began to get up again and come on. Then for seven or eight minutes ensued probably the most desperate fight ever waged between artillery and infantry at close range without a particle of cover on either side. They gave us volley after volley in front and flank, and we gave them double canister as fast as we could load. The 6th Wisconsin and 11the Pennsylvania men crawled up over the bank of the cut or behind the rail fence in rear of Stewart's caissons and joined their musketry to our canister, while from the north side of the cut flashed the chain-lightning of the Old Man's half-battery in one solid streak!
>
> At this time our left half-battery, taking their first line *en escharpe*, swept it so clean with double canister that the rebels sagged away from the road to get cover from the fences and trees that lined it ... Pender's division ... suffered terribly ... losing several hundred men ... within a few minutes ... the dauntless Davison, among the guns, cheering the men, praising this one and that one, and ever anon profanely exhorting us to 'Feed it to 'em, God damn 'em; feed it to 'em!' [9]

The Confederates wavered under the lash of the enemy guns, likened to a 'sheet of flame'. Colonel Alfred Scales fell wounded only seventy-five yards from the guns, all the field officers of his brigade being dead or wounded. His men found every wrinkle and low place in the ground in front of the Seminary from which to return fire.

---

[9] Augustus Buell, *The Cannoneer: Recollections of Service in the Army of the Potomac by 'A Detached Volunteer' in the Regular Artillery* (The National Tribune, Washington DC, 1890).

In the center Colonel Perrin rode to the front sword in hand to lead his brigade. Leadership has its price, and Perrin was offering to pay as he rode about in front of his huddled men. His courage flew across the field, and the brigade surged forward with a shout. So eager were the men to come grips with the enemy that many threw away their knapsacks and blanket rolls. The Union gunners kept up their fire, as did the infantry along the ridge, but the Confederates just kept coming, though hundreds fell to the leaden hail. They broke the line and enfiladed it, driving I Corps off the ridge and back into the town. The Union gunners, many wounded by now, served their guns until the last second, when they were ordered to limber up and get away. Rebel fire brought down men and horses, and the gallant Davison's life bled out of him, but all the guns were brought off.

The 6th Wisconsin had retreated in order into the town and opened up to let the artillery pass. Buell would write that he was 'astonished at the caution of the enemy at this time. He seemed to be utterly paralyzed at the punishment he had received from the I Corps, and was literally "feeling every inch of his way" in his advance on our front.' Buell would also relate that the retreat of I Corps was 'perfectly cool and orderly. There was not a sign of confusion, much less panic in the 1st Corps. The troops of the XI Corps were swarming into the town from the north at the same time.' [10]

'Jackson is not here'

4:30 PM, Seminary Ridge

Victory hovered over the Army of Northern Virginia as Robert E. Lee rode up to Seminary Ridge and witnessed the flight of the enemy. She offered her laurels freely. Two Union corps had been shattered, losing 5450 killed and wounded and 3620 captured out of the 16,500 men that had marched into the fight. Almost all semblance of organization among the survivors had gone as they rushed through the town and up onto Cemetery Hill to the south. Many, especially XI Corps men, just kept on going down the Baltimore Pike. The moment glistened, as scarcely a man on either side would have wagered a dime against the independence of the Confederacy.

Early's was the first division into the town. He had relatively fresh brigades, and could see the enemy rallying on Cemetery Hill. The evidence of success was pressing in on him. Hordes of prisoners being sent to the rear practically unguarded, masses of equipment strewn everywhere, and the high exuberance of his own men pushed him to go on. Even the shaken enemy's seeming intention to hold out should have triggered the natural reaction to smash them. Yet at this supreme moment, he decided to look for his corps commander to

---

[10] Buell, ibid.

receive permission to press on. He even accosted a staff officer of Hill's corps to suggest that Hill send in a division to exploit the situation that beckoned too brightly to himself.

Ewell himself entered Gettysburg about 5:00 PM and could not mistake the situation. Yet a pall of timidity fell over him, so palpable that his staff officers murmured among themselves, 'Jackson is not here,' as they shook their heads with disbelief. The arrival of the eager courier from Major General Edward Johnson relayed his commander's eagerness to throw in his division, which he said was 'in prime condition'. Brigadier General John B. Gordon, of Early's Division, seconded the proposal, saying that he could join in the attack on the hill with his brigade, and together they could take it. Gordon was seething. He had just been restrained by Ewell from pursuing the enemy, who was

> giving ground, and it was only necessary for me to press forward in order to insure the same results which invariably follow such flank movements. In less than half an hour my troops would have swept up and over those hills ... It is not surprising with a full realization of the consequences of a halt, that I should have refused at first to obey the order. Not until the third or fourth order of the most peremptory character reached me did I obey. I think I should have risked the consequences of disobedience even then but for the fact that the order to halt was accompanied with the explanation that General Lee, who was several miles away, did not wish to give battle at Gettysburg.[11]

But Ewell clung to the letter of these orders, though they were already manifestly overcome by events: 'General Lee told me to come to Gettysburg and gave me no orders to go further. I do not feel like advancing and making an attack without orders from him, and he is back at Cashtown.' His chief of staff took aside the courier, who had also served with him under Jackson, to whisper, 'Oh, for the presence and inspiration of Old Jack for just one hour!'[12]

That absence quickly became painfully evident. Major General Isaac Trimble was a general without a command but with a burning desire to serve. After Secession had been declared, he had tarried long enough in Pennsylvania to leave a trail of burnt bridges before going south. An old man, but tough and with an eye for the main chance, he had immediately understood the sig-

---

[11] Gordon, op.cit. p.154. Gordon continued: 'No soldier in a great crisis ever wished more ardently for a deliverer's hand than I wished for one hour of Jackson when I was ordered to halt. Had he been there, his quick eye would have caught at a glance the entire situation, and instead of halting me he would have urged me forward and have pressed the advantage to the utmost, simply notifying General Lee that the battle was on and he had decided to occupy the heights.'
[12] Henry Kyd Douglas, *I Rode with Stonewall* (Mockingbird Books, Marietta, Georgia, 1993) p.239. Following this remark in the text, Douglas commented: 'Yes, but it took the battle of Gettysburg to convince General Lee that General Jackson was really dead; but that did.'

nificance of the highest elevation in the Gettysburg area, Culp's Hill, just to the south-east of the town and next to the hill upon which the Yankees were repairing. Lee had attached him to Ewell as an assistant, and now Trimble thought it was about time to assist Ewell. 'Well, General, we have had a grand success. Are you not going to follow it up and push our advantage?' Ewell mumbled something about Lee's orders not to bring on a battle. 'That hardly applies to the present state of things', Trimble pointed out, 'as we have fought a hard battle already and should secure the advantage gained.'

Ewell was losing his composure in front of a strong-willed subordinate who was pushing him to do what he instinctively feared. Trimble then rode off to get a better look at Cemetery and Culp's Hills. Moments later he was back. 'General, there is an eminence of commanding position and not now occupied, as it ought to be by us or the enemy soon. I advise you to send a brigade to hold it if we are to remain here.'

'Are you sure it commands the town?' Ewell was searching for excuses.

'Certainly it does, as you can see, and it ought to be held by us at once.' By now Trimble was bristling with exasperation. Ewell just remained silent. That silence was like a match to gunpowder. Trimble was in a rage. 'Give me a division, and I will take that hill,' he said, his body shaking in anger. Ewell refused. 'Give me a brigade and I will do it.' Still no. Finally, Trimble said, 'Give me a good regiment and I will engage to take that hill.' The third no was the last straw. In disgust he threw down his sword and stormed out of Ewell's presence, vowing never to serve under him again.[13]

Lee, from whom Ewell was desperately awaiting a guiding hand, had already been on the scene on Seminary Ridge at 4:30 PM. He had planted himself with Hill's corps and seemed to feel no need to establish communications with the other half of his army on the field. He allowed subordinates to dissuade him from pursuing the battle with the enemy, huddled in shock on Cemetery Hill. His chief of artillery was afraid to fire at a whipped enemy lest he draw return fire. Hill complained that he was sick and that his corps had been too badly mauled for another fight. Yet his third division, that of Major General Richard Anderson, was fresh and at hand. In fact, Anderson had been so surprised by the order from Lee to halt that he had personally sought him out to confirm it. To his bewilderment, Lee explained that Anderson was his only reserve now that the army was not all up. It is more than coincidental that the commanders of two fresh divisions on the field, Anderson and Johnson, had to be held tightly back from an exploitation of victory. The effect of Stuart's absence was freezing up the entire chain of command. Lee was displaying the timidity of a blind man in a sword fight. Normally one of the most pugnacious and audacious of commanders, always quick to seize any advantage, he saw, without proper

---

[13] Randolph McKim, 'The Gettysburg Campaign', *SHSP*, vol.XL (1915), p.273.

intelligence, nothing but the frightening darkness around him. Had Stuart been on the field with his cavalry, surely the Union forces would never have had a chance to rally on Cemetery Hill? Stuart would have taught them that, in Homer's words, panic was indeed 'brother to blood-stained Rout.'

Finally Lee turned to Ewell for the troops to do what instinct must have been shouting at him to do. He sent a staff officer, Lieutenant Colonel William Taylor, who arrived about 5:00 PM, shortly after Ewell had rebuffed Johnson's offer to continue the attack. Taylor relayed Lee's orders 'to carry the hill occupied by the enemy, if he found it practicable, but to avoid a general engagement until the arrival of the other divisions of the army, which were ordered to hasten forward.'[14] Ewell seized upon the phrase 'if practicable' like a drowning man to a log, fully encouraged by Early, who seemed to have exerted inordinate influence on him. Jackson would never have given him such an excuse for inaction. The emphasis on not bringing on a general engagement was another easy way out. Unfortunately, Ewell gave no indication to Taylor that he had any objections to carrying out his orders.

About the time Taylor was delivering his message to Ewell, Longstreet rode up to Lee's headquarters on Seminary Ridge. Impatient at trudging behind Anderson's column with the noise of battle ahead, he had ridden forward to find out what was happening. Lee quickly pointed out the enemy positions. With his glasses, Longstreet made a careful survey for about ten minutes. Then, turning with obvious satisfaction, he said, 'We could not call the enemy to a position better suited to our plans. All that we have to do is to file around his left and secure good ground between him and his capital.'[15]

Striking the air with his fist, Lee said, 'If he is there to-morrow I will attack him.'[16]

Longstreet was taken aback. He was under the strong impression that this was the opposite of the general campaign strategy Lee and he had agreed upon as the invasion was planned. Longstreet had a realistic appreciation of the power of modern rifled firearms and artillery. The experience of the war had taught him that the perfect combination was the strategic offense and the tactical defense – you maneuvered the enemy to attack you. He therefore responded vigorously: 'If he is there to-morrow it will be because he wants you to attack. If that height has become the objective, why not take it at once? We have forty thousand men, less the casualties of the day; he cannot have more than twenty thousand.'[17]

[14] Clifford Dowdey and Louis H. Manarin, eds., *The Wartime Papers of Robert E. Lee* (Little, Brown & Co., Boston, 1961) p.576.

[15]* James Longstreet, *From Manassas to Gettysburg* (J.B. Lippincott, Philadelphia, 1896) p.357.

[16]* Longstreet, ibid.

[17]* Longstreet, ibid, pp.358–9.

Longstreet pressed him further to move around the enemy, to draw them into the attack. 'When they attack, we shall beat them.'[18] He argued that

> even if we carried the heights in front of us, and drove Meade out, we should be so badly crippled that we could not reap the fruits of victory; and that the heights of Gettysburg were, in themselves, of no more importance than the ground we then occupied, and that the mere possession of the ground was not worth a hundred men to us ... Meade's army, not its position, was our objective.[19]

Lee was by now becoming irritated. 'No,' he said, 'they are there in position, and I am going to whip them or they are going to whip me.'

It was then that Longstreet heard of Stuart's disappearance off the face of the earth. Lee was so distressed by the absence of his cavalry that he was dismissing any thought of a campaign of maneuver. Without Stuart's eyes and ears to illuminate the surrounding darkness, he would do nothing until the entire army was up. Stuart had given him the confidence at Second Manassas and Chancellorsville that he could detach half his army to maneuver with an acceptable level of risk. Yet at the same time, as Longstreet observed, 'he seemed under a subdued excitement, which occasionally took possession of him when "the hunt was up" and threatened his superb equipoise. The sharp battle fought by Hill and Ewell on that day had given him a taste of victory.'[20] He would have a victory, if not by wide maneuvers, then toe to toe, and he would have it on this field.

In the face of such determination Longstreet gave up the attempt, hoping to renew it in the morning. But he could not shake the vision of the slaughters at Malvern Hill and Fredericksburg, when just such determination had sent thousands to certain death with no chance of success whatsoever. It was at about this time that a staff officer from Ewell brought the message that Early and Rodes' divisions were able to attack Cemetery Hill if strongly supported on the right. Lee asked Longstreet where his troops were and said he wanted them brought up immediately. After being frustrated in his efforts to convince Lee to maneuver the enemy out of his position Longstreet was in no mood to be co-operative. He replied that his lead division was six miles away but then just simply did not address Lee's desire to hurry his men forward. Lee's habit of suggestion rather than definite command almost ensured such a sulking response.

---

[18] James Longstreet, 'Lee's Right Wing at Gettysburg', *Battles and Leaders of the Civil War*, vol.III (1888) p.340.
[19] James Longstreet, 'Lee in Pennsylvania', *The Annals of the War*, p.421.
[20] Longstreet, ibid.

The remaining impetus to drive the Union forces off the hill broke up like the ragged gusts of a dying storm. Half an hour after Longstreet's arrival, one of Lee's staff officers, Colonel A.L. Long, reported after a personal reconnaissance that the hill was held in strength behind a stone wall along the crest and on the reverse slope. By 7:00 PM, when Lee had ridden over to Ewell's headquarters to confer as to the advisability of continuing the attack, the narrow window of action had already closed as Union reinforcements began to crowd Cemetery Hill.

As the senior officers took counsel, the fighting men in and around Gettysburg were increasingly bewildered at the inaction. Ensign J.A. Stikeleather of the 4th North Carolina wrote to his mother of that fleeting opportunity:

> The simplest soldier in the ranks felt it ... But, timidity in the commander that stepped into the shoes of the fearless Jackson, prompted delay, and all night long the busy axes from tens of thousands of busy hands on the crest, rang out clearly on the night air, and bespoke the preparation of the enemy were making for the morrow.[21]

When Johnson's Division finally arrived on the field and nothing was done, Colonel David Zable of the 15th Louisiana remembered that 'the troops realized there was something wanting somewhere. There was an evident feeling of dissatisfaction among our men [that] we were not doing [it] Stonewall Jackson's way.'[22]

'Send every man you have got!'

4:30 PM, Cemetery Hill

As Lee was riding up to Seminary Ridge, Hancock with his small staff rode up onto Cemetery Hill into the backwash of defeat. Colonel Francis A. Walker, his assistant adjutant, was riding behind him.

> It was that afternoon, a scene of terror, strewn with the dead and dying and the wreck of battle. Even more painful for a soldier to witness, were the disordered groups of fugitives hurrying from the field or skulking behind cover. Down the Baltimore road, to the rear, poured a broad tumultuous stream of panic-stricken men, mingled with caissons, led horses, ammunition wagons, and ambulances loaded with the wounded. Here and there, in small groups, the men of sterner stuff from out the Eleventh Corps clung sullenly to their colors, and gazed downward upon the serried masses of the Confederates, who, occupying the field

---

[21] Raleigh *Semi-Weekly Standard*, 4th August 1863; cited in Tucker, p.186.

[22] Terry L. Jones, *Lee's Tigers: The Louisiana Infantry in the Army of Northern Virginia* (Louisiana State University Press, Baton Rouge and London, 1987) p.169.

of the recent battle, were threatening a fresh advance. On the left the remnants of the shattered First Corps were forming along Cemetery Ridge, under cover of Buford's brigades of cavalry, which, drawn up in a line of battalions in mass, stood as steady as if on parade.[23]

Hancock rode up to the first organized troops he had seen since leaving his own corps, the XI Corps brigade of Colonel Orlando Smith on Cemetery Hill just above the Taneytown Road. To Smith he said, 'My corps is on the way, but will not be here in time. This position should be held at all hazards. Now, Colonel, can you hold it?'

Smith could only utter a lukewarm, 'I think I can.'

Boring his eyes into Smith, Hancock repeated, 'Now, Colonel, can you hold it?'

The determination leapt from man to man as Smith straightened up and replied, 'I will.'[24] Hancock had instantly demonstrated that the purpose of leadership is to keep hope alive. So much so that Smith himself became a purveyor of hope. An XI Corps regiment passed by just then, heading to the rear. Smith called out to its colonel to about face and form line facing the enemy, but the command was studiously ignored. Smith raced over to the colonel, arrested him on the spot, and placed his regiment in the hands of a braver man.

Elsewhere on the hill General Howard had been doing his utmost to staunch the flight. Here and there a hardy regiment had held together. One such was the 17th Connecticut, which had fought a stiff rearguard action against several of Early's brigades, including that of the gallant John B. Gordon. Their acting commander, Major Allen G. Brady, recalled proudly that even in defeat

> We kept the enemy from advancing through the town until ordered to clear the street for the purpose of planting a battery. The battery not being placed in position as intended, and the regiment being in line on the sidewalk, the enemy took advantage of this, and, with a superior force, rushed through the main street, which compelled us to fall back, which we did reluctantly, but not without contesting the ground inch by inch... As we retreated, we loaded, halted, and poured destructive volleys into their ranks, which cleared the main

---

[23] Francis A. Walker, *History of the Second Army Corps in the Army of the Potomoc* (Charles Scribner's Sons, New York, 1886) p.266. Walker also wrote that upon a visit to Gettysburg in 1885, Hancock told him that 'among the most inspiring sights of his military career was the splendid spectacle of that gallant cavalry, as it stood there unshaken and undaunted, in the face of the advancing infantry.'

[24] Hartwell Osborn, *Trials and Triumphs, the Record of the Fifty-Fifth Ohio Volunteer Infantry* (A.C. McClurg & Co., Chicago, 1904) p.98; cited in Martin, p.483.

street of them several times, but we found the enemy too many for us. They poured in from every street in overwhelming numbers which broke our ranks.[25]

The regiment quickly reorganized on the outskirts of the town, just below the hill, and marched up in order with their colors and color guard at their head. A good regiment is like supple steel and will snap back into shape after the worst strain. Such were the men of the Nutmeg State. Howard, however, did not recognize the Connecticut men as he rode up, mistaking them for one of his German regiments. He called out, 'Are there men brave enough to advance to that stone wall?' pointing to one across a plot of land near the town. Brady and his men shouted back, 'Yes, the Seventeenth Connecticut will.' Then Howard said to the color-bearer, 'Sergeant, plant your flag down there in that stone wall!' The sergeant, not recognizing Howard, replied, 'All right, if you will go with me, I will!' Howard was game and took the color, placing it under the stump of his lost arm, and, accompanied by the 17th Connecticut, carried it to the stone wall, where he planted it. 'That flag served to rally the regiment, always brave and energetic, and other troops.' The 17th were better than their word. They stayed only moments at the stone wall and then moved forward to a rail fence even closer to the town, where they presented a brave front to the enemy 'until late in the evening, exposed to a galling fire from the enemy's sharpshooters.' Their gallant example convinced many a broken regiment or individual that a stand was possible on Cemetery Hill.[26]

Not all Howard's regiments were as responsive as the 17th Connecticut. When the I Corps chief of artillery asked him, 'Why don't you have them shot?' Howard answered ruefully, 'I should have to shoot all the way down; they are all alike.'[27]

Now Hancock arrived in a swinging gallop, pulling up sharply before Howard and saluting. Without ceremony, he said, 'General, I have been ordered here to take command of all the troops on the field.'[28]

Howard seemed stunned. Then he blurted out, 'Why, Hancock, you cannot give orders here! I am in command and I rank you.'

'I am aware of that, General, but I have written orders in my pocket from General Meade which I will show you if you wish to see them.'[29]

---

[25] OR, vol.XXVII, part I, p.718.

[26] OR, vol.XXVII, part I, p.718; and O.O. Howard, The Autobiography of Oliver Otis Howard, vol.1 (Baker & Taylor, New York, 1908) p.419.

[27] Charles S. Wainwright, A Diary of Battle: The Personal Journals of Colonel Charles S. Wainwright 1861–1865 (Stan Clark Military Books, Gettysburg, Pennsylvania, 1995) p.247.

[28] Lieutenant Colonel C.H. Morgan's account, Bachelder Papers p.320, New Hampshire Historical Society, cited in Martin, p.485.

[29] E.P. Halstead, 'The First Day of the Battle of Gettysburg', in Gettysburg Papers, vol.1, pp.154–5 (DC MOLLUS, 2 March 1887, pp.6–7); cited in Martin, p.484.

'No, I don't doubt your word, General Hancock, but you can give no orders here while I am here.'[30]

Hancock realized that an argument between two senior officers on this stricken field was the last thing that the demoralized men on Cemetery Hill needed to witness. 'General Meade has ... directed me to select a field on which to fight this battle ... But I think this the strongest position by nature upon which to fight a battle that I ever saw, and if it meets with your approbation I will select this as a battlefield.'

'I think it a very strong position, General Hancock.'

'Very well, I select this as the battlefield.'[31]

Howard had struck flint and realized it as he grasped the way out that Hancock had offered. 'All right, Hancock, you take the left of the Baltimore pike and I will take the right, and we will put these troops in line.'[32] He then rode off to see to his corps, which largely was on the right of the pike – just as Hancock had intended. As Doubleday was to observe, 'Howard merely used the cemetery as a rallying point for his defeated troops,' but Hancock 'immediately took measures to hold it as a battle-ground for the army ...'[33]

Hancock had only been on the scene a matter of minutes but had quickly grasped the critical nature of the ground. Riding to the east side of the hill, he saw the last I Corps battery to leave Gettysburg, the 5th Maine Battery with its six bronze Napoleon 12-pounders struggling up the hill. He called out for the commander of 'that brass battery'. Captain Greenleaf Stevens and First Lieutenant Edward Whittier, the second-in-command, rode up to Hancock and saluted. The general pointed to Culp's Hill. 'Do you see that hill, young man? Put your battery there and stay there.' The light of hero worship leapt in Whittier's eyes. He was to write: 'I shall never forget the inspiration of his commanding, controlling presence or the fresh courage he imparted, his whole atmosphere strong and invigorating.' He was also extremely impressed by the clean, white linen of Hancock's shirt cuffs and collar.[34] Stevens was more to the point, and asked, 'By whose order?' The reply was, 'General Hancock's.' With that, Stevens turned in his saddle and shouted, 'Fifth battery, forward!'[35]

For Hancock, the immediate 'commanding, controlling presence' was still Culp's Hill, and he needed more than artillery to keep it. He rode up to the

[30] Tucker, op.cit. p.193.

[31] Halstead, op.cit.

[32] Howard, op.cit. p.418.

[33] Abner Doubleday, *Chancellorsville and Gettysburg* (Charles Scribner's Sons, New York, 1882) p.152.

[34] Francis A. Walker, *General Hancock* (D. Appleton and Co., New York, 1894) p.112.

[35] *Maine at Gettysburg: Report of the Maine Commissioners* (Lakeside Printers, Portland, Maine, 1898) p.89.

acting I Corps commander: 'General Doubleday, I command this field and I wish you to send a regiment over to that hill.' [36]

The strain of the day was obvious in Doubleday's face; the courage had bled out of him, and he was all excuses. 'My corps has been fighting, General, since ten o'clock, and they have been all cut to pieces.'

Hancock literally erupted. Standing up in his stirrups and raising a clenched fist, he roared, 'Sir! *I* am in command on this field. Send every man you have got!' [37]

Shocked into action, Doubleday quickly sent not a regiment, for they were the size of companies, but the remnants of Wadsworth's entire division, including the 700 surviving men of the Iron Brigade who had rallied just behind Cemetery Hill. They arrived in time to support the 5th Maine Battery, which had positioned itself on a knoll on the western side of Culp's Hill from which it could sweep the eastern slope of Cemetery Hill and the ravine between the two. The infantry filed to the right of the battery up along the northern and western crest of Culp's Hill, where they immediately began entrenching.

Hancock continued working down the line, redirecting moving units to new positions to form a coherent defense. Howard occasionally attempted to interfere, but everyone instinctively looked to Hancock. He was taking no chances with Howard or the Confederates. It seemed inevitable that the enemy would soon come sweeping up the hill, shrieking their Rebel Yell. He could not understand what delayed them. Encountering another battery driving up to the cemetery, he ordered its guns placed to sweep the pike and said, 'I want you to remain in this position until I relieve you in person.' He turned to an aide. 'Listen to what I am going to tell you. I am of the opinion that the enemy will mass in town and make an effort to take this position, but I want you to remain until you are relieved by me or by my written order and take orders from no one.' [38]

Within half an hour of his arrival he had stitched together a defensive position running from Culp's Hill, around Cemetery Hill, and then towards Little Round Top. By 5:30 PM the two divisions of XII Corps had arrived. Hancock ordered Brigadier Alpheus S. Williams' 1st Division behind Culp's Hill and Brigadier John Geary's 2nd Division to fill in the line to Little Round Top; unfortunately, Williams' Division was to spend much of the night lost, wandering between Benner's Hill and the Baltimore Pike. At 7:00 the head of Sickles' III Corps also arrived, marching up the Emmitsburg Road. Placing the command in Slocum's hands, Hancock left the field to report to Meade, still at Taneytown. On the way

[36]* Doubleday, op.cit. p.151.

[37] Elmira Hancock, *Reminiscences of Winfield Scott Hancock* (Charles L. Webster & Co., New York, 1887) p.190.

[38] James Stewart, 'Battery F Fourth U.S. Artillery at Gettysburg', in *Gettysburg Papers*, vol.1, pp.373–4 (Ohio MOLLUS, vol.4, pp.189–90); cited in Martin, p.489.

he met his own mighty II Corps and directed it to fill in between I and XI on Cemetery Hill and the XII Corps division near Little Round Top.

Hancock had wrung hope out of defeat, an achievement felt by everyone positioned on those hills that July evening. Major General Carl Schurz, of XI Corps, said it for them all:

> The appearance of General Hancock at the front was a most fortunate event. It gave the troops a new inspiration. They all knew him by fame, and his stalwart figure, his proud mien, and his superb soldierly bearing seemed to verify all the things that fame had told about him. His mere presence was a reinforcement, and everybody on the field felt stronger for his being there. The new inspiration of self-reliance might have become of immediate importance, had the enemy made another attack – an eventuality for which we had to prepare. And in this preparation Howard, in spite of his heart-sore, cooperated so loyally with Hancock that it would have been hard to tell which of the two was the commander, and which was the subordinate.[39]

His activity had been in arresting contrast to the indecision among the Confederate leaders; only Longstreet had demonstrated a quick grasp of the situation, but he had not been in a position to influence the outcome.

9:00 PM, Marsh Creek, outside Gettysburg

Longstreet's disposition was gloomy as he rode back to his corps headquarters at Marsh Creek that night. In his mind he kept going over Lee's last statement to Hill and himself: 'Gentlemen, we will attack the enemy in the morning as early as practicable.'[40] Longstreet was sure of Lee's intention, and was also sure that Lee had not decided when and where the attack would be delivered. Riding at his side was the I Corps Medical Director, Dr J.S. Dorsey Cullen, who was talking positively of the victory won that day. Longstreet pulled his horse to a halt. Leaning over in the saddle, he shook his head and said, 'It would have been better not to have fought than to have left the Federals in control of a position from which the whole army will be needed, and then at great sacrifice, to drive the enemy.'[41] Cullen was more than surprised when Longstreet added with determination, 'I think such an attack is unwise, and I will do everything I can to prevent it.'[42]

---

[39] Carl Schurz, *The Reminiscences of Carl Schurz*, vol.III (The McClure Co., New York, 1908) pp.14–15.
[40] A.L. Long, *The Memoirs of Robert E. Lee: His Military and Personal History* (J.M. Stoddart & Co., New York, 1886) p.277.
[41] Douglas Southall Freeman, *Lee's Lieutenants: A Study in Command, vol.3, Gettysburg to Appomattox* (Charles Scribner's Sons, New York, 1944) pp.110–11.
[42]* J.S. Dorsey Cullen, 'Longstreet and Pickett's Charge', *SHSP*, vol.XXIII (1889), p.57.

CHAPTER 3

1st–2nd July 1863
Marching through the
moonbeams

Men of both armies were concentrating on Gettysburg from all directions during the afternoon and night of 1st July. The corps and detachments absent on this first day of the battle were racing toward the maelstrom. With unerring uniformity, everyone seemed to sense that this was the 'big' battle, the great blood-soaked decision that they had all spoken of for two years. Now they all sensed it, like animals before a great storm or an earthquake, with that ur-sense deep within the psyche.

Late afternoon, 1st July, Chambersburg, Pennsylvania

No-one was more elated to see Imboden's cavalry brigade arrive than George Pickett. The honor of guarding the army's trains deep in enemy territory had suddenly paled as Pickett had heard that battle had been joined at Gettysburg. He quickly turned over responsibility for the trains to Imboden and waited for orders to move on Gettysburg. As he waited, his resentment at being left out of momentous events, at being slighted, welled up again, and were directed at Lee. On the march into Pennsylvania, a girl had asked Lee for a lock of his hair. Lee had smiled and said he had none to spare, but that Pickett with his long locks should be able part with some. The officers around Lee had laughed hard, but to Pickett, who wore his feelings on his sleeve, it was not funny.

He lost no time in sending a courier to alert Lee that Imboden had arrived to relieve him. He had not been idle during his wait at Chambersburg, though. Anything useful to the enemy had been thoroughly destroyed – the railroad and its shops and depots had been reduced to ashes and twisted iron. The countryside had been picked clean of supplies. Now, if he had possessed a bit, he would have been chomping on it. The orders to move finally arrived from Longstreet between one and two in the morning. Pickett leapt to his feet. 'We must move at once to Gettysburg! Order the men into line and lead the movement!' [1] Pickett thrilled that, despite the coming thirty-mile march, his

---

[1] Edward G. Longacre, *Pickett: Leader of the Charge* (White Mane Publishing Co. Inc., Shippensburg, Pennsylvania, 1995) p.113.

men responded with 'more spirit and élan' than he had ever seen, even in this gamecock division.[2] Longstreet's order also contained the welcome news that Jenkins' and Corse's brigades were marching north and should be able to join Pickett at Gettysburg.

Early evening, on the Taneytown Road to Gettysburg

The 1200 Marylanders in Union blue were in a highly mixed state of anticipation and dread. After two years of guard duty, they were off to join the Army of the Potomac and the great battle everyone knew was in the air. These two regiments of Brigadier General Henry H. Lockwood's brigade had seen little duty other than guarding the Delmarva Peninsula of Maryland's Eastern Shore across the Chesapeake Bay and southern borders of the state. The 1st Maryland Regiment, Eastern Shore Brigade, and the 1st Maryland Regiment, Potomac Home Brigade, were unusually large, fielding 600 and 674 men respectively, having undergone none of the harrowing effects of the battlefield. They had been raised early in 1861 when it appeared that Maryland's secession was a real possibility. What action they had seen had not been of the most edifying sort. The Potomac Home Brigade men had been surrendered at Harper's Ferry during the Antietam campaign the previous year, and been returned to Federal service in an exchange of prisoners.

The Eastern Shore Regiment, as Harry Pfanz observed, 'was unique in the Army of the Potomac in that its colonel, James Wallace, and some other members were slave-owners and a few had brought servants to the field with them.' Their pro-slavery sentiments caused a number of its men to desert when the regiment occupied Virginia's Eastern Shore counties, and it was said that some joined the Confederate 1st Maryland Battalion.[3] When called to join Meade's Army, sixty-one men of Company K refused to depart with the regiment, standing on the letter of their enlistment that they would not be sent out of Maryland. They were arrested and dishonorably discharged. Thirty men of the company and their captain, Littleton Long, remained loyal and marched off with their regiment. The hard Union towns of northern Maryland gave the Eastern Shore men a decidedly enthusiastic welcome as they passed through on their way to join the Army of the Potomac in Pennsylvania.[4] The regiment arrived at Taneytown on 1st July to hear of the battle, and that Lockwood was at Gettysburg; it was given time to rest, then left all its baggage and sick and

[2] Randolph A. Shotwell, 'Virginia and North Carolina in the Battle of Gettysburg', *Our Living and Dead*, vol.IV, p.87, cited in Glenn Tucker, *High Tide at Gettysburg: The Campaign in Pennsylvania* (Stan Clark Military Books, Gettysburg, Pennsylvania, 1995) p.330.
[3] Harry W. Pfanz, *Gettysburg: Culp's Hill and Cemetery Hill* (University of North Carolina Press, Chapel Hill and London, 1993) p.308.
[4] Daniel Carroll Toomey, *Marylanders at Gettysburg* (Toomey Press, Gettysburg, Pennsylvania, 1994) p.13.

marched briskly off in the afternoon ahead of the mighty II Corps, beginning to assemble for its road march. Captain Long could not wait. The humiliation of having two-thirds of his company turn traitor was beyond bearing. The loyal remaining third and he would have something to prove.

Lee's invasion of the North had shocked both Lockwood and his command out of their comfortable rut. Two years of guard duty ended on 25th June when the brigade was added to the Army of the Potomac; the Eastern Shore regiment was added to the brigade the following day. The brigade had only been added to Williams' 1st Division, XII Corps, the previous morning. Lockwood himself was a graduate of West Point, class of 1836, and served a year fighting the Seminoles before resigning. Until the war broke out, he taught mathematics at the Naval Academy. A 'very pleasant gentlemen', he nevertheless had little field experience.

Williamsport, Maryland

Roused from his Rip van Winkle sleep around the forgotten passes in the Blue Ridge, Brigadier General Robertson had finally put his two brigades on the road after the courier on a lathered horse had clattered into his camp with orders to move north into Pennsylvania. The 6th Virginia Cavalry's three Faulkner brothers from Culpeper – James (Tom), John, and Absalom (Ab) – had never been out of Virginia, but now, as Jones' Brigade crossed the Potomac at Williamsport, they knew it was going to be a great ride. They and the rest of the brigade had been chafing at the bit as the army had left them behind weeks before. The 6th had a fighting reputation, and in the Valley Campaign had earned Ewell's accolade, 'I glory in the bloody sixth!' After Second Manassas they had the honor of providing Lee's headquarters guard, a duty they took seriously. They were therefore quick to stop two men from entering the headquarters who had no passes from General Lee, only to find that the pass-less men were Lee and his aide. The 6th Virginia had fought well at Brandy Station; they had lost fifty-five men in the wild melee, and they were proud that their commander, Major Flournoy, had come under the approving eye of Stuart himself. Many had heard Stuart's voice shout above the fray, 'Give them the saber boys!' [5] Now they feared they would miss the great adventure. The endless supply columns moving south laden with Pennsylvania's bounty had not lessened their impatience.

At twenty-six Tom was the oldest of the Faulkner brothers, and kept an eye out for his younger siblings. A family man, he had been detailed to drive the company's wagon. John was a daredevil cavalrymen, as quick to jump a fence chasing a Yankee as to draw saber and pistol and charge stirrup to stirrup. He

---

[5] Michael P. Musick, *6th Virginia Cavalry* (H.E. Howard Inc., Lynchburg, Virginia, 1990) pp.16, 21, 40.

had already served with the 9th Virginia Cavalry. But it was Tom who had to keep his promise to their mother to bring them home safe, especially young Ab, who had been conscripted less than a month before.

Hanover, Pennsylvania

The men of V Corps had eaten up mile after mile by the time they began to hear the sound of guns from the direction of Gettysburg on the afternoon of 1st July. As they approached Hanover the dead horses and trampled-down fields resulting from Stuart's battle with Kilpatrick were obvious. The corps had just made camp when a courier dashed into camp with the news that a desperate battle was being fought in Gettysburg. Reynolds was dead, and they were to march without stopping. They were needed. It had already been a day of hard marching, but there were many Pennsylvania regiments in the corps, and when they had crossed the Maryland state line with flankers and skirmishers out, these regiments found a new bounce to their step. As the 83rd Pennsylvania crossed the line – men from Crawford, Erie, and Forrest Counties – their color-bearer unfurled the regimental colors, and their brigade commander, Colonel Strong Vincent, himself a Pennsylvanian, ordered the band to play *Yankee Doodle*. The 295 voices of the regiment roared their approval.

The 83rd loved Vincent, their own former commander. He was that rarest of men, a scholar and a warrior. It was an era when a Harvard man could gladly serve his country, and when Harvard produced men manly enough to do so. An imposing, fine-looking individual, he had learned soldiering from scratch when he had enlisted at the beginning of the war. In 1862 he had stepped into command of the regiment when its colonel and major had both been killed at Gaine's Mill. Like Burgwyn of the 26th North Carolina, he had drilled his regiment to such precision that McClellan had rated it the best in the division. He had just passed his twenty-sixth birthday on the march to Gettysburg.

Now the brigade was marching through the night, and a grateful people lined the road bringing food and water. Young women gave the night a magical quality with their beauty as they waved the men on, flirted, and even bestowed a kiss here and there.

> Our dark way was illumed by groups of girls in sweet attire gathered on the embowered lawns of modest homes with lights and banners and flowers, and stirring songs waved their welcome in the ripple of white handkerchiefs – which token the gallant young gentlemen of the staff were prompt to take as summons to parley, and boldly rode up to meet with soft, half-tone scenes under the summer night; those meetings looked much like proposals for exchange of prisoners, or unconditional surrender. And others still, not daring quite so much, but unable to repress the gracious impulse of giving, offered their silent bene-

diction in a cup of water. And we remembered then with what sanction it was that water had been turned to wine in Cana of Galilee![6]

One group of girls began singing *The Star Spangled Banner*, and Vincent, overcome by the moment, bowed his head to the national colors. 'What death more glorious could any man desire than to die on the soil of old Pennsylvania fighting for that flag?'[7]

In Vincent's brigade was the new colonel of the 20th Maine, thirty-four year old Joshua Lawrence Chamberlain. A minister and college professor of natural and revealed religion, this serious and capable man had defied the disapproving faculty of Bowdoin College and marched off to war for the Union with his commission as lieutenant-colonel of the new 20th Maine regiment in August 1862. Less than a year later he commanded the regiment, a position no man grudged him. He had written to his wife: 'I study, I tell you – every military work I can find.' One of those books, heavily annotated, was in his saddlebags now, as the regiment marched through the night, and one passage in particular had recently been underlined – the use of the bayonet when two bodies of men collide in an enclosed space.

New Guilford Court House, Pennsylvania

Here, only a few miles from Chambersburg, the men of the 15th Alabama could clearly hear the cannonade from Gettysburg that afternoon. They were ordered to cook rations and be ready to move by three in the morning. They were on the road by 4:00 AM and passed a hard day and night of marching, passing the smoking ruins of Thaddeus Steven's foundry, torched by Early a few days before, still glowing with a heat the hard Republican senator would more than match in his hatred for the South. The 15th Alabama of Law's Brigade of Longstreet's Corps was commanded by twenty-eight year old Colonel William Calvin Oates, as ambitious and pugnacious a man as was ever bred in Alabama. 'Certainly William Oates was not a man to be trifled with. He was brave and reckless, to be sure, but he was also quite dangerous. His youthful appearance – he had a round, full face that made him look cherubic – was deceiving, yet there was no mistaking the stony glare of his dark eyes.'[8] As a young man he had skipped out of Alabama and Louisiana one step ahead of the law, wanted for the arguments he had settled with his fists. He had adventured in Texas, and then returned to Alabama, to a county which had no outstanding warrants for him.

---

[6] Joshua Lawrence Chamberlain, *'Bayonet! Forward!' My Civil War Reminiscences* (Stan Clark Military Books, Gettysburg, Pennsylvania, 1995) p.18.

[7] Oliver Wilcox Norton, *Army Letters 1861–1863* (Chicago, 1903) p.281; cited in Alice Rains Trulock, *In the Hands of Providence: Joshua L. Chamberlain & the American Civil War* (The University of North Carolina Press, Chapel Hill, 1992) p.124.

[8] Glenn LaFantasie, 'Introduction', Haskell and Oates, *Gettysburg*, ibid, p.9.

Within a year, the war had opened a natural outlet for his temperament and ambition. He raised a company from Henry County which was incorporated into the 15th Alabama, which he now commanded. The regiment had won its spurs as part of Jackson's Foot Cavalry in the Valley Campaign of 1862 and had suffered cruelly at Antietam. At Fredericksburg, Oates led it in a bayonet attack into the left flank of Burnside's army with the rest of the brigade. Neither Oates nor the 15th Alabama were to be trifled with.

Funkstown, Maryland

The small party of Union cavalrymen dressed in civilian clothes paused only long enough in the afternoon to rest their horses and strip a few branches of their heavy loads of ripe cherries. There were two men standing nearby, and one remarked to the other, 'I'll bet five dollars they are Union men.'

The cavalrymen's leader, a young man with a faint golden beard, asked, 'How can you tell Union men from rebels?'

The man replied, 'We are Union soldiers and ought to know.' He and his companion were James C. Moorehead and Thomas Cunningham, veterans of the 126th Pennsylvania, whose terms of enlistment, but not their pride in their service, had expired recently. The young man questioned them closely on the whereabouts and strength of Rebel forces in the area and learned that the mass of Lee's army had marched north into Pennsylvania days before. Moorehead was a resident of nearby Hagerstown but was originally from Greencastle in nearby southern Pennsylvania and was well acquainted with the roads there. There and then the young man unofficially recruited Moorehead back into the service of his country.[9]

Since yesterday, the band of ten cavalrymen had been slipping behind the rear of the Army of Northern Virginia, pausing often to let past Confederate parties and the endless wagons heading south filled with the loot of Pennsylvania. The squad had been detailed to accompany the young captain and a sergeant on a special mission. Now they watched their leader as he jotted down in his notebook the intelligence just gleaned from a loyal citizen: 'Wednesday, July 1, 1863 – Reynolds killed near Gettysburg; fell back.'[10] The horror of the note had not deterred the officer from what he was about one whit. Captain Ulric Dahlgren was what every enlisted man feared and admired at the same time. He was like the razor sharp blade of a saber that rasped as it leapt from a scabbard – all war. The thin, blond, pale-faced Pennsylvanian officer was barely twenty-one, but no one thought to presume on his youth. Son of the famous

[9] W.P. Conrad and Ted Alexander, *When War Passed This Way* (A Greencastle Bicentennial Publication, Greencastle, Pennsylvania, 1982) p.172.
[10] Rear-Admiral Dahlgren, *Memoir of Ulric Dahlgren* (J.B. Lippincott & Co., Philadelphia, 1872) p.161.

developer of naval ordnance, Admiral John Dahlgren, he had been found a position on Hooker's staff but considered that far too tame. He thrived on risk and high adventure and always arranged to get himself to whatever cavalry command was going into harm's way. He had fought at Brandy Station in the thick of the sabers, and at Middleburg and Upperville. But best of all he loved the space between and around the armies, where intelligence of the enemy is seized by daring and by cunning brains.

Meade had sought to employ him as a courier and escort officer, but Dahlgren had other ideas. There are some officers who make their own assignments, and Dahlgren was one of them. He persuaded the headquarters' intelligence officer to put him in charge of a unit of scouts. Among them he found a kindred spirit, Sergeant Milton Cline, whose talents took him in disguise into the Confederate ranks. He had joined Stuart's columns as they left Virginia and learned from conversations heard at Stuart's headquarters that critical dispatches from Jefferson Davis to Lee would be traveling by courier and escort and would cross the Potomac at a specified time, and from there would reach Lee by the Greencastle Turnpike. It had taken some forceful argument, backed up by Cline's own testimony, to convince the Cavalry Corps' commander, Major General Alfred Pleasanton, to authorize the raid to seize the dispatches. Sixteen men had been authorized; ten had shown up. Dahlgren did not care; he had a mission to die for.

The source of that mission was a new staff creature for the Army of the Potomac, the Office of Military Information. Three men, now with Meade at Taneytown, were at its core. The first, John C. Babcock, was actually a civilian, a former Pinkerton detective, hired originally by Burnside to replace the Pinkerton firm that left with General McClellan. The second was Captain John McEntee, originally of the Ulster Guards, the 80th New York. A tall, gaunt man, he was a natural interrogator and manager of intelligence operations. The third man and head of the Office was Colonel George Henry Sharpe, a lawyer, formerly commander of the 120th New York. The Office had come together as an effective organization at Hooker's prompting. Whatever other failings Hooker possessed, he had a taste for the advantages conferred by the effective collection of military intelligence. The Office had been recruited by Brigadier General Marsena Patrick, the Army of the Potomac's Provost Marshal, but it was under Colonel Sharpe's auspices that it had grown and matured. Now he controlled hundreds of agents, scouts, and other operatives. One of these was Sergeant Cline, and another was the gallant Dahlgren, attracted to it like Achilles to his glory.

Hagerstown, Maryland

To the south of Dahlgren's small band, Pickett's two lost brigades had just gone into camp north of Hagerstown as night fell, expecting to reach Pickett's

Division near Chambersburg within two more days' marching. Their fires had just begun to lick the coffee pots and camp kettles when the drums beat assembly. The fires were doused, and the brigades resumed their march for Gettysburg, where, the men were told, there had been a battle. Brigadier General Micah Jenkins' Brigade was in the lead. The South Carolinians, the only non-Virginia regiments in Pickett's Division, were as fine a brigade as existed in the Army of Northern Virginia, its six regiments consisting of the 1st South Carolina, 2nd South Carolina Rifles, 5th and 6th Carolina, the Hampton Legion, and the Palmetto Sharpshooters.

Their commander was as fine a commander as any in the army as well. At twenty-seven, the boyishly handsome Micah Jenkins had soldiering in his blood. After graduating from the South Carolina Military Academy, he had founded the King's Mountain Military School. He was elected colonel of the 5th South Carolina in 1861 and by sheer ability rose to brigade commander by the end of the year, at the age of twenty-five. He quickly became a favorite of his division commander, James Longstreet, who wrote of him: 'Besides being much liked by his men, Colonel Jenkins is one of the finest officers of this army.' [11] His list of honors was identical to the battles of the Army of Northern Virginia. At Frayser's Farm, Longstreet had ordered him to silence a battery and thought he would use his sharpshooters. To his amazement he watched the young Jenkins overrun it with his entire brigade, bringing on the battle. Promoted to brigadier-general in July 1862, Longstreet tried to get him the command of a division. He was severely wounded at Second Manassas leading from the front, one of 400 casualties in his brigade, but was recovered enough to lead it again at Fredericksburg that December. As he was carried from the field at Second Manassas, Lee rode up to him and said, 'I hope yet to see you as one of my lieutenant-generals.' He was by any measure a natural fighting man.

His men were devoted to him. A Southern war correspondent who shared his tent, F.G. de Fontaine, wrote of what it was like

to observe him calmly directing the movements of a line of battle, bearing as it were a charmed life among the flying balls; to witness him morning and night kneeling on his blanket, returning thanks to the Almighty, and invoking blessings on his command; and to be familiar with the kind of communion which existed between the humblest private and himself. Few men have had fewer enemies. No one in his position has so little occasion to punish offenders against his discipline, and when the necessity has been apparent, a tender heart has always gone out to the culprit and drawn tears from his guilty nature. Childlike, unsophisticated in the ruder knowledge which characterizes ordinary men of the

---

[11] Ellison Capers, *Confederate Military History, vol.V: South Carolina* (Confederate Publishing Co., Atlanta, 1899) pp.133, 404–5.

world, careful and polite in his conversation, pure as a woman in his thoughts, accomplished in his manners, frank, confiding and generous to a fault, he was in truth a Chevalier Bayard *sans peur et sans reproche*. As an officer he was brave, dashing, impetuous and yet prudent; had a quick military eye, knowing the strong points of a position at a glance; never ordering his men where he was not willing to lead; and rarely if ever blundered.

He returned his men's devotion, as J.B. Kershaw, a fellow brigadier, observed: 'General Jenkins was passionately fond of his men, and during his campaigns insisted on the strictest discipline as the surest means of protection and of saving them in times of greatest danger. He was the most magnetic man I ever met, and I believe the finest soldier.' Long after the war, one of his men, Sam Clinton, would tell Jenkins' son, 'We boys had to behave ourselves for the general knew every one of us by name and would spot us instantly if we did anything amiss.' The veterans repeatedly told him that his father never ordered them to 'Go', but rather, 'My men, follow me!' [12]

Behind Jenkins' Brigade were the Virginians of 'Bulldog' Montgomery D. Corse's Brigade. One of the army's older officers (he was born in 1816), he was one of the few Mexican War veterans who had not been in the Old Army, having served as a captain in the 1st Virginia Volunteers. As an acting brigade commander, he fought shoulder to shoulder with Jenkins' South Carolinians at Second Manassas and received a second wound (having been earlier wounded at Boonesboro). He led his own already decimated 17th Virginia – just fifty-six strong – at Sharpsburg, where it was reduced to seven unwounded men, a number that did not include Corse, who was left laying within the enemy's lines suffering from his third wound. He was rescued and received the highest accolade any Southern man could hope to hear, the praise of Robert E. Lee: 'Colonel Corse is one of the most gallant and worthy officers in this army. He and his regiment have been distinguished in at least ten of the severest battles of the war.' [13]

9:00 PM, VI Corps at Manchester, Maryland

As night fell on 1st July, Major General John Sedgwick's VI Corps was settling down to a well-deserved rest in Manchester, over thirty miles east of Gettysburg. At about 9:00 a courier raced through the peaceful camp, threw himself from his horse, and dashed through the headquarters' doorway. It was First Lieutenant Paul A. Oliver from Meade's staff. Covered with dust and grime,

[12] John P. Thomas, *Career and Character of General Micah Jenkins, C.S.A.* (The State Co., Columbia, South Carolina, 1909) pp.9, 11, 26.

[13] Jed. Hotchkiss, *Confederate Military History, vol.III: Virginia* (Confederate Publishing Co., Atlanta, 1899) pp.588–9.

Oliver had ridden two horses into the ground to deliver the dispatch from Meade through his chief of staff, written barely an hour and half before:

> GENERAL: The major-general commanding directs me to say that a general battle seems to be impending to-morrow at Gettysburg; that it is of the utmost importance that your command should be up. He directs that you stop all trains that impede your progress, or turn them out of the road. Your march will have to be a forced one, to reach the scene of action, where we shall probably be largely outnumbered without your presence.[14]

Grief over the death of Reynolds, a close friend, was put aside until a time when duty was less insistent. Sedgwick looked at his watch, then at the map, made a rapid mental calculation and said to Oliver, 'Say to General Meade that my corps will be at Gettysburg by four o'clock tomorrow.' Oliver briefly stared, then saluted and left, mumbling to himself, 'Well, it might just be possible, but I don't think any corps, even the old sixth, could do it.'[15] Unwittingly he had thrown down a gauntlet for VI Corps. As Oliver mounted, the 'General' was sounded, the camp came alive with the clatter of equipment and the shouting of officers ordering men to 'pack up and fall in!'

Oliver had not even passed through the door when Sedgwick turned to his adjutant, Colonel Martin T. McMahon, and said, 'Put the Vermonters up ahead and keep the column well closed up.'[16] If the corps was to march straight into a battle, he wanted his best at the head of the column. The Vermont Brigade, commanded by Colonel Lewis Grant, was, indeed, the best of the old VI Corps. One of the few Union brigades to contain regiments from only one state – the 2nd, 3rd, 4th, 5th, 6th Vermont – the men from the Green Mountain State had won a steely reputation for courage and grit from the Peninsula to Chancellorsville. Medals of Honor had fallen like leaves on this brigade. Not the least of them had gone to the 3rd Vermont's fourteen-year-old drummer boy, Willie Johnson of Salem, Vermont. Through the Seven Days' Battle on the Peninsula, when he was just thirteen, he set an example for fidelity and bravery and was the only drummer to save his drum in the hellish retreat.

The corps stepped off into the humid gloom. The moon had not yet risen, and only a few faint stars flickered in the sky. Sedgwick's last two orders from Meade directed him to arrive by way of the Taneytown Road: although the broad, well-surfaced Baltimore Pike provided a better route, it was clogged with the army's trains on their way to Westminster for safety and to be at the

---

[14] *OR*, vol.XXVII, part 3, p.467.
[15] Tucker, op.cit. p.205.
[16] G.G. Benedict, *Vermont in the Civil War*, vol.I (The Free Press Association, Burlington, Vermont, 1886) p.383.

terminus of the only railroad Meade could use for resupply.[17] The prospect of VI Corps' thirty-six infantry regiments, eight artillery batteries, cavalry contingent and trains, stretched over ten miles of road, encountering the army's other trains with their hundreds of lumbering wagons, was a nightmare.

The march took them through a still countryside, oblivious to the march of an army, and now eerily illuminated by a rising moon. The sounds of insects and the occasional clanking of a cow bell made it seem a dreamlike journey to the silent ranks plodding along the road. Only the barking of farmyard dogs acknowledged their presence. One soldier would write:

> That hot, dry, dusty, moonlit night of July 1 presented a scene of weird almost spectral impressiveness. The roads to the south and southeast of the town flowed with unceasing, unbroken rivers of armed men, marching swiftly, stolidly, silently. Their garments were covered with dust, and their gun barrels gleamed with a fierce brilliance in the bright moonlight. The striking silence of the march, the dusty-gray figures, the witchery of the moonbeams, made it seem spectral and awesome. No drum beat, no trumpet blared, no harsh command broke the monotonous stillness of the steady surge forward.[18]

Lieutenant Elisha Hunt Rhodes, barely twenty years old and commander of Company B, 2nd Rhode Island, had a less romantic memory, one that most ex-soldiers could relate to.

> We struggle on through the night, the men almost dead for lack of sleep and falling over their own shadows. But still we go on in the warm summer night. Little is said by any one, for we were too weary to talk, and only now and then an officer sharply orders the men to close up. Sometimes the column would halt for a moment at obstructions met in the advance, and then we would run to catch up.[19]

8:00 PM, Seminary Ridge

As Hancock was galloping down the Taneytown Road at about 8:00 PM to find Meade, another party of horsemen cantered up to Lee's headquarters on Seminary Ridge. Lee and Longstreet were in conversation around a small camp table covered with maps. They looked up to see Jeb Stuart ride up, doff his

---

[17] *OR* vol.XXVII, part 3, pp.484–5. This letter to Sedgwick from Major-General Daniel Butterfield, Meade's Chief of Staff, dated 2nd July, 5:30 AM, clearly states that Sedgwick had been twice ordered to take the Taneytown Road. No mention is made of any subsequent orders for Sedgwick to take the Baltimore Pike. The existence of these 'phantom' orders has been one of the minor controversies surrounding the battle.

[18] Penrose G. Mark, *Red, White and Blue Badge* (Aughinbaugh Press, Harrisburg, Pennsylvania, 1911) p.216; cited in Harry W. Pfanz, *Gettysburg: The Second Day* (University of North Carolina Press, Chapel Hill and London, 1987) p.80.

[19] Elisha Hunt Rhodes, *All For the Union: The Civil War Diary and Letters of Elisha Hunt Rhodes*, ed. Robert Hunt Rhodes (Orion Books, New York, 1985) p.115.

plumed hat in a salute, and dismount, throwing Virginia's reins to an orderly. 'General, I wish to report the return of my command with 125 fine wagons and teams filled with supplies.' His smile was cut short when Lee raised his hand for silence.

The old man's displeasure was plain to see in his face. 'Those wagons are only an encumbrance now. Do you realize, General, that we have fought a major battle here today, a battle fought in the dark, without knowledge of the enemy. It was a battle that could have ended in disaster had those people been able to concentrate here faster. Only by the grace of God did they not, and by the grace of God, the men prevailed – no thanks to the cavalry of this army, Sir!'

Longstreet sat stone silent. He had never seen Lee dress down another general officer, much less his favorite, in such terms. If anyone else but Lee had said this, Stuart would have called him out then and there. Now he only stammered, 'But, Sir, as we agreed . . .'

Lee stood up and took a step toward the now thoroughly nonplussed cavalryman. 'I held back an attack that could have driven them from the fine position they now occupy had I the cavalry present to press hard on the heels of a rout and tell me how distant their supports were. You were not here when this army needed you.'

'General Lee,' Stuart pleaded, more like a bewildered boy to the father he has somehow disappointed, 'if I have failed you so miserably, then I offer my . . .'

Again Lee cut him off. He had administered the whipping, now he must tell the boy he still loved him. 'Tomorrow, General, I will need you as I have never needed you before. We are deep in hostile territory and only your eyes, General, can see over the rocky path we must tread.' He put his hand on Stuart's shoulder and said softly, 'All will be put right now that you are here. We will not speak of this again.' Then, pausing: 'I have missed you.'

Stuart could not speak. To break the spell he had woven, Lee took him by the arm. 'Walk with me, General.' A few paces off, he said, 'We will have a greater battle tomorrow. I will drive those people from their position and break them. You must hold your command in readiness to help. See that they rest. Place one brigade north-east of the town to protect our flank. Confer with General Ewell on their placement. Place the others to watch the Emmitsburg Road to our south. I have ordered Robertson and Jones' brigades here, but I fear they will not arrive by tomorrow.'[20]

---

[20]* Charles Marshall, 'Stuart and the First Day at Gettysburg', *Military Annals of the Confederacy*, vol.X (1875), p.224. Major Marshall's account is that of an eyewitness who hovered just within earshot of this painful episode. His animosity to Stuart and his determination to protect Lee's reputation, however, became a feature of the post-war period, and did not end even with Stuart's death in 1887. He forever blamed Stuart's absence in the fighting of 1st July for the Confederate failure to cripple the Army of the Potomac at the first blow. There is some speculation that this animosity may have embroidered his account of Lee's harsh reception of Stuart.

Stuart understood the interview was over. He saluted and walked back to Virginia, his head still bent as Lee disappeared into his tent. As Stuart took the reins in his hands, Longstreet rose from his camp-chair. 'Welcome back. When you are finished seeing to your command, report to me. I have a plan that will interest you.'[21]

In his tent, Lee was doubled over on his cot as the pains shot up his left arm again and his chest ached. 'Not again,' he said to himself. 'Dear God, so much depends upon me. I must do my duty.' This and worse had happened in March – a blow like a hammer over his chest had kept him in bed. His doctors had pleaded with him to rest for months, but he had been up again in one.[22]

1:30 AM, Cemetery Hill

Barely fifty-seven minutes elapsed between the time Meade climbed into the saddle at Taneytown and his arrival at II Corps headquarters just south of Little Round Top about 11:00 PM, a distance of eight or nine miles of hard riding. He had passed an anxious afternoon and evening since dispatching Hancock to sort things out. Succeeding messages from the II Corps commander had brought clarity and hope. Gettysburg was a good place to fight. Couriers galloped from his headquarters to order the rapid concentration of the rest of the army there. Shortly before 10:00 he was surprised to see General Hancock and Gouveneur Warren, the Army's Chief of Engineers, ride up. Their briefing confirmed his decision. In minutes he was riding with such speed that all but a few aides were left trailing behind. Not even the columns of II Corps and the reserve artillery, marching through the night, delayed him.

He stayed twenty minutes at II Corps headquarters, telling Major General John Gibbon, 1st Division commander and senior officer present, to concentrate the corps there as it came up and let it rest. Hancock would be along shortly to take over. Then, back in the saddle again, he rode the final three miles to the gatekeeper's lodge by the graveyard on Cemetery Hill. The moon had come out on this last part of the ride, bathing the wooded heights of the Round Tops on his left, and the neat rows of wagons, guns, caissons, tents, and sleeping masses of troops that had filled up much of the fields between the road and Rock Creek, about a mile to the east. A shadowy figure took the reins as he dismounted by the picket fence outside the lodge; two guards at the gate smartly presented arms, the moonlight glinting off their bayonets. A soft glow came from the windows of the lodge behind them. Howard met him outside, desperate to explain that he had done everything he could that day. Meade took

---

[21]* Longstreet, *From Manassas to Gettysburg* (J.B. Lippincott, Philadelphia, 1896) p.383.

[22] Emory M. Thomas, *Robert E. Lee, A Biography* (W.W. Norton & Co., New York and London, 1995) p.278. Lee was to write in October 1863: 'I have felt very differently since my attack of last spring, from which I have never recovered.'

the time to soothe the agitated man and assure him that no blame was attributed to him. The last thing Meade needed was a corps commander whose mind was elsewhere. Inside the lodge he was joined by Slocum and Sickles. The greetings were brief; Meade threw himself onto a small chair, his hollow eyes made even deeper by the candle light and his lack of sleep. 'Well, Howard,' he asked, 'what do you think, is this the place to fight a battle?'

'I am confident we can hold this position, General Meade.' The others immediately supported him. 'It's good for defense,' offered Slocum, to which Sickles, an aggressive politician turned soldier, emphatically agreed. 'It is a good place to fight from, general!'

'I am glad to hear you say so, gentlemen, for it is too late to leave it.' [23]

---

[23] George G. Meade, *The Life and Letters of General George Gordon Meade*, vol.2 (Charles Scribner's Sons, New York, 1913) pp.61–2.

CHAPTER 4

1st–2nd July 1863
'General Lee wants the
hill taken'

6:30 PM, 1st July, Gettysburg

Ever since they had crossed South Mountain, the men of Johnson's Division could almost smell the battle down in Gettysburg. They certainly heard it; the cannon fire and musketry rumbled in the not too far distance. Before long they began to encounter the frenzied activity on the outskirts of battle. Couriers dashed up and down the column, followed by their own staff officers conveying new instructions which the line officers always seemed to translate into commands to hurry. 'Close up, men, close up; Hill's Corps is in.' Cheers rippled through the column, and the pace quickened.[1] Like Anderson's Division, they too saw the backwash of battle, the prisoners and groaning hospitals. They crossed the railroad cut and saw it filled with bodies, and the fields around were strewn with more. By the time the last brigade had reached Gettysburg at about 7:00 PM it was almost too difficult to read by the waning light. It was now obvious that the division had arrived too late for the fighting. As a result its commander, Major General Edward Johnson, was in a foul mood. He had already sent ahead a courier with the message that his men were ready, even after their long march, to pitch into the enemy. Ewell had declined the offer.

In his mind's eye Ewell could still see old Isaac Trimble throw down his sword and storm off in a perfect rage, prophesying that Ewell would live to regret his refusal to seize Culp's Hill. That hill lay like the shadow of a brooding apparition over his shoulder. Shortly after Trimble had departed, Ewell had ordered two aides, Lieutenants T.T. Turner and Robert Early, a young cousin of the division commander, to reconnoitre the hill to see if the enemy was holding it. On their return they found Ewell sitting in the corner of a fence with Rodes and Early on either side. Their report was extraordinary. They had reached the top of the hill and encountered no Federals. From their vantage point, they had been able to see the enemy's entire line in the late afternoon light. It was clear that if Confederate troops held the summit, the Union line would uncoil with a

---

[1] Harry W. Pfanz, *Gettysburg: Culp's Hill and Cemetery Hill* (The University of North Carolina Press, Chapel Hill and London, 1993) p.78.

snap. Even with his good judgement pricked by the obvious importance of the hill, Ewell still referred to his subordinates the question as to whether he should send Johnson to occupy it. Rodes was exhausted from the day's fighting and responded off-handedly that it did not matter one way or another since Johnson's command was probably tired. Exhaustion is apparently contagious. Early, as usual, was quicker off the mark. 'If you do not go up there tonight, it will cost you ten thousand men to get up there tomorrow.' Early always found it easy to recommend that the difficult job be done by someone else. Nevertheless, it was good advice, and Ewell, still under the spell of Early's forceful personality, then ordered Johnson to post his division just north of the Hanover Road and advance to occupy Culp's Hill, if it was not held by the enemy.

Then came Lee's visit to his headquarters, which had left him vaguely embarrassed. He had let Early dominate the discussion of 2nd Corps' role, which he essentially reduced to playing a diversionary part in support of Longstreet's main attack the next day. Lee had not been impressed either, and concluded that evening that he would be wasting the fighting power of Jackson's old corps in such an awkward position. He sent Major Charles Marshall of his staff to tell Ewell that he was going to move the entire Army of Northern Virginia to the right if 2nd Corps' commander did not think he could take the hills to his front. Ewell's reaction was to temporize again – and call for Early. He told Marshall that the matter was too serious for him to reply immediately. Early arrived quickly, and the party rode in animated conversation to the foot of one of the hills where their discussion continued for some time. Early strongly urged Ewell not to abandon the idea of an attack from this part of the field. Finally Marshall stated that the hour was late, and he must have an answer for Lee. Ewell stated that he must confer in person with the general commanding and accompanied Marshall to the army headquarters on Seminary Ridge. It was about 11:00 PM when he arrived, accompanied by a few aides. For the next hour they talked in Lee's tent. Ewell carefully explained the opportunity presented by the report of his aides. Without firing a shot, they would spoil the tactical basis of the entire enemy position and force a confused withdrawal. Lee would then be allowed to follow on Meade's heels and force a battle of his choosing.

Lee relented and allowed 2nd Corps to remain in its position. It had been barely ten minutes since Ewell arrived when he gave his assent. As he had not seen Ewell since the army had begun its march, there was much else to discuss, but first he suggested to Ewell that Johnson's move was best executed swiftly. Ewell then summoned Lieutenant Turner to convey his order to Johnson to take Culp's Hill with all haste. His earlier condition that this be done only if the hill was unoccupied was forgotten. It now also had Lee's support behind it.

Most of Johnson's men were asleep on their arms shortly after midnight when Turner rode up to his headquarters and delivered his message. Johnson, a careful if pugnacious man, replied that he had already sent a strong patrol from the 42nd Virginia to see if the hill really was unoccupied and was awaiting its return. Turner replied, 'General Lee's instructions are not dependent upon the hill being empty. General Lee wants the hill taken.'

'Well done, Sergeant! Well done!'
11:00 PM, Culp's Hill

At the moment Turner was admonishing General Johnson, the survivors of the patrol from the 42nd Virginia were under guard by B Company of the 7th Indiana, the Hoosiers having occupied the summit of the hill that Turner and Early had found empty hours earlier. Fate had spared them from the catastrophic battle that day which had left one of every two men of I Corps dead or wounded on the field.

The 423 men of the 7th Indiana, Cutler's 2nd Brigade, 1st Division, had been detached as the I Corps train guard at Emmitsburg when the rest of the corps followed John Reynolds to Gettysburg that morning. Colonel Ira Grover, commanding the 7th, had been given strict orders to stay with the trains until relieved by another unit. By 10:00 AM Grover had decided he had had enough of such duty and ordered the 7th forward to Gettysburg, entirely unaware that a battle was raging.[2] At first he did not push the regiment and at 2:00 PM allowed them a rest to cook dinner. Just as their fires were lit, a thunderstorm doused them. At this moment, Quartermaster Burlingame arrived from Gettysburg with news of the battle and orders for the 7th to rush forward. Grover put his men on the road, forced marching them to the sound of the guns. He sent Major Merit C. Welsh on ahead, to get orders regarding where they were to join the line. Welsh continued down the Emmitsburg Road, and as it began to pass Seminary Ridge he barely escaped Confederate pickets. Eventually he found General Wadsworth, who directed him to bring the 7th up to Cemetery Hill.

Grover arrived in time to see the backwash of defeat pouring over the hill as the shattered XI Corps, bereft of order, broke for the rear. The 7th tried to rally as many as it could while Grover reported to Wadsworth and Cutler. He found his division commander sitting on a stone wall, overwhelmed by the misfortunes of the day and mourning the slaughter of his fine division. Wadsworth eagerly greeted him but shook his head and said, 'I am glad you were not with us this afternoon.'

Cutler broke in, 'If the Seventh had been with us we could have held our position.'

Curtly, Wadsworth dismissed the bravado. 'Yes, and all would now be dead

---

[2] Grover was later court-martialed for disobeying his orders to remain with the trains, but was acquitted.

or prisoners.'[3] It was not long after this that Hancock arrived on the field to bring order out of chaos, instructing Abner Doubleday to send troops to occupy Culp's Hill. After Stevens' Battery and the survivors of his beloved Iron Brigade were sent to Culp's Hill it occurred to Wadsworth that more troops were needed: it was a big hill, and the Iron Brigade was a lot smaller now. Grover's fresh regiment moved onto the right of the 6th Wisconsin. Because the Iron Brigade was barely strong enough to cover the western slope of the hill from Stevens' Battery on the knoll, Grover had to move the 7th to the crest of the hill to cover its northern face. This left him only one company to cover the entire eastern face. B Company had to stretch so far that it became barely a picket line. Later Grover pulled the company back towards his main line. This left a half-mile gap in the army's position between the 7th Indiana and Brigadier General Alpheus Williams' 1st Division of XII Corps, bivouacked on the eastern side of Rock Creek on the Baltimore Pike.[4]

The men of the 7th found that their position reminded them of 'our Ohio River hills – its sides pretty heavily timbered, and strewn with rocks varying in size from a chicken coop to a pioneer's cabin.' Grover quickly put them to work under the direction of a civil engineer in the ranks. By nightfall, a formidable breastwork had appeared almost miraculously.[5]

On the right of this position, B Company's much shortened picket line blended into the trees. There is nothing harder to distinguish at night than a still, silent man half-hidden against a tree. On the very right of that night picket, Sergeant William Hussey and Private Harshberger heard a noise

> as of men moving cautiously in the timber some distance to their right. As they advanced to investigate, before the enemy discovered them, they got behind some boulders, permitting the officer leading to pass them. Sergeant Hussey dashed out and seized the officer, while Harshberger and Odell fired on the advancing body of troops. Other members of the company running up, poured in such a rapid fire that the enemy turned and fled in the direction of Rock Creek . . .[6]

The prisoner grabbed by Hussey was a lieutenant of the 42nd Virginia, the leader of the patrol. The young man was visibly mortified at his predicament as

---

[3] Orville Thomson, *From Phillipi to Appomattox: Narrative of the Service of the Seventh Indiana Infantry in the War for the Union* (n.p., n.d.) pp.161–2; cited in David Martin, *Gettysburg: July 1* (Combined Books, Conshohocken, Pennsylvania, 1995) pp.552–3.

[4] Williams had taken his division north of Culp's Hill on the eastern side of Rock Creek to the base of Brenner's Hill, at which point he was ordered to withdraw. Had he continued he undoubtedly would have come into contact with Johnson's Division.

[5] Thomson, op.cit. p.163; cited in Martin, op.cit. p.553.

[6] James H. Stine, *History of the Army of the Potomac* (J.B. Rodgers Printing Co., Philadelphia, 1892) p.493; cited in Martin, op.cit. p.558.

Sergeant Hussey prodded him up to Colonel Grover with his bayonet. 'Well done, Sergeant! Well done!' Turning to the lieutenant, he conducted a quick field interrogation. What was his unit? Where were they? What was he doing up here? The officer was mildly co-operative, trying to slough off his embarrassment by demonstrating a commendable pride in his regiment. He had the good sense to decline to discuss his mission. Grover knew he had obtained all he could and sent him quickly off to the Provost's prisoner cages. He took Sergeant Hussey aside and had him memorize a message for the provost; it was much too dangerous to light a candle. The message alerted the Provost to the importance of the prisoner captured while scouting out the army's right flank.

1:30 AM, 2nd July, Rock Creek east of Culp's Hill

Johnson's Division was wading across the waist-deep Rock Creek in two brigade columns, preceded by a few skirmishers and scouts. The first part of the march was relatively easy as the division crossed the fields of hay, grass, and wheat south of the Hanover Road. The clouds that blotted out the full moon and stars had nevertheless emitted a helpful if faint luminescence, but even this disappeared as the division entered the woods that led down to Rock Creek, and there in the bottom the fog lay thick. The men groped through the ghostly cloud, damp on their faces, the only sound the gurgling of the creek. Then they climbed onto the other bank and disappeared into the shadows of the thick woods on Culp's Hill. Johnson sorely missed the moonlight. Night attacks had been rare enough in this war as it was, but moonlight had usually been a prerequisite, as had open ground. He had neither. Night attacks were also almost always limited to small units, no larger than a regiment, or a brigade at the most, in order to minimize the tremendous problems of control. The larger the formation, the more control dissipated. Now Johnson was leading a division of over 6000 men through the woods in total darkness, to attack an enemy of unknown size and unknown dispositions on top of a rocky, wooded hill. Few men would have asked for such an assignment, but Johnson insisted he had wanted to fight and he still meant it as he waded through the creek, wondering how in God's name he was going to control the fight that was about to blow up in his face.

Forty-seven year old Major General Edward Johnson was a veteran of the Seminole and Mexican Wars and of considerable frontier duty in the Old Army. He was another veteran of the assault on Chapultepec and had earned two brevets in that war. He received the nickname 'Old Allegheny' for holding the crest of those mountains in December 1861, when he drove off an attack with conspicuous success. Described as a 'large and rough-looking man on horseback', he had been a favorite of Jackson. The great Stonewall jumped him to the command of D.H. Hill's Division in January 1863, even though he was still recuperating from a bad ankle wound suffered at McDowell on 8th May 1862.

As a brigade commander he had essentially directed that action during the Valley Campaign. Jackson had said that Johnson 'so distinguished himself that as to make me very desirous of having him as one of my Division commanders,' high praise indeed from 'Old Jack'. Wounds, however, kept him from that command. While recuperating, according to Douglas Southall Freeman, 'he made the best of misfortune: If he could not pursue the field of Mars, he enjoyed the domain of Venus.' [7] His recuperation was a lengthy one, and it was not until 8th May, exactly a year after receiving his wound, that he received a division, not D.H. Hill's old command, which had gone to Rodes, but Jackson's own old division, which boasted the famed 'Stonewall' Brigade. Because of his convalescence he had missed most of the great battles of the early part of the war, but the year of amorous distraction had not dulled his abilities. He played a masterful role in Ewell's crushing of Milroy's division at Winchester, Virginia, where the men gave him the title of 'Old Clubby' for the walking staff he carried, necessitated by his injured ankle.

Now, on Culp's Hill, he watched as the silent, wraith-like figures trudged past him in the gloom. It was slow going for the men, but at least he had them in the easiest formation, the column, which only required them to watch the backs of the men in the next rank of four. Brigade columns made movement easier and quicker. Even so, the columns snaked forward slowly over the uneven ground. The two lead brigades were Steuart's and Nicholls' 'Louisiana Tigers', followed by Jones' Brigade and the 'Stonewall' Brigade. The darkness was so thick that Johnson could not risk any other formation but columns; the loss of control would be just too great. He would rely on his scouts to alert him to the enemy's presence and then deploy for battle. Steuart's Brigade was on the right, with the 1st Maryland Battalion forming its own right. These 400 Marylanders, commanded by Lieutenant Colonel James R. Herbert, had been formed the previous October from veterans of the 1st Maryland Regiment, which had disbanded after its term of enlistment had expired. Brigadier General George 'Maryland' Steuart himself had been lieutenant-colonel of the regiment. It had not proved possible to find enough Marylanders to re-form a complete regiment, and they had to settle for a battalion formation. Strangely enough, however, the battalion now had more men than all but one of the 'full' regiments in the brigade, so badly had the army's line regiments been depleted.

The 'Stonewall' Brigade and Jones' Brigade followed in column, but Johnson after they had crossed the creek Johnson halted them to form a reserve. Unbeknownst to Johnson, he would be able to overlap the enemy's right with most of Steuart's Brigade. It was almost as if the half-mile gap between the 7th Indiana and Williams' XII Corps division was drawing the brigade toward it.

---

[7] Douglas Southall Freeman, *Lee's Lieutenants: A Study in Command*, vol.2, *Cedar Mountain to Chancellorsville* (Charles Scribner's Sons, New York, 1946) pp.336–7, 507–8.

1:30 AM, the Gatekeeper's Lodge, Cemetery Hill

The men of the Office of Military Information arrived in the train of Meade's staff as he rode onto the battlefield that morning. It was natural then that as soon as they arrived, they searched out the location of the Provost's head-quarters and the prisoner of war pens. They went right to work interrogating prisoners and examining captured documents, their work illuminated by the yellow glow of a lamp or two on their field tables. By morning they would be able to present Meade with a fairly clear picture of what forces Lee had on the field and what could be expected in the near future. It was slow and painstaking work involving careful questioning, the sifting of information, and the gradual piecing together of the enemy's order of battle, meticulously listing every enemy regiment and its estimated strength. In its short existence, the Office had become remarkably efficient under Colonel Sharpe's deft hand.

So it was that Sergeant Hussey of the 7th Indiana observed them at work after turning over his captive. Hussey was that wonderful example of a citizen army at its best – a man who could think critically and act on the conclusions. He had informed the officer accepting prisoners of Grover's message, but the captain had not seemed impressed. Hussey felt his duty unfulfilled and had lingered around the pens for an opportunity to convince someone of the importance of his commander's observations. He walked over to the light and to one of the men reading a pile of letters. 'Sir, my colonel had information from a prisoner he wanted someone to know.' Sharpe looked up. He had the ability to attract information, often as not by not turning away people who were eager to share it. Within two minutes one of his aides was running to the pen with orders to have the lieutenant from the 42nd Virginia brought over.

'Attention! Forward, double-quick! March!'

2:00 PM, the eastern slope of Culp's Hill

The 7th Indiana had already been awakened by the nightmare screams of one of its own men and rushed to arms when its picket line began firing. Their scattered shots were followed by a heavier blast from enemy skirmishers who cracked the night with their shrill Rebel Yell. As the Hoosier pickets scrambled to their breastworks, the enemy skirmish line began to flit through the trees, firing here and there, guided by the moonlight now sifting through the trees from breaks in the clouds. A sheet of flame fired back. In less than a minute the 'Louisiana Tigers' were rushing up through the trees in gray shadowy masses, filling the night with their cheers and shouts. Even in this poor light there were too many good targets for the Hoosiers to miss. The Rebels seemed to stop only yards from the five-foot breastworks, melt away in the fire, and then surge back to throw themselves on the walls of wood and stones again, trying to scale them. The 7th fired down on them, even throwing rocks torn off the breast-

work. In places where the Hoosiers had fallen the 'Tigers' climbed over, only to
be beaten, shot, and stabbed in wild hand-to-hand fighting. Bodies heaped up
at the base of the wall as the 'Tigers' broke themselves against it. The fiery
spouts of musket discharges to his front told their commander, Colonel J.M.
Williams, where the enemy's line ended, and he now directed his reserve, the
tiny 15th Louisiana's 186 men, to flank it. They curled around the Hoosiers'
right flank just as the 6th Wisconsin came down the slope to extend the line.
General Wadsworth had immediately ordered the 6th to Grover's aid when the
attack began. After its losses the previous day the Wisconsin regiment was not
much bigger than the 15th Louisiana. But they were quicker off the mark, and
were barely yards away when they fired. The 15th seemed to melt away from
the impact. The survivors fled back deeper into the woods.

Steuart's Brigade had lost its alignment and drifted to the left in the dark,
losing contact with the 'Tigers'. The noise of their fight flared then grew fainter
and fainter as the brigade continued to move through the woods. Steuart was
plainly lost by then, but the empty night seemed to draw them on. Adding to
his difficulties, the 1st Maryland had apparently lost contact with its flank
regiment and wandered off into the darkness somewhere. More runners disappeared into the night to find the lost Marylanders. It was depressingly
obvious why night attacks were so rarely attempted. But though rarely used,
they sometimes provided a cloak of darkness for actions that would never even
have been attempted in clear daylight. Before long his skirmishers began
reporting that they had descended the hill to its rear and found themselves on a
major highway crawling with the enemy's trains, hospitals, and artillery
reserves. From being bewildered, Steuart suddenly realized he had found what
every commander had dreamed of – the enemy's exposed rear. Homer's 'Panic,
brother to blood-stained Rout' would multiply the power of his brigade, which,
with over 2100 men, was already large. He called a halt and sent his staff
officers down the column to inform the regimental commanders of the situation. They would come up the edge of the trees and halt to determine where to
strike, then burst out to raise havoc. At the same time he sent runners back to
General Johnson to urge him to direct his reserves this way.

At that moment Johnson was preoccupied with the fight for the 7th
Indiana's breastworks. As the 'Tigers' swept forward once again, he roared
encouragement and waved them on with his walking staff like an Old Testament prophet until a bullet snapped it in two. He just laughed and continued to
wave the stump. Before long, he realized, he would have to pass Jones' Brigade
through the 'Tigers' to renew the assault. He expected Steuart's Brigade to lap
around the enemy any time now. As the minutes ticked off, he became more
and more impatient. Where was he? This was not like Steuart, who had served
him so well at Winchester. The runners he sent off could find no trace of him to
the 'Tigers' left.

Steuart was, in fact, readying his brigade to plunge like a sword into the guts of the Army of the Potomac – the concentration of trains, artillery, and headquarters securely nestled behind Cemetery and Culp's Hills, all well-lit by numerous camp-fires, lamps, and the suddenly generous moon itself. Running only several hundred feet in front of them, as they hid at the edge of the woods at the base of Culp's Hill, was also the enemy's principal artery – the Baltimore Pike, busy with traffic even at this early hour. As he expected, the fighting above him had thrown much of the enemy below into heightened activity, but there was still time. Time, he thought; he had lost track of it. Had he been able to see well enough, his watch would have told him it was almost 2:15. Looking about him in the gloom, he felt his whole brigade tensing up for the moment – four regiments in line with one in reserve. He drew his sword. 'Attention! Forward, double-quick! March!'

'What made you so brave?'

2:00 AM, the Gatekeeper's Lodge

Colonel Sharpe galloped up to the house and almost leapt off his horse, throwing his reins to an orderly and running through the gate before the guards could present arms. Meade had just opened the door to go on his first inspection of the army's position when Sharpe ran up the garden path and reported. Slocum had come out just behind Meade, who turned to him and asked, 'General, what troops do you have that can get up there fastest?'

'Williams' Division is encamped only a few hundred yards away on the other side of Rock Creek.' Doubleday added that his old 3rd Division was in reserve near the Cemetery but that they were fought out.

To Slocum, he said, 'Send them all, immediately. Position them yourself.' Slocum rushed past them, shouting for his horse and his staff officers. One of his aides dashed off at a gallop. To the Army's Chief of Artillery, Brigadier General Henry J. Hunt, Meade continued, 'We will need some more artillery up there as well.' Then, turning to Doubleday, he added, 'Get them ready to move; even tired men can find one more fight in themselves.'

As Slocum and Doubleday were rousing their sleeping divisions, Steuart's Brigade burst out of the treeline with cheers that echoed down the valley. In a few minutes they had reached the Baltimore Pike and came on in line of battle, the 1st North Carolina on the right followed by the 3rd North Carolina and the 23rd and 37th Virginia, with the 10th Virginia following in reserve. Crossing the Pike they found themselves in among the tents and wagons. A few hundred yards up the Pike two batteries of the XII Corps artillery battalion were rushing to their guns.[8] After Slocum's aide had alerted him, First Lieutenant Edward D.

---

[8] *OR*, vol.XXVII, part 1, p.870.

Muhlenberg of F Battery, 4th US Artillery, had barely had time to rouse his
men from sleep before the Rebel Yell echoed across the Pike. Nearby Second
Lieutenant D.H. Kinzie of K Battery, 5th US Artillery, was shouting for his
teams as well. Between them they had ten 12-pounder Napoleons.

A stampede of support troops – teamsters, cooks, quartermasters, servants –
fled south past Power's Hill, Slocum's headquarters, with Steuart's men in
pursuit, their line of battle now badly broken up by the mass of the camp,
clumps of open woods, and the small stream they had waded through. Here
and there men stopped to loot, but their officers drove them on. The pursuit is
an intoxicant, and every man was drinking his fill. A small group of infantry
emerged out of the chaos before the 23rd Virginia and fired a volley that
slammed into the Virginians. They were the 169 men of Companies A, B and D
of the 10th Maine, the XII Corps Provost Guard. They held their ground as
Steuart's regiments worked around their flanks and poured a steady fire into
them. For ten precious minutes these Maine companies absorbed the impetus of
the Confederate assault, time enough for the two 10-pounder Parrott batteries
on Power's Hill to begin firing into the dark Confederate masses, outlined by
the light of burning tents and wagons. Henry Hunt had rushed to the hill and
alerted the gunners and was personally directing their fire with the deadliness
expected of America's foremost artillerist.

Muhlenberg and Kinzie's batteries quickly harnessed and galloped the short
distance that placed them in the right rear of Steuart's brigade. Up out of the
dark a sheet of flame transformed Kinzie's four gun-teams into a bloody wreck
as horses collapsed in their traces and men spilled from the caissons. The 10th
Virginia had come up. Muhlenberg deployed his guns as the Virginians surged
past the broken battery. They saw his gun teams swing around and unhitch as
the gunners rushed to their pieces. The Virginians and the Redlegs[9] fired
simultaneously, but Muhlenberg's punch was double canister at fifty yards. The
small regiment staggered and disintegrated from the blast – rifles, body parts,
bits of uniforms, hats, all flying into the air.

Behind Muhlenberg's guns a brigade of Doubleday's old 3rd Division
rushed down the Pike, their rifles low over their shoulders, cheered on by the
surviving gunners as they began deploying in line of battle. This brigade was
another shrunken survivor of the first day of the battle. Its commander,
Brigadier General Thomas A. Rowley, had been drunk in the battle and was
arrested by a lieutenant of the 6th Wisconsin and escorted into oblivion by
fixed bayonets. Now it was being led forward by Colonel Chapman Biddle, a
man of sterner habits who put his 600 men into line of battle as he passed
Muhlenberg's guns. The remnants of the 10th Virginia gave way before

---

[9] 'Redlegs' is a US Army nickname for artillerymen, alluding to the red stripe – the branch of
service color – which ran down their trouser legs.

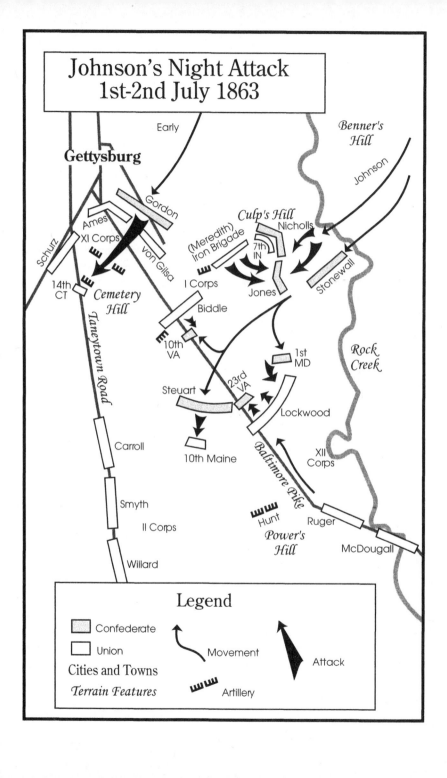

them. At the same time Williams' 1st Division was double-timing up the Pike across the bridge over Rock Creek with Slocum at its head. Spearheading Williams' Division was Brigadier General Henry H. Lockwood's 2nd Brigade; one of its three big unblooded regiments, the 1st Maryland, Eastern Shore Brigade, had only just arrived.[10] Two jaws were about to close on Steuart's Brigade.

Over the hill, at Ewell's headquarters in a red barn, Brigadier General John B. Gordon, unable to sleep, had arrived to urge Early and Ewell to let him try to take Cemetery Hill:

> My thoughts were so harrowed and my heart so burdened by the fatal mistake of the afternoon that I was unable to sleep at night... Much of my time after nightfall had been spent on the front picket-line, listening to the busy strokes of Union picks and shovels on the hills, to the rumble of artillery wheels and tramp of fresh troops as they were hurried forward by the Union commanders and placed in position... I expressed the opinion that, even at that late hour... by a concentrated and vigorous night assault we could carry those heights, and that if we waited till morning it would cost 10,000 men to take them.[11]

No sooner had he expressed his misgivings than the noise of Johnson's attack on Culp's Hill turned every head in that direction.

Gordon implored Ewell, 'Let me attack now to support Johnson, General. One more blow may be all it takes to drive them off that hill now that they are looking over their shoulders.'[12] Gordon was a compelling advocate. The charismatic thirty-one year old Georgian was one of the army's most promising commanders, obviously destined for greater things. His clear, commanding voice was the same one that had inspired his brigade with 'Forward, Georgians!' that afternoon when he fell on XI Corps' flank so that it 'shriveled up like a scroll.' So skillfully had he handled his brigade that when an officer asked where his dead were, he replied in a roar, 'I haven't got any, sir. The Almighty has covered my men with His shield and buckler.' His men were devoted to him and gloried in his leadership. On that same field, a wounded man said, 'Did you ever see the gin'ral in battle? He's the most pretties thing you ever did see on a

---

[10]* Henry J. Lockwood, *Lockwood's Brigade at Gettysburg* (Barnes & Sons, Philadelphia, 1879), pp. 76–7. Lockwood explains that he received orders to force march the 1st Maryland Potomac Home Brigade and the 150th New York to Gettysburg to arrive on the evening of 1st July. Had these orders not been received, he would have arrived at 8:00 the following morning. The 1st Maryland Eastern Shore had arrived independently at Taneytown early on 1st July and had been sent on to Gettysburg by Meade later that day.

[11] John B. Gordon, *Reminiscences of the Civil War* (Louisiana State University Press, Baton Rouge and London, 1993), p.170.

[12]* John B. Gordon, 'Three Days at Gettysburg', *MAC*, vol.XXV (1890), p.76.

field of fight. It 'ud put fight into a whipped chicken just to look at him.' [13]

The noise of battle from Culp's Hill grew louder. Gordon looked to Early, his division commander, for support, and, strangely, so did Ewell. Early had twice this evening shifted the fighting away from his command, first in the early evening to Longstreet then in the night to Johnson. A third time would be one too many, and Early was clever enough to realize that the time had come for him to play a part. He warmly supported Gordon's plea, Ewell agreed, and Gordon wasted no time riding off to ready his command.

Johnson desperately needed support. As far as he knew Steuart's Brigade had disappeared off the face of the earth. He had plenty of fight in front of him on the north-eastern crest of Culp's Hill. Jones' Brigade was going in on the left of the 'Tigers' where Steuart should have been. He ordered the 'Stonewall' Brigade brought up in order to exploit the breakthrough he hoped to make. At the same time, Wadsworth had arrived on the scene and made the decision to shift the remaining regiments of the Iron Brigade to the Union right, leaving only the 100 survivors of the 24th Michigan to support Stevens' Battery on the knoll. Both Johnson and he had instinctively identified the open flank as the key to the fight. Wadsworth's problem was that there was not much left of the Iron Brigade. Already the 6th Wisconsin had strung out on the right; together with the 2nd and 7th Wisconsin and the 19th Indiana, they would add fewer than 600 men to the line while Jones' Brigade numbered over 1500 and the 'Stonewall' Brigade another 1300.

Johnson had found himself another walking stick and was hobbling along on it, personally leading Jones' Brigade of Virginians to cave in the enemy flank. His scouts had found the end of the 6th Wisconsin's line and were guiding Jones' regiments around it when firing broke out from that direction. Where there should have been an open flank there were now more Federals. As Jones' regiments move up the slope the firing extended into the night. If it had been daylight, Jones' Brigade would easily have overlapped the end of the shrunken Iron Brigade, but Jones, in order to control his troops more closely in the dark and close terrain, had put only three of his six regiments in the lead, with the second three directly behind. As it was they still had two men in line to every one in the Federal regiments, which had spread their men out. Now, as the firefight flared up and down the line in the dark, the only way to tell the two sides apart was by the direction of the muzzle flashes: the Confederates pointed up and the Federals pointed down. But Jones had another advantage besides numbers: his regiments were comparatively fresh and had not been savaged once already in the same twenty-four hour period, as the Iron Brigade had. Even iron becomes brittle when beaten and twisted too long. Human courage is

---

[13] Robert Stiles, *Four Years Under Marse Robert* (R. Bemis Publishing Ltd., Marietta, Georgia, 1995) pp.211–12.

a depletable resource, and, by any standard, the Iron Brigade had used up most of even their great store that day.

As Jones struck the Iron Brigade, the jaws were closing on Steuart. Lockwood's Brigade shook out into line of battle as they came up the Pike abreast of Power's Hill. With a shout, they struck the unsuspecting 37th Virginia and crumpled it before it could refuse the brigade's flank. Next the 23rd Virginia was struck and pushed back. The Marylanders may have been inexperienced, but they had been in service long enough to shake down as cohesive, well-trained formations, which now paid off handsomely as the Virginians gave way. Just before Lockwood's Brigade had attacked, Steuart had finally swept away the last of the 10th Maine, their bodies lying in formation where they had stood. Now, suddenly, it was his own flank that was being crushed by a superior force. He desperately tried to pull back the flank, but Lockwood's attack was coming on too strong. The 23rd Virginia was barely holding on as the dark blue mass swept forward. Steuart's control of the fight was slipping away; his attack through the cluttered camp had disorganized his command, and his two North Carolina regiments were on the other end of the line. He ordered up his reserve, only to find it gone except for a few survivors roaming the field. An aide brought a captured horse up to him, a Godsend. He mounted, rode over to the Carolinians, and ordered them to face about and attack. These had been two strong regiments totalling over 900 men when the attack had begun, but several hundred had trailed off into the darkness and could not be found. The Carolinian regiments were joined by disorganized companies of the 23rd Virginia, and the shrunken brigade marched for the safety of the woods. It was then that they collided with Colonel Biddle's command. The fire flashed between them in continuous sheets, but the I Corps men would not let the Confederates pass, and Steuart's men would not back off. Muhlenberg's guns arrived and unlimbered to throw canister into the ranks of the North Carolinians as well. Steuart looked behind him to see Lockwood's Brigade surging across the field in the dark, almost invisible in their blue uniforms except for the glint of brass and polished steel in the moonlight.

It was only now that one of his runners finally found Johnson on Culp's Hill to tell him that Steuart had debouched into the enemy's rear. Steuart begged for support to spread the panic he had created. In an instant Johnson's whole frustrated picture of the battle was reversed. His sword had skidded along a wall on Culp's Hill. Success appeared elsewhere by sheer chance. He made up his mind in an instant. His orders had been clear – take the hill. They had said nothing about attacking the enemy's rear unsupported. But the whole purpose of the attack on Culp's Hill was to prize the enemy's grip off this end of his line and so drive him away. Attacking into his rear was an even more direct way to send him packing from the field, which was General Lee's basic intent. Johnson chose to follow the intent rather than the letter of his orders. His disobedience saved the Iron Brigade, whose thinning ranks had been on the point of melting away completely. For the second time a few men stood among the bodies of their comrades, mere companies where there had been regiments the day before. But almost by magic the firing from downhill ceased, and they could hear the enemy moving deeper into the woods. Rather than relief, they felt dread, thinking the enemy was going to again go around their flank; this time they had no more to give. Instead, Jones' Brigade disengaged and began following Steuart's runners directly south. The 'Tigers' would remain to pin down the enemy on the hill. The 'Stonewall' Brigade was ordered to follow Jones.

For Steuart it was too late. He could not break away from Biddle, and Lockwood was closing on his rear. Then, from the treeline above him, the bayonets of the 1st Maryland Battalion appeared. After wandering over the hillside lost in the darkness the Marylanders had only now found the edge of the woods. For their commander, the battle below was a lurid scene from hell. Burning tents, wagons, and stores flickered eerily. The muzzle flashes of artillery bathed the struggling brigades in instants of clarity, revealing the mass of Lockwood's Brigade closing fast on Steuart.

Rarely has an unblooded unit been presented with such a chance to immolate itself in glory. The Marylanders emerged unseen from the woods and formed line of battle. Captain William Murray, commanding A Company, quickly walked the line. He was well-liked by his men and had served with the old 1st Maryland Regiment from the start of the war. He had been around enough to know a forlorn hope when he saw it. Shaking the hand of every man, he said, 'Goodbye, it is not likely that we shall meet again.' Then the 1st Maryland attacked.

Only later would both sides grieve at what fate had cruelly arranged for them. Lieutenant Colonel Herbert halted the battalion at forty yards and ordered it to fire on the dim mass marching past unaware of the threat to its flank. Their volley streaked a sheet of flame, lighting up the darkness for an instant, shredding the flank of James Wallace's 1st Maryland (Regiment), Eastern Shore Brigade. For the first time, death had whistled into their ranks. More would have been pitched into the grass had their been light to aim better, but it was bad enough. The regiment came to a confused halt. Groans and shouts in the darkness now took their toll on the regiment's lack of combat experience, adding fear to confusion, a deadly mix for new troops. Two more volleys came out of the night before Herbert sent his men forward with the bayonet. They drove the disintegrating Eastern Shore men back upon the Potomac Home Brigade regiment. Herbert could feel them about to break as he slashed with his sword at dim shapes that seemed to recede into the dark as fast as they appeared.

As the Eastern Shore men fled past in the dark, Captain Long and the thirty men of Company K stood unmoved. They fired into Herbert's oncoming men and saw the first rank fall into the darkness. But others, howling, leapt over them. Long shouted for the charge, and the remnant of Company K collided with the enemy in a melee of bayonets, rifle butts, fists, and teeth. They were like a rock that breaks a wave, which washes around them, dissipating its power. That was all the time Wallace needed to rally enough of his men. They stopped just long enough for training to override fear, then more rote training got them firing at the enemy's gun flashes. Once they started firing, they kept it up, assured by the automatic motions that kept fear at bay. Lockwood had swung the Potomac Home Guards at right angles to their first line of attack. They stumbled over the uneven ground to form and fire. Now it was the Confederate Marylanders turn to stagger as the bullets came back at them out of the night. The officers of the Eastern Shore regiment brought their companies back up in line on the right of the Potomac Home Guards. Both sides were striking blindly in the dim light of their muzzle flashes, but Lockwood's command overlapped Herbert's considerably on both flanks. One of Herbert's survivors wrote: 'The death shrieks rend the air on every side.' Herbert himself went down with three wounds and command fell to Major William Goldsborough, who walked the thinning line of dim shapes encouraging them to keep up their fire, all the time watching the fight to the right to see if the rest of his brigade could extricate itself. Then he felt 'a violent shock' and fell to the ground. Raising himself on one elbow, he sensed more than watched as the firing line unravelled and its survivors rushed back towards the woods. Company A's Captain Murray tried to rally them, waving his sword, but pitched over dead with a bullet in the neck. At his side, his brother, Lieutenant Alex Murray, tried to catch him but was knocked unconscious by an exploding shell. Goldsborough watched all this as in a dream. Seconds later more shapes, this time in greater numbers, rushed over him. Then he fainted. Next to him in the bloody grass was Captain Long of Company K, his glassy stare peering up into the night.

The sacrifice of the 1st Maryland Battalion was enough for Steuart to wrench his surviving men away from Biddle's hard embrace. They made for the woods as fast as they could, in small groups, all cohesion lost, men stopping individually to fire into the gloom while others helped the wounded along. Steuart was shot off his horse while shepherding his command back to the safety of the woods and was carried from the field by a half-dozen of his men. As they bore him off, he cried out, 'My poor boys! My poor boys!'[14]

On the field south of the Baltimore Pike where the 1700 Marylanders had torn at each other in fratricidal strife, Confederate Private D. Ridgely Howard waited to die. During the fighting, a bullet had broken his leg, and he made a tourniquet with his handkerchief and bayonet and tied it around the limb. As

---

[14] Daniel Carroll Toomey, *Marylanders at Gettysburg* (Toomey Press, Baltimore, 1994) p.28.

he lay wounded another bullet had struck his hip. After the enemy had run over him and the fighting receded, he arranged his body so that others would see he had died well. But Union soldiers found him as dawn began to light up the morning sky, and he was carried to a field hospital. They asked him, 'What made you so brave?' Then they asked him his unit and were amazed, saying in return, 'Did you know that you are fighting your own men?' They were from the Eastern Shore Regiment. He was still game and replied, 'Yes, and we intend to fight them.' [15]

'His eyes burned with a terrible anger'

4:00 AM, Cemetery Hill

On Cemetery Hill the survivors of the Pennsylvania Bucktails, Doubleday's 2nd Brigade, had forced the XI Corps men back to their positions at bayonet point. They were feeling downright hostile, already blaming the 'Half-Moon Men' for the losses they had taken during the day. Many would gladly have bayoneted one of them rather than a Reb. However, they would have the chance, shortly, to reconsider that choice. Gordon's Georgians were coming.

Had he attacked half-an-hour sooner, or had Ewell or Early thought to co-ordinate his attack with Johnson's, chance would have had him striking the XI Corps just as Steuart was spreading panic in the rear, and the Germans would have bolted for sure. But now Steuart was being borne off the field wounded, and his bloodied brigade was crawling into the shelter of the woods. If there still remained a worthwhile opportunity for Gordon's attack it would be as a second blow to the one Johnson was trying to organize on Culp's Hill. It was almost 4:00 AM, and dawn would soon be fingering the horizon. The minutes were slipping away. Meade had meanwhile put his time to good use. The rest of Williams' division had flooded over the Rock Creek bridge and was being directed up onto Culp's Hill. Meade had also ordered up Geary's 3rd Brigade of New Yorkers, under Brigadier General George S. Greene, from the southern end of Cemetery Ridge. II Corps had also been ordered up, but Hancock, who had directed his corps to stop a mile south of Little Round Top, heard the sound of the guns and pushed on his First Division before Meade's order arrived. Meade therefore put them in reserve.

Steuart's survivors met Johnson's other brigades in the woods. Their tale of the brigade's defeat and the swarm of Yankees behind them immediately made Johnson cautious. His skirmishers quickly confirmed the presence of the enemy, and a lively firefight lit up the woods in the last hour of darkness before dawn. Johnson realized the game was up at that point. Two of his brigades had been savaged, the rest of the men were staggering on their feet, not having rested for

---

[15] Pfanz, op.cit. pp.320–21.

over twenty-four hours. He also faced an enemy force large enough to have wrecked Steuart's Brigade. He pulled back along the eastern slope of the hill.

Within minutes of Johnson's order to withdraw, Gordon gave the command to advance. The Georgians had barely 700 yards to go from their starting point beyond the small hill to the south-east of the town which had masked their assembly. Gordon rode at their front, his brigade eagerly stepping out behind him; they were game for anything John Brown Gordon led. When they were 200 yards from East Cemetery Hill, the Georgians rent the air with their cheers and advanced out of the last of the morning's darkness.

Their objective was that part of the Union line held by Brigadier General Adelbert Ames' 2nd Brigade of the 1st Division of XI Corps. The brigade was now commanded by Colonel Andrew L. Harris, former commander of the 75th Ohio, since Ames had been promoted to division command after the loss of Brigadier General Francis Barlow in the fighting north of the town. Ames, a 28-year-old West Point graduate of the class of 1861, had been jumped by promotion and chance from command of a regiment to that of a division in just six weeks. Serving initially in the artillery, he was severely wounded at First Bull Run but refused to be evacuated and continued to command his battery until too weak to sit up on the caisson where he had been placed; years later he would receive a Medal of Honor for his courage on this occasion. He had subsequently trained and led the 20th Maine into battle at Fredericksburg, and served as Meade's aide at Chancellorsville, after which he was promoted to brigade commander. It was at Gettysburg that he led his brigade in action for the first time. One of his men from the 75th Ohio, Lieutenant Oscar D. Ladley, would write that Ames was possessed of good judgement and was 'far superior to any Dutchman in the Army.' [16] The I Corps chief of artillery, Colonel Wainwright, observed that Ames did not indulge in any sort of profanity, something decidedly odd in the army. His forbearance was more than made up for by the legendary abilities of the 1st Brigade commander, the German immigrant Colonel Leopold von Gilsa, a veteran of the Prussian Army. Von Gilsa was uncommonly brave and able, and as uncommonly unlucky. His brigade had been on the army's right flank at Chancellorsville.

Ames' brigade, called the Ohio Brigade because of its three Ohio regiments (the 25th, 75th and 107th), was no longer overwhelmingly German in its make-up. It had lost more than half of its 1300 men in the first day's fighting and now numbered barely 500, some of them deserters rounded up by Slocum on the Baltimore Pike and returned to their regiments. The thin line it formed was barely one man deep, and in some places consisted of just one man every five yards. Barely twelve hours earlier most of them had fled through the town,

[16] Carl M. Becker and Thomas Ritchie, eds., *Hearth and Knapsack: The Ladley Letters, 1857–1880* (Ohio University Press, Athens, Ohio, 1988) p.147; cited in Pfanz, *Gettysburg*, p.243.

and they remained edgy as the fighting flared to their east and rear. In all fairness, two regiments – the 75th Ohio and 17th Connecticut – had retreated stubbornly, helping to inflict heavy losses on Gordon's veterans. The 17th Connecticut had been as hard as the symbol of the their state, the Nutmeg, and had shot down many of Gordon's men. But now, along the wall on Cemetery Hill, more than a few of the brigade (though only a handful of the 241 surviving Nutmeggers) had taken off to the rear in the darkness, only to be returned at bayonet point, some for the second time in less than half a day. The brigade was positioned along Brickyard Lane (now Wainwright Avenue), bending west just below the crest of east Cemetery Hill. On its right along the lane was von Gilsa's 1st Brigade, which had not suffered as much as the 2nd, retaining 650 of its original 1100 men. At 10:00 on the evening of 1st July, von Gilsa's brigade was augmented by the 218 men of the 41st New York.

Though the Ohio Brigade's attention had been on the fighting raging to their rear and right, it was suddenly jerked around to their front when the Georgian paean rang out. In the darkness they did not know that it was the Georgians who were coming, the very men who had bludgeoned them into near ruin the day before. A tremor ran through the line, then the brigade's skirmishers came bounding over the stone wall to join their regiments. Colonel Harris walked down the line, steadying his men as they fired into the dark mass almost on top of them. The first volley was wild; the Georgians were still hard to see. Only a few men were able to reload by the time the Georgians closed on the stone wall, firing as they came up to it and jabbing with their bayonets. At their head Gordon jumped the wall on his fine bay howling, 'Forward, Georgians!' His men swarmed over in the gaps where the Ohio men had fallen, widening the holes in the line as whole companies poured through. The 75th Ohio regiment dissolved in the hacking close combat along the wall, swamped by the Georgians. Sergeant Josiah Anderson parried aside Colonel Harris' sword and struck him across the face with his rifle's butt stock. As Harris fell to his knees and fumbled for his pistol, Anderson finished him with his bayonet.

The 17th Connecticut held out a few minutes longer against the 13th Georgia, which had suffered forty per cent losses the previous day. Their acting commander, Major Allen T. Brady, wrote: 'We fired several volleys by battalion, after which they charged us. We had a hand-to-hand conflict with them, firmly held our ground, and drove them back.' [17] But in that time, the 500 men of the 60th and 31st Georgia had broken over the wall and swallowed the 75th Ohio. The 60th swung right behind the 25th and 107th Ohio on the angle of the Ohio Brigade's line, and the 31st swung left trying to wrap itself around the 17th Connecticut. The Ohio Brigade died then. The two regiments at the angle surrendered as the Georgians came up behind them; the Connecticut men,

---

[17] *OR*, vol.XXVII, part I, p.718.

fighting front and rear, were all that was left. But they held steady under Major Brady's firm hand as the Georgians swept around them. Awaiting them was Brady's reserve, Company D, kneeling in the high grass. They stood up on command and fired into the oncoming enemy at ten yards. The Georgian front rank went down in a bloody heap. 'Now at 'em, lads!' a high voice rang out. Lieutenant Martin Frasier, a faint golden down on his young face, waved his sword and ran straight into the enemy, his men right behind him. The Georgians recoiled, but for only moments; then the Southerners came on again. Brady watched as company D, now providing the regiment's rearguard, doggedly contested every backward step they took with bayonet and rifle butt. 'The coolness and bravery displayed by the officers and men of Company D exceeded anything I ever saw.' [18] Behind the gallant company, he pulled the regiment back up the hill, firing as it went.

Gordon was everywhere, directing one clump of men after another into the fight. The darkness, even when lit by musket flashes, limited vision to no more than a few men rushing past. But Gordon's voice could be heard where his Mars-like form could not be seen, and the three Georgian regiments pressed forward. Ames had just ridden up to this most threatened part of the line when a hail of bullets riddled his right arm and mortally wounded his horse. He was thrown from the saddle, and his horse fell dead across his legs. He lay under the dead animal as the Georgians leaped over him, baying their rebel yell like hounds.

Von Gilsa's brigade had another three of Gordon's regiments in front of them. Two of them had been badly shot up the day before, so the odds were even, but whereas von Gilsa's men had already drunk deep of defeat, Gordon's were intoxicated by victory. The Georgians here too closed on the wall after absorbing casualties from the enemy's volley, but here the Union line was deeper and the fight had piled bodies on both sides before the news spread down the line that the Ohio Brigade had broken. In an instant von Gilsa's command collapsed and his 'Dutchmen' either threw down their arms or fled to the rear. The Georgians fired into their backs and scrambled over the wall after them. Von Gilsa rode among them, even his formidable profanity unable to halt his men. Save for the Nutmeggers of the 17th Connecticut, in fifteen minutes Gordon had destroyed the remnants of the 1st Division, XI Corps, and was sweeping his brigade up towards the crest of the hill.

With the Georgians on their heels, the survivors of the 1st Division ran through their batteries, posted 200 yards up the hill behind them. Two batteries of 3 inch rifles, 200 yards apart and just below the Baltimore Pike, fired canister as the last of the men in blue ran past. The Georgians in front of them melted away in the blast, which sent a great flare of illumination over the blood-spattered hillside. But those behind came on as the 13th Georgia rushed

---

[18] *OR*, vol.XXVII, part I, p.719.

through the wide gap unscathed, with Gordon urging them on. They fell on the gunners as the other Georgian regiments, their men hopelessly mingled, surged forward up towards the crest. Gordon stopped only long enough to send his second aide in five minutes to urge Early to send up Hokes and Hays' Brigades. Grabbing Lieutenant Charles Mason by the arm, he shouted, 'Tell General Early to waste no time; they are breaking; supports will secure the hill. I can take it but cannot hold if they counterattack. Now, boy, ride!' Mason's horse was already bleeding from two wounds, but he spurred the creature and was over the stone wall in a clean bound.[19]

The disintegration of the 1st Division left the right flank of Major General Carl Schurz's 3rd Division, on the west side of Cemetery Hill, wide open. It had already been whittled down to the size of a brigade (1500 men) the day before. Schurz had witnessed the debacle to his right and was desperately trying to redeploy to throw one of his brigades across Gordon's path before he reached the crest of the hill. Colonel Wladimir Krzyzanowski's 2nd Brigade swung back at a right angle from its reserve position and onto the Baltimore Pike just as Gordon's men overran the guns. The small brigade was quickly outflanked on its right and fell back onto Colonel George von Amsberg's 1st Brigade, still along its stone wall position facing west. Gordon's advance was sweeping everything before it, collapsing one brigade of XI Corps after another. Already Schurz's Division was unravelling, with the Georgians moving past them up towards the top of the hill. There they would be above and behind Major General Adolph von Steinwehr's 2nd Division. The 'Half-Moon Men' were about to be driven from Cemetery Hill entirely. Nothing stood in Gordon's way except his own victory-disordered command, fewer than 150 men of the 17th Connecticut, and Battery G, 4th US Artillery.[20]

Lieutenant Eugene Bancroft, commanding Battery G, had also watched the irresistible rush of Gordon's Brigade, and had shifted his five 10-pounder Napoleons to face west. They were on the top of Cemetery Hill, the last Union resistance before the high ground was lost. The Nutmeggers had drawn up on either side of the battery, frantically reloading. Only a dozen yards ahead of the Georgians, the last few men of Company D broke into a run for the safety of the guns. The last man was Lieutenant Frasier, limping, his face bleeding from a slash through the scalp and blood soaking his left arm. In his right he carried his sword, the blade broken but the stump red. He stopped in front of the guns, turned, came to attention, and presented his broken blade – then limped

---

[19]* Steven R. McClellan, ed., *The Wartime Papers of Gordon's Aide, Captain Charles Mason* (Georgia University Press, Boston, 1933) p.164.

[20] *OR*, vol.XXVII, part I, p.719. The 17th Connecticut had marched into battle on 1st July with seventeen officers and 369 men; by the end of the battle on the 3rd, there were barely nine officers and 120 men.

behind the guns. In that instant, as dawn threw light over the horizon at their
backs, Bancroft screamed to fire. The five guns recoiled, spewing double canister into the Georgians. This time Gordon went down. His horse's forelegs
blown off, he was thrown to the ground. He heaved himself up as men rushed
to his side. 'Shoot the gunners,' he shouted above the din. Outlined against the
new light, Bancroft was one of the first Redlegs to be hit, slumping against the
wheel of a gun and quickly bleeding to death. His second in command was also
down, but the gun sergeants kept their crews at work, even as they started to
drop. Their places were taken by Connecticut men. The rest of the shrunken
regiment kept the Georgians from enfilading the guns. Brady was the senior
officer and walked along the gun line encouraging the men. One enemy
company dashed forward and surged over the two guns on the left. The gunners
fought back with rammers and pistols, joined by the infantry, who added
bayonets to the melee. Brady threw his last reserve into the deadly swirl, led by
a lieutenant with a broken sword. For a moment the struggle balanced on a
hair. Then the enemy broke and fell back to their firing line. More canister
followed, and now the Georgians groaned at the impact, unable to move forward.

Early and Ewell could now begin to make out the fighting in the new light.
Gordon's aides faithfully delivered his pleas for support. Lieutenant Mason did
so dramatically, by riding his wounded horse right up to the two generals and
leaping from the saddle as the dying animal collapsed. Still Early did nothing,
which meant Ewell did even less. Early maintained that Gordon was only
conducting a supporting attack for Johnson and had done just fine in drawing
strength away from that fight. He insisted that the silence form Culp's Hill
meant that Johnson had taken the heights and that now Meade would begin to
abandon the field without further effort. The hundreds of prisoners Gordon had
sent stumbling back from the hill gave every evidence that success was to be
expected any moment. When it was too late to order forward his other two
brigades near Cemetery Hill, Johnson's staff officer arrived at Ewell's red barn
headquarters with the news that the attack on Culp's Hill had failed.

Meade had suffered no such indecision. As the fight in front of Power's Hill
had receded back onto Culp's Hill, Meade's attention turned to the fight just
beginning on Cemetery Hill. The reserves he had ordered two hours earlier were
now at hand as Hancock rode up, with his 3rd Division marching rapidly
behind at the double-quick up the Taneytown Road. 'On time, as usual,
General Hancock.' Then, pointing to Cemetery Hill and the guns blazing away
at Gordon, Meade said, 'We must keep that hill or give up this position. Go in
now!'[21] Hancock hurried two brigades up the Taneytown Road; Hancock's

---

[21]* Winfield Scott Hancock, *From West Point to White House* (Charles L. Webster & Co., New
York, 1882) pp.226–7.

veteran brigades swung up the hill as Bancroft's guns fell silent, deployed in line of battle, and came forward. The third brigade marched along the base of the hill and onto the Baltimore Pike, deployed, and likewise attacked. Caught from front and flank by 3600 fresh protagonists, Gordon looked once more to his rear for support, saw none, and ordered a retreat. 'No battle of our Civil War – no battle of any war – more forcibly illustrates the truth that officers at a distance from the field cannot, with any wisdom, attempt to control the movements of troops actively engaged,' he wrote years later. What he thought at that moment of the lack of Early and Ewell's support can only be guessed.[22] The Georgians had to fight hard just to escape from II Corps; they were closely pursued back over the stone wall by Hancock's men and stopped only when the Confederate artillery covered them with a heavy fire.

Twice in the early hours of 2nd July, Ewell's Corps came close to rupturing Meade's position, but each attempt had been as unsupported as it had been heroic. Ewell essentially failed to exert any effective control or co-ordination of the two attacks. Meade, on the other hand, had not panicked and had instead masterfully committed his reserves and thereby dominated the battle as it swept over the hills. Gordon had lost another 500 men in his ferocious attack and was out of the fight for good. Had Early's other two brigades been sent in at almost any time, it is likely that the Union position on Cemetery Hill would have crumbled. Gordon had almost single-handedly defeated the remnant of XI Corps. He would never forgive Early for failing to support him, and this bad blood would pursue them to their graves. 'His face was set hard as granite,' wrote Lieutenant Trace Wilcoxen of the decimated 13th Georgia, as the brigade trudged past him, 'but his eyes burned with a terrible anger. Our splendid brigade had been carelessly used and destroyed. There had been no divine shield and buckler that awful morning.'[23]

Gordon's blood-drained brigade stumbled to the rear in the early morning, past the other brigades of Early's Division, which had had a clear appreciation of the Georgians' glorious yet wasted sacrifice. The news of Johnson's failure was also running through the ranks. On top of the failure to press hard on the heels of yesterday's rout, officers and men were saying plainly that if Old Blue Light had been here, such follies would never have been committed. Jackson never let his men down or threw their lives away, they said. He would always find a way out of a tough spot. Bitterly, they said among themselves that the old 2nd Corps was no longer fighting in 'Stonewall Jackson's way'.

---

[22] Gordon, op.cit. p.153.

[23]* Trace J. Wilcoxen, *Gordon's Georgia Brigade* (Confederate Publishing Co., Atlanta, 1891) p.188.

CHAPTER 5

2nd July 1863
'They will soon stir up a fight'

7:30 AM, Pitzer's Woods

A hundred figures in dark green uniforms with emerald green piping crossed the Emmitsburg Road. They deployed through a peach orchard surrounding the Snyder Farm, and spread out into a skirmish line as they moved into the adjoining Pitzer's Woods. They were a detachment of the 1st US Sharpshooters, assigned to III Corps. Armed with the Sharps breech-loading, single-shot rifle, and dressed in green to blend with nature, they had become a deadly force in wooded country where stealth and accuracy were vital. Major General David D. Birney, commanding the 1st Division of Dan Sickles' III Corps, had sent them out to guard the corps' left flank and find the enemy. They had a reputation for finding the enemy. As they passed other regiments, men would say, 'There goes Berdan's men, they will soon stir up a fight.' And they were right, every time. This time it was not as if they had not been forewarned:

> As we approached these buildings a lad then living there, who had just returned from an errand to a neighbor's close by, seeing our handful of men about to attack a large force of rebels concealed here, whom he had seen but a little while before as he was returning to his father's house, remarked almost with a sneer, in the hearing of several of us: 'Look out! there are lots of rebels in there, in rows' – pointing towards the woods. We ridiculed the boy's remark and discredited his statement, thinking that he knew nothing about war and was talking nonsense. It is now stated that the lad, young as he was, had been at Antietam the year before, witnessed a part of that battle, and was not, consequently, so unsophisticated as we thought him to be. At any rate, the words were hardly out of his mouth before we advanced rapidly into the woods, and were almost immediately briskly challenged and disputed by the rebel pickets.[1]

They had stumbled upon Cadmus Wilcox's brigade of Anderson's Division, moving into position with the woods on its right. The Sharpshooters drove in

---

[1] C.A. Stevens, *Berdan's United States Sharpshooters in the Army of the Potomac 1861–1865* (The Price McGill Co., St Paul, Minnesota, 1892) pp.303–4.

his pickets and poured a heavy fire into the 10th Alabama, the right flank regiment.[2]

They had riled a hornet's nest. In the next few hours the Sharpshooters, reinforced by more of their own men and the 3rd Maine, played havoc with the Confederates who had been massing to the rear of Pitzer's Woods. They did not have it all their own way, though. Private Bailey George McClelen of the 10th Alabama was lying down with the rest of the regiment listening to the

> racket between our skirmishers and the enemy. The orders were to reserve our first shots until the enemy advanced close enough to make our shots effective. In short time the enemy moved our skirmishers back into retreat. Thomas Mackey before returning received a gunshot wound in one of his legs, his associate, John Nathanial Harrelson assisted him in his efforts to fall back and get back. The enemy charged up and shooting at us all they could until they got within 30 or 40 yards of our line before we arose from the ground and gave them a sound volley. [That] seemed to produce a consternation in their ranks whereupon they made a right about for their rear and with a rebel yell we pursued them some distance and then fell back where we were lying in line of battle.[3]

By the time the Union men retired, the sharpshooters had fired an average of ninety-five rounds a man, an enormous rate of fire compared to the muzzle-loading muskets carried by the ordinary soldiers on both sides. Peter H. Kipp of Company D was captured and taken to the rear when he refused to abandon his wounded captain. 'It is impossible for me to describe the slaughter we had made in their ranks. In all my past service, it beat all I had ever seen for the number engaged and for so short a time. They were piled in heaps and across each other. When I got to where the surgeons were dressing the wounded, I found hundreds of wounded men.'[4]

The only man to panic amid all this slaughter was Colonel Hiram Berdan, the founder of the Sharpshooters and supposedly the best shot in the country. Normally, as combat approached, Berdan would discover that his presence was vitally required somewhere in the rear, but this morning fate had trapped him there in the woods with his men. His first impulse was to call for help, and the nearest help was Colonel Thomas Devin's 2nd Brigade of Buford's 1st Cavalry

---

[2] *OR*, vol.XXVII, part 2, p.617. Wilcox stated that he moved into position at 7:00 AM and that the severest casualties were taken before 9:00, when the brigade had formed in line of battle on the division's right. At this time, McLaws' Division of Longstreet's corps began to fill in on his right at a right angle.

[3] Bailey George McClelen, *I Saw the Elephant* (White Mane Publishing Co., Shippensburg, Pennsylvania, 1995) pp.40–1.

[4] Stevens, op.cit. p.310.

Division. Devin had already been out scouting the right rear of the enemy when the firing started; he immediately threw two squadron's into the fight.

As the fighting progressed, Buford made the strangest of requests to his superior, Major General Alfred Pleasonton, chief of the Cavalry Corps. Explaining that he desperately needed to rest and refit his command, he requested permission to retire to the supply base at Westminster. Perhaps he was responding to the cavalryman's traditional concern for his horse; the animals were worn out after unceasing marching. Pushing them further would simply incapacitate the brigade as a cavalry formation. Still, it was an astounding request, unexplained fully to this day, to permit the only available Union cavalry to quit the battlefield, especially when Buford's command had only suffered five per cent casualties in the first day's fighting. Pleasonton's reaction was even more astounding – he granted permission. Meade confirmed the order. By 9:00 AM Colonel William Gamble's Brigade was already on the Taneytown road heading south. A few hours later, Devin's Brigade was withdrawn from the skirmishing to follow. Only one squadron of the 9th New York Cavalry was left to guard Sickles' open flank. As the division moved away from the battlefield, the men were openly questioning Buford's decision. They wanted to fight.[5]

Sickles began screaming to army headquarters almost immediately that his flank was bare. Only then did Meade understand the import of what had happened. Meade had given Pleasonton general instructions to guard both flanks with cavalry. When Pleasonton made his request to retire Buford, Meade had assumed that Brigadier General David Gregg's 2nd Cavalry Division had arrived on the field and that Pleasonton had moved part of it to the left flank. In fact Gregg was not to arrive until after Buford had departed. Meade now sent a stiff note to Pleasonton at 12:50 PM, saying that he, 'had not authorized the entire withdrawal of Buford's force from the direction of Emmitsburg, and did not so understand when he gave the permission to Buford to go to Westminster; that the patrols and pickets upon the Emmitsburg Road must be kept on as long as our troops are in position.' Another agitated note followed in five

---

[5] Edward G. Longacre, *The Cavalry at Gettysburg* (University of Nebraska Press, Lincoln, Nebraska, and London, 1986) p.205; Longacre, *General John Buford* (Combined Books, Conshohocken, Pennsylvania, 1995) p.206; *OR*, vol.XXVII, part I, pp.185, 927–8, 939, 1032. It is curious that Buford considered his horses too worn out to guard the flank at Gettysburg when they were in good enough condition to move a dozen miles to Taneytown, and then to Westminster, a total of thirty miles. Lieutenant Calef offers only the smallest glimmer of an explanation why the division moved first to Taneytown – 'to obtain supplies and forage'. However, since his division assumed the role of guarding the army's trains at Westminster, this may have been a major factor in Meade granting permission for his departure from the battlefield. Whatever the reason, his departure was one of the major blunders of the battle, so strangely at odds with his wonderfully good judgement and aggressiveness of 1st July. (Perhaps not so strangely, if the dulling effects of sleep deprivation are taken into consideration.)

minutes. Meade said that his permission for Buford's departure was based on Pleasonton's assurance that all of the Cavalry Corps was up and that another unit would automatically be sent to replace Buford, which manifestly had not happened. Pleasonton then waited almost another hour to direct Gregg, whose cavalry division had just arrived on the army's opposite flank, to detail a regiment for that purpose.[6]

The flank was wide open

7:30 AM, Stuart's headquarters, Seminary Ridge

Jeb Stuart had been far more attentive to the movements of Buford's Division than Pleasonton. His scouts had been up before dawn as well, feeling out Meade's left flank – and finding Buford's pickets stretching almost to Fairfield. He had planted his own headquarters in Macmillan Woods, about three-quarters of a mile south of the Seminary, to be able to easily receive the reports of the scouts on both flanks. Anderson's Division had moved onto the army's right flank nearby in the early morning.

While he waited, he turned over in his mind again the interview with Lee that had been crushing to a man who valued so highly the 'bubble of reputation found in the cannon's mouth'. It had been bitter beyond all measure to hear Lee's reprimand in such terms. He was still bewildered – had he not simply used the discretion that Lee had given him? When he had arrived at Longstreet's headquarters late that night, he was still burning with the shame of it, unable to criticize Lee despite the unjustness of it all. Longstreet was leaning back in his camp chair, his blouse on the bed, and enjoying his pipe. Stuart just stood there, still too agitated to sit down. Longstreet pushed a chair over to him with his foot. 'Sit down, General. I think I have something to take your mind off of this evening.' He called to his orderly, 'Bring us some of that fine Yankee coffee.'

As they savored the fresh coffee, now quite rare in the South, Stuart relaxed a bit, intrigued by Longstreet's laconic statements but sensing an opportunity. He leaned back in his chair, ostentatiously emptying his cup. Longstreet smiled and puffed on his pipe. 'It's going to be a bloodbath tomorrow. You'll see it as soon as the sun comes up in the morning and you see where the Yankees are. I wish we had their position, and they were going to attack us tomorrow, just like Fredericksburg.' He let the import sink in. 'It's going to be a bloodbath unless we do our best to support the Old Man. We had a complete victory in our hands today. But General Lee would not grasp it.' Stuart sat up sharply. Even after this evening, he instinctively rose to Lee's defense. 'Now, just wait,' Longstreet said. 'He did not grasp it because with the whole army not up, he

---

[6] OR, vol.XXVII, part III, p.490; OR, vol.XXVII, part I, pp.927–8. According to Buford, his pickets extended almost to Fairfield before his division retired to Taneytown.

did not know whether he was going to put his hand around a bunch of laurels or a wildcat.' Stuart's face reddened at the implied rebuke. Longstreet went on. 'I suggested that he simply move to get between the enemy and Washington. Without a shot we would have prised him out of that wonderful piece of ground he's got himself dug into. But again he would not maneuver in the dark. You see, General, without you Lee is a blind giant, something I thought he made clear this evening.'

'But, General, I acted on the discretion he gave me to ride around the enemy and gather supplies. I sent a half-dozen couriers to inform him of my progress! He had three brigades of mine at his call. What was Jenkins doing?'

'Well, none of the couriers got through, and I don't know why Jenkins and, for that matter, Robertson and Jones were never called up. But that is spilled milk. Like I said, tomorrow will be a bloodbath unless we do something about it. There is the opportunity to erase today by whipping the enemy tomorrow. And we can only do it now that your cavalry has returned. Look at this map. These Northern people make such good maps we hardly need scouts. See how these two hills make a hook and the shank runs down to these wooded hills a mile or so to the south? It is a wonderful position, and the Yankees have it; you can hear their axes and shovels making a fortress out of it. See this creek, Rock Creek, that runs about a mile behind the position. Now look at how the roads all feed into the town. The Emmitsburg Road runs straight between our two positions. The Baltimore Pike feeds in between behind these two northern hills where it crosses Rock Creek. The other important road is the Taneytown Road that also runs behind the enemy position. It is their direct road to Washington, and, I suspect, to their main supply depot.'

Stuart was instantly transformed. He positively glowed. 'All I have to do is swing my cavalry, followed by your corps south of these hills, and the enemy will pop out of their position like a knot in a burning log.'

'Yes, and we can do it without a shot, just sit on their communications with Washington. I'd say about three miles south of Gettysburg at, let's see, at Barlow. You could then send a brigade to cut the Baltimore Pike at Two Taverns. But you scout it out, find me the best and fastest way to move without the Yankees seeing us.'

Stuart was jarred from his recollection of the meeting with Longstreet by the sound of gunfire to the south; from his vantage point he could see Wilcox's Brigade in action around some woods. His scouts had departed before dawn on their mission to find a way to get onto the enemy's communications. He feared that Longstreet's plan may have already been overtaken by the enemy's drive to flank the army's right. He had kept the two brigades well back that Lee had ordered him to put on this end of the line. Only a few well-hidden pickets were guarding the open flank. If this was a strong enemy attack, he would have to counter it with the two brigades and thereby alert the Yankees to their presence. He ordered Virginia brought up and leapt into the saddle. He would see for himself.

He found the picket commander and joined him in the shady gloom on the edge of the treeline. The young officer immediately pointed out the Union cavalry on the field. 'Sir, the enemy was working around our flank, but as soon as the firing started, several hundred dismounted to support the fight going on in those woods.' Stuart could see most of a brigade deployed behind the woods. From the accounts of yesterday's battle, he gathered that at least two brigades were in the field. By now there were probably more. It seemed that Wilcox had accidentally flushed an attempt to flank them. Just in case the enemy resumed this attempt, he turned to an aide: 'Order General Hampton to bring up his brigade but keep it out of sight.' To another aide he said, 'Inform General Lee that enemy cavalry was working around our flank but has become engaged with General Anderson's Division and has stopped.'

He kept this position for several hours, watching the powder-smoke drift up from the woods. His scouts quickly found him to report that a second cavalry brigade was on line with the one behind the woods. He wondered why they just stayed there. He would have been raising hell if he had commanded them. By 9:30 they began bringing word that this second brigade had begun to withdraw from the front; by noon the first brigade and its artillery had also withdrawn. His scouts had slipped through the woods south of the Round Tops and trailed them from hiding as they disappeared down the Taneytown Road. Quite simply, it was a breathtaking blunder. The flank was wide open.

A few of his scouts, who had a good idea of the opportunities that lay on the enemy's main communications, had set an ambush to waylay any couriers. Their judgement was rewarded when they observed a single horsemen galloping toward them in a cloud of dust.

'Bring up every round of ammunition'

4:45 AM, Meade's headquarters, Cemetery Hill

Like the good engineer he was, Meade could not wait to inspect the geography of his position after his arrival the night before. But a conference with his corps commanders had come first, while the darkness of an overcast night draped the terrain in black. Colonel Sharpe's warning had arrived just then, and Meade gave his orders to bring up the reserves. Then he took a few moments to ride up to Cemetery Hill and walk among the silent batteries. Looking to the west and north, he saw the thousands of campfires around which the enemy huddled in their own exhausted sleep. If it gave him any pause, he did not show it. It was then that the night battle had begun. He chose to stay at his headquarters, the Widow Leister's House, barely a third of a mile from the crest of Cemetery Hill, and there he stayed through the fighting, committing his reserves as they were needed.

As soon as the light of dawn showed on the horizon behind him, and Cemetery Hill was back in Union hands, he began his ride along the line amid the broken litter of war, and the thousands of sleeping men beginning to wake. The shape of the field was vaguely discernible in the humid first light: Cemetery Hill and Cemetery Ridge, with the brooding heights of Culp's Hill and Little Round Top at either end, two rocky anchors. As the sun rose higher, he became even more pleased with the position. Nature had provided him with a great gift. The obvious fishhook shape gave him not only a natural rampart but a relatively short distance over which to switch troops from one part of the field to another if necessary. Lee's position wrapped around his, making the movement of the Confederate troops potentially three times as long. The Union position was also excellently supported by roads. Culp's Hill protected the Baltimore Pike, the main communications route to the army's supply base at Westminster. The Taneytown Road, which also ran to Westminster, ran behind the army's positions, providing the perfect lateral means of moving troops across the field. However, no position is perfect, and Meade could see the dangers of this one. Rock Creek, running a mile behind the Union line, was a barrier that would trap much of the army if it was driven off the high ground; retreat for the whole army across a few bridges or down the Taneytown Road would be difficult at best; and if the Taneytown Road was cut, his only route of retreat would be across the same few bridges.

Nevertheless, it was a splendid position for a commander determined not to retreat. It gave the inestimable advantage of gravity. Most of the mile-and-a-half length of Cemetery Ridge rose twenty to thirty feet higher than the ground in front of it. The hills were like towers in a mediaeval castle's curtain wall. Edwin Coddington summed up its advantages: 'Though not to be exaggerated, the Union positions did offer some real advantages to determined and trained troops who were willing to improve them by building stone walls or throwing up breastworks. They also afforded Federal artillery excellent fields of fire, especially along Cemetery Ridge which overlooked open and cultivated country.'[7]

Someone had noted how tired Meade seemed when he walked through the gate at the Gatekeeper's Lodge. That fatigue seemed to melt away as he rode over the field. Meade was the type of man, unobtrusive but quietly able, who seemed to draw strength from the very burden of responsibility. As the morning progressed, his chief of engineers, Major General Gouveneur K.

---

[7] Edwin B. Coddington, *The Gettysburg Campaign: A Study in Command* (Charles Scribner's Sons, New York, 1968) pp.330–3. Big Round Top reached 305 ft, Little Round Top 170 ft, Cemetery Hill 60 to 80 ft, and Culp's Hill 140 ft.

Warren, saw him as 'quick, bold, cheerful, and hopeful, and he so impressed others.'[8] His spirit matched that of the men. They had awakened to the feeling that this would be the great battle, and had thrown themselves into their tasks with a will and eagerness amazing for men who had tasted defeat to its dregs. If ever an army knew that destiny was in the air, it was the Army of the Potomac. Despite its defeats, the army still had faith in itself and its cause. Like an electric current, the knowledge of today's importance ran from man to man; the fate of the republic was in their hands, a heady thought, the kind to make a man gird his soul. For the thousands of Pennsylvanians in the army, it was even more important. They were defending their native state, a revelation that explained the matchless valor of the Virginians in the first two years of the war.

After riding over the field Meade stayed at his headquarters except when an emergency called him to some threatened spot. His firm hand made the house the nerve-center of the army. Aides and couriers swarmed in and out. He took pride in the swift efficiency of his staff, which quickly set to work to sort out the countless details necessary to put an army in fighting shape. He particularly relied on his chief engineer, Warren, and his chief of artillery, Brigadier General Henry Hunt. Both were superb officers, and Meade trusted their judgement absolutely. Warren was proving invaluable in identifying every important military feature on the ground. Hunt was organizing the artillery, the Army of the Potomac's iron and bronze fists, for maximum effect.

The Union artillery was both more numerous and better-served than its Confederate counterpart. The hard science of the artilleryman had come more easily to the business- and technically-minded Northerners, abilities which also resulted in the manufacture of better and more consistently lethal ammunition. At West Point, Hunt had trained the very men who were commanding the Confederate artillery, the best of whom was Colonel Porter Alexander, chief of Longstreet's artillery. Meade was particularly worried that there would not be enough artillery ammunition to see them through the battle. Both I and XI Corps had exhausted their supplies, and other corps were deficient. He was immensely relieved when Hunt informed him that he had brought twice the amount of ammunition normally carried by the Reserve Artillery, in order to make good any shortages that might occur in the artillery of the corps. 'I . . . was prepared for this, having directed General Tyler, commanding the Artillery Reserve, whatever else he might leave behind, to bring up every round of ammunition in his trains, and I knew he would not fail me.'[9]

What Hunt had not told the new commander of the army was that he had created a 'Ghost Train' of over seventy wagons of ammunition and other

---

[8] Emerson G. Taylor, *Gouverneur Kemble Warren* (Houghton Mifflin, Boston, 1932), p.123.
[9] Henry J. Hunt, 'The Second Day at Gettysburg', *Battles and Leaders* (The Century Co., New York, 1888) p.299.

artillery-related supplies over the last several months. Hunt had knowingly exceeded the army's table of allowances by the carte blanche Hooker had given him to order supplies and ammunition. He had done so for just such an emergency as this.

Unfortunately, Meade had not taken the same precautions with other supplies that the army would need in a sustained battle. He had halted the rest of the army's trains at Taneytown on 1st July, and ordered that 'corps commanders and the commander of the Artillery Reserve will at once send to the rear all their trains (excepting ammunition wagons and ambulances), parking them between Union Mills and Westminster.' On the 2nd he ordered them further back, to Westminster, fully twenty-five miles from the area of Gettysburg.[10] In effect he had permitted the army only ammunition and emergency medical treatment. Perhaps it was a mental hedge, because he did not want to fight a prolonged battle at Gettysburg and fully expected to fall back on his trains, which were much better placed after their withdrawal to support a defensive battle on the Pipe Creek positions he had obviously preferred. The field hospitals that would provide vital care for the wounded, following emergency treatment from medical personnel in the corps, were sent to the rear. The corps medical personnel were fully equipped with dressings, chloroform, and similar supplies, but little else. The army's rations were also on their way back to Westminster. Meade was concentrating over 80,000 men, who would have to eat what they carried in their own haversacks and could scrounge from the local area.

That morning the roads leading into Gettysburg from the east and south were filled with tens of thousands of men marching through clouds of dust to reach the battlefield. The first to arrive, between 5:30 and 6:30, were the remaining two divisions of Hancock's II Corps. Meade placed the entire corps behind Cemetery Hill because he thought heavy skirmishing with Ewell's Corps indicated an attack. By 8:00 AM the danger had passed, and the corps went into line on Cemetery Ridge, tying into I Corps on Cemetery Hill on its right and into III Corps on its left. Four out of five of Hunt's brigades of the Artillery Reserve were also on the field, having accompanied Hancock's corps. They were placed in a central position behind Cemetery Ridge on a cross-roads running between the Baltimore Pike and the Taneytown Road. After a gruelling march from Hanover, the last of a succession of forced marches, V Corps marched over Rock Creek on the Baltimore Pike at 8:00.

VI Corps, the biggest in the army, was now the only one which was absent. For Meade, the presence of VI Corps was the key to the battle. It was his reserve in case of disaster and his spearhead should he go over to the attack. Just as importantly, VI Corps' commander, Major General John Sedgwick, 'Uncle

---

[10] *OR*, vol.XXVII, part I, p.197.

John' to his devoted men, was the only corps commander of real stature other than Hancock. Slocum of XII Corps and Sykes of V Corps were dependable professionals, but neither had the quick grasp and initiative of the late Reynolds. Sickles, commanding III Corps, was a politician turned soldier. He had achieved fame for gunning down his young wife's lover and then getting off scot-free by using the temporary insanity plea for the first time in US history. An aggressive man, he could be depended upon to fight, but his judgement left much to be desired. Of all the corps, III Corps was the most sloppily administered, and its staff the most careless. Sickles was also not a subordinate man and, to the disgust of many of the Regular Army professionals, engaged in the sordid conspiracies that continually hamstrung the army. Meade simply did not trust him.

By noon the army's position was well-defended, but Meade still chaffed at the absence of VI Corps. He should not have worried. The corps was making probably the greatest forced march in the army's history.

A little present from General Meade

11:00 AM, Lee's headquarters, Seminary Ridge

Longstreet noted that it was eleven in the morning when Lee returned to his headquarters from a visit to Ewell on the left flank. 'Old Pete' – the nickname coined for Longstreet back at West Point, by none other than Ulysses S. Grant – was not surprised when Lee explained that Ewell and Early had not supported the idea of 2nd Corps beginning the attack that day on the left, or itself shifting all the way to the right for an attack. He was even less surprised when he learned that Early recommended that 1st Corps be given the honor of such an attack. Ewell was not even a shadow to Jackson, and Early was an open enemy. He could tell from Lee's laconic understatement that he had not been happy about the uncoordinated and bungled attack on the hills the previous night that had cost several thousand casualties and contributed to Ewell's plea that he could neither redeploy his corps nor initiate the main attack.

Longstreet had arrived at Lee's headquarters just north of the Seminary while 'the stars were still shining brightly', having left his own headquarters at three that morning. Almost immediately he had renewed his urging that the army move around the right and put itself athwart Meade's communications. Lee dismissed the proposal as he had the day before. A.P. Hill arrived to join the conference. To Longstreet's distress, Lee decided to attack Meade's left with his own 1st Corps. By 7:30 Major General John Bell Hood's Division, the van of the corps, was approaching the battlefield, with Major General Lafayette McLaws' Division in column behind. It would take several hours for the tail of the column, still far back on the Cashtown road, to pull up and make the concentration of the corps complete. Nevertheless, Lee was satisfied that the forces to make the assault would soon be available. His determination to strike Meade and drive him off his position was evident when he greeted Hood by saying, 'The enemy is here, and if we do not whip him, he will whip us.' Hood recalled how eager Lee was for the fight. 'General Lee – with coat buttoned to the throat, saber-belt buckled round the waist, and field glasses pending at his side – walked up and down in the shade of the large trees near us, halting now and then to observe the enemy. He seemed full of hope, yet, at times, buried in deep thought.' [11]

By the time McLaws arrived, Lee had devised his plan. His concept of the attack centered on the apparently unoccupied depression in Cemetery Ridge just where it met Little Round Top. Longstreet's Corps would attack it obliquely from the Emmitsburg Road. Once astride the ridge, the corps would sweep up its length, driving the enemy off and into the trap formed by Rock Creek behind it. Speaking to McLaws, Lee asked, 'Can you do it?'

'I know of nothing to prevent me, but I will take a party of skirmishers and go in advance and reconnoitre,' McLaws replied.

'Captain Johnston of my staff has been ordered to reconnoitre the ground, and I expect he is about ready.'

'I will go with him...' but McLaws got no further before Longstreet interrupted him. He had been walking nearby and heard Lee giving McLaws directions.

With an edge to his voice that surprised McLaws and Lee, Longstreet jabbed his finger onto the map and said, 'I wish your Division placed so.'

With the quiet majesty of which only he was capable, Lee said, 'No, General, I wish it placed just opposite.' Longstreet was stung and backed off. When McLaws suggested that no matter how his division was positioned, he still needed to make a personal reconnaissance, Longstreet sharply forbade it.[12]

For the next hour Lee sat on a fallen log with Longstreet and Hill and discussed the plan of attack. Hood's Division was then concentrating on the edge of the very woods in which the generals were conferring. As they approached the battlefield, they had passed crowded field hospitals, acres of captured Yankees, and finally the fields strewn with human wreckage. Word passed quickly, and the Texans of Hood's old Texas Brigade quietly massed at a respectful distance, peering through the trees and pointing in whispers at the demigods. Private John J. Evans of the 4th Texas remembered the moment: 'Even the officers crowded around with us to watch the generals talking on that log, with our own Hood nearby. We hadn't been on the hottest part of a dozen fields not to know that we were in for something.' [13]

---

[11] John Bell Hood, *Advance and Retreat: Personal Experiences in the United States and Confederate States Armies* (Published for the Hood Orphan Fund, New Orleans, 1888) p.57.

[12] Lafayette McLaws, 'Gettysburg', *SHSP*, vol.VII (1879), p.68.

[13]* John J. Evans, *A Private with the Fourth Texas* (Privately printed, Tyler, Texas, 1902) p.97.

Finally, the generals were in motion – the critical piece of information had arrived with Captain Johnston, who had just returned from his reconnaissance. He confirmed that the enemy did not occupy the two Round Tops as of 5:30. Lee, whose reputation had been made in the Mexican War for his daring reconnaissances over impassable terrain, was extremely interested in this report, although he did not comment on the fact that the information was three and half hours old. His own visual examination of the enemy opposite his headquarters did not indicate they were in strength. When he was satisfied, he turned to Longstreet and said, 'I think you had better move on.' It was evident that he now expected Longstreet to put the attack he had just outlined into operation as 1st Corps moved up.[14] Longstreet said that he would prefer to wait until Pickett's division arrived, to which Lee made no comment.[15]

Longstreet had been hoping that Stuart would arrive to take part in the conference. After all, Lee had directed him as well to protect the army's flanks and to throw out patrols to ascertain the enemy's strength on the field. But Lee seemed so anxious to strike the enemy that he seemed to have forgotten Stuart, or perhaps was satisfied that there would be no surprises now that the man who embodied the army's security was on the field. 'Sir, don't you think it would be wise to wait for General Stuart's report before we commit to this attack? Already we have discovered that the enemy's V Corps is only a few miles from here, and XII Corps is already near or on Culp's Hill. How much more of the Army of the Potomac is on the field or within striking distance?'

'We will proceed with this plan. General Stuart will undoubtedly keep us informed of any serious obstacle to your attack. But you are right, General, we should consult Stuart. But first I must see General Ewell.' It was about 9:00 when he rode out of his headquarters to visit 2nd Corps' headquarters. He had left with the clear impression that Longstreet would begin preparations to attack.

After Lee's departure, Longstreet's bad mood was palpable to everyone around him. To Hood he said, 'The General is a little nervous this morning; he wishes me to attack; I do not wish to do so without Pickett. I never like to go into battle with one boot off.'[16] To his Chief of Staff, Major G. Moxley Sorrel, he said, 'Find Stuart. Tell him if he doesn't report here to support my plan, I will have to attack this afternoon.'

But there was no sign of Stuart as the hours dragged on, and Longstreet, with some annoyance, thought to himself that he now understood Lee's impatience with the dashing cavalier over the past few days. Now Lee was

[14] Douglas Southall Freeman, *Lee's Lieutenants: A Study in command*, vol. 3, *Gettysburg to Appomattox* (Charles Scribner's Sons, New York, 1944) p.113.
[15] Hood, op.cit. p.57.
[16] Hood, ibid.

dismounting on his return from his meeting with Ewell, and Longstreet faced the bitter possibility of having to attack that awful position. He saw the blood run in torrents down that slope.

Lee for his part was barely containing himself. At Ewell's headquarters, one of his staff officers had found him listening intently for the sound of Longstreet's attack. After making a personal reconnaissance of the Cemetery Ridge, he had stated at 10:00 with some irritation, 'What can detain Longstreet? He ought to be in position now.' [17] Back at his own headquarters, Lee dismounted and walked over to him. 'I have discussed with General Ewell the possibility that he attack this morning, but he has concluded it would have little chance of success as the main effort.' The implied rebuke was not lost on Longstreet who merely nodded.

Lee had finally lost patience. His reconnaissance had revealed most of the Union position bristling with troops and guns. He felt the opportunity for a successful attack on a not yet fully-concentrated enemy ebbing rapidly away. He dropped his gentlemanly style of merely suggesting a course of action. 'General Longstreet, you will attack with what portion of your corps is at hand.'

Words seemed to stick in Longstreet's throat. Sheer willpower was forcing obedience, however unwilling, upon him. The seconds ticked by, and Lee began to look at him curiously. 'General, did you hear...'

'Yes, Sir, but I only ask that Law's Brigade be allowed to come up to join Hood's division; he should be here within the hour.' Lee agreed and issued orders that Anderson's division extend itself to the right and that Hood and McLaws then fall in on his right. It was then that Stuart's courier arrived to tell of the movement of the enemy cavalry around Hill's Corps. Lee left to personally investigate, leaving the deployment for the attack to Longstreet. Lee's command style was simple in its elegance. He left immense discretion to his chief captains once they had received his orders.

With Captain Johnston acting as a guide, 1st Corps began its march to the right of the line. Lee rode along with Longstreet in the middle of the column. Longstreet was almost beside himself at this point. Not only had his plan fallen apart because of the absence of Stuart, but Lee and he had had their first serious disagreement. His response was to sulk, not obviously in Lee's presence, but, as Douglas Southall Freeman described, 'the dissent of Longstreet's mind was a break on his energies.' [18] He was letting himself be carried along by events, and not breaking them to his will as Lee had come to expect of his 'Old Warhorse'.

Lee and Longstreet were in animated conversation when both were suddenly distracted by the arrival of several horsemen in a cloud of dust. No-one could

---

[17] A.I. Long, *The Memoirs of Robert E. Lee: His Military and Personal History* (J.M. Stoddart & Co., New York, 1886) p.281.

[18] Freeman, op.cit. p.115.

mistake the beautiful mare Virginia, nor her master. Stuart leapt from the saddle with a grace most men never even dream of, a leopard among cows.

'General Lee,' he said brandishing a leather dispatch case, 'a little present from General Meade. My scouts picked it up on the Taneytown Road.' He could not repress a grin at Longstreet as he pulled out a handful of papers, and handed the top sheet to Lee. The general slowly pulled his glasses out his breast pocket. It was a dispatch from Meade's headquarters to the officer in charge of the army's trains on their way to Westminster. There was no grand strategy in it, nothing as dramatic as Lee's orders for the movement of his army captured in the invasion of Maryland last September. It concerned the purely mundane information needed by supply officers to ensure the support of fighting men. For Lee, though, it was a blow. The dispatch listed the corps to be supplied at Gettysburg: I, II, III, V, VI, XI, and XII – all seven infantry corps of the Army of the Potomac, as well as the Cavalry Corps.[19]

'I fear, General Longstreet, I have been premature in ordering this attack. Meade has his entire army up.'

Longstreet suddenly came back to life. 'Sir, we could never hammer them out of that position with their entire force there. Now is the time to do as I suggested earlier – move around his left and cut his communications with Westminster and Washington at the same time. He will fly from that position, and we can fight him on better ground.'

Stuart chimed in, 'General Lee, that plan is entirely feasible. As incredible as it may sound, the enemy cavalry on their left has left the battlefield and is departing down the Taneytown Road. His pickets south of the Round Tops are also being withdrawn. It doesn't make sense, but, just the same, they are leaving. My boys don't see any Federals south of that big, wooded hill on Meade's left. They have also found a route whereby the army or at least one corps can shift south,' pulling out a folded map, he pointed, 'to here, at Barlow, about three miles south on the Taneytown Road. You see how Rock Creek cuts west to parallel the road just at this point. It is a perfect choke point.'

Lee examined the map intently. Longstreet and Stuart exchanged glances. Stuart added that his men had also captured Federal soldiers walking around Big Round Top towards the Emmitsburg Road. They were greatly surprised at their capture; they had surgeon's certificates allowing them to proceed to the rear, to which they pointed in the direction of Emmitsburg. They said they had come from the medical train on the other side of the mountain, indicating Big Round Top. They also stated that the 'medical and ordnance trains around the

---

[19]* *OR*, vol.XXVII, part IV, p.137. This supplemental volume includes the dispatch probably intercepted by Stuart. At this time, VI Corps had not yet come up, but the dispatch was written on the assumption that it would be present shortly, a subtlety that did not communicate itself to Lee.

mountain' were poorly guarded; no attack was expected at that point. They also said that the other side of the mountain could be easily reached by a good farm road, along which they had just traveled, the distance being little more than a mile.[20] Stuart added that there was also an excellent, well-surfaced main road that ran another half-mile south, the Barlow-Greenmount Road. 'Sir, my men have confirmed this intelligence.'

Then Lee looked up from the map, his brown eyes hard-set. 'General Longstreet, it seems you will have your way at last.' Then he thought for a moment, and added, 'But that would still require me to divide this army in the face of the concentrated enemy, a risk I could take in Virginia but not here deep in the territory of the enemy.'

'Sir, I must disagree. The enemy . . .' Lee had raised his hand.

'General Longstreet, I cannot divide the army, and I cannot afford to fight the enemy at another place and time. The longer we wait, the stronger he becomes, and the weaker we will be. I must destroy him on this field. But you are correct that a direct attack on his position would be too fraught with danger. You will have your envelopment, which I see as vital to the destruction of the enemy.' Looking to Stuart, he asked, 'You are sure the flank is wide open, that this main road, this Barlow-Greenmount Road, is open?' Stuart assured him emphatically that it was. 'Then, gentlemen, this is what we will do.'

'John, you are needed'

1:00 PM, Taneytown

The sweating columns of VI Corps continued to trudge through the dark early hours of the day and the heat of the morning. Men began straggling and falling out in increasing numbers. Barely one short halt an hour was permitted, and only once did Sedgwick allow a stop long enough to brew coffee. Even that was brief. Barely had a cup been drunk when the officers were bawling to get their men back in ranks. There was no time to lose. Men who thought they could dawdle suddenly found an officer kicking over their coffee pots and chasing them into their ranks. Lieutenant Rhodes was feeling the heat:

> Daylight brought no halt and what little hard bread we had was taken from the haversacks and eaten as we marched on. On the morning of July 2nd we heard the firing in front and then we understood the reason for such great haste. I was taken sick upon the road and fell helpless to the ground. The surgeon, Dr. Carr, gave me a remedy and a pass for admittance to an ambulance. I lay upon the road side until several Regiments had passed when I began to revive. I immediately hurried on and soon came up with my Co. 'B.' The boys received me well,

---

[20] E.M. Law, 'The Struggle for the Round Top', *Battles and Leaders*, p.321.

and I went on without further trouble. At Taneytown, we saw large numbers of our wounded men, and all kinds of carriages were being used to take them to the hospitals.[21]

VI Corps poured north through Taneytown just as Buford's cavalry were coming south through it, interspersed with ambulances and carriages full of wounded from yesterday's battle, creating a major traffic jam. Sedgwick forced his way through the head of the stalled blue column, yelling for the commander of the cavalry. Buford rode up. Sedgwick was struck by the exhaustion written all over the man's face, 'Good God, John, what are you doing going south?' The thought that the army could be retreating briefly unsettled him. 'John, I have had no word from the General Commanding since last night. I was ordered to reach Gettysburg by forced march. Is the army in retreat?' He could hear the noise of battle in the direction of Gettysburg. 'Has something happened?'

'No, General, things were quiet when we left this morning. The army is massed on excellent ground, and Meade has things well in hand. The enemy will probably attack today.' The sound of the guns showed that statement to have been overtaken by events.

The robust Sedgwick seemed to tower over Buford, who slouched in the saddle. 'Then why are you here and not on the field?'

Buford seemed to sag even more. 'My command is worn out and my horses near blown. I must rest them and have been ordered here to Taneytown and then to Westminster where we will guard the army trains.'. Sedgwick caught the eye of Colonel Gamble, who turned away as he overheard Buford's account.

Sedgwick leaned over in the saddle. 'John, you left a battlefield because your men and horses were tired?' Buford almost flinched from the words. Sedgwick could hardly believe that this was the same man he had come to know and respect as the best cavalryman in the army: tough, determined, and unflappable, the man Meade's dispatches had said had held off the enemy all morning with two small cavalry brigades. Something was wrong. 'Well, General, I suggest you get your tired men and horses off this road, so I can get my tired men and horses to the battle.'

'General . . .' Buford began, but Sedgwick cut him off.

'Either get off the road or turn around and precede my corps back to Gettysburg. If the battle is about to begin, and the sound of those guns means it damn well already has, we may well be marching into it, and I could use the best cavalry in the army to screen ahead of us.' Then, putting his hand on Buford's arm, he said softly, 'John, you are needed.'

---

[21] Elisha Hunt Rhodes, *All For the Union: The Civil War Diary and Letters of Elisha Hunt Rhodes*, ed. Robert Hunt Rhodes (Orion Books, New York, 1985) p.115.

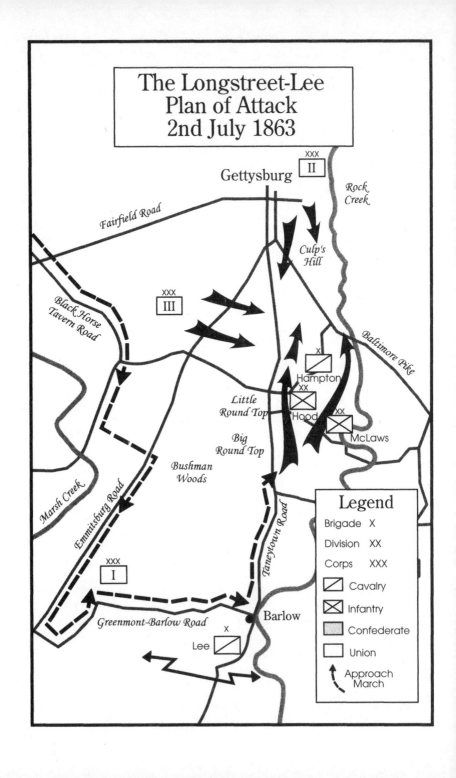

'Not on my authority'

2:00 PM, the Peach Orchard on the Emmitsburg Road

Major General David G. Birney, commanding 1st Division of III Corps, had dispatched the reinforced Sharpshooters into Pitzer's Woods about noon and watched as the smoke drifted up from the trees and the racket of the fire-fight grew in volume over two hours. Suddenly figures in Sharpshooter green and regular Union blue burst from the woods heading his way. One of the first to find him was Colonel Berdan, who warned him of the masses of moving Confederates on the other side of the woods. Birney quickly sent Berdan to report in person to Sickles on the saddle of Cemetery Ridge. It was just the news Dan Sickles was waiting for. He had chafed at the position of his corps in the low ground at the end of the ridge. His attention was focused on the high ground to his front. At the same time he was oblivious to the dominating high ground to his left, Little Round Top. Sickles had assumed responsibility for the army's left that morning, relieving Brigadier General John W. Geary's 2nd Division of XII Corps, which had been stationed on Little Round Top since yesterday evening. As Geary organized the movement of his command, he had recommended three times, with increasing vigor, that Sickles occupy the height. Concentrating on the high ground to the front, Sickles had ignored him.

Sickles had had his eye on the jumble of granite boulders directly across from Little Round Top, as well as the other high ground that stretched a few thousand yards north-west towards the Sherfy Peach Orchard on the Emmitsburg Road. He had already asked Meade that morning for permission to move his corps forward to occupy this ground, and Meade had asked Hunt to examine it. The artilleryman had quickly concluded that the advantages it offered did not outweigh the dangers of such an extreme lengthening of the line, which still had to be grounded on Little Round Top. Such a line could not be held by III Corps alone and would form a salient, the two sides of which could be assailed at the same time. Hunt also pointed out that the position would be difficult to occupy if the enemy had himself already occupied the woods to their front across the Emmitsburg Road. At Hunt's insistence, Sickles had dispatched the Sharpshooters to see if the woods were occupied. Then Sickles asked if he should move his corps out. Hunt was quick to reply, 'Not on my authority; I will report to General Meade.' He returned directly to Meade's headquarters and advised against it but recommended that Meade personally examine the ground himself before ordering its occupation. Meade nodded in agreement.[22]

---

[22] Hunt, *Battles and Leaders of the Civil War*, vol.III, p.302.

Black Horse Tavern Road

2:00 PM, Pitzer's School

If Brigadier General Fitzhugh Lee's 1900 Confederate cavalrymen rode past the white country school with less than the usual gay canter they had shown on other fields, it was because they were tired, man and beast. Stuart waved them by with a flourish of his black-plumed hat, which never failed to raise a shout from the men of his division. And it did not fail on this occasion either as the 1st Virginia Cavalry waved their hats and cheered. He knew he had pushed them hard these last two weeks. Today, by all rights, they should have been resting, but one more great effort was needed, and they were game for it. He did not want to think what one more day's hard marching would have done to the men and horses. Behind Lee's Brigade were the 1700 men of Wade Hampton's Brigade. Jenkins' Brigade and Rooney Lee's Brigade, the latter commanded now by Colonel John R. Chambliss, had been left by General Lee's orders to guard the army's northern flank. Hampton's and Fitzhugh Lee's brigades had turned off the Chambersburg Pike to follow Willoughby Run down to the school. There, after passing Stuart, they continued south along the run. This route, Stuart's scouts had assured him, would provide a route protected from a Union observation point on Little Round Top.

Longstreet had concentrated his corps behind Herr's Ridge and marched it down to Marsh Creek, then south along the creek to Black Horse Tavern. Hood's Division, which Longstreet always considered the better marcher, was in the van, with McLaws behind. At the tavern, the van of the column took Black Horse Tavern Road, which led directly to the Pitzer School. That route would have taken the column over a bare hill easily visible from the Union signal station on Little Round Top. Instead, Stuart's guides turned them left across country which took them around the hill to the south and then directly across fields to Willoughby Run and the Millerstown Road opposite the school. It was here that 1st Corps picked up the Black Horse Tavern Road again, where it was intersected by the Millerstown Road, which ran east through the Union position just north of Little Round Top. Black Horse Tavern Road continued almost due south, hidden in the depression of Willoughby Run. Longstreet and Stuart had worked out this route to avoid congestion and, more importantly, to avoid detection by the enemy. Stuart's cavalry would be past Pitzer's School before the first of Hood's men reached it.

The movement of Stuart and Longstreet's commands was working smoothly, much as it had when they had fallen upon John Pope's open flank at Second Manassas. Here, though, it would be trickier. They were in an alien land among a hostile people. Still, Longstreet could not have been happier. If the Confederate operation was functioning like a well-oiled machine, it was because Longstreet had become his usual energetic and totally involved self. His attention to his corps was all-consuming. He had sent his staff up and down the columns ensuring that the pace was maintained and that everyone knew his part. It was a foolhardy officer or man who dawdled under the corps commander's gaze.

Longstreet's confidence was high, something his staff and subordinates noted, a remarkable turn-around from only two hours before. He was executing much of the plan he had so fruitlessly advocated all morning; there would be no Southern bloodbath on the slopes of those hills and ridges. He would strike the enemy before he could even turn to defend himself, and make him collapse like a house of cards.

Maybe Lee was right, that they could not afford to delay the showdown. Well, Longtree had three subordinates who would carry out an assault on the moon itself if need be. Stuart would do anything to redeem himself in Lee's eyes, and this plan was the very thing to appeal to the cavalier. John Bell Hood and Lafayette McLaws were the other two of the trio. Hood, at the age of thirty-two was 'blond, towering, blue-eyed and handsome,' standing six feet two inches with broad shoulders and a voice with a 'booming, musical richness of tone.' He had led the Texas Brigade, initially as the commander of the 4th Texas, and given it his name forever. A Kentuckian by birth, he had been disappointed when his native state failed to secede and declared himself a Texan, having served there in the Regular Army and become greatly attached to it austere beauty. This self-identification gained him command of the 4th Texas early in the war:

> I lost no opportunity whenever the officers or men came to my quarters, or whenever I chanced to be in conversation with them, to arouse their pride, to impress upon them that no regiment in that army should ever be allowed to go forth upon the battlefield and return with more trophies than the Fourth Texas – that the number of colors and guns captured, and prisoners taken, constituted the true test of the work done by any command in an engagement.[23]

He was utterly devoted to his men and they to him. The brigade historian was to write that none of the brigade's subsequent commanders was to have 'the personal magnetism of Hood, nor the swinging dash and reckless yet cool disregard for danger, which from the outset, won the love and admiration of a brigade largely composed of boys just flowering into manhood.' [24]

McLaws, a Georgian, was in his forties, short, powerful, compact, swarthy, black-haired, dark-eyed, and honest. An early division commander in the army, his career had shown more dependability than fire. At Sharpsburg and

---

[23] Hood, op.cit. p.19.
[24] J.B. Polley, *Hood's Texas Brigade* (Neale Publishing Co., New York, 1910) pp.204–5.

Chancellorsville he had failed to make the extra effort and take the risks that marked a great soldier. 'In dealing with him one thought more of his tenacity than his grace, for impassiveness and unflinching fortitude seemed to show all over him.' [25] If he had little fire, he was nevertheless dogged. It would not be enough to kill a man like this; you would have to knock him down as well.

'Are you not too much extended, general?'

3:00 PM, III Corps headquarters

Dan Sickles made his decision. All morning and afternoon he had worried about the low ground his corps had occupied. He was desperate to move forward to the higher ground ahead. It seemed a replay of Chancellorsville. There, he had been held back from seizing just such high ground to his front at the Hazel Grove. The Confederates had been quicker off the mark, seized the high ground, and from there had tormented the Federal line. He had watched the Sharpshooters and the 3rd Maine bolt out of the woods, and now Colonel Berdan had come running up to him, ahead of all his men, panting with the run. Between gasps, Berdan told him that huge masses of the enemy were concentrating behind Pitzer's Woods, readying themselves for an attack.

He would beat them to the punch. The 10,000 men of III Corps marched off Cemetery Ridge in a grand display, flags flying and music playing. The men of II Corps, up on the ridge, dropped what they were doing to crowd forward and watch. They were impressed with the military display. 'How splendidly they march!' 'It looks like a dress parade, a review.' Hancock's first reaction was to laugh and tell the officers around him, 'Wait a moment, you will see them tumbling back.' [26] But he also had a more practised eye for the consequences of such maneuvers. He had been completely surprised. Sickles had given him no warning of his intentions. III Corps' abandonment of its position on the ridge had opened a massive gap on II Corps' flank. Leaving a flanking unit in the lurch was a military sin of the first order. Sickles was about to get everybody into trouble.

III Corps quickly moved onto the high ground so much admired by its commander. Brigadier General Andrew A. Humphreys' 2nd Division, on the right, moved out to the Emmitsburg Road, down to the Peach Orchard on the Sherfy Farm, and there formed an angle. Birney's 1st Division positioned itself on a line running from the Wheatfield on the Rose Farm to the Devil's Den, a jumble of boulders directly across Plum Run from Little Round Top. The shape of III Corps' new position was a spearhead, with its point at the orchard. Sickles

---

[25] Tucker, op.cit. p.270.

[26] John P. Nicholson, ed., *Pennsylvania at Gettysburg*, vol.2 (William Stanley Ray, Harrisburg, Pennsylvania, 1914) pp.622–3; quoted in Tucker, p.241.

now had his high ground, but upon examination it proved an illusory advantage. Although a slightly higher elevation than the saddle of Cemetery Ridge, the Peach Orchard was open and exposed. It could be swept by artillery and assailed from the woods nearby, which would form a short-distance assembly area for the enemy. It was less a position to hold than to deny the enemy. The Wheatfield was much the same, with its elevation in its bare center. Houk Ridge backed onto woods, making much of its elevation useless for fields of fire. The Devil's Den was also deceptive. As seen from Cemetery Ridge it was high ground, and would certainly have been deadly to any Union attack from that direction. However, once in occupation of it, Birney's men found that the rear of the rocky pile was essentially level with the woods behind it.

Meade was holding a council of war with his corps commanders when Warren rode up and informed him that III Corps had abandoned its position and moved forward. It was then that Meade turned to George Sykes and ordered him to move V Corps from its place in reserve to the left and to hold it 'at all hazards.'[27] Sickles, who had ignored repeated summonses to attend the conference, eventually obeyed the last peremptory one and had just ridden up. Meade met him outside. One of his aides recalled: 'I never saw General Meade so angry if I may so call it. He ordered General Sickles to retire his line to the position he had been instructed to take. This was done in a few sharp words.'[28] Just then Humphreys' right flank and center along the Emmitsburg Road was assailed by gunfire. The firefight begun by the Sharpshooters had escalated significantly as each side had added more troops, and Anderson had now upped the ante by throwing in some of his artillery. The crash of the guns interrupted Meade's dressing down of Sickles. He collected himself and said, 'General, I will not ask you to dismount. The enemy are engaging your fronts. The council is over.'[29]

Sickles and his staff rode off. Meade followed with General Warren. When they topped Cemetery Ridge, Warren pointed up to Little Round Top and said, 'Here is where the line should be.' Meade replied that it was too late but gave Warren permission to inspect it. As Warren rode off, Meade continued on to find Sickles at the Peach Orchard. He had taken in the situation during his ride and immediately asked Sickles, 'Are you not too much extended, general? Can you hold this front?' Sickles was quick to assure him that he could. But, he said, he would need more support and more artillery. These Meade promised him, with II and V Corps and the Reserve Artillery.[30] Meade told Sickles that he had

---

[27] *OR*, vol.XXVII, part I, p.592.

[28] Harry W. Pfanz, *Gettysburg: The Second Day* (University of North Carolina Press, Chapel Hill and London, 1987) p.140.

[29] 'Historicus' in the New York *Herald*, 12th March 1864.

[30] 'Historicus', ibid.

made an unwise move but that it was too late to correct it. They would have to do the best they could. Then he asked him why he had not maintained his flank connection with Hancock's II Corps. Sickles said it was because he needed the higher ground to his front. It was then that Meade put his finger on the whole fallacy of Sickles deployment. 'General Sickles, this is neutral ground, our guns command it as well as the enemy's. The very reason you cannot hold it applies to them.' Sickles then asked if should return his corps to Cemetery Ridge. Meade paused briefly and replied, 'You cannot hold this position, but the enemy will not let you get away without a fight, & it may as well begin now as at any time.'[31]

'I would pay you to be here now!'

3:00 PM, south of Big Round Top

Stuart's brigades followed Willoughby Run south about three miles, then due east another mile-and-a-half, past the farm of George Bishop to reach the Emmitsburg Road. Ripples of laughter broke out as the column passed Bishop's farm and a sign that said, 'Go Away – And That Means You!' At the Emmitsburg Road, the two cavalry brigades turned south. If they looked back to their left rear, the men could see the forested heights of Bushman Woods and behind it Big Round Top. Behind them the van of 1st Corps had passed the school. From there the march was on a good but narrow country road lined with fences that restricted the marching columns. The division commanders were forced to narrow the columns down by ordering them to 'break files to the rear,' stretching out the columns and, slowly, the rear brigades.[32]

Still, 1st Corps was making good time, eating up the miles in the rich Adams County countryside. Hood's Division pulled ahead with their renowned gait. Even here the pretty girls seemed to come out to the roadside in places, to watch the soldiers march by. As the Texas Brigade at the head of the division passed, the girls would call out, asking which brigade or regiment. 'At the answer "Texas," there seemed to be the word "Law" well drawn out.'[33] The girls would have a lot more to wonder at as the rest of the 15,000 men of 1st Corps marched quickly by along the narrow lanes.

When they reached the Emmitsburg Road, they too turned south. Here Longstreet galloped ahead with his staff to find the cavalry. As they turned down the road, Big Round Top was barely a thousand feet to the north. It was eerie; just on the other side of these heights a mile-and-a-half away, a heavy skirmish was taking place, but he could hear nothing. He had been on too

[31] Pfanz, op.cit. p.144.
[32] McLaws, op.cit. p.69.
[33] William A. Fletcher, *Rebel Private Front and Rear: Memoirs of a Confederate Soldier* (Dutton Books, New York, 1995) p.77.

many fields to be surprised at the tricks sound could play. It was a short half-mile ride to the intersection of the Emmitsburg and Barlow-Greenmount roads and then another two miles to the intersection with the Taneytown Road. There he found Stuart and his brigade commanders. Stuart smiled and motioned with a cigar to the road that paralleled the treeline they were in. 'There it is, General. Just like I promised – the Taneytown Road.' A few enemy moving north had already been captured, but otherwise it was tranquil. They had achieved complete surprise.

Longstreet looked at his watch. It was almost 3:30. 'The lead brigade of Hood's Division will be arriving in about forty minutes at worst.' He looked at Hampton. 'As soon as they reach the tail of your column, you know what to do?'

'Hell, yes, General. I would pay you to be here now!' Longstreet nodded, saying to himself, 'Yes, if anyone can do this, it will be Hampton.' This fellow South-Carolinian[34] was well known, not only as the richest planter in the South, but as a superlative cavalry commander. At the age of forty-six, he was in his prime: 'Just under six feet in height, he had the balance of a horseman and the smooth muscles of the athlete.'[35] In conversation with Longstreet only the night before, Stuart had described his conduct at Upperville on 21st June, as he led his command against a stubborn enemy, as 'brilliant'. Major Henry McClellan, one of Stuart's staff officers, had added, 'Drawing his saber, and raising himself to his full height, he cried, "First North Carolina, follow me!" and those North Carolinians could as little resist that appeal as iron can fail to obey the magnet.' His success 'was mainly due to that personal influence which . . . has marked Hampton a leader of men.' He had that ability to weld a body of men into a unified fighting force.[36] That is just what Longstreet would need – bold courage and iron control, a man who could drive in a sword to the hilt and not let it turn in his hand.

Hood rode up with his staff. 'General, my men are here.' Longstreet looked at his watch again. It was 4:05. 'Well, Gentlemen, I guess we shouldn't waste any more time.' Hampton ordered his brigade forward, and they thundered north up the Taneytown Road. Turning back to Hood, he said, 'Sam, bring your division up fast. Now break 'em, Sam, break 'em.'[37]

[34] Longstreet was raised in both Georgia and South Carolina and claimed both as his home.
[35] Freeman, op.cit. vol.I, p.93.
[36] H.B. McClellan, *The Life and Campaigns of Major-General J.E.B. Stuart* (Houghton Mifflin, New York, 1885) p.313.
[37] John Bell Hood, 'The Attack Around Big Round Top', *SHSP*, vol.XXVII (1879), p.37.

CHAPTER 6

2nd July 1863
'Remember, at all costs!'

A band of angels

4:00 PM, Emmitsburg, Maryland

As Longstreet gazed down upon the Taneytown Road, Captain Dahlgren galloped through the streets of Emmitsburg, just across the state border in Maryland, his horse lathered white with sweat. Strapped to his saddle was a valise, lately in the charge of a Confederate courier. Its contents were pure gold, and he would ride his horse and others to death to get it to Meade.

The day had begun quietly as Moorehead, the veteran of the 126th Pennsylvania, had slipped out of Dahlgren's camp and ridden into his old home town of Greencastle to scout out any Rebel presence. The Union band had changed back into their uniforms by the time he had returned. He reported that conversations with old friends indicated only small squads of Confederates had passed through the town since Lee's army had marched north a week ago. Dahlgren ordered the men into their saddles.

As they rode into Greencastle, Dahlgren sent Moorehead and three men south out of town to reconnoitre the road. His own problems were more immediate, as is apparent from a resident's record of his arrival:

> If a band of angels had come down into the town they could not have been more unexpected or welcome. It required only a few minutes to apprise the people of their presence, when all Greencastle seemed to be in the street. Hats flew into the air and cheer followed cheer. Even the old and staid ministers forgot the proprieties and many wept for joy.[1]

Dahlgren was in his element, the savior of his fellow Pennsylvanians, and he loved every moment. It was then that Moorehead raced back into town to report that a company of Confederate cavalry were about half a mile away on the Williamsport Road, approaching the town. Laurels or no, Dahlgren had still kept his wits about him and ordered the townspeople off the streets, which

---

[1] Jacob Hoke, *The Great Invasion* (W.J. Shuey, Dayton, Ohio, 1887) pp.180–1; reprinted Thomas Yseloff, New York and London, 1959.

emptied as quickly as they had filled. It was just in time. He hid his small force behind a public building, then rode back to the Reformed Church on East Baltimore Street and climbed the bell tower to scan the area for any more Confederate parties. To his surprise he saw an enemy wagon train trundling into Greencastle from the north. This was more than a complication. The train's infantry guard upped the odds even more against his little band.

For a young fire-eater like Dahlgren, the opportunities dismissed the odds. He raced down the stairs to join his fifteen men and waited, leaning forward until he touched the horse's neck, cocked pistol in hand, until the enemy cavalry company and the head of the train had almost met, some seventy-five yards from where he was hidden. He felt the icy, controlled thrill mount within him, just as it had at Brandy Station when he rallied a retreating cavalry regiment and led it back into the fray.

Then, with a yell, he led his small detachment around the building in a wild charge. 'Cutting through he supply train, they stampeded the lead teams, causing some vehicles to overturn. In minutes, the center of Greencastle was bedlam'. The Rebels panicked; the Union cavalry seemed to be everywhere, shooting with pistols, waving sabers, and yelling fit to raise the dead. Train guards and cavalrymen ran for their lives, except for three officers and fourteen infantrymen who threw up their hands in surrender.[2]

Two of the captured officers were couriers, whose cavalry escort had bolted in the attack; two large bags of mail they were carrying were scattered on the side of the street. A quick search showed they contained only personal letters. It was then that Dahlgren noticed a leather valise tied to the saddle of one of the couriers, whose behavior was nervous in the extreme. For the second time in a span of minutes he was surprised, but this time far more agreeably. The contents were dispatches from Jefferson Davis for General Lee. He tore open the seals and scanned them, and even this cursory look told him what a treasure glittered in his hands.

In minutes they were riding out of town down the Waynesboro Road. On the outskirts of Greencastle, Dahlgren ordered half of his force to stay behind to barricade the road in case the enemy recovered their courage and came after them. He left the rest of the men behind to march the prisoners to Emmitsburg, and sped on alone, crossing the mountains at Monterey Pass and heading east to Emmitsburg. Greencastle had been only twelve miles by the direct route from Gettysburg, but Lee's army barred the way. He would have to ride around it thirty miles. In Emmitsburg he rested his horse momentarily, and heard from local citizens that the army and Meade were still at Gettysburg. Then he rode on into the afternoon, to find Meade and present his prize.

---

[2] Edward G. Longacre, *The Cavalry at Gettysburg* (University of Nebraska Books, Lincoln, Nebraska, and London, 1986) p.209.

'It couldn't have worked out better'

4:00 PM, the Lutheran Seminary

Lee sat on a tree-stump waiting for Longstreet's attack to begin. Hill was the only senior officer in attendance, and he too was waiting for Longstreet. At the first sign of frantic movement on the ridge in front of him, he would throw Anderson's and Pender's Divisions straight up the slope, to cave in the enemy's front as Old Pete struck them from behind. He felt confident; the same crushing envelopment had worked wickedly at Second Manassas and Chancellorsville. Today it would net them the entire Army of the Potomac. His thoughts were dazzled at the consequences of the stroke. Washington, Baltimore, Philadelphia even, all at their mercy – Southern independence assured, victory, home.

At first Lee was concerned that the enemy had observed Longstreet's march around the flank and had decided to strike Hill's now open flank when Sickles moved off the ridge. But only Anderson's artillery and skirmishers had become engaged as Sickles stopped his command in the form of a salient on minor high ground. Lee did remark, however, 'I am surprised that General Meade would do something so foolish. I thought him too calculating and prudent for such a move that has no apparent purpose. I do not believe they will attack.'

Hill said, 'It couldn't have worked out better. If they had stayed on the ridge, they could have about-faced and attacked Longstreet in the flank.' He was confident that Anderson's flank was secure.

'Nevertheless, General, we only have a few regiments of cavalry to Anderson's right. Kindly alert General Heth's Division to be ready to march should those people become more energetic.'

When Dan Sickles threw the dice

4:00 PM, the Peach Orchard

Sickles was watching the skirmishing and artillery duels between the Peach Orchard and Pitzer's Woods, when Major General Birney rode up to him. 'General, I am afraid that Berdan's reports of Longstreet's Corps to my front were wrong. I have sent the cavalry squadron Buford left as well as sharpshooters and skirmishers forward to find the enemy. They are simply not there.' The only Rebels he could find were the same ones in Pitzer's Woods that he had been skirmishing with since dawn.

Sickles' face reddened. He had received a tongue-lashing from Meade for moving off the ridge. His excuse had been that a large force was threatening him and he needed a better position. With that rationale manifestly wrong, his political instincts were all alive to what this could mean to his position in the army and even to his continued command of III Corps. He was completely aware of Stanton's letter giving Meade the authority to relieve or assign any officer as he saw fit. Meade was no friend, and with Hooker gone, he had no protector in the army. Then it occurred to him that there is no armor like success, in war or in politics. 'Are you saying, General, that we are overlapping Lee's flank?'

'It appears to be the case. We have only dismounted cavalry skirmishers to my front, and none too many at that. My men have crossed the Emmitsburg Road and pushed the enemy's skirmishers into the treeline.'

'Meade is sending V Corps to my support. Together we can wheel around Lee's flank and crush it.' He stood up in his stirrups to look south over the young peach trees, down the road and into a large open space – fields of corn, oats, and hay. He could see a few puffs of smoke from the treeline and the dark forms of Birney's skirmishers in the fields. He weighed the prospects. Meade was too cautious. Butterfield, his old friend, had taken him aside already and blurted out that Meade's first concern was retreat; he had ordered him to spend all morning preparing orders to retreat to the Pipe Creek positions he had so dearly set his heart upon. Meade had not wanted him to move to where he was now and certainly would not countenance an attack from this position. But if the attack was launched, he would have to support it. Then how far would the star of the man who broke Lee rise? Beyond this duplicitous calculation, there was a fire in Sickles, the fire of an aggressive fighting man, sick of cautious commanders. When Dan Sickles threw the dice, you could hear the clank of iron.

'The whole Fifth Corps'

4:00 PM, south of Power's Hill

Sixty-four guns of the Artillery Reserve – three brigades – were massed just south of Power's Hill in the open fields along the cross-roads between the Taneytown Road and the Baltimore Pike. Another two brigades with forty-six guns had already been positioned to support III Corps. At that moment Brigadier General Robert O. Tyler's Artillery Reserve of the Army of the Potomac was the most powerful artillery command in the Americas. Thanks to Brigadier General Hunt, they packed twice the ordnance called for by the army's normal allowances. The two brigades supporting Sickles included the 1st Regular Brigade, commanded by Captain Dunbar R. Ransom, and the 1st Volunteer Brigade of Lieutenant Colonel Freeman McGilvery, which had arrived in the early morning. The remaining three brigades had departed Taneytown at dawn and arrived by 10:30. To their south and around them were stretched the crowded rear of the army, supply wagons and field hospitals stretching south down the road that made for such excellent lateral communications behind the front. It was from these hospitals that a few walking wounded had been given medical certificates to walk to Emmitsburg. When these men left in the morning, the three artillery brigades had been resting along the road behind the Round Tops before moving on to their position in reserve below Power's Hill.

Each of the thirteen batteries waited for the command 'Battery, forward!' that would send them galloping into the fight they could hear beginning over the ridge. Around them they could feel events moving towards that moment. The infantry and guns of V Corps were streaming south past them, down the Taneytown Road and across towards the ridge, to the sound of the guns and the support of III Corps. The lead brigade of V Corps was Vincent's and the lead regiment, Joshua Chamberlain's 20th Maine:

> So the awakening bugle, sounded 'To the left! At utmost speed!' Down to the left we pushed – the whole Fifth Corps – our brigade nearest and leading; at the double-quick, straight for the strife; not seeking roads, nor minding roughness of the ground, thorn-hedges, stone-fences, or miry swamps mid-way, earth quaking, sky ablaze, and a deepening uproar as we drew near.[3]

'Wait here and cool off til they pass'

4:15 PM, the Taneytown Road, south of Big Round Top

Lieutenant Joseph Beecham was the surgeon escorting a small train of ambulances south down the Taneytown Road. The Round Tops were to his right. He had noticed that when he had come abreast of them the sound of battle had faded completely. He did not have to speculate on that phenomenon long when a flood of gray cavalrymen galloped up the road, wild yells ripping the afternoon quiet. As a physician, Beecham was unarmed, and did not even bother to raise his hands. The ambulances were evidence enough of his non-combatant status. The enemy poked into the vehicles nonetheless to make sure. Their officer saluted and ordered him to stay where he was. It was then that he saw Hampton gallop by with his staff in a swirl of dust and dash. He clenched his teeth at the thought of the blow his army was about to receive.

Hampton's Georgians and Carolinians were shooting up whatever traffic they accosted on the road and sending detachments to the right up the country lanes, to spread panic among the trains that seemed to sprawl over every open field. John Weikert was sitting on his porch to get away from the misery inside his farmhouse; it had been commandeered as a field hospital for the wounded of last night's fighting. The farmyard was full of ambulances. A Union officer rode up and asked to fill his canteen from the well. Weikert nodded assent, but the

---

[3] Joshua Lawrence Chamberlain, *'Bayonet! Forward!' My Civil War Reminiscences* (Stan Clark Military Books, Gettysburg, Pennsylvania, 1994) pp.20–1.

young man watered his horse first. The horse was a fine gelding, a gift from his father, a Philadelphia banker who had also secured his son's appointment, through his considerable connections, to the staff of the Commander of the Army of the Potomac. His father had foreseen all the political advantage that would accrue to his son rubbing shoulders at that level. It had never really occurred to him that even an aide would have to put his life on the line. But the young man had his father's sharp wits and also possessed the courage of a great grandfather who served with Washington, marching with bloody feet through the snow at Trenton. So twenty-two year old Charles Scofield Mariner III had been through Fredericksburg and Chancellorsville and had learned a thing or two as well. Under his dark blue tunic, made by the best tailor in Philadelphia, a ragged purple scar from a jagged piece of shell at Chancellorsville marred his alabaster skin. He had refused a long convalescence in the comfort of his own home in favor of a field hospital and his own tent.

As he wiped the sweat from his forehead with a handkerchief, Mariner explained that he was a courier from General Meade. Weikert, who had noted the young man's quality horseflesh, fine uniform and, well-stitched boots, laughed. 'Well, if you are going to Taneytown, you might as well wait here for fifteen more minutes.' He said that the road in front of his farmhouse had been full of traffic. An empty supply train going south had passed just a few minutes before, clogging the road. Five hundred feet south the road crossed a small creek, and it would be difficult to get past them. 'Wait here and cool off til they pass,' Weikert suggested. He had calculated that the wagons would be just about crossing the creek when all hell broke loose from that direction, a fusillade of shots, shouts, and screaming horses. Mariner dropped his handkerchief and was riding in that direction in one fluid motion.

In moments he saw the cause. The wagons had indeed clogged the road over the stream and others were overturned in the drainage ditches along the road. Rebel cavalry rode around, shooting the drivers who had not already abandoned their wagons, and the few escorts who had survived. One of the escorts had demonstrated the presence of mind to shoot the mules of the wagon in the creek. The road beyond, though, was full of the enemy. He could see more riding down the creek to the east to find a crossing. A few had already made their way across. Mariner took this all in within a few seconds, then turned his horse and brutally drove his spurs into the animal. A few Rebel cavalrymen saw him and gave chase, firing their pistols. He bent low on the horse's neck and rode for his life. Passing the Weikert farm, he saw out of the corner of his eye the farmer still sitting on his porch, this time with his mouth wide open. Almost simultaneously he passed more wagons heading south, and shouted an alarm. He had barely ridden by when he heard shots as the train guards and the pursuing Rebs ran into each other.

'I will take the responsibility'

4:15 PM, to the east of the Wheatfield

Vincent's Brigade had followed Sykes' over Cemetery Ridge and down into the little valley of the Plum Run, double-quicked past the Peach Orchard, and came to a halt behind Rose's Wheatfield, the forward edge of which was held by III Corps. Vincent's horse pawed the ground in anticipation; his veterans were outwardly more calm but also waited with barely subdued anticipation for the order to join the line. Humphreys' men at the Peach Orchard were under a well-directed artillery fire which had not yet sought out Birney's units in front of the V Corps men. Vincent may have seen the lone figure of Warren's aide, Lieutenant Mackenzie, riding down from Little Round Top and up to George Sykes and his group of aides, but he could not have heard what was said. Mackenzie put Warren's words squarely to Sykes: 'That hill is key to this position, General. The General Commanding specifically entrusted it to you. While I don't see the enemy at this moment, that hill should be held by at least a brigade. Our position is strong but can be easily turned, as you can see.' He swept his hand to take in the hills. Sykes was no fireball of initiative, but he was astute enough to realize that no blame could accrue to him for obeying orders. There was, indeed, safety in that. As usual, his 1st Division commander, Brigadier General James Barnes, was nowhere to be seen. Sykes sent an aide to find Barnes and order him to send a brigade to the hill.

Corporal Oliver W. Norton was Vincent's bugler and brigade color-bearer and remembered what happened next:

> Vincent was sitting on his horse at the head of the column, waiting orders. Seeing Sykes' aide approaching, he rode forward to meet him. I followed with the flag, and distinctly heard the following conversation: 'Captain, what are your orders? Give me your orders.' The captain answered, 'General Sykes told me to direct General Barnes to send one of his brigades to occupy that hill yonder,' pointing to Little Round Top. 'I will take the responsibility of taking my brigade there.' [4]

Vincent ordered his senior regimental commander, Colonel James C. Rice, 44th New York, to bring the brigade forward while he rode ahead. First he quickly skirted the hill's rocky western slope and found it too difficult to ascend on horseback. Then he rode back up onto the ridge at the base of the hill and then down the road that connected with the Taneytown Road. He was about to enter the woods to scout out positions on the hill for his brigade, when he

---

[4] Oliver Wilcox Norton, *The Attack & Defense of Little Round Top, Gettysburg, July 2, 1863* (Konecky and Konecky, New York, 1996, reprint of 1913 edition) p.264.

detected gunfire to the east. Yelling and waving his cap, a horsemen galloped off the Taneytown Road a few hundred feet away on the road to the east, pulling his horse to a sharp stop in front of him, breathing hard. Blood ran down the rider's face from an obvious close shot just above the ear. 'Rebel cavalry, sir, in large numbers . . . coming up the Taneytown Road . . . nobody to stop them.'

Vincent looked behind him. Chamberlain's 20th Maine quickly came into view at the head of the column. His brigade had lost no time in moving out: 'We broke to the right and rear,' Chamberlain later recorded, 'found a rude log bridge over the Plum Run, and a rough farm-road leading to the base of the mountain. Here, as we could, we took the double-quick.'[5]

Turning to Mariner, Vincent said, 'Well done, lieutenant, now ride for all you are worth to tell General Sykes, the V Corps commander. Tell him Vincent has gone to close the road and to send help.' Mariner shook the blood out of his eyes, and was off. Chamberlain had just ridden up at the head of his regiment. Vincent said 'with a voice of awe, as if translating the tables of eternal law, "Place yourself at the southern end of this hill. This is the left of the Union line. You understand. You are to hold this ground at all costs!" He smiled then, "The Rebs have turned our flank with cavalry, and I must hammer them out with the rest of the brigade. Goodbye, Chamberlain, remember, at all costs!"'[6]

'Strike them hard, or this flank will crumble'

4:45 PM, the Emmitsburg Road, south of the Peach Orchard

Sykes had been looking for Birney ever since he had ridden to this part of the field but to no avail. When he saw Birney's whole division abandon its position and move forward, he realized why. But he was more than puzzled, for Meade had given him no idea that the army was going to attack.

That was the last thing Lee and Hill had expected either. They were not used to a great deal of intelligent, or, at least, unexpected initiative on the part of their opponents. But Sickles had their full attention now as his 10,000 men surged forward across the Emmitsburg Road. Humphreys' Division immediately engaged Wilcox's Brigade as they pushed into Pitzer's Woods. Birney's Division drove the enemy's cavalry pickets back into the woods west of the road. Sickles maintained his position on the slight elevation of the Peach Orchard, his *Feldherrnhügel* (Warlord's Hill), as Humphreys' men advanced.

From his vantage point in Spangler's Woods, Major General Anderson watched in disbelief as Sickles' Corps swept out of its defensive positions

---

[5] Chamberlain, op.cit. p.21.

[6]* Strong Vincent, *Reminiscences of Major General Strong Vincent* (J.B. Lippincott, Philadelphia, 1878) p.302.

towards his own command. Sickles' right division would crash into his own two right flank brigades, Wilcox and Perry's 'Florida' Brigade, but Sickles' second division to the north would sweep around his open flank like a barn door and crash into his rear. The few cavalrymen out there would be brushed away easily. Wilcox on his right would have to be the pivot of the army's flank. He would have to hold while Anderson rushed reserves to refuse that flank. If anyone could do it, he thought, Wilcox's 1700 Alabamians were up to it. His real worry was the small 'Florida' Brigade in Spangler's Woods, only three regiments and 742 men. Perry was sick with typhoid fever, and today his brigade would be commanded by Colonel David Lang of the 8th Florida. Anderson's aides were barely off to appraise Lee and Hill of the situation when Humphreys' two lead brigades, Brewster's 'Excelsior' 2nd and Carr's 1st, approached the treeline, flags flying and regiments well aligned. If Anderson had known who was opposing him at that moment, it would have done his self-possession little good. At the age of fifty-two, Humphreys was an old Regular Army engineer who had proven himself from Antietam to Chancellorsville as one of the army's best division commanders.

At least Wilcox had one good surprise for him. Poague's Artillery Battalion of Pender's Division had been placed in reserve behind Wilcox. Numerically his sixteen guns were a match for Humphreys' seventeen, but he had only three rifled guns to the enemy's thirteen. But the situation was so manifestly critical that the artilleryman needed no orders to commit his guns in support of Wilcox. Brewster's six New York regiments wheeled into the meadow and cornfield and into the murderous fire from Wilcox's Alabamians and Poague's guns. Brewster's regiments recoiled, leaving hundreds of dead and wounded. Wilcox's Brigade had a breathing space. Carr's Brigade was luckier than Brewster's. Anderson's own artillery had been posted further north along the ridge and had little time in which to adjust and fire on Carr, while the Union artillery poured its fire into Spangler's Woods and the thinly stretched Floridians within. Wood splinters from shattered trees caused more casualties than the shells themselves, but every man down was a serious loss for such a small brigade. Shells were exploding in the trees as Carr's men reached the edge of the field, their ranks thinned insignificantly by the Floridians, who were more intent on sheltering from the shellfire and wood splinters. The Union brigade kept its alignment as bayonets came down. The Floridians fell back further into the trees as Carr's men lunged forward. Carr himself led an attack that overwhelmed the small 8th Florida, and captured its colors, its major and thirty more men. The colors were seized by Sergeant Thomas Hogan of the 72nd New York under Humphreys' own approving eye.[7]

As the 'Florida' Brigade disintegrated in the woods, Wright's Brigade of

---

[7] *OR*, vol.XXVII, part I, p.559.

Georgians on its left quickly filed through woods in its rear and wheeled right. Groups of Floridians fled through them, then Carr's men appeared through he trees. At twenty yards both brigades fired. Lee and Hill rode into the northern edge of Spangler's Woods just as this volley crashed out barely a few hundred feet away. Lee seemed to gain power from his proximity to the battle. Even his horse Traveler noticed the surge and danced. Mahone and Posey's Brigades of Anderson's Division should already be on their way. Now aides were galloping to bring Heth's wounded Division onto Anderson's right. Lee's staff tried to suggest that he move further away from the fighting, but his brown eyes thundered no. He turned to Hill. 'General, I suggest you see to the placement of Heth's Division yourself.' He knew that Heth's men had been severely handled the day before and would need Hill's personal leadership. 'Strike them, General, strike them hard, or this flank will crumble.' Turning to his staff, he said, 'Colonel Taylor, ride yourself around the enemy, and find General Longstreet. Tell him he must come up on our flank to trap the enemy, even if he must curtail his own attack.'

The Pennsylvanians went in with a rush

4:45 PM, Taneytown Road, below Big Round Top

Longstreet was starting to relax a little now that his plan had worked well thus far. There was hardly any opposition at all – and that was part of a small but nagging problem. He had expected to be overrunning the Yankee trains by now, but very few of them had been located south of the Round Tops. Hampton's cavalry had nevertheless raised havoc among those that were there. Yankees were running everywhere in the mile-wide countryside between the hills and Rock Creek as Hood's Division double-quicked up the road amid evidence of the cavalry's murderous romp. Private James Wilson, 4th Texas, remembered:

> We passed overturned wagons, dead horses in their traces, and others struggling to escape. Dead Yankees were strewn over the road, in the fields. We passed one abandoned camp with untouched tents where the coffee still boiled over a camp fire. Any other time nothing would have kept us out of the Yankee camp and from that coffee, but today we knew we could win the war. Not a man fell out of ranks.[8]

The plan was working, and Longstreet could not have been more pleased. Compared to this morning's deep depression, fed by the prospect of assaulting the enemy's natural fortress, he was now riding on a tide of elation. When the men began to cheer him, his hard-headed fighting style came through. 'Cheer less, boys, and fight more!' He would wait for the arrival of McLaws' Division,

---

[8] John Stewart French, *With the Fourth Texas to Glory* (Lone Star Press, Fort Worth, Texas, 1893) p.199.

which would follow Hood. McLaws would file off to Hood's right when the enemy situation dictated.

Colonel Vincent was about to dictate some changes in those plans. He had rushed his brigade, minus the 20th Maine, down onto the Taneytown Road. He was fifty yards ahead of the brigade with his staff when a company of Rebel cavalry came howling up the road from behind the Bricker farm, firing at them. An aide pitched out of his saddle. Vincent drew his sword, 'Steady!' Behind them Colonel Rice of the 44th New York had taken in the same scene and deployed his first two companies across the road into a cornfield. Their fire ripped through the cavalry, emptying saddles and bringing down horses. He rushed his regiment forward past the imperturbable Vincent. 'Thank you, Rice; now down to those farm buildings and hold them. We must hold this road.' As Rice's men rushed forward, Vincent threw the 83rd Pennsylvania and 16th Michigan on line to the east of the farm buildings.

Vincent rode forward as the crash of more firing erupted from the New Yorkers. He found Rice on the firing line spread between the farm buildings and across the road. 'The cavalry tried another charge just as we came up,' Rice reported. He pointed to the dead and wounded horses and men scattered over the road and farmyard, and the half-dozen prisoners being escorted to the rear with a few good prods of the bayonet. Vincent thought that would be about the last of that. Cavalry always left well-ordered infantry alone. They had only tried in the hope of breaking him up on the march. But their skirmishers were active in the orchard next to the farm east of the road. Vincent rode over to the left to look for the 16th Michigan and its attached element of Michigan Sharp-shooters, Brady's Company, and found them coming through the cornfield behind the farmhouse. Enemy cavalry were riding around the fields and country roads in large numbers.

He was about to send them in when Colonel Rice rode up to him, saying, 'In every battle in which we have been engaged the 83rd and 44th have fought side by side. I wish it might be so to-day.' Vincent understood the unique bond between the two regiments, formed two long years ago when they were first brigaded together. Although two separate organizations, they were, in spirit, one regiment. He replied, 'All right, let the 16th pass you.'[9] As the 83rd's

---

[9] Norton, op.cit. pp.265, 271–2. Shortly after being formed, the 83rd Pennsylvania arrived and went into camp across the Potomac from Washington in September 1861, to join a new brigade forming under the command of Colonel Daniel Butterfield. A few days later the 44th New York arrived. As they stacked arms, a delegation of officers from the 83rd invited the 44th's officers to dinner. A delegation from each of the 44th's companies, headed by its first sergeant, similarly invited their counterparts in the 83rd to dinner. From that first courtesy, an inseparable bond was formed between the two regiments, which were henceforth 'called "Butterfield's Twins". A generous rivalry sprang up, each regiment striving to outdo the other in drill, discipline, and all the manifold duties of a soldier's life.'

commander, Captain Orpheus S. Woodward, came up at the head of his regiment, Vincent pointed his riding crop at the orchard. 'Drive them out of the apple trees, Captain.' The Pennsylvanians went in with a rush. Next, Vincent rode up to the 16th Michigan as it came up, directing its commander to seize the buildings of the J. Group farm. 'Hold that farm. It is our shoulder. I think there will be infantry up here soon.' The cavalry was bad enough. They had dismounted enough men to give Woodward a hard time in the orchard, but dismounted cavalry have no stomach for a knock-down-drag-out fight with good infantry determined to use the bayonet. Woodward led his men in among the gnarled apple trees. 'We went in with the bayonet, and the Rebs ran out with their carbines.' In five minutes the orchard was cleared, and Woodward's men had the road in their sights. They ran up to the orchard's edge, shooting down the enemy as they ran for their horses. Vincent, known for his quick grasp of terrain, had seized an extremely good position, running from woods at the base of the northern end of Little Round Top to the Bricker Farm south-east, a few hundred feet along the edge of the orchard, and then east to the Group Farm. A good farm road ran from the Taneytown Road south-east through the orchard and past the Group Farm all the way to a loop of Rock Creek, a mile-and-a-quarter away. The ground between the Bricker Farm and Little Round Top was marshy from the creek that flowed off the hill. Boulders emerged out of the marshy grass here and there. At least Vincent had a secure right. To the east of the Taneytown Road, in front of the orchard and Group Farm, the ground was open pasture for 200 to 400 feet before being bisected by the creek. Behind the creek was yellow corn and then more marshy ground to the right. Though it was good ground for Vincent, his left hung in the air.

It had seemed only seconds since the Rebels charged him on the road. Now for the infantry. Vincent looked up just as they came down the road and splashed across the stream in line of battle, the Rebel wolf's yell preceding them.

Hampton was waiting for Hood as the Texan's lead regiment came up the road. They were just south of the Weikert Farm, barely a thousand feet from Vincent's Brigade. 'Well, General, they have got some infantry ahead of me that I can't budge. They are all yours. They extend about three or four hundred yards to the right. I have some of my boys riding around them.' [10] He pointed to the right and indicated that he had already sent several of his regiments in that direction as the road had become increasingly clogged with overrun wagons and marching units. The enemy might not be in great strength yet, but they were uncommonly good shots at this range, he remarked. A few men in the front ranks had already been hit as they waited on the road. The rest had been ordered to kneel.

---

[10]* Wade Hampton, *For the Glory of South Carolina* (D. Appleton, New York, 1881) p.243.

'Hampton's cavalry maneuver was all well and good,' Hood thought, 'but I will have to rely on my own infantry.' His only comment to Hampton was, 'I am going on while I can.' [11] He turned to Brigadier General Jerome B. Robertson, whose brigade was first in column, and ordered him forward. He was exactly where he always wanted to be – at the front of a good fight. Robertson wheeled his brigade in line behind the creek with the 4th and 5th Texas and the 3rd Arkansas, in that order, and the 1st Texas in reserve. He would have over 1700 men to Vincent's 950. Hood waved his hat to the men of his old 'Texas' Brigade as they double-quicked by, raising clouds of dust, and they cheered him in return.

The flower of Virginia

4:45 PM, Barlow, Pennsylvania

John Buford thought of Brandy Station as he sent his regiments into the attack. Sabers rasped from almost 2000 scabbards as the bugles sounded the advance. Across the field he heard the answering trumpets and the same flash of steel and roar of defiance from the enemy.

Sedgwick's entreaty had put him on the road back to Gettysburg. His own exhaustion had evaporated when the men cheered as the column turned about. Barely an hour later he had run smack into Fitzhugh Lee's Brigade just outside of Barlow, a dozen houses strung along the Taneytown Road. They had skirmished for an hour with little effect. Now Sedgwick was coming up fast on his heels. He had to break through this cavalry for him. Fitzhugh Lee just needed to make Sedgwick deploy from column to be successful; that would eat up time. Buford decided he could not let that happen. He could hear the guns; something terrible was happening to the north. Something terrible enough had happened right here – the enemy had cut one of the army's main lines of communication. For that reason alone he had to dislodge them. Fitzhugh Lee was not about to budge through mere skirmishing either. Buford's dragoon tactics, which had revolutionized Union cavalry operations, were laid aside in this desperate moment when cavalry faced cavalry. As his aides rushed up and own the firing line, the regiments rushed back to their horses and mounted. As he rode along, Buford said a silent thank you to Sedgwick for knocking him out of his funk.

Across the field, Fitzhugh Lee had mounted his own brigade, almost 2000 men, against what appeared to be a similar number of Yankee cavalry. A nephew of the army commander, he was a solid though not very imaginative leader of cavalry. His brigade was the flower of Virginia, what the Yankees mocked as 'the gentry' – the 1st, 2nd, 3rd, 4th, and 5th Virginia Cavalry

---

[11]* John Bell Hood, 'Hood's Division at Gettysburg', *MAC*, vol.XIV (1879), p.18.

Regiments. Accompanying Fitzhugh was Stuart himself, with the Cavalry Division staff. Stuart had been painfully aware of the accusations of glory-hunting against him. He had consciously chosen not to accompany Hampton's Brigade in its drive against the enemy's rear. The glory lay there, but Hampton was capable of reaping it. The more responsible place was here. Longstreet's attack would only succeed if his back was guarded. His only regret now was that he had not brought Chambliss' Brigade along too.

Just as much as John Buford wanted to drive him away, Fitzhugh Lee was determined to stay, for as long as Longstreet needed to close the trap on the enemy. Stuart and he were confident he could do it with his fine, big cavalry brigade. They had held the Yankees off Lee's army on its retreat from Sharpsburg the previous year, held off not only the Yankee cavalry but his infantry as well, held them off long enough for his uncle to safely cross the Potomac with his wounded army. And for that his uncle, always careful to mute the praise of his relatives in the army, had thrown laurels to him not once but three times in his reports. If ever there was a time for a man to live up to his reputation, it was now. Besides, he had missed the great saber battle at Brandy Station, lying a convalescent in his bed. He drew his saber and waited for John Buford to begin.

'I must find General McLaws, Sir!'

5:15 PM, the Emmitsburg Road

The last regiment in Hood's Division had just marched onto the Emmitsburg Road when a pair of horsemen galloped down the from the north. They barely slowed as they turned west onto the side road that led to the George Bishop Farm, scattering the front rank of McLaws' van regiment. Curses and a few stones followed them. The commotion brought the old white-manned Brigadier William Barksdale to the head of the column. 'By God, Sir, stop!' he shouted at them, waving his fist. His Mississippians crowded around the horsemen, bringing them to a stop. Barksdale's men parted before him as he rode up. 'By God... Why, Colonel Taylor, what are you doing here, Sir?' Barksdale never cringed before anyone, but he was genuinely curious to see Lee's aide here.

'I must find General McLaws, Sir! I bear General Lee's orders for your division to counter march.' By reputation Taylor was cool under pressure, but he was now desperately anxious to find McLaws. 'The enemy has flanked Hill with at least a corps and possibly two. Your division, General, is to counter-march north and save the army's flank!' Here was meat for Barksdale's warlike appetite. 'I will countermarch my brigade immediately, Colonel.' Turning in his saddle, he shouted, 'Off the road, make way for this officer!' [12] His

---

[12]* Walter H. Taylor, 'Lee at Gettysburg', *MAC*, vol.XV (1880), pp.34–5.

Mississippians parted into the trees and field, and Taylor sped off to find McLaws. A few more thunderous bellows, and Barksdale's Brigade marched onto the Emmitsburg Road, turning north instead of south.

'The fighting is coming from the east'

5:15 PM, Little Round Top

Colonel Chamberlain's 20th Maine had double-quicked through the woods on the northern slope of the hill and then slowed to cross its rocky, clear-cut western slope. From this vantage point, Chamberlain had the best view of the battlefield and III Corps' attack across the Emmitsburg Road. Obviously, there was little immediate threat from this direction. But the noise of fighting was coming from the eastern side of the hill, just about where Vincent would be with the rest of the brigade. It was unnerving to think how the enemy could have got himself in the army's rear while that same army was off charging in the opposite direction. He called his officers to him. 'Gentlemen, the orders that took us here intended us to guard the western and northern face of this hill. As your eyes and ears can tell you, the situation has changed. The fighting is coming from the east.'[13] Already every face had turned to look down the rough, wooded slope behind them.

'We are making out badly up there'

5:15 PM, Ewell's headquarters at the Red Barn

While Longstreet and Hill were desperately engaged, Ewell seemed to inhabit a dreamworld in which time stood still. Through the long morning and afternoon before the fighting began, he did practically nothing to prepare for his role in the day's battle. Lee had committed the same error as the day before by giving Ewell instructions to conduct a supporting attack for Longstreet and to develop it into a 'real attack' should the opportunity dictate. He had left too much room for Ewell's fears to dictate his actions, and so the hours ticked by, and nothing happened. The absence of a firm, guiding hand was felt everywhere. One of Johnson's officers remarked, 'Greatly did the officers and men marvel as morning, noon and afternoon passed in inaction – on our part, not on the enemy's, for, as we well know, he was plying ax and pick and shovel in fortifying a position which was already sufficiently formidable.'[14]

Even Early had been ready and eager for the attack and had positioned his division on his starting line, from which it could rapidly assault Cemetery Hill.

---

[13]* Joshua Lawrence Chamberlain, 'Destiny on Little Round Top', address to Grand Army of the Republic annual banquet, New York, 2nd July 1889, New York *Herald*, 3rd July 1889.

[14] Champ Clark and the Editors of Time-Life Books, *Gettysburg* (Time-Life Books, Alexandria, Virginia, 1985) pp.113–14.

Rodes attempted to co-ordinate his attack with Pender's Division on his flank, but nothing came of it. Johnson had moved into line for another attack up that rocky, wooded slope. Lee had told Ewell that Longstreet would be engaged about then; this was a clear enough instruction. The corps commander ordered Johnson to provide the diversion. At his direction, Major Joseph W. Latimer, commanding the division artillery battalion, was ordered to place his sixteen guns on Benner's Hill north-east of Culp's Hill and 'open fire with all his pieces.' Latimer, at the age of twenty-one, was another Southern prodigy, a scion of war, so skilled and daring that he was cheered by the infantry, an accolade they usually reserved for Lee and Stonewall Jackson. Unfortunately, Benner's Hill was badly exposed to Union counter-battery fire and had insufficient room for the massed batteries that would be necessary to dominate the coming duel. It was also badly exposed, with no shelter for the caissons and horses. This pointed to a greater problem – the lack of good artillery positions in the 2nd Corps area. One of the few things Ewell had done that day was survey possible artillery positions with his chief of artillery; they found only enough for forty-eight of the Corps' seventy-eight guns.

Latimer's batteries with their sixteen guns rode smartly onto the hill, passing the four 20-pounder Parrotts of the Rockbridge Artillery already posted there. Latimer rode along the front of the guns sword in the air, called his battalion to attention, and ordered, 'Fire!' With a crash the first salvo streaked over to strike the Union positions on Cemetery Hill. Confederate batteries west of Gettysburg also joined in. The enemy's response was immediate. To John Hatton of Dement's Battery, 'Benner's Hill was simply a hell infernal.'[15] The guns of I and XI Corps on Cemetery Hill had been reinforced by batteries from Hunt's Artillery Reserve and were plying their expert work. Stevens' Battery, on the knoll between the hills, joined in with its Napoleons, and later in the fight guns were dragged up to Culp's Hill to add their weight to the pounding. A war correspondent on Cemetery Hill wrote:

> Then came a storm of shot and shell; marble slabs were broken, iron fences shattered, horses disemboweled. The air was filled with wild, hideous noises, the low buzz of round shot, the whizzing of elongated balls and the stunning explosion of shells overhead and all around. In three minutes the earth shook with the tremendous concussion of two hundred pieces of artillery.[16]

Almost the first shot from Cooper's I Corps battery struck one of Latimer's ammunition chests, and the resulting explosion was met with a cheer from the

---

[15] John William Ford Hatton 'Memoir', pp.454–5, Library of Congress; cited in Pfanz, *Gettysburg: Culp's Hill and Cemetery Hill*, p.180.
[16] Pfanz, ibid.

Union side heard all the way to Benner's Hill. Almost immediately one of Latimer's guns hit and blew up a caisson of Stewart's Battery. This time the Confederate cheer was heard on Cemetery Hill. The Union battery commander was thoroughly impressed.

> It was the cleanest job I ever saw. The three chests were sent skyward and the horses started off on a run toward the town, but one of the swing teams got over the traces, throwing him down and causing the rest of the team to halt. The men ran after them and brought them back; every hair was burnt off the tails and manes of the wheel horses.[17]

Colonel Wainwright was roving among the I and XI Corps' batteries, directing their fire and leading a charmed life amid the storm of jagged metal. He recalled the deadliness of the 20-pounder shot being thrown by Latimer's battalion and the Rockbridge Artillery:

> One of these shot struck in the center of a line of infantry who were lying down behind a wall. Taking the line lengthwise, it literally ploughed up two or three yards of men, killing and wounding a dozen or more. Fortunately it did not burst, for it struck so near where we were sitting that it covered us with dust. The other was a shell which burst directly under Cooper's left gun, killed one man outright, blew another all to pieces, so that he died in half an hour, and wounded the other three.

Despite the hot work, Wainwright had much cause to be proud of his gunners that day and readily forgave them 'their utter unmilitariness and loose ideas of discipline in camp.' Five new men immediately stepped forward to serve the gun before its slaughtered crew could be dragged away. The man who had been 'blown all to pieces' was dragged just inside the Cemetery Gate to die of his hideous wounds. His brother, the battery bugler, would not leave his post without permission even though he had no immediate duty. His battery commander would not grant it without Wainwright's permission so desperate was the action. 'Yet were they in camp, hardly a man in the battery but would go off for all the day without permission to see a well brother, and Cooper would think it all right.' [18]

Such men were throwing their iron with deadly effect back into Latimer's batteries. Captain William D. Brown, commanding the Chesapeake Artillery, had exhorted his Marylanders to do their duty as the fight began and was hit

---

[17] James Stewart, 'Battery F Fourth U.S. Artillery at Gettysburg', in *Gettysburg Papers*, eds. Ken Bandy and Florence Freeland, vol.1, pp.374–5; cited in Pfanz, op.cit. p.181.

[18] Charles S. Wainwright, *A Diary of Battle: The Personal Journals of Colonel Charles S. Wainwright 1861–1865* (Stan Clark Military Books, Gettysburg, Pennsylvania, 1962) p.243.

almost immediately by a round shot that struck his right leg, ploughed through his horse, and struck his left leg. The horse broke three of his ribs as it fell upon him. As he was being carried away, he said to a friend, 'Captain, if you should get home, tell my poor father I died endeavoring to do my duty.' Then, indicating Benner's Hill: 'We are making out badly up there.' Up there they were falling quickly around their guns; and death found its way even more effectively among the exposed ammunition carriers and horses behind the guns. When no ammunition reached his gun, Private Jacob Cook of Brown's Battery ran back to the limber to see why:

> Cpl. Daniel Dougherty was cut in half, Pvt. Frederick Cusick's head was torn off, Doctor Jack Brian had lost his head, and there were other wounded lying nearby. As they spoke, another shell hit the ground in front of Pvt. Thaddeus Parker, driver of the limber's lead pair. He stood at their heads holding them and the rest of the team in place. The shell exploded, disemboweling Parker and killing both lead horses.[19]

Latimer realized the uneven contest was grinding up his battalion and requested permission to withdraw, which Johnson granted. The surviving elements fell back behind the hill, and their misery was witnessed by Robert Stiles:

> Never did I see fifteen or twenty guns in such a condition of wreck and destruction as this battalion was. It had been hurled backward, as it were, by the very weight and impact of metal from the position it had occupied on the crest of a little ridge, into a saucer-shaped depression behind it; and such a scene it presented – guns dismounted and disabled, carriages splintered and crushed, ammunition chests exploded, limbers upset, wounded horses plunging and kicking, dashing out the brains of men tangled in the harness; while cannoneers with pistols were crawling around through the wreck shooting the struggling horses to save the lives of the wounded men.[20]

As Latimer's battalion fired and burned on that exposed hill and Longstreet lunged up the Taneytown Road, Ewell's Corps remained still.

---

[19] Harry W. Pfanz, *Gettysburg: Culp's Hill and Cemetery Hill* (The University of North Carolina Press, Chapel Hill and London, 1993) p.185.
[20] Robert Stiles, *Four Years Under Marse Robert* (R. Bemis Ltd, Marietta, Georgia, 1995) pp.217–18.

CHAPTER 7

2nd July 1863
'There is a price for leadership'

5:00 PM, Cemetery Ridge

In the last few minutes the world had come apart for George Meade. He stood speechless as Sickles again defied the general commanding and threw his corps into an attack. Sickles' aide, who had just ridden up to explain his corps commander's 'initiative', had been subjected to one of the army's most withering tirades, which was considerably cleaned up for the history books by his own staff. 'Support his attack? I will court-martial him! I will break him! The miserable politician will destroy this army!' [1]

He was about to ride down and deal with Sickles once and for all when Sykes rode in with a wounded member of Meade's own staff. Behind them he could see Sykes' brigades turning about and heading back over Plum Run and towards the saddle of the Ridge at the base of the hill. 'I'll be damned, General!' Sykes almost shouted. 'The enemy is behind us. Tell him, Lieutenant.' Mariner, the wounded staff officer, blurted out his story as firing exploded behind them, over the ridge and behind the hill.

'Men of the 83rd, keep it hot!'

5:15 PM, the Bricker Farm

Vincent watched the enemy's regiments file down the opposite bank of the creek in front of him, hidden by the cornfield but for the silvery gleam of their bayonets rushing above the yellow stalks. Directly in front of the Bricker Farm, skirmishers were trying to cross the marshy ground, but his sharpshooters were picking them off easily. They would be upon him any moment, coming down the road and across the stream, and they would outflank the 16th Michigan at the Group Farm. Their bayonets continued to extend beyond his flank. An officer rode up then to tell him that more brigades would be filling in on his left, and the officer was to guide them. An artillery officer came up next, wanting to know where to post his two batteries; Vincent directed him to the cornfield on the left of the Group Farm.

Hood was not about to wait that long. Time was priceless, and deploying his

---

[1]* Edwin R. Smith, *An Aide to General Meade at Gettysburg* (D. Appleton, New York, 1886)

first brigade had already used up too much of it. He had directed Benning's Brigade, his second in column, to deploy on Robertson's right, but had told Robertson to attack immediately and not wait for Benning. He wanted his third brigade, Law's, to push up the road as soon as Robertson cleared it. His fourth and last in column, Anderson's, was his reserve.

'Now, General, now!' Hood shouted to Robertson. The Texas Brigade rose from the corn and rent the air with their Rebel yells, which they had borrowed from the Commanches, an unconscious compliment to the only people they truly feared. In an instant the 5th Texas and the 3rd Arkansas were splashing through the creek and up on the other bank, almost running, preceded by the fire of their artillery, which sent shells into the trees. Despite the iron fragments and wood splinters that flew among the apple trees and farm buildings, Vincent's men fired as the Rebels came up, sending scores of them toppling backwards into the shallow creek bed. But the others pushed forward and across the grassy meadow. The sharpshooter company in the orchard accounted for a man with almost every shot, while the rest of the 83rd Pennsylvania took their toll from behind the apples trees, blasting wide gaps in the 5th Texas. To the left, the 4th Texas came rushing down the road and through the marshy ground next to the hill.

Private William A. Fletcher, Company F, 5th Texas, saw the first color-bearer tumble back down into the creek. Fletcher was a member of the color guard, but an unwilling one. Afflicted with too much common sense, he had tried to get out of the detail but had failed. Now, through the fight, he would count the color-bearers as they went down. He would take his chances, but shied away from lowering them by picking up the colors himself. As the 5th Texas charged across the meadow to the orchard, he remembered:

> Our men near me commenced falling rapidly and especially color bearers ... I saw the colors fall five times, the last time in the hands of the sergeant who had ordered me to act as color guard. In falling, the flag staff struck my head in front of my face. As it went down my forward motion caused my feet to become somewhat tangled. I gave a kick and said a curse word, and passed on.[2]

He never knew who finally rescued the colors, and probably did not care. He was too busy firing and advancing. The charge across the meadow littered the grass with the 5th's dead and wounded but did not stop their rush into the orchard. The Pennyslvanians fell back through the rows of trees, firing as they went, their numbers thinning now that the Texans were on even terms.

The 4th Texas came quick-timing down the road with a thick line of

---

[2] William A. Fletcher, *Rebel Private Front and Rear: Memoirs of a Confederate Soldier* (Dutton Books, New York, 1995) p.79.

skirmishers ahead of them, but Rice's New Yorkers poured such a hot fire into the head of the column that the attack fell apart. The regiment was on too narrow a front to use its numbers well, and the marshy ground to their left was more a trap than a field to charge over. Vincent rushed into the rear of the orchard and found Woodward by the stand of his color guard, where the regiment had halted along the farm road that ran through the trees. 'Colonel, hold them here. Not a step back.' The 83rd Pennsylvania's colors were conspicuous, as were the officers around them. An enemy officer ordered his company to fire on the group around the flag. Just as Vincent finished speaking, shots ripped through the little group, bringing down Woodward, the color-bearer, and five of the guard. Vincent himself picked up the colors. 'Men of the 83rd, keep it hot!' He seemed to live a charmed life. The men fell around him, and his clothes were torn by bullets, but not one so much as brought a trickle of blood. Another man took the colors and fell at his side, then another. Finally he passed the colors to a fourth man, whose luck was a little better. Captain Woodward, blood trickling down the side of his face and matting his dark hair, came back into line, tying a handkerchief around his head. Vincent looked on admiringly as the young man resumed command.

To the left the fighting swirled around the Group Farm buildings. The barn was on fire as detachments from the 3rd Arkansas rushed forward into the yard, to be shot down by the Michiganders in the farmhouse and in refused line to the left around the farmyard's rail fence. The Arkansans had found the flank, and moved half their companies around it into a cornfield. Vincent came running up to the flank with three companies of the 44th in time to build up the flank at right angles. Robertson, though, had a bigger reserve, the 400-plus men of the 1st Texas, which was now passing around the right of the Arkansans.

'The biggest guns I had ever seen'

Artillery Reserve, south of Power's Hill

Hampton's cavalry had swept all the way to the massed batteries waiting south of Power's Hill just as Vincent's Brigade had rushed into position. Fugitives had barely alerted them before the 400 troopers of the 1st North Carolina came pounding down upon them, pistols firing. They hit the twelve guns and 241 men of the 2nd Volunteer Brigade of artillery as it stood in column ready to deploy. An artillery brigade thus organized takes up a lot of ground, with its twelve guns, thirty-six limbers, and twelve caissons, each with its own horse team. The mass itself was a military obstacle.

The Carolinians shot the artillery horses in their traces and the gunners on their caissons. Some teams tried to drive off, but were brought to a stop or even a crash by the killing and wounding of their animals. Among the North Carolinians was Captain Timothy Wheeler:

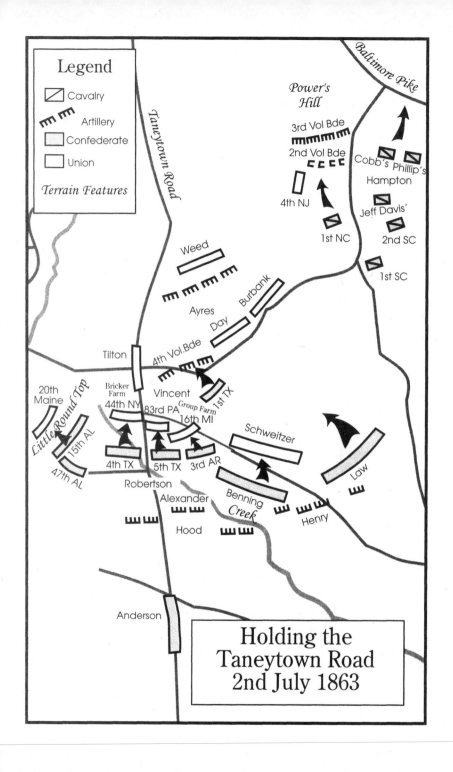

Holding the
Taneytown Road
2nd July 1863

Before they met at Gettysburg, General Robert E. Lee (left) had commanded the Army of Northern Virginia for over a year, leaving a trail of victories behind him, while Major General George Meade (right) had only commanded the Army of the Potomac for four days. Neither would leave the field in command.

Lieutenant General James Longstreet (left), Commander, I Corps, Army of Northern Virginia, and Major General Winfield Scott Hancock (right), Commander, II Corps, Army of the Potomac, were the most trusted subordinates of Lee and Meade. Fate thrust the command of their respective armies upon them.

Major General J.E.B. Stuart, Commander, Cavalry Division, Army of Northern Virginia. He put victory within Lee's reach by arriving in time to support Longstreet's envelopment of Meade's left flank.

Brigadier General John Buford, commanding the 1st Division of the Army of the Potomac's Cavalry Corps, intervened decisively three times at Gettysburg.

Brigadier General Henry J. Hunt, Chief of Artillery of the Army of the Potomac. Thanks to Hunt, who was captured briefly on 3rd July, the full advantage of the Union artillery was brought to bear on the second and third days of the battle.

Major General Daniel E. Sickles, Commander, III Corps, Army of the Potomac, started the battle on 2nd July against orders and nearly crushed Lee's right. *(MOLLUS Collection)*

Buford's cavalry division opposing the Confederate advance on Gettysburg.

I Corps' 2nd Maine Light Battery, commanded by Captain James A. Hall, resisted the Confederate advance on the Chambersburg Road.

Buford's cavalry division opposing the Confederate advance on Gettysburg.

Corps' 2nd Maine Light Battery, commanded by Captain James A. Hall, resisted the Confederate
advance on the Chambersburg Road.

Brockenbrough's Brigade (Heth's Division) of Virginians attacks the stone barn at the McPherson Far

Colonel Hiram Berdan's 1st US Sharpshooters opened the battle in Pitzer's Woods on the second day.
would be only the beginning of their strange odyssey under a despised commander.

(Left) Major General Jubal Early, commanding a division in the Confederate II Corps, broke the Union's right flank on 1st July, but over the next two days his activities were always too little too late.

(Below) Major General Abner Doubleday took command of the Union I and XI Corps when Reynolds fell on the morning of 1st July, but lost control of the battle in the afternoon.

ne-armed Major General Oliver P. Howard had no faith in his largely German-immigrant XI Corps. The 'Ialf-Moon Men' had run at Chancellorsville and ran again at Gettysburg on 1st July. Here Howard llies the remnants on Cemetery Hill, where he and they would redeem themselves.

Union dead of III Corps. *(MOLLUS Collection)*

Captain John Bigelow's 9th Battery, Massachusetts Light Artillery, advances at a gallop to support the Union III Corps. *(MOLLUS Collection)*

While Hood was held up on the Taneytown Road, Brigadier General Joseph B. Kershaw's South Carolina Brigade swept over Cemetery Ridge at the base of Little Round Top to link with him.

Major General John Sedgwick's VI Corps made the greatest forced march in the history of the US Army to join Meade at Gettysburg on the afternoon of 2nd July. *(MOLLUS Collection)*

Major General John Bell Hood, Longstreet's finest division commander, led I Corps' drive up the Taneytown Road on 2nd July. *(MOLLUS Collection)*

Colonel Joshua Lawrence Chamberlain had been with the 20th Maine since its formation, but Gettysburg was his first battle in command.

Fourteen-year-old M[...]
of Honor winner Wil[...]
Johnson beat the cha[...]
as VI Corps' Vermon[...]
Brigade trapped
Longstreet behind the
Round Tops.

Colonel Porter Alexander's artillery of I Corps goes into action to support the drive up the Taneytown Road on 2nd July.

The great cavalry fight at Barlow, south of Gettysburg, on 2nd July, where John Buford's 1st Division smashed through Fitzhugh Lee's brigade in the last great saber to saber engagement of the war. J.E.B. Stuart was badly wounded here trying to protect Longstreet's rear.

FARNSWORTH'S CHARGE.

the moment when Hampton's Brigade was crossing the Rock Creek Bridge, Union cavalry under Brigadier General Elon Farnsworth charged and swept them back.

The 1st Minnesota charges to drive off a Confederate attempt to break through the Union position on Cemetery Ridge and returns in triumph with several hundred prisoners. From an oil painting by Rufus Zugbaum, *c* 1905, original in the Minnesota State Capitol. *(Courtesy Minnesota Historical Society)*

Early's belated attack on Cemetery Hill almost washes over Rickett's Battery, but the courage of the Union gunners and the XI Corps counter-attack drives them back into the darkness on the second day.

e Virginians, led by Brigadier General Montgomery D. Corse (left), and the South Carolinians, under gadier General Micah Jenkins (right), were Pickett's third wave in Longstreet's charge on 3rd July.

jor General George Pickett would earn eternal ry in Longstreet's Charge on 3rd July as he jumped horse over the stone wall on Cemetery Ridge, ing on his division's second and third waves.

Captain Ulric Dahlgren, a staff officer who always seemed to be in the thick of the action. He would pull off one of the greatest intelligence triumphs of the war.

Brigadier General Louis Armistead led Pickett's second wave over the stone wall and broke through Webb's division of II Corps. *(MOLLUS Collection)*

First Lieutenant Frank A. Haskell, Gibbon's able aide, led II Corps' last-gasp counter-attack before being overwhelmed by Pickett's Division. *(MOLLUS Collection)*

Meade's headquarters at Widow Leister's house behind Cemetery Hill was rendered untenable by the Confederate cannonade preceding Longstreet's Charge.

nfederate soldiers of Pickett's Division sheltering in Seminary Woods from Union counter-battery fire
or to Longstreet's Charge on the third day.

nnard's 2nd Vermont Brigade of the Army of the Potomac's I Corps flanked Pickett's column as it
red Cemetery Ridge during Longstreet's Charge. *(MOLLUS Collection)*

The arrival of Henry Hunt's 'Ghost Train' of the Reserve Artillery was an act of decisive initiative that provided the Army of the Potomac with all the artillery ammunition it would need for a prolonged battle.

Arnold's Battery A, 1st Rhode Island Light Artillery, defends the flank of Hays' 3rd Division of II Corps against Pettigrew's Division during Longstreet's Charge. *(MOLLUS Collection)*

...nistead's breakthrough of II Corps' position on Cemetery Ridge. Jenkins' and Corse's Brigades were ...t behind and helped push a strong battle-line over the crest.

...dgwick's grand counter-attack with the entire Union center and reserve on the third day was the killing ...ke. *(MOLLUS Collection)*

We rode in, killing everyone, but the Yankees were downright possessive about those guns, the biggest guns I had ever seen. The mounted Redlegs and their officers fought on horseback, and the others with pistols, swords, and rammers. I saw more than one jump off a limber and drag one of our men off his horse. An officer rode by swinging his saber, but I was faster with my pistol, and he fell off as his horse ran past.

Wheeler and his men had just run into the enemy's heavy artillery brigade. The pandemonium was confined only to the slaughtered brigade which had absorbed the attention of the North Carolinians. The other nearest batteries had manned their guns. The rest drove away from the congestion to find better fighting space. The infantry of the 4th New Jersey, the train guards, rushed up just as the artillery section leaders shouted, 'Fire!' The concentration of canister and rifle fire into the mass of horsemen sent sprays of blood and flesh into the air, and the survivors of the Confederate cavalry scattered back down the road.

Meade came riding up with General Hunt just as the Carolinians were being swept from the field. About a mile to the south the firing was raging along Vincent's front and the smoke from the burning Group Farm drifted back up towards Little Round Top. Hunt did not wait for orders, but sent the batteries of Captain Robert Fitzhugh's 4th Volunteer Brigade towards the sound of the fighting. It was Fitzhugh who rode up to Vincent asking where his batteries should be placed.

The cornfield behind the Group Farm

Fitzhugh rode ahead of his galloping batteries to place them in line, but saw Confederates swinging well past the position he had chosen. He swung the lead battery, the 6th Maine, into line in a meadow north of the cornfield, its guns and caissons throwing up chunks of sod as they each turned almost on a dime. As the 1st Texas emerged from the tall corn, the 6th Maine's six 12-pounder Napoleons mowed them down with canister at less than 400 yards. Battery G, 1st New York Light Artillery, came pounding into the artillery line next to the Maine men with six more Napoleons. But the range was good for the Texans as well, who were close enough to begin shooting down the gunners and horse teams. Nevertheless, the fire was so hot that the 1st Texas drifted away to the right as they tried to get behind the artillery.

The arrival of Fitzhugh's batteries had saved Vincent from being outflanked, but Hood's gunners were blasting away at his three shrinking regiments as the 4th and 5th Texas came at his front again and again. The fighting in the orchard was hand-to-hand as the Pennsylvanians of the 83rd were pressed back from one row of trees to another. Their flank was losing touch with the 16th Michigan around the burning Group Farm. Vincent's observers had reported another Confederate brigade on the road behind the Texans and a third going across country to his left. Hood's battle fury was up; he could sense the enemy to his front ready to break. He would lead in the next brigade, Benning's Georgians, himself, straight up the road. He would smash through, and at the same time swing wide to the right to outflank whatever was coming. Then, on his right, Law could fill in all the way to Rock Creek. He rode up to Benning. 'Are your Georgians ready for glory!' The lead troops of the 2nd Georgia shouted back with a roar. 'Then, General, forward!'

'A more gallant officer or perfect gentlemen cannot be found'

The Baltimore Pike bridge over Rock Creek

At that moment other Georgians were already reaping glory by the bushel. Hampton had led Cobb's and Phillip's Legions of Georgians, and the Mississippians of the Jeff Davis Legion, through the fields of corn and oats along Rock Creek. To their left were woods, on the other side of which the 1st North Carolina was at that moment charging into Hunt's Reserve Artillery Brigade. Behind the three legions came the 1st and 2nd South Carolina Regiments. The oats gave way to more fields, bound by low stone walls for 300 yards, and just beyond was the prize dreamt of by every cavalryman that had ever lived. Hampton was riding at the head of the legions, trotting forward in line. He had been expecting to find what lay before him, but not without a desperate fight. The Baltimore Pike drew closer with every second, and it was crowded with traffic, most of it streaming east. A crowd had developed at the stone bridge as the army's provost guards attempted, with little success, to stem the fainthearted. Hampton drew his saber, turned and gave the command to increase speed to a gallop. The mass of horsemen sped forward, leaping the low wall like a tidal wave. Every man had seen the same prize. The enemy had left his own throat unguarded. The sabers came out with a roar.

About a mile east of the bridge, Judson Kilpatrick's 3rd Cavalry Division was awaiting orders as the sound of battle drew quickly nearer. Kilpatrick had been summoned to Gettysburg earlier that day by courier from Meade. The sound of the morning's fighting had carried for miles and quickly became audible as his column came up from Abbotstown. He was not known as 'Kill Cavalry Kilpatrick' for nothing, and turned his division from the road to a more direct but rougher path across country as he was drawn to the sound of the guns. The division had arrived by two in the afternoon[3] and had received orders placing them in reserve. Now Kilpatrick paced across the road listening with growing apprehension. At the same time, he was still immeasurably pleased with himself for having bested the famed Stuart a few days ago. The tension and the arrogance were a bad mix and the resentment he felt for his two young brigade

---

[3] *OR*, vol.XXVII, part I, p.992.

commanders, both jumped from captain to brigadier-general by the sweeping power granted to Meade by Stanton, now made him foolish. He could not help needling his 1st Brigade commander, Elon Farnsworth, over something trivial, but something he was sure would provoke a response – a veiled allusion to Farnsworth's courage. He was pleased to see the young man flare. Had they been Southerners, Kilpatrick would have felt the sting of a gauntlet in his face. He had also been careless enough to insult Farnsworth in the presence of his subordinates, who held an infinitely greater opinion of the young man than they did of Kilpatrick. His senior regimental commander echoed the opinion of anyone who served under Farnsworth, even for a short time. 'A more gallant officer or perfect gentleman cannot, in my opinion, be found.'[4]

The unseemly episode was brought to a sudden halt by an abrupt burst of shots from the direction of the Rock Creek bridge. Kilpatrick may have been an ass, but at that moment he did the right thing. 'General, take your brigade forward and secure that bridge!' Farnsworth was already ahead of him and leapt into the saddle in one fluid motion, shouting commands that rippled in trumpet calls back down the dismounted column. The head of the brigade column was in motion before the command to mount reached even halfway back. Sabers by the hundreds were rasping out of scabbards.[5]

In minutes Farnsworth reached the bare top of the hill overlooking the bridge. He took in the situation at a glance and kept on going. Hundreds of Union troops were streaming up the hill along the Pike in terrified flight. On the other side of the bridge, Confederate cavalry were swarming all over the place. But the bridge itself was a congested mass of fugitives and cavalrymen. In moments the gray horsemen would hack their way through and flood across the creek. Farnsworth just picked up speed coming down the hill, hearing, no, feeling the thundering column of the 1st Vermont behind him. The men running up the road, stared and blinked, and then dove off the road into the cornfield on one side. A few were too slow and simply ridden down by the Vermonters. On the bridge, the Georgians had just cut their way through the last of the press, leaving piles of corpses to clog the roadway. They were a handful of seconds too slow. It was then that Farnsworth and the head of the column crashed into them on the bridge. The momentum of their impact tumbled a dozen of the enemy and their mounts onto the bridge pavement. More were knocked over the bridge railings into the creek. Farnsworth sabered his way to the center of the bridge, the Vermonters keeping up with him. A Confederate loomed up in front of him and fired his pistol. Suddenly Farnsworth and his mount fell into the hacking, shouting melee.

[4] *OR*, vol.XXVII, part I, p.1005.
[5]* Ellon Farnsworth, *The Wartime Letters of Brigadier General Ellon Farnsworth* (The Charter Company, New York, 1900) p.216.

The fight on the bridge involved barely a few score men with hundreds more backed up on either end as mere spectators. That is, until Colonel Nathaniel P. Richmond of the 1st West Virginia, the second regiment in Farnsworth's column, took in the situation and figured out how to get his men into the fight. He ordered them off the road and down the grassy slope toward the river. They jumped a small rivulet and rode into a wheatfield, where he ordered them to dismount. With one out of four holding the horses, the rest ran across the wheatfield to the bank of Rock Creek, lined by only a few trees on either side, and began a rapid fire into Hampton's cavalry packed on the Pike and in the fields south of it. A battery of 3-inch rifles from the 1st Horse Artillery Brigade now appeared on the hill overlooking the river, and began lobbing shell and case shot into the enemy, and a battery remaining on Power's Hill joined in. In moments bloody lanes had been driven through the packed horsemen. The wounded and the dead were trampled underfoot as the stalled regiments began breaking up to escape the barrage. Richmond now directed the fire of several of his companies on the enemy on the bridge and quickly brought them down, allowing the Vermonters to burst across with a whooping holler. In the few desperate minutes since Farnsworth had charged down the hill, Hampton's high hopes had turned to ashes. So close, so very close. The cavalry had done all it could do; now it would be up to the infantry.

'Sam Hood will just have to do it'

Taneytown Road below Big Round Top

Colonel Taylor thought Longstreet was about to have a stroke when he delivered Lee's order. 'Old Pete' came out of his stunned silence and shouted above the sound of his batteries rolling north on the road next to them. 'I am engaged, Sir, can you not hear the guns ahead? Hood is cutting his way through to victory! I cannot and will not disengage now!'

'General Longstreet, I must repeat General Lee's orders...'

Longstreet leaned over in the saddle until he and Taylor were within cigar distance. 'No! Even if I could, it would be better for Hill to just hold on until Hood and McLaws have...'

Now Taylor interrupted Longstreet. He was harder than most men thought and loyal to Lee unto death. He would see Lee's instructions carried out. 'General, McLaws, on my explanation of General Lee's order, has counter-marched to aid Hill. I told him I would inform you, that time would not allow the order to go through you.' At that moment, Taylor thought that the 1st Corps commander was going to strike him as he watched the balled fist rise. Then it fell, and Longstreet seemed to slump in his saddle.[6]

---

[6]* Walter H. Taylor, 'Lee at Gettysburg', *MAC*, vol.XV (1880), p.36.

'You understand, Colonel, that should God Almighty command me now to completely disengage I could not do it. Sam Hood will just have to do it.' He thought briefly and then straightened up. His assurance had returned. 'Tell General Lee that McLaws will save Hill, but I cannot disengage and will continue to press the attack. Now, go, Sir. I have work to do.' With that, he galloped off up the road.[7]

As he passed Law's Brigade halted along the road, the men listening to the battle ahead, he looked to his left. Big Round Top hovered above the road, its woods creeping down to the base of the slope. It was too steep and too wooded to be of any tactical use. To the north of it was the smaller hill.

'Forward, boys! General Lee is watching!'

Behind Pitzer's Woods

A.P. Hill was riding up and down behind the firing line ensuring that the men of Heth's Division, now commanded by James Pettigrew, saw their corps commander up front with them. He had led them at the double-quick from their place in reserve while Wilcox, his flank now bent back to anchor on the Pitzer's Run, had held on for dear life holding the army's flank.

Birney's Division had swung across the Emmitsburg Road and pivoted north to strike Hill's open flank, while Humphreys' brigades had struggled unsuccessfully to break through Spangler's Woods, now held by Wright's Brigade. With Hill bringing up Heth's Division, Anderson was the senior 3rd Corps officer on the spot, and, under Lee's direct observation, this often sluggish officer was performing well. He had led up Wright's Georgians when Perry's 'Florida' Brigade had been overwhelmed and stopped Carr's advance cold. He was riding through the woods encouraging his men. Private Josiah Williams of the 72nd New York saw him flitting through the trees behind the Confederate firing line. He pointed him out to the men on either side, and they all fired at him. One bullet tore through his left shoulder and another into his left leg; a third struck his horse in the chest, bringing both to the ground in a heap. The horse screamed in agony, flailing around with its iron-shod hooves until a soldier shot it. As some of Wright's Georgians attempted to pull Anderson to safety, Humphreys committed his third brigade.

Colonel George C. Burling's five New Jersey regiments charged through the opening between Carr and Brewster and burst out of the woods and into the meadow behind. Burling led his men forward in pursuit, sweeping over one of Poague's batteries and around Wilcox's flank, held fast by Brewster's Brigade.

The flank of the army was about to collapse, as Lee rode out from Spangler's Woods and into the fleeing Floridians in the field behind. His presence was

---

[7]* James Longstreet, *From Manassas to Gettysburg*, p.423.

unmistakable on his white horse. In small groups and individually the fugitives stopped and faced about. Reserves were nowhere in sight, and Burling's men were closing. 'General Lee, please, Sir, do not expose yourself,' implored Colonel Armistead Long, his military secretary. Already men were falling around him as Burling's regiments surged forward. He should have saved his breath. Lee was majestic as Lang's broken regiments magically coalesced around him. The men might as well have been around an angel of the Lord, so transformed were they. Colonel Lang, his right arm soaked with blood and his left clutching his sword, placed himself at Lee's right. Again Long implored him to come away. Lee simply said, 'There is a price of leadership, Colonel.'[8] Private Shelby Carter of the 5th Florida, carrying his regiment's colors nearby, was amazed to see that Lee did not carry a weapon of his own, and that he had to borrow Colonel Long's sword.

The situation was not lost on Lang: he would never live it down if Lee died redeeming his brigade's honor. Stepping out in front of the denuded regiments, he shouted, 'General Lee, never let it be said that the men of this brigade needed the commander of this army to stiffen their courage.' Then to his Floridians, 'Forward, boys! General Lee is watching!'[9] They stepped forward with a cheer and advanced a dozen yards as Burling's Brigade came up and fired. The Confederates staggered at the blow. The tiny regiments seemed to disintegrate; all the colors and the surviving field officers went down. Colonel Lang fell dead with the last of his staff in a jumbled heap. Of the 400 men who had rallied on Lee, every second man was down, but the survivors stood and returned fire, feeble though it was. Burling ordered the advance, sword in hand, as the wall of bayonets behind him leveled and surged forward, colors waving along the unbroken line. His charge through the woods had left Wright's flank wide open. The Georgian pulled it rapidly back, disengaging from Carr. Humphreys was quick to spot the gaping ruin to his front, and sent Carr's Brigade through Spangler's Woods to join Burling's advance. Humphreys rode forward and placed himself in the center of his two advancing brigades. There was only what seemed to be a skirmish line in front of his 3000 men.

The skirmish line was the dying 'Florida' Brigade. Behind them were Lee and his staff. Even Lee could see no point in hanging on before the irresistible blue tide. Anderson was missing, and the brigades he had ordered forward were nowhere to be seen. Brigadier General Carnot Posey had, indeed, received Anderson's orders to move to support the right, but three of his four regiments

---

[8]* A.L. Long, 'There is a Price of Leadership', *MAC*, vol.XVI (1881), p.193. Colonel Long here continues his hagiography of Lee, but his account is well-supported by the numerous eye-witnesses in Wright's Brigade, for many of whom fighting under the direct eye of Lee was a singular honor.

[9]* Long, ibid, p.195.

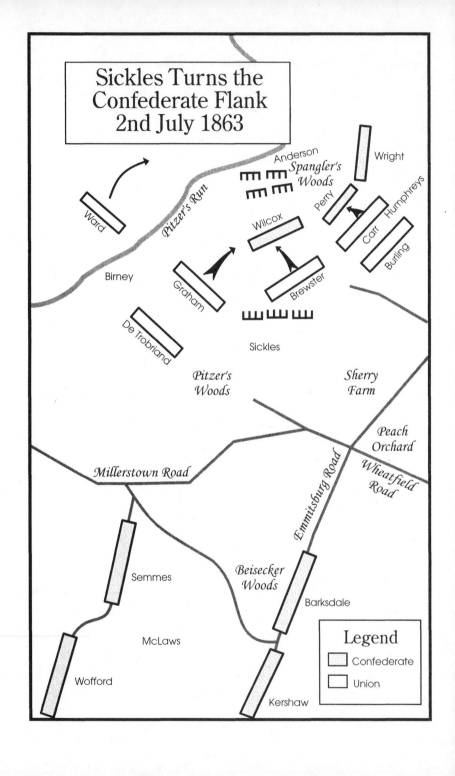

were dispersed across the corps front as skirmishers; he had no brigade readily at hand to move. Brigadier General William Mahone's brigade was waiting in the woods in readiness to move. Anderson's aide was relieved to see them so as he rode up to Mahone and delivered his message. To his amazement, Mahone merely replied that he had orders to hold his position and would not leave it. The aide answered, 'I am just from General Anderson and he orders you to advance.' Mahone replied, 'No, I have my orders from General Anderson himself to remain here.' [10] Nothing the aide could say would move Mahone from his position that an order given in person by his division commander took precedence over one transmitted by an aide. It was cold comfort for Lee to turn his back on the advancing Federals at the last minute to find that Wright had run his brigade out into a cornfield in the path of the onrushing enemy. No other reserves were in sight.

The odds against Lee were piling up even higher as Birney's Division of 5000 men swung around the disintegrating flank. Now facing north, they came on quickly. Colonel Charles K. Graham's 1st Brigade broke into Pitzer's Woods from the south, forcing back the one regiment that Wilcox could spare from his fight with Brewster. Colonel J.H. Hobert Ward's 2nd Brigade splashed across Pitzer's Run unopposed into the meadows beyond. The 3rd Brigade under Colonel P. Regis de Trobriand was in reserve to the rear. Sickles rode up elated with his attack and the splendid alignment of his corps. Aides from Humphreys found him in the woods and passed on to him the equally splendid news of the 2nd Division's success. The whole Confederate flank was crumbling, and he was now behind it as well. To his staff, he said, 'This is the end of the mighty Lee. This is repayment for Chancellorsville and Second Bull Run. By God, we have got him, boys!' The heady moment was too much for what little discretion he had. 'And now that I have won Meade's battle for him, there is nothing anyone can do.' [11]

'Sitting like a God Almighty atop Traveler'

E. Pitzer's Farm

A.P. Hill rode up past the farm of E. Pitzer, leading the first of Heth's brigades, that of Brigadier General Joseph R. Davis. Davis' only recommendation for command had been his family relationship to the Confederacy's president. His conduct on the first day of the battle had been scandalous. He had lost control of his command and stayed conspicuously out of the way. It was now Davis' Brigade in name only. Hill had made it clear that its senior regimental com-

---

[10] Freeman, op.cit. pp.127–8.
[11]* John W. Campbell, *The Court Martial of Major General Dan Sickles* (Swinton and Sons Publishers, Boston, 1927) p.201.

mander would command, and Davis was now as inconspicuous as he had been the day before. Brigadier General Pettigrew, the acting division commander, was welcome at Hill's side. The other shrunken brigades were all under new commanders since the slaughter of the previous day. He had to handle these men carefully. Most of the brigades had taken terrible losses. Davis and Archer's had been badly led. Losses had almost reached forty-five per cent for the division. As Jomini wrote in his classic on the art of war, the Spanish have a saying: 'He was a brave man that day.' That day was yesterday, and most of the survivors were still stunned at the shredding of their regiments. Lee had recognized, as did Hill, that the reservoirs of courage were low. But were they too low for the work ahead? He would find out shortly. The smoke and noise from a desperate fight was only just ahead as he passed the Pitzer Farm.

He knew it would be a hospital. Already dozens of wounded men had converged on it by instinct. One of them was Private Bailey McClelen of the 10th Alabama. He had been shot in the right leg charging a battery. Two of his comrades tried to take him to the rear but were ordered by the regiment's commander to put him down and get back into the firing line. For McClelen, it was safer to move on than remain where he lay:

> I did not really know at the time whether I could walk or not. Seeing our wounded passing me for the rear so numerously, I did not lie there long until I concluded to make an effort to walk. I left that spot faster than any walk. I made several stations on my way to the rear by reason of the shells I heard coming towards me from the enemy's batteries. I would fall flat until they passed me, then I would rise and try it again. I repeated this kind of tactics several times on my retreat ... At one station I had stopped at a fence, the shell that caused that stop exploded so close to me that the pieces flew all over and around me and hit the fence within two feet of me, and just after I crossed the fence another round shell came nearly over me but was some feet higher than my head. By this time I was nearing a stone building which was a good protection.[12]

Luckily he had found the brigade surgeons just behind the building. He did not record whether he saw Hill and Heth's Division marching past.

Wright's Georgians had held up Humphreys' men for fifteen minutes of dreadful pounding. He was outnumbered more than two to one as the volleys flamed across the small deadly space. His men in the edge of the corn field were dropping fast. Carr's New Jersey regiments were tough, but blue-clad bodies were piling up in their firing line as well. Wright was never prouder of his men,

---

[12] Bailey George McClelen, *I Saw the Elephant* (White Mane Publishing Co., Shippensburg, Pennsylvania, 1995) p.42.

especially now that they were under the eye of Lee himself, who would not leave the fighting. 'Please, General Lee,' Wright asked him, just as Long had, 'kindly move to the rear, to a safer position until reserves come up. I will not have it said that you were hurt on my firing line, Sir.'

Lee replied, 'General, I suggest you move a regiment to the right. Those people will flank you otherwise.' [13] Burling's Brigade had extended around Wright's right flank and was getting ready to close in on him. Wright took one look and shouted for the major commanding his last reserve, the 2nd Georgia Battalion of 150 men. The little band did a right face and ran off to the flank, beating Burling's men by seconds. Lee stayed where he was, and Wright did not presume to offer any more suggestions. He had other things to worry about. The close nature of the fighting left little room between the enemies, and Carr's Brigade came on in a rush that closed the gap almost instantly. They were fresh, and fell on the Georgians with a determination and ferocity the Confederates were not used to from their enemies. In places the fight was hand-to-hand, with bayonet and fist, sword and pistol, as the blue lines surged forward and blurred with the gray to stain the ground red. The mass of struggling men heaved back into the cornfield.

During all this Lee rode behind the line, inciting the men to a ferocity of their own by his mere presence. Colonel Long had long since stopped urging him to remove himself from danger; his body lay behind the line among the dead and wounded. Only one lieutenant remained at Lee's side, and he was bleeding from a head wound that left a crimson smear through his red hair. It seemed to those who saw him amidst this maelstrom that Lee bore a charmed life. Captain William S. Johnson, who led the 3rd Georgia's small reserve – Company B – into the bloody breach that the 1st Massachusetts had driven through the regiment, saw Lee at his most magnificent. He was sitting on Traveler, alone, behind the very point where the Baystaters broke through in their Puritan fury. The haze of smoke in front of them blew away to reveal the great old man, sword in hand at his side, majestically still. There was not a man in the Army of the Potomac who had not seen countless likenesses of Lee. Many knew him better than their own army commanders. They stopped cold, the white heat of battle somehow frozen. He stared them down for a heartbeat, before Johnson's men came howling at them with the bayonet and rifle butt, rushing past Lee to smash the enemy back. 'I will never forget Lee sitting like God Almighty atop Traveler as we attacked past him,' recalled Johnson. 'The boys cheered at the sight of him, desperate more to save him, I think, that to drive back the enemy.' [14]

---

[13]* Long, op.cit. p.96.
[14] William S. Johnson, *A Georgian in Gray: The Civil War Memoirs of William S. Johnson* (Stars and Bars Press, Savannah, 1967) p.162.

It was this scene that Hill and Pettigrew saw – Wright's Brigade turned at right angles being bent back by a blue vice of two brigades. In the van of Hill's reserve was the 11th Mississippi, fresh and rowdy, almost 600 strong. Alone of all the regiments in Heth's Division, it had lost not one man in Thursday's slaughter. Instead it had idled as the division train guard. Now it was out to avenge yesterday's losses. No scrappier regiment existed in the Confederate service. Raised among sharpshooting, wild backwoodsmen, it also had one company of university students who prided themselves on being 'always undisciplined and impulsive', an apt description of the entire regiment, of which it was written: 'No more disorderly mob of men ever got together to make an army.' Indeed, a former brigadier was reported to turn the air blue on the numerous occasions when the 11th's deeds off the battlefield were reported, but always ended by saying, 'Damn 'em! I wouldn't go into battle without 'em.' [15]

The Mississippians double-quicked from column to line in a fluid motion that impressed Hill; they had not been in his old Light Division, but they would have done it proud. He could work on the discipline later.

'Sparkling sabers'

Barlow, Pennsylvania

Buford had no time to reflect on the fact that the impending crash of cavalry against cavalry was the opposite lesson to that he had taught the horsemen of the Army of the Potomac. If he had, he would have agreed with Thoreau that 'foolish consistency was the hobgoblin of little minds', if he had ever read Thoreau. But Fitzhugh Lee was a Gordian Knot only the saber could cut. Buford cantered at the head of his division and felt the mass of men and horses trotting behind him knee to knee, sabers at the rest on every man's shoulder. The bugles blared, and the pace accelerated into a limited gallop. A hundred yards later the buglers sounded the charge, and the mass broke into a full gallop. The sabers arched up and then down, pointing straight at the enemy, as the flags and guidons fluttered overhead like a mediaeval host. All along the thundering line the deep roar of a Union shout boomed. Across the shrinking interval, the keening Southern yell echoed back in defiance as the gray host lowered its own saber hedge.

Adrenaline pumped through the veins of 4000 men, the very sensation described by an officer at Brandy Station: 'Who can describe the feelings of a

---

[15] George W. Stewart, *Pickett's Charge: A Microhistory of the Final Attack at Gettysburg, July 3, 1863* (Houghton Mifflin, Boston, 1983) p.43. Stewart relates an incident that highlighted the regiment's renowned marksmanship: 'Someone once came to report the loss of a hog within their lines, testifying that a shot had been heard and a squeal. General Whiting replied soberly, "I am satisfied you are mistaken. When an 11th Mississippian shoots a hog, it don't squeal."'

man on entering a charge? How exhilarating, and yet how awful! The glory of success in a charge is intoxicating! One forgets everything, even personal safety, in the one grand thought of vanquishing the enemy. We were in for it now, and the nerves were strung to the highest tension.' [16] Even the horses caught the fiery spirit of their masters and strained every muscle to race forward.

Confederate and Union horse artillery batteries had positioned themselves on the flanks and fired into the oncoming tides, slamming horses and men into bloody jumbles into which rear ranks crashed. Yet the hurtling masses still surged around the kicking heaps and into each other with a mighty crash. The impact brought scores of horses to the ground, their riders thrown into the trampling storm. Everywhere the combat immediately disintegrated into hundreds of individual duels, as a Confederate participant recounted:

> A passage of arms filled with romantic interest and splendor to a degree unequaled by anything our war produced ... Not a man fought dismounted, and there was heard but an occasional pistol shot and but little artillery, for soon after the opening of the fight the contest was so close and the dust so thick that it was impossible to use either without risk to friends ... It was like what we read of in the days of chivalry, acres and acres of horsemen, sparkling sabers, and dotted with brilliant bits of color where their flags danced about them, hurled against each other at full speed and meeting with a shock that made the earth tremble. [17]

Buford's horse had gone down in the initial shock, spilling him to the ground. He threw himself free and rolled to avoid the hooves of the close-packed horses around him. A Rebel cavalryman leaned over to hack at him but fell back as a bullet exploded into his forehead. Buford pushed the corpse out of the saddle and leapt up. An aide, forcing his way through the press, offered him his own red-stained saber, but before he could take it more of the enemy swarmed around them. The aide fell in the glittering flash of steel as Buford swung down on one side of his horse, Plains Indian fashion, to avoid the same fate. As he came up again, Stuart himself was a short distance ahead of him, trading blows with a Union sergeant, who collapsed and fell forward in the saddle even as he watched. Stuart looked about him for another challenge, and almost instinctively Buford spurred forward, reached out his open hand, and struck him on the shoulder. Stuart jerked around to see Buford glide past, the sweep of his own saber too late to catch him. Buford had counted coup on Stuart in imitation of, and admiration for, the heroism of a lone Brule Sioux warrior

---

[16] Samuel Carter III, *The Last Cavaliers: Confederate and Union Cavalry in the Civil War* (Saint Martin's Press, New York, 1979) p.157.

[17] W.W. Blackford, *War Years with JEB Stuart* (Louisiana State University Press, Baton Rouge and London, 1993) pp.215–16. This account is also of Brandy Station.

during the Battle of Blue Water Creek in 1855, who had similarly ridden up weaponless to touch him, in the supreme act of Lakota chivalry and courage. Buford's warrior heart had been touched as well. Stuart turned to him, a strange look on his face, then charged. Buford drew his pistol, aimed coolly, and shot him out of the saddle. Stuart's staff rushed up and lifted him bleeding back onto his mount while three troopers went after Buford, but the swirl of battle engulfed them as men of the 3rd Indiana swarmed around amid the screams of horses, shouting of men, and clang of steel on steel.

As Buford's men fought their way to their beleaguered commander, his trump card played itself. The division reserve, the almost 600-strong 8th New York Cavalry, came crashing into the right rear of the melee, while up the Taneytown Road from the south, in plain sight, came a bristle of bayonets above a human river in Union blue, the van of VI Corps.

Struck from the rear, and with a mass of approaching enemy infantry only minutes away, Lee's Brigade began to unravel and stream away north. Buford's men were after them, the exhilaration of the fight fed by the even greater astonishment that they had driven the gray cavalry from a fairly fought field.

'For God's sake, hurry'

The Taneytown Road, east of Little Round Top

Meade could not be in two places at once, but no commander had such a desperate need to be as he did at that moment. Sickles' second feckless act of disobedience that day, as destructive of Meade's plans as it was, had taken second place to Longstreet's sudden appearance in the army's rear. Vincent's plunge into the face of that attack had given him time to speed the rest of V Corps in support and to order XII Corps down from Culp's Hill, leaving only one brigade to man the defenses. From his vantage point on a small rise just east of the Taneytown Road 250 yards north of the Bricker Farm, he watched the rest of the 1st Division rush into battle. Colonel William S. Tilton's 1st Brigade came up to bolster Vincent's sagging defense. Colonel Jacob B. Sweitzer's 2nd Brigade came in on Vincent's left just as Hood was extending his own line in the direction of Rock Creek, with Benning's Brigade filling in on Robertson's right.

The Bricker Farm buildings, like those of the Group Farm, were burning as the Texas Brigade heaved and battered against Vincent's depleted brigade like a bull against a stubborn gate. Vincent's men later recalled that their colonel seemed to be everywhere, resolute as iron and as impervious to the enemy's fire. Armed only with a riding crop, he walked the firing lines in his high riding boots. 'Not one inch' he thundered as a group of men began drifting away – and they came scurrying back shamefacedly.

Colonel Tilton found Vincent on the outer edge of the shattered apple orchard behind the last thin line of the 83rd Pennsylvania. 'Bill,' he called out, 'put a regiment in here! For God's sake, hurry!' [18] That was the 118th Pennsylvania, just 233 men, but enough to stiffen their fellows of the 83rd. They filed into line just in time to deliver a volley at close range to the Texans, who thought they had only to make one more good thrust forward to break through. Tilton's two other small regiments, the 18th and 22nd Massachusetts, reinforced the 44th New York and 16th Michigan. Tilton had been just in time to blunt the Texan rage. Especially welcome was the 2nd Company, Massachusetts Sharpshooters, who took an extra toll of the enemy. Still, Tilton's small Brigade had added only 400 men to the fight. He had kept in reserve the 145 tough veterans of the 1st Michigan.

Sweitzer's Brigade came into line in the large cornfield to the east at the double-quick just as Benning's Georgians swept across the meadow to the south, aiming for that same cornfield. Both brigades, of almost identical strength – 1422 men to 1420 – were on a collision course. As the Union men burst out of the corn it was to see the enemy barely twenty yards away. As if on command, both brigades stopped in their tracks, leveled rifles, and fired. The flame swept its scythe through both brigades, a pall of black smoke boiled up over the firing lines to blind the protagonists. Artillery batteries unlimbered and fired into the roiling clouds rent only by the flames of muskets. The men kept on firing into the blackness until a slight breeze began to tear away the smoke, revealing a scene of carnage neither of these two veteran brigades had witnessed before. The dead and wounded were strewn thick enough to cover the ground where the firing lines had stood, the rear rank men now up front. They just kept firing – with most of their officers down they did not know what else to do, and were just too obstinate to do anything else anyway.

One of the few field officers still on his feet was Colonel Harrison H. Jeffords, commander of the 4th Michigan, on the brigade's left. A twenty-nine year old lawyer from Dexter, he had risen quickly, like so many other capable young men, from lieutenant to colonel in less than two years. He possessed a deep and abiding love for his regiment and had proclaimed, when the regiment had been presented with new colors, that he would defend them with his life. He looked for the colors and found them still flying but with only two of the color guard left. Then, to his horror, as he looked back towards the enemy he saw another brigade coming up on the flank of Benning's Georgians.

These were Brigadier General Evander Law's Alabamians, over 1400 men, aiming to crash into Sweitzer's flank and sweep around it. That flank was the 4th Michigan. Jeffords tried to refuse his flank, but his decimated command was groggy from the punching match with the Georgians and did not move in time. It would not have mattered. Law's men were just too numerous. The 4th and

---

[18]* Edwin Carter Bolling, *Strong Vincent, Pennsylvania's Glory* (D. Appleton, Philadelphia, 1899) p.226.

44th Alabama seemed to shrug off the thin volley delivered by the Michiganders and just kept coming. Unable to get out of the way, Jeffords men were hit by the gray tide and carried backwards by the rush, fighting back with bayonet and rifle butt in small groups. Jeffords shot one man with his pistol and killed another with his sword before he saw his flag fall into the trodden cornfield, its bearer dead. As a jubilant Confederate attempted to wrest it from the dead man's frozen grip, Jeffords ran forward, shouting, 'Save the colors, Boys!' A group of his officers and men followed him. Jeffords leapt onto the man now holding the colors and drove his sword into him. With a shriek, the man fell, and Jeffords grabbed the falling staff. A look of fiery joy flashed across his face for an instant, just an instant, before another Confederate bayonetted him through the chest. Lieutenant Michael Vreeland shot the attacker but was then himself shot in the chest and arm and clubbed to the ground with a rifle butt. More Michiganders came shouting to club, shoot, and stab in the red-eyed dance of death, until, like warriors on the Plains of Troy, they retrieved the body of their fallen hero and his precious standard. Thirty-nine of them had fallen in the desperate effort. Jeffords died in their arms, his last word 'Mother'.

Law's Brigade swept on around Sweitzer's wrecked command, which dis-integrated as it was taken in front and rear. Hood rode behind them with Law whooping his men on, his features flushed with battle joy and his blond beard shining in the sun as the Union flank died. Prisoners were being hustled to the rear as other Yankees fled in the opposite direction. A few small groups fought on, but they were mere pebbles that would soon be engulfed in the Confederate flood. This scene had been paralleled on so many fields in this war, that the Confederates had come to believe it was the natural order of things. Hood, however, had not previously encountered the calm resourcefulness of George Meade and the brilliant Henry Hunt. Instead of a collapsed flank, their fore-sight now presented Hood with an entirely new battle-line. Coming towards Hood's brigades were the two Regular brigades of V Corps' 2nd Division, flanked by the massed batteries of the Artillery Reserve. No volunteer regi-ments from the states, some of the 2nd Division's regiments had been in the pre-war Army. Although many new Regular regiments had been raised, and all of them had been diluted with new recruits, there were nevertheless a few grizzled long-service veterans in the older regiments who had wet-nursed future Confederate generals when they were no more than second lieutenants.

'The most destructive fire I ever saw'

Little Round Top

Not all of Law's Alabamians were now facing the Regulars. Colonel Oates' 15th Alabama had been the regiment marching past Longstreet when he had looked up and reflected upon the wooded hill to his left. 'General Law, send two good regiments to take that hill.' He pointed towards Little Round Top. 'We can sweep around the enemy from both directions.'[19] Law immediately detached Oates' 15th Alabama and Lieutenant Colonel Michael Bulger's 47th Alabama, putting Oates in overall command. In the lead, Oates quickly marched his men off the road and onto a farm track running up into the saddle between the two hills. Every man's head turned right to watch the fighting explode as the Texas Brigade attacked: Benning's column rushed to the flank, and their own brigade moved on. More than a few complaints were heard that they were going to miss the fight. At least their canteens were full; most of the men had refilled them from the ponds and creeks that came down off Big Round Top while they waited for Hampton's Brigade to began this business.

Company B of the 20th Maine was hiding behind the stone wall at the base of Little Round Top. They had watched in awe the thick columns of Hood's Division marching north on the Taneytown Road and knew that the rest of the brigade was fighting desperately only 400 yards away. Captain Morrill quietly withdrew his men up the hill ahead of the enemy. A runner reached Colonel Chamberlain quickly with the news. Though Chamberlain was new to command of the 20th Maine, he was no stranger to his regiment, having been its lieutenant-colonel since it was raised, and the mantle fell easily on his shoulders. He had deployed the 20th around the southeasterly pointing spur of the hill. Pickets extended north along the hill's slope. It was against this very spur that the Alabamians were climbing. Morrill arrived, panting from the speed of his return, to confirm that two regiments at least were coming. Chamberlain put Morrill's company in reserve up the slope, behind the center of his position. He had every confidence in his Maine men – even the 120 mutineers of the 2nd Maine who had been sent to him under guard at the end of May. Unlike the rest of the regiment, whose term of enlistment had expired after Chancellorsville, these men had signed three-year enlistment papers. Even so, they expected to be allowed to go home with the other men, having shared in all the same hardships as their comrades-in-arms. The Army had thought otherwise, and handled the matter so clumsily that these independent Yankees had simply mutinied, refusing to obey orders. Meade had sent them to the only other Maine regiment in V Corps, Chamberlain's, with instructions to 'make them do their duty, or shoot them down the moment they refused.'[20]

Too much the Christian to ever entertain shooting such men, Chamberlain had distributed them among his understrength companies and then

---

[19]* James Longstreet, *From Manassas to Gettysburg*, p.376.

[20] Joshua Lawrence Chamberlain, *'Bayonet! Forward!' My Civil War Reminiscences* (Stan Clark Military Books, Gettysburg, Pennsylvania, 1994) p.24.

called them together and pointed out to them the situation: that they could not be entertained as civilian guests by me; that they were by authority of the United States on the rolls as soldiers, and I should treat them as soldiers should be treated; that they should lose no rights by obeying orders, and I would see what could be done for their claim.

His gallant heart warmed when all save one or two stepped forward gladly. These were Maine men, all grievances forgotten when duty and the honor of the North Star state were at stake. Chamberlain described the next few moments.

The exigency was great. I released the pioneers and provost guards altogether, and sent them to their companies. All but the drummer boys and hospital attendants went into the ranks. Even the cooks and servants not liable to such service, asked to go in. Others whom I knew to be sick or footsore, and had given a pass to 'fall out' on the forced marches of the day and night before, came up, now that the battle was on, dragging themselves along on lame and bleeding feet, finding their regiment with the sagacity of the brave, and their places where need is greatest and hearts truest. 'Places?' Did any of these heroic men ever leave them? [21]

Heroic they might well be, but even with the men of the 2nd Maine, Chamberlain had only 358 all told — Colonel Oates had 499 men in the 15th Alabama, and the 47th Alabama had another 347, a total of 846 men, outnumbering the 20th Maine five to two. In addition both were veteran regiments, and had known nothing but victory from battlefield to battlefield. But they had not previously encountered that stubbornness which distinguished Maine troops.

Coming from a state blessed by more than its fair share of rocks, the Maine men had instantly recognized the value of the jumble of gray, worn rocks protruding from the earth and lying scattered down the slope among the trees. As soon as Chamberlain had deployed his men, they went to work building a breastwork wall, reinforcing it with whatever substantial pieces of timber were at hand. They had raised the wall to a height of two feet in some places when Captain Morrill and Company B arrived to take its place in the line. Chamberlain was worried despite the intelligent activity of his men. The slope behind them on the other side of the hill would have been better by far to defend. It was even steeper and rockier and had been logged and brushed recently, so fields of fire were good, and between the two hills there was a smooth dale of which he could have made a great killing ground. The slope he defended, on the other hand, was less steep and wooded with second growth forest, though it was

---

[21] Chamberlain, ibid, p.24.

filled with rocks and boulders 'thicker than gravestones in a city cemetery'. Fields of fire were not as good, but the enemy would have a difficult time rushing forward in a coherent body, and the rocks did offer a good measure of concealment. Chamberlain placed himself and the colors in the center of the line behind a jumble of immense boulders protruding from the soft forest floor, from where he could survey the entire line easily.

Oates deployed his command in line with the 47th Alabama in column to the rear, ready to flank whatever force he encountered. It was slow going for the 15th, picking over the jumble of rocks and through the trees. As with most woods in the well-farmed areas of the Eastern United States, this one on Little Round Top had been cleared of fallen trees and brushed regularly so that the going, save for the rocks and the steep ascent, was not all that daunting. There was no sight of the enemy, only what seemed in places like a farmer's wall ahead up the slope, something to prevent animals grazing too far. Behind that wall, in heart-pounding silence, the men of the 20th Maine crouched. In the center of the line, Corporal Albert Tozier cradled the regiment's colors in his arms as he lay on the ground. Chamberlain himself was the only man on his feet, standing behind an oak and peering carefully around it as the Alabamians inched forward with a soft rattle of equipment and the occasional snap of a dry branch. He did not twitch a muscle as they closed the distance – fifty yards, forty yards, thirty yards – they had to get closer – twenty yards, ten yards. Now! 'Up, men!' he shouted, 'Fire!'

His men jumped to their feet and fired into the surprised faces of the 15th Alabama. Oates wrote:

> unexpectedly to us, because concealed, they poured into us the most destructive fire I ever saw. Our line halted but did not break ... As men fell their comrades closed the gap, returning the fire most spiritedly. I could see through the smoke men of the Twentieth Maine ... running from tree to tree.[22]

The Union fire had brought down the first rank of his regiment, spilling the bodies among the rocks, their ancient, dull gray now splashed with bright red. Their comrades crowded forward to take their places as the fire grew hot. Bodies in blue now began to pitch forward or back to line the wall. The 15th Alabama's supports came up in a rush that carried the firing line with it. Chamberlain described how

> the two lines met and broke and mingled in the shock. The crash of musketry gave way to cuts and thrusts, grapplings and wrestlings. The edge of the conflict

---

swayed to and fro, with wild whirlpools and eddies. At times I saw around me more of the enemy than of my own men; gaps opening, swallowing, closing again with sharp convulsive energy; squads of stalwart men who had cut their way through us, disappearing as if translated. All around, a strange mingled roar – shouts of defiance, rally, and desperation; and underneath, murmured entreaty and stifled moans; gasping prayers, snatches of Sabbath song, whispers of loved names; everywhere men torn and broken, staggering, creeping, quivering on the earth, and dead faces with strangely fixed eyes staring stark into the sky. Things which cannot be told – nor dreamed. How men held on, each one knows, – not I. But manhood commands admiration.[23]

For Chamberlain, the fight seemed to last an eternity.

The edge of the fight rolled backward and forward like a wave. The dead and wounded were now in our front and then in our rear. Forced from our position, we desperately recovered it, and pushed the enemy down to the foot of the slope. The intervals of the struggle were seized to remove our wounded (and those of the enemy also), to gather ammunition from the cartridge-boxes of the disabled friend or foe on the field, and even to secure better muskets than the Enfields, which we found did not stand service well.[24]

He was talking about the US Springfield rifled musket calibre .58, Model 1855 or 1861. From their numerous captures, the Confederates were well-armed with this accurate, clean-killing rifle, superior to the British Enfield. One of these rifles in the hands of an Alabama sniper was aimed right at Chamberlain's heart as the battle swept up and down the slope. The sniper had found a safe vantage point between two rocks and saw Chamberlain as he stood fully exposed in the center of the line, easily recognized as the enemy commander by his dress and actions; pleased at finding such a target, he laid his rifle on the rock to steady it, and 'drew bead fair and square'. His finger began to squeeze the trigger, then a 'queer notion', as he later described it, made him pause. 'Then I got ashamed of my weakness and went through the same motions again. I had you, perfectly certain. But that same queer something shut right down on me. I couldn't pull the trigger, and, gave it up.'[25]

[23] Joshua Lawrence Chamberlain, 'Through Blood and Fire at Gettysburg', *Hearst's Magazine* 23 (June 1903) p.903.
[24] *OR*, vol.XXVII, part 1, p.624.
[25] Chamberlain, *'Bayonet! Forward!' My Civil War Reminiscences*, p.31. The sniper wrote this to Chamberlain after the war. Chamberlain invited him north to 'see whether I was worth what he missed. But my answer never found him, nor could I afterwards.'

CHAPTER 8

2nd July 1863
Dominus noster Jesus Christus vos absolvat

5:30 PM

Post-war studies of the battle of Gettysburg have consistently dwelled, most often in academic amazement, on the fact that by 5:30 the battle had shifted from its natural east-west axis to one facing almost north-south. Each army was turning a flank of the other. Sickles' Corps was wrapping around Anderson's right, while Longstreet had driven up almost behind Meade's left. At the time, neither Meade nor Lee were in any position to reflect on it. Each was trying to deal with the wreck of his plans as the battle, like an unbalanced blade, twisted in his hand. Each had been carried to this point by the hubris of a subordinate, and each was fulfilling his worst nightmare. Lee was struggling with just the catastrophe he had foreseen in separating the army in the face of the enemy in hostile territory. Meade was finding his strong reservations about fighting at Gettysburg savagely confirmed by Longstreet.

At the moment, Meade's situation was the more critical. Lee, at least, could continue to pull his threatened wing back, even if it meant leaving Longstreet to his own devices. There was still a good chance 'Old Pete' would pull it off, especially if Ewell chimed in at the right time. Meade, on the other hand, was in an extremely tight situation. Longstreet was pressing him north back up against Cemetery Hill and Culp's Hill. If he pushed him far enough back to threaten the Baltimore Pike, the Army of the Potomac was trapped – and the war was over. To Meade's advantage was his clearly superior leadership in battle. If ever a Union commander tightly controlled all his forces on a battlefield – with the lamentable exception of Sickles – it was Meade. He was there parceling out brigades as the situation demanded, keeping his fingers on the pulse of the action. In contrast, Lee had allowed himself to become involved personally in the tactical play on his left. This had happened at Sharpsburg as well. But in all fairness to him, if a commander has no other resources to throw into the fray, then he has no option but to lead by personal example. Still, he found himself in such straits because he had not cracked the whip on his corps commanders. Hill had neglected his own and the army's flank; and Ewell was simply doing nothing. It says much for Meade that he had such a firm grasp of the army after less than a week in command.

Meade had another vital advantage. The staff work of the Army of the Potomac was generally very good. Perhaps it was the Northern penchant for organization, but the staffs at army, corps, and division level alike were actively seeing that the orders of their commanders were carried out efficiently and promptly. Thousands of bits of information were being sifted, evaluated, and shared. Meade had already been well-served by the thoroughness and initiative of his Office of Military Information. He was even now being served equally well by his Chief of Artillery, Brigadier General Hunt, who was surveying the situation on Cemetery Hill. It was plain to see that XI Corps would be hard pressed to stretch its dwindling infantry to cover the ground that Ames' destroyed division had held. Hunt conferred with Colonel Wainwright, I Corps' Chief of Artillery, and on his own initiative ordered up six more batteries from the Artillery Reserve to ring the slope of East Cemetery Hill. In contrast, Confederate staff work was practically non-existent, and failure to co-ordinate concerted action was already a problem. For example, Lee's Chief of Artillery, Major General Pendleton, was a complete cipher. He gave no thought to the co-ordinated use of the army's artillery to support Lee's plans, and, more critically, no-one, including Lee, thought to tell him to do so.

5:30 PM, Hancock's headquarters, Cemetery Ridge
The dreadful cannonade to their right did not disconcert the veterans of II Corps as they stood in their ranks along and behind Cemetery Ridge. They had complete faith in Hancock. Already word had spread of how their corps commander had single-handedly stopped yesterday's rout and put iron back into the spines of the defeated. But they, no less than Hancock, were now spectators of Sickles' awesome maneuver around Lee's flank, and naturally nervous about the noise of battle to their left rear.

Meade easily found Hancock in the center of his line. Wherever the white trefoil on the corps commander's flag waved, he was sure to find Hancock. The watching thousands saw Meade ride up over the ridge followed by his cloud of aides, each ready to dash off with a vital message or supervise the execution of a critical order. His confidence was such that he had left Sykes, with Slocum coming up in support, to hold off Longstreet while he turned his attention to the mess Sickles had made. He quickly briefed Hancock on the overall situation along the Taneytown Road and expressed his belief that the line would hold with the entire V Corps either engaged or in reserve. He had also ordered up most of XII Corps. Ewell's inactivity in the early morning hours had convinced Meade that not much would be heard from him today; consequently it was safe, or at least an acceptable risk, to denude Culp's Hill. He needed a reserve, especially as there was no word from Sedgwick and the mighty VI Corps, even though he was expected at any moment. Meade was clearly in control of the situation, but his temper was more than frayed by Sickles' monumental insubordination. The air around them was blue with his opinion of that 'wretched politician', confirming to everyone in earshot the accuracy of his epithet as the 'old snapping turtle'. That out of the way, he got down to business. 'Hancock, I cannot be in command of this battle on two sides of the same hill at one time. I am placing you in overall command of all forces along this ridge to include I and XI Corps and those damn fools out there.' He waved his hat in the direction of III Corps. 'Make sure that Sickles doesn't stick his head into a noose. Recall him if necessary. Support his attack if the opportunity presents itself.' He grew silent for a few moments as he watched III Corps grinding away at Lee's flank. 'I'll be damned, but he may succeed. Right now it is a coin toss over which I would enjoy more – beating Bobby Lee or court-martialing Dan Sickles.'

And then, quite suddenly, the attention of the two generals, along with their staffs and the whole of II Corps, was called to a new actor on the stage.

'Attention, Mississippians! Battalions, forward!'

5:35 PM, the Emmitsburg Road at Beisecker Woods

The new actor was the lead brigade of McLaws' Division, emerging from Beisecker Woods on the Emmitsburg Road, its red battle-flags dancing over the rapidly moving column. The gasps and oaths among the commanders on Cemetery Hill were accurate predictions of the impending trap about to be sprung on Sickles. By this time, Sickles' two divisions were facing roughly north, pushing Hill's men ahead of them, utterly ignorant of the storm about to break upon their rear. From Cemetery Ridge staff officers raced down to warn them. Meade was cursing Sickles again. Then he stopped abruptly and turned to Hancock. 'Send in a division now. It must hold off the enemy long enough for III Corps to extricate itself.'

On the Emmitsburg Road, McLaws rode at the head of Barksdale's Brigade. The situation described by Lieutenant Colonel Taylor was too fluid and critical for a set-piece preparation. He would have to see it with his own eyes. For a reserved, methodical sort, he was not in his best element at times like this. He had expected that the best he could hope for was to prevent a catastrophe, but what he saw instead was enough to excite even him. The line of smoke rising from the fighting was perpendicular to the road. Not only would he strike an unsuspecting enemy from the rear, but he would cut him off from his main line at the same time. At that moment he was mightily glad he had taken Taylor's advice to advance in two columns, one by the Emmitsburg Road and the other by a parallel farm road. His division was advancing in columns of brigades. On the Emmitsburg Road, Kershaw's South Carolinians followed Barksdale's

Mississippians with the division artillery battalion of sixteen guns; on the farm road were Semmes' and Wofford's Brigades, all Georgian regiments, supported by the Washington Artillery Battalion of ten guns.

Meade's frantic staff officers arrived at breakneck speed just as McLaws announced himself with his artillery. The shot from the Washington Artillery's 12-pounder Napoleons came ploughing into the rear of de Trobriand's brigade in reserve, gouging bloody lanes through the packed ranks. One of the shot had continued on, spattering flesh and blood through the ranks before tearing into the cluster of officers around the III Corps flag. A horse was down, its entrails looped over the ground, kicking and screaming in its death agonies before an orderly put it out of its misery with a shot. Then officers rushed to the stricken corps commander, laying half under the dead weight of the horse. Sickles' right leg was hanging by a few strips of flesh as his staff pulled him out from beneath the dead horse.

De Trobriand had more to worry about just then than his wounded corps commander. Semmes' and Wofford's Georgians were closing fast on his rear. His regiments shook off the shock of the artillery and reversed front barely in time to get off a volley as the Georgians closed on them in that rushing, impetuous style that put Confederate infantry amongst the finest assault troops of the century. Ahead of them flew the Rebel Yell, to fall like panic-tipped arrows into the enemy's ranks. The volley did not even slow them down. At twenty yards they stopped barely long enough to fire a deadly volley of their own that left gaping holes in de Trobriand's regiments. Then with a roar they came forward again, bayonets levelled. The Yankee brigade wavered, but not its commander. Regis de Trobriand was the younger son of French aristocrat and had sought his fortune in America, where he had married well and become a successful lawyer. When the guns were fired in 1861, this descendent of a warrior house became an American citizen and colonel of the 55th New York on the same day. He commanded good, veteran regiments, and was not about to let them be swept away. Riding up to the 17th Maine, he called on them in his accented English to fire. They got off a ragged volley that caught the first rank of the 50th Georgia almost point-blank. The 3rd and 5th Michigan followed suit, but the Confederates leapt over their dead and into the Union ranks. Sword in hand and shouting in French, de Trobriand led the brigade reserve, the 40th New York, forward into the melee that had been his center and right.

De Trobriand's brigade had held long enough for Birney to pull most of Graham's 1st Brigade out of Pitzer's Woods and their grim fight with Wilcox's Alabamians. He fed them into the line on de Trobriand's left, which saved it for the moment. De Trobriand's right was in much more serious trouble as Wofford's Brigade swung around and onto the flank and rear of the 17th Maine, which melted away in the crossfire. The fighting swung south. As his two Michigan regiments and the New Yorkers were pushed back towards the woods, Hancock's courier finally found him to order him to pull back. More Confederates were coming down the Emmitsburg Road and would shortly cut him off. Birney realized he was too closely engaged to retreat and begged for support. The courier was off again in the opposite direction. Birney also realized that Ward's Brigade, which had crossed Pitzer's Run to envelop Hill's left, was his only reserve. If Ward could be recalled, he could turn the tables on the enemy and take him in the flank with his most powerful brigade, almost 2200 men, including most of the 1st and 2nd US Sharpshooters. Aides dashed away to find him.

McLaws' attack was only the beginning of worries for Birney, now the acting III Corps commander. The two divisions of the Corps had been fighting two essentially separate actions. Birney was desperately engaged in the first, while the second was Humphreys' successful drive through Spangler's Woods. Now that effort too had suddenly come to a halt and was barely holding its own. Just as at Sharpsburg, Hill had arrived in the nick of time to save the army's disintegrating flank. Of course, this time the flank had been his own, but it was a dramatic rescue nonetheless. He had personally led the 11th Mississippi, the sharp spearpoint of Davis' Brigade, splashing across Pitzer's Run and into the flank of Burling's Brigade as it was about to crush Wright's hard-pressed men, the inspiring presence of Lee notwithstanding. Poague's surviving guns were firing into Humphreys from the rear. He also saw heavy enemy columns pouring down the road over Herr's Ridge only 400 yards to the north, the other brigades of Heth's Division. Artillery was pulling off the road as well and going into action. The first shots were ranging his hard-pressed brigade as he watched. The terrible impact of the hard-fighting 11th Mississippi had heaved Burling's men back, trailing a thick carpet of blue-clad dead and wounded. How could he have known that they were merely the sharp point of a shivered spear? The rest of Heth's Division was in no real shape for desperate fighting; the courage-draining ordeal of the previous day was still too fresh in their minds, though that was not apparent as their columns flowed over Herr's Ridge. Hancock's courier found Humphreys as he gathered in the same appalling scene. The news that the enemy would soon be behind him as well made up his mind in an instant to pull his division out of this fight and back across the Emmitsburg Road.

It was too late. Barksdale's Brigade was coursing up the road and approaching the Peach Orchard. In ten minutes the fiery white-maned Mississippian would cut both Birney and Humphreys off. Barksdale halted the brigade only long enough to throw out skirmishers and deploy in line of battle. His spirited steed danced. The forty-five year old Mexican War volunteer veteran, brawler, and former Congressman had been a man to fear in the heated House debates before Secession. One of his men said that 'he had a thirst for battle glory'. In moments like this it suffused him with a white-hot glow. He rode out before his old regiment, the 13th Mississippi, in front of the colors. Behind him his men dropped their packs and blanket rolls in piles, to be guarded by a single man from each regiment. Colonel Benjamin Grubb Humphreys, commanding the 21st Mississippi on the right, had one of the finest command voices in the army; when he brought his regiment to attention, it stiffened every pair of shoulders 'like an electric shock'.[1]

Barksdale's voice rolled over the regiments like a crack of thunder. 'Attention, Mississippians! Battalions, forward!' The piercing Rebel yells, as sharp as razors to the minds of their enemies, rose from the ranks as they sprang forward, Barksdale in the lead waving his hat, his long white hair streaming behind.

6:00 PM, Cemetery Ridge

If Hancock's men had originally been no more than awed spectators of III Corps' lunge across the valley, they were fast becoming participants as Sickles' broken units reeled back. Private Roland E. Bowen, 15th Massachusetts, in Harrow's Brigade, was also experiencing a sensation less exalted than awe:

> The shot and shell went screaming through the air, and again and a gain I thined my-self down to that old five cent piece crowding my nose into the sand out of sight. It seemed every shell burst nearer and nearer. I fancied they just skimed over my back and then exploded. I turned my face up to see how much longer I had got to live, and to my great joy I found they were bursting 200 feet above the ground. I cracked the next man on the head, who I see was trembling, if posible, worse than myself, at the same time saying look up, see the smoke, they are bursting 2 or 300 feet above us. We were congratulateing ourselves on their wild shots when down came one right into the 1st Min. sending one man's legs flying into the air and tareing a foot from another poor fellows. Howe they did take on. One of them bled to death in a few minits, the other was taken to the rear. In a minit another fell in the 82nd N.Y. kiling 2 men instantly.[2]

Heedless of the stray shells, Hancock rode down the line of his corps to the left, where he found the 1st Division commander, Brigadier General John C. Caldwell. The 1st Division had been Hancock's old command not too many weeks before, and he was fond of it. 'Caldwell, get your division ready.' Caldwell was to lead it to the relief of Sickles' forlorn command. As the

[1] J.S. McNeilly, 'Barksdale's Mississippi Brigade', *Publications of the Mississippi Historical Society*, vol.XIX, p.236; cited in Glenn Tucker, *High Tide at Gettysburg: The Pennsylvania Campaign* (Stan Clark Military Books, Gettysburg, Pennsylvania, 1995) p.276.

[2] Roland E. Bowen, *From Ball's Bluff to Gettysburg: The Civil War Letters of Private Roland E. Bowen, 15th Massachusetts Infantry 1861–1864*, ed. Gregory A.Coco (Thomas Publications, Gettysburg, Pennsylvania, 1994) p.197.

ranks rustled in preparation to move, Father William Corby, Chaplain of
Caldwell's 2nd 'Irish' Brigade stepped forward and climbed a three-foot high
rock. The brigade commander, Colonel Patrick Kelly, commanded, 'Order
Arms.' Irish-born Major St Clair Mullholland of the 116th Pennsylvania was
an eyewitness:

> Now ... help is called for, and Hancock tells Caldwell to have his men
> ready... The Irish Brigade ... whose green flag has been unfurled in every
> battle in which the Army of the Potomac has been engaged ... formed part
> of this division... The Chaplain of this brigade, Rev. William Corby, pro-
> posed to give a general absolution to all the men before going into the fight.
> While this is customary in the armies of Catholic countries in Europe, it was
> perhaps the first time it was ever witnessed on this continent ... Father
> Corby stood on a large rock in front of the Brigade. The Brigade was stand-
> ing at 'Order Arms!' As he closed his address, every man, Catholic and non-
> Catholic, knelt on his right knee, his head bared, hat in left hand, right hand
> upon his rifle, and bowed his head. Then stretching his right hand toward the
> Brigade, Father Corby pronounced the words of absolution: 'Dominus noster
> Jesus Christus vos absolvat'.

The scene was more than impressive; it was awe-inspiring. As Mullholland
knelt with the other 531 men of the battle-shrivelled Brigade, the rest of II
Corps watched in respectful silence.[3]

Father Corby's last words were a hard injunction, befitting the tradition of
Holy Crusade: 'The Catholic Church refuses Christian burial to the soldier who
turns his back upon the foe.' With Corby's deep voice lingering in the air,
Caldwell gave the order to advance at the double-quick, and his 3320 men
began to snake down the slope in a race to hold open the door for III Corps'
escape.

Barksdale and Kershaw's 3800 men had a head start and were about to slam
that door shut and shoot home the bolt. Barksdale had sent ahead a thick line of
skirmishers on both sides of the road, and Kershaw had veered off the road to
the south, his own skirmishers pushing on towards the Rose wheatfield aligned
with Barksdale's men on the left.

---

[3] John B. Bachelder Papers, New Hampshire Historical Society, Concord, notes of a conversation
with Colonel Mulholland, n.d., cited in Harry W. Pfanz, *Gettysburg: The Second Day* (University of
North Carolina Press, Chapel Hill and London, 1987) p.269; John E. Carey, 'Priest went to war
armed with the Word of God', *Washington Times*, 14th September 1996, p.B3. Corby was the
first Catholic priest to serve as a chaplain with the Army of the Potomac and achieved a reputation for courage and personal ministry. At Antietam he rode along the battle-line with Colonel
Meagher, the brigade commander, offering encouragement and absolution.

'Limber up and get out'

6:00, the J. Staub farm, west of the Emmitsburg Road

Lieutenant Colonel Freeman McGilvery, commanding the 1st Volunteer Brigade of the Artillery Reserve, could not tear his gaze away from the oncoming Mississippians of Barksdale's Brigade. They had just filed off the Emmitsburg Road into line of battle and were coming his way. Already bullets from their skirmish line were impacting amid Captain John Bigelow's 9th Massachusetts Battery. 'Captain, abandon this position. You have no infantry support, and those people will simply overrun you. Limber up and get out.'

It was going to be a grim introduction to battle for the Baystaters. Fresh from the comfortable defenses of Washington, where they had spent the last year, the 109 officers and men of the battery now found themselves literally on their own as Gilvery rode off to see to his other batteries in support of III Corps. His order was absolutely correct, but it was advice easy to give and not so easy to execute. Bigelow reasoned that if the battery simply limbered up and rode off, it would escape. But it would escape its duty to fight as well, and it was obvious that III Corps was in for a disaster with that howling gray horde flooding up the road. Bigelow's Battery, Captain Charles Phillips' 5th Massachusetts, and Judson Clark's III Corps 2nd New Jersey Battery, had been firing in support of Brewster's Brigade from the open fallow field west of J. Staub's farm, and had engaged in some sharp dueling with Poague's batteries in the last few hours. Bigelow had been pleased with the cool performance of his battery in its first action. Only moments before, an order from McGilvery had brought the batteries to a position perpendicular to the Emmitsburg Road, just north of the Peach Orchard. He knew that if he took the time to limber up, the enemy would get close enough to slaughter his men and horses with rifle fire. He ordered them instead to retire by prolonge. Ropes on the trails of the guns were quickly hooked up to the limbers. This tactic did not require the gun to stop firing; instead the recoil of the gun propelled it backwards guided by the ropes attached to the limbers. As soon as the gun halted, the crew would dash forward, reload, and fire, then stand aside as the recoil 'withdrew' the gun further back.

It was Clark's Battery that was closest to the oncoming enemy, though. Clark had not waited for McGilvery to order a retreat. He ordered his six 10-pounder Parrotts limbered up as soon as he saw the Confederates coming out of the high ground of the Peach Orchard to his left rear. He could do little now; he had used up all his canister against Wilcox's stubborn men in Pitzer's Woods. As his limbers wheeled around for the gunners to hook up their pieces, the 21st Mississippi fired into them, killing the lead horses of one team. As the drivers cut them free, the Mississippians got closer and called out, 'Halt, you Yankee sons of bitches; we want those guns!' Corporal Samuel Ennis shouted in reply, 'Go to hell! We want to use them yet awhile!'[4] As the battery sped away, McLaws' artillery lashed out at them, wounding some gunners and all the horses of the fourth gun's caisson and four horses of the third gun's caisson. Leaving the caisson behind, the 5th New Jersey rode out of the battle.

Phillips' battery pulled out next. The enemy was now so close that their rifle fire was picking off men and horses. When the lead and swing pairs' drivers were shot down, Lieutenant Scott and a gunner ran to No. 2 gun to hook it up to its limber. As they did so, Scott was shot in the face by a ball that smashed his cheek bones and the roof of his mouth. No. 1 gun had worse problems. In response to Phillips' order to retire by prolonge and firing, the crew had

> toggled the rope to the trail and stretched it back ready to be hooked up. When the limber swung around, Corporal Benjamin Graham, the gunner, hooked the prolonge into the limber's pintle and shouted, 'Drive on!' It did not move. Graham stepped to the side to see what was wrong and saw that in the few seconds it had taken him to hook up, the Confederates had shot down the five remaining horses of the piece's team.[5]

Phillips then ordered Graham to break the sponge staff in the muzzle and abandon the gun. A true gunner, Graham announced that the crew would drag the gun away and immediately grabbed the prolonge and started to pull. Phillips dismounted and lent a hand, holding his horse with the other. When they eventually stopped at the Trostle Farm, they discovered that they had dragged the piece over half a mile.

Bigelow's ordeal was last. He had turned his guns in the enemy's direction and continued to fire as Clark and Phillips had made good their escape. With bullets pinging off the bronze guns, he ordered the battery to fall back. By this time Brewster's New York regiments had broken contact with Wilcox in Pitzer's Woods and were streaming out of action just to the north of Bigelow's guns. Seeing the oncoming Rebels, they quickened their pace. They had been fighting Wilcox's stubborn Alabamians for two hours and were spent. All they could think of now was getting out of the way. Humphreys was too pre-occupied getting his other two brigades out through Spangler's Woods to turn Brewster south to support Bigelow. Ironically it was Bigelow, slowly recoiling his guns backwards, who was buying time for the 2nd Division's escape:

> No friendly supports of any kind, were in sight; but Johnnie Rebs in great numbers. Bullets were coming into our midst from many directions and a

---

[4] Michael Hanifen, *History of Battery B, First New Jersey Artillery* (Republican Times Printers, Ottawa, Illinois, 1905) p.76.

[5] Pfanz, op.cit. p.340.

Confederate battery added to our difficulties. Still, prolonges were fixed and we withdrew … We moved slowly, the recoil of the guns retiring them, while the prolonges enabled us to keep the alignment; but the loss in men and horses was severe.[6]

'See, that is Longstreet!'

6:10 PM, Seminary Ridge

If it was to be an escape it would be a narrow one, because the remaining Confederates along Seminary Ridge, so inactive all day, suddenly came alive. When the 11th Mississippi had come to Wright's rescue, Lee had left the fighting in Hill's hands, assigning McLaws to him for the attack. Riding north up the ridge, he applied fire to Posey and Mahone's resolve and left them quivering to leap forward into action. Finding Pender, he ordered him to take charge of these two brigades and two of his own to sweep around Humphreys' flank. Lee was filled with more than the normal exultation of battle; he felt positively incandescent. The ache in his chest and the sense of dullness that had clung to him since his illness was suddenly gone. Despite the hot and oppressively humid day, he felt like that vigorous captain in the cool, thin air of the high mountains around Santa Anna's capital so many years before. Today he had thunderbolts in his fists.

He returned the salute of Pender and his staff as they rushed off to ready the attack. 'Quickly, quickly, General,' he had urged Pender, 'We have them now! See the smoke behind those hills?' He pointed to the pall that hung above the burning Bricker Farm just behind Little Round Top. 'That is Longstreet! All we have to do is press our attack here, and they will break.'

Indeed, as Meade had foretold, Sickles had marched III Corps into an enormous trap, with McLaws as one hinge and Hill as the other. Semmes and Wofford had finally driven Graham's and de Trobriand's brigades back and followed them into Pitzer's Woods. The regiments melted away into crowds of fugitives. Here and there, clumps of men still crowded around a forlorn color, and remnants of batteries that had managed to slip through the woods kept together. The mass streamed out of the woods on the eastern side, into the fields just vacated by Clark, Phillips, and Bigelow's batteries, to provide perfect targets for Poague's surviving guns. On the receiving end for two hours, the grimy gunners plied their pieces with a new enthusiasm. They fired spherical case, shell which exploded overhead, and solid shot which tore through the crowds, all of which hurried the survivors on towards safety on Cemetery Ridge. They ran straight into the unequal fight between Bigelow's Battery and Barksdale's Brigade. Like a herd of stampeded cattle they surged around the

---

[6] *Voices of the Civil War: Gettysburg* (Time-Life Books, Alexandria, Virginia, 1995) p.93.

battery and kept going, despite the slaughter inflicted by the Mississippi riflemen. Graham had kept a few of his regiments in hand – the 57th, 68th, 105th and 114th Pennsylvania – and threw them into the path of the oncoming Mississippians. Defending their own soil, the Pennsylvania regiments steeled themselves to face Barksdale's thunderstorm. The 114th was a dash of vivid color on the field, being a Zouave regiment, dressed in short red-piped blue jackets, baggy red trousers, and a red, yellow-tasseled fez. The trousers, tied around the waist with a robin's egg blue sash, were tucked into white canvas leggings, sometimes covered with short leather greaves. The 114th could fight, too.

One of McLaws' aides, Captain G.B. Lamar Jr., described Barksdale as he saw him at that moment, racing at the head of his brigade, his face 'radiant with joy'. His white hair streaming behind recalled to Lamar the white plume of Henry of Navarre. 'I have witnessed many charges marked in every way by unflinching gallantry ... but I never saw anything to equal the dash and heroism of the Mississippians.'[7]

The 57th Pennsylvania rushed into and around the buildings on the Sherfy Farm along the Emmitsburg Road to form a strongpoint, with the 105th forming on its right. The 114th, now commanded by Captain Edward R. Bowen, ran through the farmyard to take up position on the eastern side of the road, while the 68th came up on its left. But Graham's new battle-line started to come apart almost at once. Barksdale personally led the attack, the 13th and 17th Mississippi driving Bowen's men north up the road, leaving brightly-clothed bodies in the sunken roadway. Colonel Humphreys' 21st Mississippi's fire cut down the 68th's colonel, lieutenant colonel, and color-bearer in a single volley. Then their charge swept the dazed 68th away. On Graham's right, the 18th Mississippi scattered the 105th and drove into the farmyard. The 57th sold out more dearly, blasting away from the windows of the house and the barn loft with a heavy fire that dropped many of the Mississippians in the yard. The Rebel fire was even heavier, shredding the windows and doors into pulp. Fire curling up from the barn and house did even more damage, and the survivors threw out their weapons and surrendered. Graham himself went down in the fighting and was captured.

McGilvery had been watching from Cemetery Ridge, hoping to find infantry support for his guns. Finding none, he saw that only Bigelow's slowly recoiling guns stood between Barksdale and the ridge. Driving spurs into his horse, he raced back through a storm of artillery and rifle fire; his horse staggered as it was struck several times, but the faithful beast gathered its strength and plunged forward. He reached Bigelow, who had arrived at the angle of the stone wall at Trostle's house and was hoping to limber up and get away.

---

[7] Tucker, op.cit. pp.276–7.

McGilvery shouted above the din that between the Round Top and the left of II Corps there was a 1500-yard gap with no reserves in sight. 'Hold your position at all hazards, and sacrifice your battery, if need be.'

Into this misery, Caldwell's division struck. As Birney's men ran from the woods, Caldwell's four small brigades had come up in line with their right on the Trostle Farm and their left at the Wheatfield, and immediately collided with Kershaw's Brigade. That did little good for Bigelow. He still had no infantry support, just 'Johnnie Rebs in great numbers'. As McGilvery rode off, Bigelow prepared to fight it out with the 21st Mississippi. 'Orders were given to unlimber, take the ammunition from the chests, place it near the guns for rapid firing and load the guns to the muzzle. They were hardly executed before the enemy appeared breast high above the swell of ground 50 yards in front . . . and firing.' The enemy crowded to the very muzzles of Lieutenant Erickson's and Whitaker's sections but were blown away by the canister. Erickson, a twenty-eight year old Norwegian, had lost so many men that his section was now out of action; he rode over to help Whitaker, who, though shot through the lung, kept shouting orders as blood poured from his mouth, then fell dead as six bullets riddled his body. Just before the enemy closed, Bigelow saw that Lieutenant Milton's section could not bear on the enemy due to some large boulders. He ordered him out of the action through a gate in the stone wall, hoping to save at least two guns. The first gun careened so wildly through the gate that it overturned. Milton jumped from his horse amid a hail of bullets to help the crew right it, and soon it was flying to the rear. The other gun-crew simply drove its team straight at the stone wall; they leapt over and crashed the gun right through the wall. Bigelow had ridden over to get some of Milton's men to widen the hole, so that he get a few more guns out, when his bugler, Corporal Charles Reed, suddenly reared his horse on its haunches next to him, trying to shield him from the attentions of six Mississippi riflemen. It was not enough; Bigelow and his horse fell, each struck by two bullets. Reed put him on the back of his own horse, but the captain still had one last duty to perform. 'I then saw the Confederates swarming in our right flank, some standing on the limber chests and firing at the gunners, who were still serving their pieces; the horses were all down; overhead the air was alive with missiles from batteries, which the enemy had now placed on the Emmetsburg Road.' He saw that they had only four rounds of canister. 'Cease firing,' he ordered, 'and get back to your lines as best you can.' [8] They scattered back to the ridge, where infantry and artillery had plugged the gap McGilvery had seen only thirty minutes before. The faithful Corporal Reed lagged behind to help Bigelow to safety.

Colonel Humphreys' Mississippians swarmed over their captured guns, great

[8] *Voices of the Civil War: Gettysburg*, p.95–6; Don Troiani and Brian Pohanka, *Don Troiani's Civil War* (Stackpole Books, Mechanicsburg, Pennsylvania, 1995) pp.118–21.

and honored trophies in this war. He wanted to move to the left to rejoin the rest of the brigade's advance north of the Trostle Farm, but just then a battery rode up and unlimbered its four 3-inch rifles opposite his regiment across Plum Run. Colonel Humphreys ordered his gun-takers forward.

Commanded by Lieutenant Malone Watson, West Point Class of '61, Battery I, 5th US Artillery, had been ordered up by a III Corps staff officer as it was on its way to support its own V Corps. Almost immediately Watson was shot in the knee, and command devolved upon Lieutenant Charles C. MacConnell, who quickly realized how perilous their position was.

> The battery was without support of any kind. The enemy appeared shortly – say twenty minutes – after taking position, nearly in front, at a distance of about 350 yards, and the battery immediately opened up on them with shell. As they approached nearer, the battery poured canister, some twenty rounds, until men and horses were shot down or disabled to such an extent that the battery was abandoned.[9]

Half the horses and twenty-two of the battery's seventy-one men were killed or wounded. The survivors fled ahead of Humphreys' charging men, one of them, Lieutenant Samuel Peeples, fruitlessly searching the ridge and surrounding area for infantry to help recapture the lost guns.

'Like devils incarnate'

6:30 PM, the Codori Farm on Emmitsburg Road

Bigelow's thirty-minute delaying action had bought precious time for Brigadier General Humphreys' two brigades retreating through Spangler's Woods. They had their hands more than full with Hill's determined pursuit, that had pulled Wright's and Wilcox's battered but still game brigades along with Davis' and Pettigrew's. Hill had sent Brockenbrough's and Archer's Brigades to counter Ward's Brigade north of Pitzer's Run.

Humphreys shepherded his brigades back across the fields to the Emmitsburg Road, where, planting his flag at the Codori Farm, he formed them in line of battle to the north and south. The Confederates had followed closely, with their batteries unlimbering outside Spangler's Woods. The brigades of Wilcox, Davis, Pettigrew, and Wright seemed to flood out of the trees, the red battle-flags at the center of each regiment waving with the speed of their advance. Just to the north more masses of infantry emerged to advance obliquely to strike Humphreys' flank. These were the brigades of Posey and Mahone from Anderson's Division, and the Georgians and North Carolinians of Thomas' and

---

[9] OR, vol.XXVII, part I, p.660.

Scales' Brigades from Pender's Division. A.P. Hill was riding along the front of the advancing brigades, waving his hat to cheer the men on. To the south, Barksdale's Mississippians had overrun Bigelow's battery and were coming in behind Humphreys' left rear. Behind Barksdale, Semmes' and Wofford's Brigades had emerged suddenly from Pitzer's Woods. Hill now had twelve brigades in the attack against the two-brigade remnant of III Corps and Caldwell's four small brigades of II Corps. The hardest punch was coming straight for the gap between them. Lieutenant Adolpho Cavada, the son of a Cuban patriot, was on Humphreys' staff. He was in the thick of what came next:

> A copious shower of shell and canister from the enemy was followed by a dia-bolical cheer and yell and 'here they come' rang along our line. At this moment my horse was shot in the leg and pranced around frantically. Our batteries opened, our troops rose to their feet, the crash of artillery and the tearing rattle of our musketry was staggering and added to the noise on our side. The advancing roar and cheer of the enemy's masses, coming on like devils incarnate. But our fire had not checked them and our line showed signs of breaking. The battery enfilading us redoubled its fire, portions of Birney's command were moving to the rear broken and disordered. Our left regiments took the con-tagion and fled, leaving a wide gap through which the enemy poured in upon us. In vain did staff officers draw their swords to check the flying soldiers and endeavor to inspire them with confidence.[10]

Humphreys was everywhere, riding up and down his fraying battle-line, trying to hold the men steady. His gallant horse was wounded five times but stayed on its feet, until, struck for a sixth time, the poor animal reared and threw Humphreys to the ground. He was back on his feet in an instant, and, bor-rowing the mount of an aide, resumed his ride along the line. But the best he could do was to fend off destruction by falling back stubbornly. To have stood his ground would have meant annihilation. 'Twenty times did I bring my men to a halt and face about.'

'We must retreat'

6:30 PM, Pitzer's Run

Ward had received his recall as Wofford and Semmes were slugging it out with Birney's other two brigades. He immediately countermarched his brigade and attempted to withdraw across the run and strike Wofford as the Georgians battered Birney. Wofford had refused his left flank along the run with the 16th Georgia. The water course strengthened the flank, but it was shallow, and

---

[10] *Voices of the Civil War: Gettysburg*, p.97.

against a fresh brigade of almost 2200 men Wofford would be quickly out-flanked and overrun. That was exactly what Colonel Ward had in mind as he sent the 3rd and 4th Maine forward, covered by the fire of a battery and the two Sharpshooter regiments, with the 86th and 124th New York working down the run south of the Georgians. The attack went in briskly with the Maine men unflinching as they advanced into the enemy's fire, Ward on horseback riding among them. The Georgians were dropping quickly in the heavy and expertly delivered fire as they stood along the bare banks of the run. Colonel Goode Bryan went down as he walked the firing line, too conspicuous a target for the green-clad Sharpshooters. But the Georgians had good shots as well. One of their company commanders made out Ward, waving his hat, with the brigade colors flying behind him. 'There, men, direct your fire at that officer.' Twenty-two men took aim and fired in ragged succession as they brought their rifles to bear. They saw Ward, his horse and the color-bearer all go down.

The attack pressed up to the run as the Maine men and Georgians blazed away at each other. Here and there Maine officers were jumping into the shallow water and leading their men up the other side to meet the Georgians hand to hand. The Confederate line was marked more by the sprawled bodies of its dead and wounded than by its hale fighting men. They would crack, and soon.

As the senior colonel, Ward's death put Colonel Hiram Berdan in command. Notice of his promotion took a little longer to reach him than it should have because the aide carrying the news had to search him out in the brigade's rear. He was not entirely inactive: he was facing in the opposite direction, watching through his field-glasses as Heth's two brigades debouched from Herr's Ridge. In minutes they could be attacking the rear of the brigade. 'We must retreat,' he said to the young aide who was also taking in the picture. He rode back to the reserve 99th Pennsylvania and ordered it to cover the brigade. He sent runners to the engaged and flanking regiments with orders to disengage and retreat south through the woods that lined the bank of the run south of the fighting.

His runners found the two New York regiments already crossing the run unopposed to flank the enemy. The rest of Wofford's Brigade had disappeared through Pitzer's Woods to the east in pursuit of Birney's men. The order to retreat did not save the Georgians. The Maine regiments fought their way across the run and crushed the last thin line. The survivors fled, and the Maine regiments reformed, cheering as one of their men waved the captured colors of the 16th Georgia. It therefore came as a shock when they were ordered not to pursue but to march off the field. The grumbles and curses of hundreds of men turned the air blue as the regiments stumbled through the woods and then waded through Willoughby Run just where it was joined by Pitzer Run. The Sharpshooters, however, were silent; for them this was just another example of their colonel's shameful conduct. They had seen it all before. That did not mean they had become used to it. For some it had become too much to bear, and more than one man vowed to put a bullet in the coward. Only the moral authority of Lieutenant Colonel Trepp of the 1st Sharpshooters saved Berdan's life that day. Trepp was the real commander of the 1st Sharpshooters, the man who held the regiment together in the face of its colonel's inadequacies. Walking through the woods, he found the men who were threatening to shoot Berdan and calmly talked to them one or two at a time. They would not do it, they said, for his sake.

'In excellent style'
6:30, the Wheatfield

A lieutenant of the 17th Maine trailed behind the stampeding mass of fugitives from III Corps, dragging a wounded leg. As he limped up the slope of Cemetery Ridge, where his division had been stationed that morning, he saw a Union column coming up to the large Wheatfield on his left. They wore the red trefoil cap badge of Caldwell's 1st Division of II Corps. They were too late to help Birney's Division, but now they were all that stood between Cemetery Ridge and Kershaw's large brigade, two-thirds the size of Caldwell's entire division. The brigades disappeared into the woods ringing the field, and in moments a crash of musketry echoed across Plum Run. The lieutenant turned around and hurried as best he could up the slope.

Hancock had forged a tough division and had left it in good hands with Caldwell. His brigade commanders were also hard as nails. Brigadier General Samuel K. Zook 'was an able and valuable officer, with long militia service and an active interest in military affairs.' He was well thought of and good-natured but merciless to those who shirked their duty. Colonel Edward E. Cross was an eccentric, a disciplinarian, and, in his own critical and outspoken way, paternally concerned about the welfare of his men. As commander of the 5th New Hampshire, he had stated that the regiment 'dared not fall back without orders'. These traits brought him no love but much obedience. He had had a presentiment of death for days; when Hancock had seen off the brigade, he had said to him, 'Colonel Cross, this day will bring you a star.' Cross replied, 'Too late, too late, General, this will be my last battle.'[11] Colonel Patrick Kelly of the 'Irish' Brigade, a Regular Army officer, had come to command after Chancellorsville from his own 88th New York, and to his men 'he was the father to the brigade, as he was always to his own regiment, a brave, gentle, splendid soldier.'[12] Colonel John Rutter Brooke was barely twenty-five years

---

[11] *Pennsylvania at Gettysburg*, vol.2, p.624.

[12] Elmira Hancock, *Reminiscences of Winfield Scott Hancock* (Charles L. Webster & Co., New York, 1887) p.203; *New York at Gettysburg*, vol.II (J.B. Lyon Co. Printers, Albany, New York, 1900) pp.481, 521.

old, a boy-colonel with no prior military experience who had joined up in April 1861 and risen through merit.

Kershaw's South Carolinians were waiting for them across the Wheatfield, along a stone wall to the south and on the Stony Hill to its east. Caldwell's men were entering the open jaws of an almost 90 degree angle, but also overlapped the Rose Woods on either arm of the angle. They charged out of the woods with Cross' Brigade on the left, and Brooke and Kelly's Brigades in line heading straight for the apex of the angle. Zook's Brigade on the right clipped the northern edge of the Wheatfield and attacked into the Trostle Woods towards the flank of the Stony Hill. Major Peter Nelson was with the 66th New York of Zook's Brigade:

> Very soon we were under fire of musketry, but, nothing daunted, we pressed steadily forward through wheatfields, woods, over rail fences 10 feet high, stone walls, ditches, deep ravines, rocks, and all sorts of obstructions, every one of which served as cover for the enemy, and from which a murderous fire was poured upon us as we advanced, but without avail, as nothing could stop the impetuosity of our men, who, without waiting to load or even fix bayonets, rushed eagerly forward at a run, their cry being constantly, 'Forward! Charge!' We passed large numbers of rebels in our advance, of whom, however, we took but little notice, so interested were we in our pursuit of the retreating foe.[13]

Their charge had dislodged the 7th and 3rd South Carolina, and that was not the end of Kershaw's troubles. Cross, Brooke, and Kelly's men poured across the Wheatfield towards the stone wall from behind which the rest of his regiments fired furiously. Major Mulholland, Father Corby's blessing still on him, attacked with the 116th Pennsylvania:

> Our brigade returned fire with good effect. After firing for about ten minutes, the order was given to advance which the brigade did in excellent style, driving the enemy from their position, which we at once occupied. We took many prisoners at this point, hundreds of the enemy laying down their arms and passing to the rear. We found the position which our foe had occupied but a few moments before thickly strewn with dead and wounded. Here we again opened fire, the enemy having rallied to oppose our further advance.[14]

Private William Ratliff of the 2nd 'Palmetto' South Carolina was one of the riflemen along the stone wall as the Union brigades came across the Wheatfield. A young farmer with a taste for books and an equal taste for fine shooting,

---

[13] *OR*, vol.XXVII, part I, p.398.
[14] *OR*, vol.XXVII, part I, p.392.

he would go on to a distinguished career as a lawyer and only lose his ability to hit a mark at 200 yards when his eyes dimmed late in life. Right now he was carefully drawing a bead on a mounted officer coming through the wheat accompanied by a great, billowing, emerald green color, the Stars and Stripes streaming beside it. The men to either side of Ratliff were slumped down in death behind the wall. Another lay half over it. Around him bullets were knocking chips out of the stones, but he was utterly calm as he slowly squeezed the trigger. However, instead of the smooth report he expected there was an explosion as the rifle breach blew apart in his face. He lurched backwards and stumbled away among the trees, blood running through the fingers he pressed to his eyes. Miraculously, he would get his sight back, though the scars on his face never disappeared.[15]

The sniper who fired on Colonel Cross from behind a boulder in the woods on Stony Hill suffered no such interference. Cross jerked forward in the saddle, shot through the stomach, and slipped off his horse. The commander of the 5th New Hampshire, Lieutenant Colonel Charles E. Hapgood, saw the muzzle flash and directed one of his own marksmen, Sergeant Charles Phelps, to shoot the sniper. Phelps was the better hunter; he waited until the sniper peered around the rock for another victim, then shot him dead.

Kershaw was trying to rally his regiments, which had been pushed into the Rose Woods and off the Stony Hill on his left and beyond.

By this time the enemy had swung around and lapped my whole line at close quarters, and the fighting was general and desperate. At length the 7th South Carolina gave way, and I directed Colonel Aiken to reform them at the stone wall, some 200 yards in the left rear. I fell back to the Third Regiment, then hotly engaged on the crest of the stony hill.

There the Carolinians swung around left to form a new flank. Zook's men came on from the right through the Trostle Woods, and the Irish Brigade through the Wheatfield, and among the rocks and trees, within a few feet of each other, a desperate conflict ensued. The Confederates were up in the high boulders above the heads of their attackers and consequently were firing down at such a steep angle that they fired high. This allowed the Irish to get so close that their officers were able to use their pistols with some effect. Zook's Brigade could not dislodge the 3rd South Carolina from the Stony Hill but worked around its left. Kershaw wrote: 'I feared that the brave men about me would be surrounded by the large force pressing around them, and ordered the Third Regiment ... to fall back ... whither I followed them.' At this critical point, the great tide of

---

[15]* William Ratliff, *The Life of a Southern Sharpshooter* (Palmetto Press, Charleston, South Carolina, 1890) pp.119–20.

McLaws' two lead brigades, led by Barksdale's Mississippians, swept past the Wheatfield beyond the Trostle Woods. For Kershaw they had arrived in the nick of time.

> On emerging from the wood, I saw Wofford coming in splendid style . . . The enemy gave way at Wofford's advance, and, with the whole of my left wing advanced to the charge, sweeping the enemy before them, without a moment's stand, across the stone wall, beyond the wheat-field, up to the foot of the mountain.[16]

Cut off from Cemetery Ridge and struck by Wofford's Brigade and Kershaw's counter-attack, Caldwell immediately pulled his division back from the woods, across the Wheatfield strewn with his casualties, and south-east across Plum Run towards the hill, with its steep face thick with boulders.

'Remember Harper's Ferry!'
6:45 PM, Plum Run

After Caldwell had gone into action in the Wheatfield, Hancock led the 3rd Brigade of his 3rd Division to the left of Cemetery Ridge to reinforce the deteriorating situation. Instead of shoring up the line, he found Birney desperately trying to rally the few small groups of his men who still clung to their colors. Birney frankly said he needed help, and it was obvious that these men would scatter at the first enemy blow. It was even more apparent that the blow was about to be delivered by the gray brigade that was just crossing Plum Run.

The 1500 New Yorkers of Colonel George L. Willard's brigade had a grudge to settle. For nine months they had had to live with the shame of their surrender at Harper's Ferry during the Antietam Campaign, the last time Lee had invaded the North. This was the chance they had been looking for to redeem themselves. Aged thirty-five, Willard was the scion of Revolutionary War and War of 1812 generals and had enlisted to fight in the Mexican War, where he won a commission. He was a captain when the War started in 1861. One month after taking the colonelcy of the 125th New York he had had to surrender his regiment to Stonewall Jackson. Therefore he too had a score to settle.

Already the enemy were shooting at his men from the brush in the rock-strewn swale of Plum Run. As he ordered the brigade to ready for the attack, a few of his men nervously started returning the enemy's fire. He sternly ordered them to stop: they would fight as a unit, on order. His officers and NCOs ran up and down the lines to steady the men. He had three regiments in the first line, from north to south the 126th, 125th and 39th New York. The 111th was

---

[16] OR, vol.XXVII, part II, p.369.

in the second line. Three of Barksdale's regiments, the 13th, 17th and 18th Mississippi, had hung together, but, tired by their rapid approach march and long charge, they had halted in the swale. The fourth regiment, Colonel Humphreys' 21st, had veered to the south after overrunning Bigelow's Battery at the Trostle Farm.

When Willard gave the order to advance, his men stepped off quickly with the shout of 'Remember Harper's Ferry!' Captain Aaron P. Seeley, commanding the 111th, recalled that 'at the command, the regiment with the brigade – not a man in the whole line faltering or hesitating for an instant – hurled themselves upon the advancing foe.'[17] At ten paces from the swale, the Mississippians fired into the advancing New Yorkers, who stepped over their fallen and just kept coming with lowered bayonets. They dashed through the thicket and into the swale, firing and stabbing. Barksdale's men recoiled at the shock, and many, robbed of their courage by fatigue, threw down their rifles. The rest fell back stubbornly as Barksdale, 'almost frantic with rage', rode up and down the line damning his men to stop and attack. Legend has it that one of Willard's company commanders ordered his men to fire at the white-haired officer on the spirited horse. He fell riddled through the chest and legs.[18] But as he was carried from the field his regiments fought on, making the New Yorkers pay for every foot of ground. Every backward step the Mississippians took, though, was bringing Willard closer to a trap. Almost as soon as they started up the western slope of the run, they were struck at 400 yards by the concentrated fire of McLaws' massed batteries in the Peach Orchard. Still they pressed forward, however, despite the carpet of blue-clad bodies they left behind, forcing Barksdale's regiments beyond the Emmitsburg Road and recovering four guns lost to the Mississippians from Turnbull's Battery. As they reached the guns, they saw a fresh brigade through the tattered ranks of the Mississippians. It was Semmes' Georgians, and they were charging. Willard's line coolly delivered a volley even while the artillery continued to rake it. The Georgians were checked momentarily, but these redoubtable fighters blazed back with deadly volleys of their own. Willard's attention was now directed by an aide to the Confederate brigade moving towards his left rear. It was Kershaw, who had pulled his command together and led it out of the Wheatfield towards the New Yorkers' flank. It was Willard's turn to retreat stubbornly. Between Semmes' blows and the continuing destruction wrought by the artillery, Willard's losses mounted seriously. But he kept his dwindling regiments in hand, and must have been proud of them in their first serious fight of the war. Then, as he rode back across Plum Run, a shell fragment tore away his face and part of his head. The body, a

---

[17] OR, vol.XXVII, part I, p.475.
[18] Barksdale died of his wounds that night, but not before gasping out, 'Tell my wife I am shot, but we fought like hell.'

crimson mess above the collar, fell into the already wine-colored water of the run. Whatever else was to befall them, Willard's Brigade had indeed redeemed itself, and in the words of their division commander, Alexander Hays, 'The history of this brigade's operations is written in blood.' [19]

'Barksdale, Barksdale!'
7:00 PM, Cemetery Ridge

As Willard attacked, Hancock immediately saw another Confederate mass coming in on their right. He ordered up Willard's 111th New York in the second line to take these troops – probably Wilcox's men who had done so well in Pitzer's Woods – in the flank. He then rode along the ridge with his two remaining aides, Captain William D. Miller and First Lieutenant Arthur P. Seeley, and found Brigadier General Humphreys with the sad remnant of his division. Hancock noted that this small command was 'scarcely equal to an ordinary battalion, but with many colors', being composed of the fragments of many shattered regiments. 'I directed General Humphreys to form his command on the ground from which General Caldwell had moved to the support of the Third Corps, which was promptly done.' [20] However, the line was still too thin, and he turned to Seeley. 'Go to General Doubleday and order him to immediately bring up one of his divisions to the right of this position. Tell him there is no time to lose.' Then he rode on along the ridge as Seeley spurred his horse back over the ridge and onto the Taneytown Road, to find Doubleday's corps concentrated behind Cemetery Hill. Through the smoke that hung along the run, Hancock saw a regiment awkwardly pushing through the thick brush in the swale. 'Here,' he said to Miller, 'what are these men falling back for?' [21] Hancock's chief of staff would write that, 'Believing these to be some of his own troops driven in from the front, the general rides forward to halt and post them, but is undeceived by a volley, which brings down his aide, Captain Miller.' Hancock and Miller, the latter bleeding from two wounds, rode through a low place in the ground and escaped, just as Wilcox's men began to ascend the slope above the ridge, now empty of defenders. [22]

Up the ridge to the north, Hancock's two other division commanders were bracing for the impact of four Confederate brigades. Wright's right wing brushed the Codori Farm; on his left in echelon were Posey, Mahone, and Thomas, and in support was Scales' depleted brigade. Major General Pender

---

[19] *OR*, vol.XXVII, part I, p.453.

[20] *OR*, vol.XXVII, part I, p.371.

[21] Frank L. Byrne and Andrew T. Weaver, eds., *Haskell of Gettysburg: His Life and Civil War Papers* (The Kent State University Press, Kent, Ohio, and London, 1989) p.124.

[22] Francis A. Walker, *History of the Second Army Corps* (Charles Scribner's Sons, New York, 1886) p.283.

was leading the attack in person. South of the Codori Farm, Pettigrew and Davis' Brigades were also sweeping forward in line with Wilcox's men, who had just missed bagging the II Corps commander himself as the gray brigades, red battle-flags whipping at the center of countless gray and butternut regiments, topped by a sea of bayonets, crossed the valley and began to ascend the ridge. Lieutenant Haskell of Gibbon's staff was watching in amazement. 'The whole slope in our front is full of them; – and in various formations, in line, in column, and in masses which are neither, with yells, and thick vollies, they are rushing towards our crest. – Now we are in for it.'[23]

Colonel Humphreys watched Willard's battered brigade retreating back across Plum Run, turning every few yards to fire another volley at Semmes' Brigade hard on its heels. After adding Watson's four guns to his growing collection, he found that Willard's attack had prevented him from rejoining his brigade. Instead he could only watch through gaps in the thick powder smoke as the rest of Barksdale's regiments were beaten back and the old warrior himself shot out of the saddle. Now the tables were turned as the enemy staggered back to the safety of their own lines. His attention was turned at that moment to the ranks of Kershaw's Brigade emerging from Trostle Woods to Plum Run on his right. Kershaw himself rode up to Humphreys and pointed to the plight of Willard's Brigade. 'Do you see what I do, Colonel?' he asked. As Humphreys nodded, Kershaw added, 'Wheel to the right and strike them as their flank comes up to you. You will protect my flank as I take my brigade over the ridge.' Then he was off to his own brigade. Humphreys' voice rang out with great satisfaction, clear as a bell, bringing his men to attention. The ranks had been thinned by a great deal of Union canister, but

> my boys had one more strong effort in them and that was fuelled to furnace heat by the loss of their brigade commander and the worsting of their brigade. I told them their battle cry was 'Barksdale!' They roared their approval. It was not for nothing that a foreign visitor had deemed the Texas and Mississippi regiments as the most determined and vicious in battle.[24]

Kershaw had just enough time to return to his brigade before Humphreys' moment came. He ordered the charge, and the shout of 'Barksdale! Barksdale!' smote the sky. He led them forward across a grassy field to wheel up against Plum Run from the east, just as Willard's men were scrambling through its brush. They looked up just in time to catch a volley in their upturned faces that tumbled scores back down into the crowded shallows of the run. Semmes'

---

[23] Byrne and Weaver, ibid, p.125.
[24] Benjamin G. Humphreys, *Reminiscences of Barksdale's Brigade* (Walker, Evans & Cogswell, Charleston, South Carolina, 1883) p.265.

Brigade had closed up and fired into the packed mass in the swale, already filled with Barksdale's dead, turning it once more into a slaughter pen. One more volley, and hands by the hundred starting pointing skyward as the rest fled up and over the ridge. Kershaw gave a last look at the destruction of Willard's Brigade as he wheeled his own brigade in line of battle up the slight slope of the ridge at the base of Little Round Top. He had thought they were finished at the Wheatfield and the Stony Hill. Now the sound of battle just around the hill grew louder and closer. He headed straight for it.

And then Ewell struck.

CHAPTER 9

2nd July 1863
'Ten G-d d——d minutes'

The Union position had cracked in half in a dozen places from the hammer blows of Southern valor. Despite his superior control of the ebb and flow of the fighting, Meade felt the battle slipping away from him. The audacity of Longstreet's envelopment, Lee's personal presence at the defining moment of Sickles' disobedience, and the ferocity of the Confederate infantry in the attack, had brought the Army of the Potomac to the edge of ruin. Even now as the gray tidal wave rushed upon Cemetery Ridge and surged up the Taneytown Road, the weak of heart were slipping away in droves to flee down the Baltimore Pike. When it seemed that the Federals could fend off no more calamities, Ewell finally threw his sword onto the scales of battle.

For three-and-a-half hours of the severest fighting Longstreet and Hill's Corps had struggled, waiting for Ewell to add his weight to the contest. The attacks of the Confederate 1st and 3rd Corps had so unbalanced Meade that a determined blow from a third direction would have sent his army toppling. But for three-and-a-half hours that blow had waited, suspended in the air by nothing more than Ewell's indecision. His only positive action had been to place Latimer's artillery battalion to support the attack, but even there the guns lost the duel before the infantry were to advance. Where Jackson would have lunged like a snarling mastiff a split second after Lee had slipped the leash, Ewell hung back. Indeed, he even disregarded Lee's orders to strike when he heard the roar of Longstreet's guns. And Colonel Porter Alexander's artillery had begun the attack with a crash of artillery that would have done Thor's Hammer proud. The noise washed over Cemetery and Culp's Hills in a wave that assaulted the eardrums of every man on both sides and was clearly remembered years later by all who experienced it. Yet Ewell waited as the last precious afternoon hours of daylight seeped away. By his own subsequent admission, he did not even think to co-ordinate his attack with Major General Pender's Division of Hill's Corps on his right.[1] Neither did he find much for his own remaining division, that of Rodes in Gettysburg itself, to do to support the attack. Rode's only instruction was to co-operate with any attack made by Pender's Division on his right. Neither

---

[1] *OR*, vol.XXVII, part 2, p.556.

did Ewell's staff do much, if anything, to knit the details of co-ordinated action together. And Lee, in his strangely detached command style, did nothing to prod Jackson's successor either, as Meade would certainly have done in his place. Only when the last daylight began to filter through the trees on the western horizon did he finally give the word to attack. Still, it was not too late. Southern battle frenzy had turned such scraps of advantage into victory many times before.

And the enemy had done much to help him. Meade had already pulled Williams' 1st Division of XII Corps off Culp's Hill to shore up the collapsing battle lines to the south. For a general with such a reputation for prudence, moving this division had been the ultimate risk. Having been an eye-witness that morning, he was fully aware of the effect of the enemy sweeping down from the heights into the army's rear. But the crisis was elsewhere, and he desperately needed a reserve. So as Williams' brigades filed out of their positions, Geary's extended to the right to take over the entire corps front. The north-eastern crest of the hill, which the 7th Indiana and the Iron Brigade had held so grimly, was now occupied by the upstate New York brigade of Brigadier General George S. 'Old Pop' Greene, which tied in with Wadsworth's I Corps division on the north slope of Culp's Hill to the left. Greene was another West Pointer the war had brought back to the colors from civilian life. An accomplished engineer, he had insisted to Geary that the division throw up a formidable breastwork. In the morning and afternoon after Johnson's repulse the woods had echoed with the thud of axes and the slice of shovels as the breastwork grew.

On East Cemetery Hill, the defenders were weaker than when Gordon had nearly taken the position in the early morning hours of that same bloody day. What was left of von Gilsa's Brigade, fewer than 400 men, had been rounded up by the Provost guards and kept in reserve. Ames' Brigade, except for the battered 17th Connecticut and a few survivors of the 75th Ohio, had been destroyed. These survivors of XI Corps' 1st Division were assigned to Schurz's 3rd Division, which extended itself to fill in the line left empty by the destruction of the 1st Division. Steinwehr then extended his right to make up for the front given up by Schurz. Howard's position, so weak now in infantry, had been strengthened with six batteries from the Artillery Reserve during the day to add to the two I Corps batteries and the survivors of old Wiedrich's battery. A seventh battery had been added to Captain Stevens' on the knoll to the east. The restless Hancock, though, had ridden through the reorganized defenses and, recognising the eggshell thinness of the line, had then earmarked one of his brigades to reinforce Howard if need be. The only reserve were the remnants of Doubleday's and Robinson's Divisions of I Corps, each only the size of a brigade. He spoke briefly to General John Newton, the corps' new commander, who had arrived from VI Corps at a gallop that morning, alerting him to the probability that his corps, as beaten up as it was, would probably be called upon as a reserve. Also that morning, however, Doubleday's Division had been reinforced by a Vermont Brigade of nine-month men, commanded by General George J. Standard, who had force-marched his five regiments directly from Washington. Against this fragile defense Early aimed the tough Louisiana and North Carolina brigades of Brigadier General Harry T. Hays and Colonel Isaac E. Avery. Avery was the commander of the 6th North Carolina and had replaced Brigadier General Hoke, wounded at Chancellorsville. In reserve was the small Virginia brigade of Brigadier William 'Extra Billy' Smith. In all, Early would be throwing over 3000 fresh men against the thousand Howard had on East Cemetery Hill. And this thousand had licked its wounds too often already in this battle.

But as Ewell gave the order to let slip the mighty 2nd Corps, the Confederate tide crashed against Cemetery Ridge.

'What regiment is this?'

7:30 PM, Cemetery Ridge

As Kershaw overran the saddle of Cemetery Ridge, Layfayette McLaws was leading his last two brigades up the undefended slope to the north of the George Weikert Farm. Wilcox's Brigade was keeping up on his left, and further north the ground in front of the ridge was alive with surging masses of Confederates. Longstreet's plan, despite the last minute changes and the interference of chance, was working. The enemy's positions was crumbling with each successive shock.

To no-one was this more starkly apparent at this moment than to Winfield Scott Hancock. Riding north along the ridge, he had just barely escaped from Wilcox's men, whom he had mistaken for Union troops. Looking behind him, he saw the enemy wave within minutes of crashing over the ridge. He turned his horse to watch the brigade that had nearly caught him. Brigadier General Humphreys' burned-out regiments were in no shape to stop the attack; they would shatter at the first contact. There seemed to be no Union men on the ridge except the masses of fleeing III Corps men. He turned to Captain Miller, bleeding from the two wounds suffered when the two had nearly ridden into the Alabamians. 'Bill, you must get to Newton and tell him to come up now with his whole corps. Can you do it?' Miller had thought he was going to faint from the loss of blood, but the call of his chief for this desperate service revived him. He straightened himself up in the saddle, managed to get a grip on his animal, and spurred away without a word.[2] Now looking desperately around, Hancock

---

[2]* W.D.W. Miller, *With Hancock at Gettysburg* (Merriweather Publishing Co., Boston, 1880) p.122.

saw one lone Union regiment nearby, standing firm as the fugitives fled around and through its immobile ranks. This was the lead regiment of Brigadier General William Harrow's Brigade of Gibbon's 2nd Division, II Corps; Hancock had ordered Gibbon to extend a brigade south along the ridge after Caldwell had attacked into the Wheatfield.

These men of the 1st Minnesota had been silent, horrified spectators to the ruin of III Corps. Colonel William Colvill III recorded the moment:

Gen. Hancock was with us and immediately dismounted and with all his energy sought to rally them. Our field and staff [officers] also dismounted and aided him. It was useless; they were perfectly demoralized. The rebel line, following, came in sight across the hollow, looming through the smoke, and pushed down the slope into the bottom, their left extended out on the terrace – we could not see how far. The last of Sickles' men had passed, and this skirmish line opened a scattering fire upon us. Then over the ridge came the rebels' first line and moved rapidly down into the hollow.[3]

The crisis was obvious to everyone in the ranks as well. Sergeant Alfred Carpenter saw the enemy coming

in two splendid lines, firing as they advanced, capturing one of our batteries, which they turned against us, and gained the cover of the ravine. The plain was strewed with dead and dying men. The Rebs had advanced their batteries and were hurling death and destruction into the ranks of the retreating men. They were nearing the hill, which if gained, the day was lost to us.[4]

As the last of Sickles' men dashed past, Hancock turned to the 1st Minnesota and was stunned at how small the regiment was, barely 262 men to stem the Confederate tide. 'My God! Are these all the men we have here?' Colvill replied that he was correct. 'What regiment is this?'

Colvill straightened up and replied, 'First Minnesota!' He caught a glimmer of recognition in Hancock's eye. The 1st Minnesota had been on just about every battlefield on which the Army of the Potomac had bled and on every one of them had established a reputation for fidelity and coolness in the hottest moments.

'Do you see those colors?' Hancock asked.

'Yes, Sir.'

---

[3] William Colvill, 'The Old First Minnesota at Gettysburg', Minneapolis *Daily Tribune*, 28th July 1884, Goodhue County (Minnesota) Historical Society; cited in Richard Moe, *The Last Full Measure: The Life and Death of the First Minnesota Volunteers* (Henry Holt and Co., New York, 1993) p.268.

[4] Alfred P. Carpenter, letter, 30th July 1863 (Minnesota Historical Society); cited in Moe, ibid.

'Well, capture them.' [5]

Colvill stepped out in front of his regiment and asked if they would follow him. They roared back, 'Yes!' He shouted, 'Forward, double-quick.' Already the enemy had their range, and men began to fall as the regiment – only 100 yards from flank to flank – advanced downhill, perfectly aligned; the pace quickened as the men raced down into the Plum Run swale, filled with smoke and Confederates. Everyone understood that speed would offer some measure of protection as the Alabama brigade and the Confederate artillery focused on them. They headed straight for the center of Wilcox's Brigade. Carpenter remembered: 'Bullets whistled past us, shells screeched over us; canister and grape fell about us; comrade after comrade dropped from the ranks; but on the line went. No one took a second look at his fallen companion. We had no time to weep.' [6]

For Wilcox and his Alabamians, the charge was a total surprise. They had driven all before them and were reaching out for victory. 'This stronghold of the enemy, together with his batteries, was almost won, when still another line of infantry descended the slope in our front at a double-quick, to the support of their fleeing comrades and for the defense of the batteries.' Their very advance was too much for Wilcox. He recalled this moment and the 'contest so unequal'. [7]

The Minnesotans advanced with no hurrahs or cheers to egg on their courage. Now every man was silently determined on his desperate work. The pace did not slacken. Three color-bearers and one quarter of the regiment had fallen, and still the Minnesotans had not closed with the enemy. Now, as they approached the enemy's first line, with only 150 men left, Colvill gave the command 'Charge', and the advance broke into a run as the bayonets came down with a glinting sweep. The enemy's first line had been disordered in crossing a dry brook, and it was there that the 1st Minnesota ran them down, pursuing the survivors, who fled through the second line, confusing their brigade's own advance and bringing it to a halt. For the first time, Colvill gave the command to fire, and a murderous volley cut into the Alabamians. Then his voice rang out again, 'Charge!' This time the men let out an exultant cheer, like a roar ripped from the guts, as they lunged forward into the ranks of Wilcox's second line in a blur of bayonets and rifle butts. Beneath that assault the second line too gave way.

Wilcox's men were tired; all afternoon they had fought against superior odds before going over to the attack that had carried them so far. But even courage is

---

[5] Elmira Hancock, *Reminiscences of Winfield S. Hancock* (Charles L. Webster & Co., New York, 1887) p.199.

[6] Carpenter, op.cit. p.269.

[7] *OR*, vol. XXVII, part II, p.619.

an exhaustible commodity, and they had been called upon to use too much of it that day. Already four of Wilcox's five regimental commanders had been wounded. The brigade had been stunned when the 1st Minnesota had charged down the slope. They were even more surprised when they kept coming after Minié balls and artillery had cut down so many. Now the brigade's nerve gave way to split-second herd instinct. The center regiments broke. One of the flank regiments had wrapped around the Minnesotans and was pouring fire into their rear when the 82nd New York, the 1st Minnesota's companion regiment, and the 15th Massachusetts came charging down the hill onto their flank, turning the tables on them. Hancock had personally led them up and thrown them into the fight. Had they been any longer arriving, the Alabamians would likely have recovered and crushed Colvill. At this moment, Humphreys led his small surviving bits of regiments, each clustering around its colors, to the edge of the ridge. From the swale, they looked like massed regiments in columns with flags at the head. That was enough. In minutes the Confederates were streaming back across the fields to the safety of the woods, the victorious Minnesotans still firing into their backs as they went.

The collapse of Wilcox's Brigade checked Davis' and Pettigrew's nervous brigades as well. Pettigrew, as acting division commander, did everything to move them forward, but they hung back. Here and there a few companies would advance, only to fall back as the bullets and canister from the ridge toppled man after man into the grass. Only the 11th Mississippi still had plenty of fight left in it, and tangled with the 82nd in a short but vicious fight. Despite adding to the butcher's bill, this action did nothing but satisfy the pugnacity of the Mississippians, who had drunk deeply already of success that day. But the damage had been done; the impetus had gone out of the two brigades so badly cut up the day before. They disengaged and retreated back to the woods as well, with the Mississippians acting as a defiant rear guard. Now masters of the field, the 1st Minnesota and the 82nd New York slowly withdrew back up onto the ridge, their bayonets prodding more than 200 prisoners ahead of them.

'We were now complete masters of the field'

7:30 PM, the Copse of Trees, Cemetery Ridge

Hancock had barely had time to watch the 1st Minnesota begin its charge when he had found the 82nd New York and 15th Massachusetts and waved them on in turn. Then he had raced north up the line with the uncanny ability to place himself at the place of greatest danger. That danger was personified by Major General Dorsey Pender, leading three of his brigades (Thomas and Lane, with Scales in support) and two of Anderson's (Posey and Mahone) straight for the Copse of Trees in the center of II Corps' line. Save for Scales' Brigade, savaged on the first day's fighting and numbering barely 500 men, the other four were fresh. In all Pender was leading over 6400 men straight at II Corps. On his right, Wright's Georgians, bloodied but game, added another thousand men to the assault.

Only twenty-nine, Dorsey Pender, like Odysseus, had to be torn away from his family to go to war. Nothing else but duty would have driven him to it, but once committed, he was determined to be in the forefront of the battle. According to Douglas Southall Freeman, 'in battle he forgets all else in persistent, flaming combat.'

So far today he had avoided his 'habit of getting himself wounded in almost every fight.' [8] As a soldier he knew that it made sense to carry the war to the enemy but was nagged by his wife's warning that God would turn away from the Confederacy if it invaded the North. A.P. Hill had the fullest confidence in Pender, who he had marked for promotion. That confidence was fully shared by Pender's subordinates; Brigadier General Scales said of him, 'The higher [Pender's] promotion, the better fitted he seemed for his position.' [9]

Hancock rode north up the ridge and got a magnificent view of the 7500 Confederates sweeping towards his two remaining divisions. He had infinite faith in the men of the old II Corps, but he would have been less sanguine had he known that Early was about to unleash almost another 4000 at right angles to Pender's attack. The Confederates he could see through the clouds of black powder smoke drifting between the ridges were problem enough at the moment.

Gibbon's detachment of Harrow's Brigade to fill in to the south had left a gap in his own front, towards which Wright's Georgians were heading. The gap was about 200 yards south of the Copse of Trees upon which Gibbon's Division was centered. Colonel Norman Hall's Brigade was on line while Brigadier General Alexander Webb's 'Philadelphia' Brigade, save for the 69th Pennsylvania, was in support and out of sight just behind the ridge. Wright's Georgians split around the Codori Farm buildings and then closed ranks and continued forward. Half of Harrow's Brigade had been waiting there for several hours until Hancock had ordered them to the south. Now nothing impeded the Georgians in their rapid advance, preceded by the wild rebel yell, except Battery C, 5th US Artillery, commanded by First Lieutenant Gulian Weir, just beyond the Codori Farm. Weir ordered the guns to limber up before he saw a nearby Union regiment fire into the Georgians. Then, hoping to continue fighting from that position, he ordered the guns back into action. The Union infantry support then disappeared, and the Georgians were immediately on top of the half-deployed battery. At this moment Weir was dazed by a spent round,

---

[8] Douglas Southall Freeman, *Lee's Lieutenants: A Study in Command*, vol.2, *Cedar Mountain to Chancellorsville* (Charles Scribner's Sons, New York, 1946) p.xli.
[9] *SHSP*, vol.XL, p.214.

and in the confusion three of his Napoleons were abandoned to the enemy and the rest barely escaped. As the Georgians swept on, Posey's Brigade of Mississippians on their left closed up quickly, coming straight for Gibbon and the Copse of Trees.

While Posey steered towards the Copse of Trees, Wright aimed at Battery B, 1st Rhode Island Light Artillery, commanded by First Lieutenant T. Fred Brown. The keening battle-cry raced ahead of the Georgians, cutting over the roar of Brown's guns, whose crews were firing double canister from their six 12-pounder Napoleons for all they were worth. The canister tore blood-spattered holes in the oncoming line, but they magically closed up again. The men were using up the last of that magical battle energy that all good troops have. The advance turned into a forward-loping half-run, like a wave rushing up a shore. 'On they came like the fury of a whirlwind,' remembered Captain John E. Reilly of the 69th Pennsylvania. The guns fired more double canister, again and again, but it was not enough – the wave leapt over the broken front ranks and in among the guns. Wright exaggerated the steepness of the slope but not the high pitch of valor.

> My Brigade now climbed up the side of the mountain nearly to the enemy's guns . . . but my brave men passed rapidly and steadily on, until we approached within fifty or sixty yards of the enemy's batteries, when we encountered a heavy body of infantry posted behind a stone wall. The side of the mountain was so precipitous here that my men could with difficulty climb it, but we strove on, and reaching the stone fence, drove the Yankee infantry from behind it, and then taking cover from the fence we soon shot all the gunners of the enemy's artillery, and rushing over the fence seized their guns.[10]

Captain Miller had raced to find Newton, who was then speaking to Doubleday and Robinson, their divisions waiting in reserve behind Cemetery Hill. The crescendo of fighting could be plainly heard as the Confederate waves raced up the slope of the ridge and crashed into the defenders. They were barely 500 yards from the fighting on the ridge. Newton had been mindful of Hancock's warning earlier that day. When Miller pulled up before them, he fell out of the saddle into the arms of the generals. As they lowered him to the ground, he blurted out Hancock's order between gasps. Both divisions were immediately ready to move. Newton, new to the corps, was visibly impressed as the divisions moved out. 'I was deeply gratified at the promptitude with which these divisions moved at this period, their movement not consuming one-half the time it would have taken on drill.'[11]

---

[10] Freeman, op.cit. vol.3, p.126.
[11] OR, vol.XXVII, part I, p.261.

The first regiment ready to go was the 13th Vermont of Standard's Brigade. Its commander, Colonel Francis Randall, was already mounted and ready when he saw Doubleday ride up. 'Colonel, what regiment do you command?'

'The 13th Vermont, Sir!'

'Where is General Standard?' Randall indicated a grove of trees too far to reach quickly. Doubleday realized he could not waste time on the chain of command; he was also concerned now that he realized that this was an unblooded nine-month regiment. 'Colonel, will your regiment fight?'

'I believe they will sir.' He explained that he had been in plenty of fights but his regiment not one, but expressed such faith in his men that Doubleday asked him to introduce him to the five companies assembled there. He gave the men a rousing talk, and they responded with cheers. Then he ordered Randall to move out with all speed and reinforce Hancock's line on the ridge.[12]

As the Vermonters quick-timed down the Taneytown Road, Wright rode right into the slaughter around the guns. 'Come on, boys, come on! Forward! Forward!' The Georgians rushed forward past the guns. Gibbon was in the middle of Hall's Brigade as the Georgians overran the guns and just as Posey's Brigade crashed into his front. It seemed as if the roof had fallen in. Most men would have scrambled free of the debris and run off, but Gibbon was that rare jewel in a crisis – a man with ice water in his veins. His horse went down just then, spilling him to the ground. He was up in an instant, trailing a hurt leg, but hobbled over immediately to Colonel Paul J. Revere, commanding the 20th Massachusetts in Hall's second line. The grandson of the great patriot of the Revolution, Revere had already wheeled his 243 men to form at a right angle to the front, refusing the flank. Already his men were firing desperately into the Georgian tide rushing past them over the ridge. Revere saw his division commander limping toward him and rushed over to support him. 'Charge them, Colonel!' Gibbon shouted above the din. 'Charge them, or the day is lost!' Revere raced to the front sword in hand. 'Twentieth Massachusetts! Charge!' Without looking back, he raced forward. He heard a cheer and felt the mass accelerating behind him.[13]

Just then Wright topped the crest of Cemetery Ridge. Spread before him was the Union rear, as roiled as an overturned ant hill. He could see thousands of blue troops below him, but what thrilled him was the large number fleeing down the Baltimore Pike and, to his far right, the evidence of a fierce battle raging east of the Round Tops. For the second time in less than twenty-four hours, the Army of Northern Virginia had broken into the enemy's rear. But for

[12] G.H.G. Scott, 'Thirteenth Vermont', *Proceedings of the Vermont Historical Society*, vol.I (1930) pp.62–3; cited in Harry W. Pfanz, *Gettysburg: The Second Day* (The University of North Carolina Press, Chapel Hill and London, 1987) p.416.

[13] John Paul Revere, *Massachusetts at Gettysburg* (A.J. Merrifield and Sons, Boston, 1882) p.236.

the second time it was by a single brigade. Steuart's attack had failed, not for lack of audacity, but for lack of support. Wright, though, could look to his right and left and see the rest of the army hammering away at the tottering structure of the Army of the Potomac. He had driven his Georgian bayonet through the enemy line, but more bayonet blows all along the line would be needed to turn the single wound into gaping death for the Union army. 'Forward! We've broken 'em!' he shouted as he spurred his horse down the gentle reverse slope of the ridge.

> We had now accomplished our task. We had stormed the enemy's strong position, had driven off his infantry, had captured all his guns in our front, except a few which he succeeded in carrying off, and had up to this minute suffered but comparatively little loss ... We were now complete masters of the field, having gained the key, as it were of the enemy's whole line.[14]

Wright's vision of victory was about to be sharply contested. As the 20th Massachusetts stepped forward with a shout behind its colonel, Hancock rode up to Colonel Webb and pointed at the breakthrough, saying, 'Send in a regiment now!' One regiment – the 106th Pennsylvania – was all Webb had left, his others being all committed to support Hall's small brigade against the impact of Posey's Brigade. He shouted the command to wheel to the left, and attack.

Revere struck first. Revere himself was the first into the enemy's ranks, shooting with his pistol and laying about with his sword. A Georgian closed in behind and swung his bayonet, but the blade's arc was stopped as a Massachusetts man shot him and rushed by to fight at his colonel's side. Revere's attack quickly crumpled the 2nd Georgia Battalion, sending the survivors scrambling into the ranks of the 48th Georgia. Wright's attention was suddenly arrested by the attack of the Philadelphia Brigade, which had come up on the left front of his own disorganized regiments. A well-delivered volley swept away the men in the lead. One of those to fall seriously wounded was Wright himself, conspicuous on horseback and at the head of his men. Others paid the price as well: 'Colonel Hall of the Twenty-second had been killed, Colonel Gibson of the Forty-eighth seriously wounded, and while at the enemy's guns with his hands on the horses, Major Ross of the Second Georgia Battalion had just been shot down. Nearly all my company officers had been killed or wounded.'[15]

That was not the end of misfortune for the Georgians, only the beginning. Humphreys' little regiments, which had done so much to demoralize Wilcox's

---

[14] Freeman, op.cit. p.126; OR, vol.XXVII, part II, p.623.
[15] Freeman, op.cit. p.127.

men by their appearance alone on the ridge, now took delight in firing into the right of the brigade, sweet revenge for all they had suffered in the long day's fight against the same regiments. The seventh color-bearer of the 48th Georgia fell, and the colors were lost. By ones and twos at first, then by squads and finally by companies, the Georgian regiments began to drift back past the guns they had bought so dearly, over the stone wall, and then down the gentle slope into the valley they had crossed with such impetuous valor. Many defiantly walked backwards, firing as they retreated, refusing to show their backs to the enemy. Webb followed closely, picking up Revere's 20th Massachusetts on the way. As they crossed the stone wall, he sent the two regiments to take Posey's Brigade in the flank and rear. With the pressure off, the Georgians began reforming.

Colonel Randall arrived and reported to Hancock. 'The enemy are pressing me hard,' shouted Hancock, 'they have just captured the battery yonder . . . and are dragging it from the field. Can you take it?'

'I can, and damn quick too, if you will let me.' Hancock waved him on, with some reluctance, just as Randall's five companies came up.[16] Randall formed them in line, told the company commanders what he intended to do, then ordered them forward. The 13th double-quicked down the slope toward the Codori Farm. As they approached, one of the companies gave a fine 'Irish yell' just as a bullet brought down Randall's horse. Pinned beneath the animal, Randall urged his men on, vowing to catch up as soon as he freed himself of 'this damned saddle'. A few men stopped to help, and the colonel was off running after the rest, whose momentum had slowed. Randall limped around the end of the line and ordered them forward again. They leapt straight into a volley fired by a line of reformed Georgians. Few were hit; the volley just drove the Vermonters forward faster with the bayonet. Such was the ferocity of their attack that many of the stunned Georgians threw themselves into the grass and surrendered. When Randall brought them back to the ridge, they escorted over a hundred prisoners and dragged back Weir's lost guns.

After sending in Randall, Hancock rode to the front of Hall's Brigade, locked in the deadly embrace of Posey's Mississippians. The space between them had shrunk to barely ten yards and was filled with black smoke pierced only by the flames of discharging rifles. On the right the line was held by Battery A, 4th US Artillery, commanded by 1st Lieutenant Alonzo Cushing. His six 6-inch rifles were firing so fast that the 16th Mississippi could approach no closer behind its mound of dead and dying. Hancock's horse pranced behind the guns. 'Keep it up, Cushing. They must not get through!' The young officer barely took time to grin to himself as the corps commander watched the battery's machine-like

---

[16] Pfanz, op.cit. p.421.

efficiency with evident approval. Satisfied that Gibbon would hold, he galloped north to find Hays' Division of his corps.

'Everything is in'
7:45 PM, Cemetery Ridge

As Hancock rode among the guns, A.P. Hill was only yards away across the small, deadly space, made invisible by roiling clouds of smoke. Gone was the sick man of the day before; now he was the A.P. Hill of Frasyer's Farm and Second Manassas, infusing his men with his own flaming will. But even through the smoke, he could see the bodies piling up as the firing line wilted under Cushing's fire. The Yankees were unusually tough here, he concluded. With the coolness that was the other part of his nature, he tore himself from the fight to find a reserve and a new opportunity. He rode parallel to the ridge to the north, where the smoke cleared, and found it empty of the enemy save for a single Union officer racing north. He spurred his horse back down the slope where it seemed as if the smoke was thicker, and almost ran down the right flank file of the 12th Virginia of Mahone's Brigade. Riding along the front of the brigade, he found Mahone, explained the situation, and ordered the brigade forward at the double-quick. He rode part of the way with Mahone to ensure he was on the right course, then rode north again to find Pender to reinforce the attack.

The gap towards which Hill ordered Mahone had been held that morning by Robinson's Division of the battered I Corps, and then by Willard's Brigade of II Corps. When Willard had been sent to the left, Hays had not filled in the gap.

Now it was a race for Mahone's 1500 Virginians. Any successful penetration of the Union position on the ridge, especially if it was reinforced, would ripple through the whole position like the masonry-shivering wave of an earthquake. If a second blow fell elsewhere, the whole structure would collapse. Wright had come close, but Mahone's chances were better. His brigade was fresh and had suffered few casualties from Union artillery as it emerged from the woods along Seminary Ridge, being partially masked by the hanging powder smoke clouds in the valley between the ridges. The gap towards which he was driving was defended only by the six 3-inch guns of Captain William A. Arnold's Battery A, 1st Rhode Island Light Artillery. To Mahone's right, Cushing's Battery and Gibbon's Division were locked with Posey's Mississippians, lost in their own immediate combat and its enfolding smoke. To Mahone's left, Hays' Division was preparing for the impact of Pender's brigades, which were more visible due to the thinning smoke in that part of the field.

Despite 'Billy' Mahone's earlier petty standing on the authority of his orders, once the sword had been drawn he was 'fierce action' personified. Described by Freeman as 'small, and as lean as a starvation year', he had the soul of a great fighting man, imperceptible to others but awaiting only the opportunity to reveal itself.[17] Now he led his five Virginia regiments straight toward the greatest opportunity of the war, that beckoning gap between Gibbon and Hays. Hill had pointed it out as the smoke cleared here and there, but now it was shrouded again as the Union battery there was firing straight at him as fast as it could. The shell and case shot were wiping bloody smears through the ranks behind him, but the drifting smoke hid part of the line. He ordered the double-quick to give his men the best chance he could, knowing that the gunners would have trouble adjusting their fire if he moved fast. He looked around for supports, but could see little to his right but more smoke where Wright and Posey should have been. The thundering racket that came from that roiling cloud, and the waving Confederate battle-flags that pierced the smoke, told him those brigades were doing their best. To his left, where Pender's brigades should have been, he could see little at all. 'Where are my supports?' he asked himself.

At that moment Hill had found Pender and directed him to angle his attack to the right to follow Mahone. Pender's brigades were only halfway across the valley between Seminary and Cemetery Ridges. They had further to go than Posey and Mahone and had also started out a bit later. Thomas was on the right and Lane on the left, with Scales' tiny brigade behind Thomas. For Pender, the order to follow Mahone was a mixed blessing. The massed artillery on Cemetery Hill, Pender's original objective, had already inflicted heavy casualties. Angling away from that line of attack now offered the enemy artillery his flank instead, which was a deeper, more packed target. And the Union gunners were quick to take advantage of their opportunity, gouging long, gory holes through the ranks of North Carolinians and Georgians in the three brigades. Hill kept pace with Pender. 'I will ride with you, Dorsey. I have no more reserves. Everything is in.' Pender rightly took it as a compliment that the corps commander had chosen to fight with his command.

Hill had not been exactly accurate. All the infantry was in; that was true, but the 3rd Corps artillery, eighty-four guns, was still a powerful force at the corps commander's disposal. Particularly well-sighted to support the attack were the twenty guns of Lee's youngest artillery commander, William R. J. Pegram. Like Latimer in 2nd Corps and Alexander in 1st Corps, Pegram was a born artillery officer of exceptional ability. At Fredericksburg, Hill had said, 'Pegram, as usual ... managed to find the hottest place.'[18] After Chancellorsville, one of his men had written: 'He was everywhere on the field, encouraging and cheering the men to do their duty, he is the bravest and noblest fellow I ever saw, has won the confidence & esteem of

---

[17] Freeman, op.cit. p.xxxviii.
[18] *OR*, vol.XXI, p.650.

the whole command.'[19] Pegram instantly understood what the change of direction of Pender's Division meant. They were following Mahone toward that point on the enemy ridge devoid of infantry. Within minutes he was directing the fire of his guns at that point.

For all Mahone could tell, Pender might as well have been on the face of the moon. His brigade had been stopped by the high, plank fence along both sides of the Emmitsburg Road. The planks were nailed on the field side to keep cattle from pushing them out, and they served to foil infantrymen just as well. The enemy's guns now had a beautifully stationary target. First Lieutenant Arnold's Rhode Island battery had been having things all its own way up until then, only worrying about keeping Mahone's Brigade under fire. Arnold's delight in catching the advancing enemy at the plank fence, fortunately for Mahone's Virginians, was short-lived. Pegram's guns quickly poured a concentrated fire straight into the gap occupied by Arnold's battery. A shot struck the breech of gun No.1 just as Sergeant Jeremiah Wilson was about to pull the lanyard. The shot gouged through the touch-hole and took off Wilson's head. Shells exploding above guns Nos.3 and 4 killed four men and wounded ten. Gun No.4 was struck on the axle and dismounted by a shot that killed two more men. Another shot disintegrated a limber into splintered pieces of wood and burning powder bags. One of the latter fell into another limber, from which Private John Bunting was lifting ammunition. Arnold shouted a warning just as the limber blew up. Across the valley, Pegram's gunners raised a cheer at the explosion, then went back to serving their guns.

The case shot and canister that Arnold had sent into Mahone's men packed by the plank fences had at least blown holes through the barrier. Rallying his men on the other side, Mahone led them forward at the double-quick up the slight slope. They bent forward instinctively as Pegram's iron hail shot overhead to smash the battery on the ridge. They saved their breath for the rush. Mahone was buoyed by the sight of the heavy fighting going on at the crest of the ridge to his right as Posey continued to battle with Gibbon along the stone wall.

As he galloped over to Hays' Division, Hancock wondered what more could happen to threaten II Corps' grip on Cemetery Ridge. He was directly behind Arnold's Battery when he found out. An overshot round skidded right in front of his horse, spraying them both with dirt. Riding on, he could now see that between Cushing's Battery with Gibbon, and the left flank of Hays Division, there was 400 yards of ground empty of defenders save for

---

[19] John H. Munford to Sallie Munford, 14th May 1863, Munford-Ellis Papers, George W. Munford Division, William R. Perkins Library, Duke University, Durham, North Carolina; cited in Peter S. Carmichael, *Lee's Young Artillerist: William R.J. Pegram* (University Press of Virginia, Charlottesville and London, 1995) p.91.

Arnold's dying battery. He rode up along the crest and through the artillery
fire. The smoke was thinner here, and it would have been clear even to a
blind man that Pender's assault was heading straight for the gap, despite the
pummeling his brigades were receiving from the Federal artillery. Their
battle-flags streamed above forests of glittering bayonets. For a moment he
paused to admire the order and speed of their formation and the skill of the
commander who was directing the attack towards the softest spot on his
front. But only for a moment. He had more important things to worry
about – reinforcements. Gibbon was fully occupied with Posey, and Hays'
two remaining brigades were small (Carroll 941 men, and Smyth 1105) and
barely equal to the part of the enemy assault that would overlap their front.
The only men about were wounded gunners from Arnold's Battery stumbling past him to the rear, but his mounted color-bearer proved to be a
beacon to the staff at his nearby headquarters. Major W. G. Mitchell, his
senior aide-de-camp, rushed up to him with the news that they had
moments to intercept the last of I Corps rushing to the far end of the II
Corps line. 'Order everything within reach up to this spot with all speed.
Seconds count!' Mitchell galloped the few hundred years down to the Taneytown Road and found Robinson at the head of his small division of barely
1400 men, all that was left of the nearly 3000 that had gone into the first
day's slaughter. Even as Robinson's turned off the road and ran up the rear
slope of the ridge, it was evident to Hancock that the enemy had a clear
two-to-one advantage in numbers at his weakest point, although the artillery
was doing its best to whittle down the odds. The enemy's guns were also
ranging the front after driving off Arnold's last two pieces, and were being
handled with uncommon skill.

7:30 PM, Winebrenner's Run

It was almost sunset as Early finished giving his last minute instructions to
Hays and Avery, whose brigades rested along Winebrenner's Run about 700
yards to the north of Cemetery Hill. As senior officer, Hays would have overall
command of the two brigades. They would be attacking over the same ground
that Gordon had attempted in the early hours of the morning. The fields were
still strewn with his dead and wounded Georgians. The hot day had already
started to bloat the dead and had killed off a number of the wounded. The cries
of the survivors had carried down the slope to the waiting brigades and done
little for their composure, already unsettled by their exposure all day to the
enemy's snipers and skirmishers.

Early kept looking at his watch. 'I was ordered by General Ewell, a little
before sunset, to advance to the assault of the hills in front of me as soon as
Johnson should become engaged on my left, being informed at the same time
that the attack would be general, Rodes advancing on my right and Hill's

division on his right.'[20] Early must have shaken his head in disbelief that his corps commander had seen fit to communicate his plan only minutes before the attack. If he was trying to imitate the great Jackson, he had chosen one of his less endearing traits. Still, his attack was contingent on Johnson beginning the dance. At least Rodes had attempted to co-ordinate his attack. Only minutes before, the blonde, six-foot general, looking like a 'Norse god', had ridden over to Early and explained that Pender's Division had issued from Seminary Ridge into the attack and that he would follow. With any dispatch, Rodes' men would be striking the west slope of Cemetery Hill as Hays and Hoke's Brigades struck its northern slope. Early looked at his watch again and calculated that he had, at best, another hour of declining visibility. After that, his men would be groping in the dark, not quite the right conditions for accomplishing a decisive rupture of an enemy position. While he waited for Johnson, he could hear the sound of battle coming closer and closer down the ridge to the south of Cemetery Hill. So Hill was doing his part, it seemed. He began to fret about Johnson. What was taking so long? Ewell had told him that Johnson's losses in the night attack had been severe, but he had not so far to go as last night. He had retreated to the base of Culp's Hill.

Finally the noise of Johnson's attack exploded on Culp's Hill. The time had come. 'I ordered Hays and Avery to advance and carry the works on the height in front. These troops advanced in gallant style to the attack.'[21] The troops left no record of seeing Early in conference with their brigade commanders. More deeply impressed on them was the rapid riding up and down their front of staff officers, the presage of action, and the shouts of command. Having been tormented by the enemy's skirmishers and sharpshooters for hours, the men were eager to go forward. Both brigades were led by seasoned and aggressive officers. Hays, aged forty-three, had seen service in the Mexican War in a volunteer Mississippi cavalry regiment and had recruited his own 7th Louisiana from New Orleans when war broke out in 1861, and had commanded this brigade for a year. His was one of the two Louisiana brigades in 2nd Corps, both nicknamed the 'Louisiana Tigers'. Hays' five Louisiana regiments (5th, 6th, 7th, 8th, and 9th) numbered about 1200 men. Avery was thirty-five and had originally commanded the 6th North Carolina. He was an imposing man, tall and powerful, an officer stating that 'there was no fallback' in him. His three North Carolina regiments had taken over 300 casualties in the first day's fighting and now had only some 900 men fit for action. The brigade of 'Extra Billy' Smith was in support, and would add a further 900 men to the attack if committed.

On East Cemetery Hill, Howard had been expecting just such another

[20] Jubal Early, *Autobiographical Sketch and Narrative of the War Between the States* (J.B. Lippincott, Philadelphia, 1912) p.273.
[21] *OR*, vol.XXVII, part II, p.470.

attempt. His skirmishers had reported the three brigades when they moved into position early in the morning. He had worked his men unceasingly to dig rifle pits behind the low stone wall that ran along the Brickyard Road. The stone wall had not been enough for the 1st Division that morning, a lesson not lost on the 3rd Division now defending the same ground. With each spadeful of earth heaped up in front of them, their confidence grew. A pile of protective earth or stone rampart does wonders for the defending soldier's morale and steady marksmanship. This attack would come as no surprise either. Howard was painfully aware of how thin his battered corps had been stretched. He had no reserve other than the remnants of the 17th Connecticut and 75th Ohio, not more than 120 men. He impressed upon both Schurz and Steinwehr that each should be ready to detach a brigade if a crisis threatened the other division. Howard also had been prowling the lines all day, warning the men to be ready and seeing that they were. Their confidence was further reinforced by the arrival of almost forty guns from the Artillery Reserve, the equivalent of an entire brigade. Combined with the I and XI Corps batteries already in place, they seemed to stretch hub to hub in two iron bands up the slope behind them. More than one reference was made to Malvern Hill by the grinning 'Half-Moon Men'.

Among the guns to arrive from the Artillery Reserve were Combined Batteries F/G of the 1st Pennsylvania Artillery — six 3-inch ordnance rifles commanded by Captain R. Bruce Ricketts. That afternoon, after his guns were placed on the hill, Colonel Wainwright, commanding all the guns on Cemetery Hill, had made something deadly clear. 'Captain, this is the key to our position on Cemetery Hill, and must be held, and in case you are charged here, you will not limber up under any circumstances, but fight your battery as long as you can.' Ricketts assembled his men and repeated every word to them.[22]

As soon as Early's brigades emerged into the open, the full fury of the massed batteries responded. Hays said that his brigade

had gone but a short distance when my whole line became exposed to a most terrific fire from the enemy's batteries from the entire range of hills in front, and to the right and left; still both brigades advanced steadily up and over the first hill and into a bottom at the foot of Cemetery Hill . . . Here we came upon a considerable body of the enemy, and a brisk musketry ensued; at the same time his artillery, of which we were now within canister range, opened upon us.[23]

On the knoll of Culp's Hill, Lieutenant Whittier, now in command of the 5th Maine Battery after the wounding of Captain Stevens, had to work fast to take

---

[22] Pfanz, *Gettysburg: Culp's Hill and Cemetery Hill*, p.253.
[23] *OR*, vol.XXVII, part II, p.480.

advantage of the fast-moving attack. The battery had been alerted by a sergeant who yelled, 'Look, look at those men,' as the enemy brigades emerged
from Winebrenner's Run.

The order, 'Case 2½ degrees, 3 seconds time,' had hardly been heard before up
went the lids of the limber-chests, the fuses were cut in another moment, and the
guns were loaded as if on drill. Slap went the heads of the rammers against the
faces of the pieces, almost a welcome sound, for at the same moment came the
order 'Fire by battery,' and at once there was the flash and roar of our six guns,
the rush of the projectiles, and along the front of the enemy's charging line every
case shot – 'long range canister' – burst as if on measured ground, at the right
time and in the right place above and in front of their advance.[24]

Whittier described the frenzied action:

At dusk opened with the whole battery at 1,200 yards on the enemy's line
advancing from the edge of the town, and, by changing front and firing to the
left, enfiladed their lines, at a distance of 800 yards, with spherical case and shell,
and later with solid shot and canister, expending the entire contents of the
limber chests, which contained upward of 46 rounds of canister repacked from
caissons.[25]

The new battery which had joined them from the Artillery Reserve that
morning worked their guns with equal fervor.

The Union guns firing on Early's attack were entirely unopposed by Confederate artillery except for two batteries on Benner's Hill, all that remained of
Latimer's valiant effort. They interfered little with the massive and accurate fire
directed at the charging Louisiana and North Carolina brigades. The only relief
the attacking brigades could find was in the smoke drifting down the hill from
the Union batteries. Hays, who, like his men, had chafed under the enemy's fire
all day and wished for the attack, now wished they had waited another half-
hour so that enfolding darkness would have hidden them from the enemy's
guns. Colonel Wainwright was delighted, on the other hand, that there was
still enough daylight left for the almost fifty guns under his command to pour it
on. And his men were tearing great gaps in the oncoming Confederate regiments as they ascended the hill. The hillside was becoming wreathed in smoke
as the guns belched a steady stream of fire downward. The Confederates found
some small measure of protection as they descended into the low ground at the

---

[24] Maine at Gettysburg Commission, *Maine at Gettysburg*, p.94; Edward N. Whittier, 'The Left
Attack (Ewell's) at Gettysburg', *Gettysburg Papers*, Ken Bandy and Florence Freeland, eds., vol.2,
p.87.
[25] *OR*, vol.XXVII, part I, p.361.

base of the hill, but almost as soon as they began the ascent the guns found them again, and now Schurz's infantry fired a well-directed volley that brought down the first Confederate ranks. Colonel A.C. Godwin of the 57th North Carolina was on the left flank of his brigade:

> We continued to advance ... under terrific fire, climbed a rail fence, and still farther beyond descended into a low bottom... The enemy's batteries now enfiladed us, and a destructive fire was poured into our ranks from a line of infantry formed in rear of a stone wall running at right angles with our line of battle and immediately below the batteries.[26]

Major James Beall of the 21st North Carolina, next in line, remembered that 'like an unbroken wave our maddened column rushed on. Four or five color-bearers went down. The hour was one of horror.'[27]

Already Colonel Avery had fallen. Riding a horse in order to command better, he had marked himself for a target and was one of the first to be hit. His regiments pushed on over him, and it was some time before anyone knew he was down. While he lay there, right arm and shoulder shattered, he drew a lead pencil from his blouse and painfully scribbled a note on a piece of paper – rapidly staining with his blood – to Major Samuel Tate, who had succeeded him to command of the 6th North Carolina: 'Major: Tell my father I fell with my face to the enemy. I.E. Avery.'[28]

At the other end of the line, the 5th and 6th Louisiana charged directly up the north spur of the hill and against the angle of Schurz's defense, held by the 74th Pennsylvania of the brigade commanded by Colonel von Amsberg. The 74th, recruited from the German population of the counties of Philadelphia and Allegheny, had been badly handled in the first day's fighting, losing ten dead, forty wounded, and sixty prisoners out of its 326 men, but compared to most of its sister regiments its losses had been relatively light.[29] By this time the two Louisiana regiments coming up the hill did not overly outnumber the 74th, whose steady fire was reducing the odds even more. From his vantage point higher up the hill, Howard saw that these regiments, which had had the shortest distance to go, would strike first. What Howard could not see was the mounting fear that had gripped the young captain commanding the 74th after the loss of all its field officers the day before. Captain Henry Krauseneck was

---

[26] *OR*, vol.XXVII, part II, p.484.

[27] Walter Clark, ed., *Histories of the Several Regiments and Battalions from North Carolina in the Great War, 1861–1865* (State of North Carolina, Raleigh, North Carolina, 1901), vol.2, pp.136–8.

[28] This note, on blood-stained paper, is in the North Carolina Department of Cultural Resources, Division of Archives and History, Raleigh, North Carolina; cited in Pfanz, *Culp's Hill and Cemetery Hill*, pp.259, 451.

[29] *OR*, vol.XXVII, part I, p.183.

fast succumbing to the crushing sum of his terrors. He already had a poor reputation in the regiment and had done nothing to improve it in the last twenty-four hours. When the howling Tigers came within thirty yards of his position he snapped, yelling 'Retreat! Retreat!' and then fled up the hill. He had thrown confusion into his own ranks. Half the men started to fall back from the stone wall or climb out of their rifle pits. Their fire slackened just enough for the Tigers to come bounding like deer over the stone wall. But this time the 'Half-Moon Men' did not break. Forced back from the wall, they retreated stubbornly up the hill, firing steadily or grimly striking out with bayonet and rifle butt when the Tigers closed with them.

In the center of Schurz's line, where his brigades joined, the Confederate tide broke over the wall as well. Here was the 74th's sister regiment, the 75th Pennsylvania. It too had suffered cruelly the day before, losing 108 dead and wounded, but had then broken and fled with such alacrity that it lost only a further three men as prisoners. With only 97 men left, it held on grimly as the center of the enemy line – the 9th Louisiana and 6th North Carolina – neared the wall. The Pennsylvanians were stretched thin here. Seventy-five Carolinians and twelve Louisianans, led by sword-waving officers, leapt over the wall as the thinly-spread defenders emerged from their shallow rifle pits to fight back. Major Tate of the 6th North Carolina recalled that 'the enemy stood with a tenacity never before displayed by them, but with bayonet, clubbed musket, sword, and pistol, and rocks from the wall' they overwhelmed the defenders.[30]

7:45 PM, Gettysburg

Major General Robert E. Rodes was having more difficulty than he had anticipated moving his division through the streets of Gettysburg to position it for the assault on Cemetery Hill he had promised Early. This battle had become a series of misfortunes for Rodes, whose career to this point had marked him as one of the Confederacy's rising stars. On the first day, he had handled his division awkwardly; it had been badly roughed up by Robinson's Division of I Corps and lost a third of its almost 7500 men. Now he had badly miscalculated how long it would take to move through the town. Already he could hear the noise of Early's assault, and his men were not even near their assault position on the other side of the town.

7:55 PM, The Angle, Cemetery Ridge

Mahone's Virginians were pouring through a gap between Gibbon's and Hays' Divisions formed by an inward angle in the stone wall that ran in front of much of II Corps' position. Neither the stone wall nor the broken guns and dead of

---

[30] *OR*, vol.XXVII, part II, p.486.

Arnold's battery slowed them much. They came racing forward over the crest of the ridge, officers and color-bearers vying to take the lead, the Rebel yell echoing before them. Rushing up to them with a deep Northern shout came Robinson's Division, its flags thickly dotting the front of its battle-thinned regiments. The distance between them shrank to forty, thirty, then twenty yards before the two masses almost instinctively halted and fired. What seemed like a solid sheet of flame filled the small, deadly space. The smoke roiled between them, hiding the carnage at first, but did not stop either side from automatically keeping up the fire. It was not immediately obvious, but Mahone's regiments had taken the heavier blow. They had been more disorganized from their charge and the heavy losses from the Union artillery that had enfiladed them. Mahone had also dropped off the 12th Virginia on his right to aid Posey by manning the stone wall in the angle perpendicular to the enemy's line. The gap had also not been wide enough to accommodate all the brigade, and the 61st on the left had come up against Colonel Thomas B. Smyth's Brigade. That left just the three smallest regiments, the 6th, 16th, and 41st Virginia, as the only part of his brigade that had actually broken through the gap, giving him fewer than 700 men against Robinson's 1500-plus. The Union advantage quickly began to tell as the I Corps men kept up a hot and rapid fire.

Hays had rushed up the 7th West Virginia from Colonel Samuel Carroll's small 941-man brigade to cover Smyth's open flank and to enfilade Mahone's left flank. Hancock was with Hays when he ordered the 7th up; he realized that Carroll's three remaining regiments – the 14th Indiana and 4th and 8th Ohio, barely 700 men – were the only reserve left on this part of the field. Mahone had jammed himself into the gap in his corps front, while Posey hung on trading hammer blows with Gibbon on the left. To their front, strong enemy brigades were following Mahone and should be impacting within minutes. The artillery was doing all that it could but had not been able to stop the rapid and almost parade-ground order of the enemy's advance, despite the trail of broken bodies it had left. If the enemy widened his lodgement, the game would be up. Hancock could do nothing more. As he contemplated the approach of Pender's brigades, and heard the continuous thunder of the massed batteries on Cemetery Hill, he remembered just how thin Howard's men were along that stone wall. To himself he thought, 'Hold on, Howard, hold on,' as if the will behind the thought was all the help he could send.

Right now he realized the crisis of the action on his front had arrived. If the new enemy lines attacked into the gap, they would surely burst through. He drove his spurs into his horse and galloped to the left to set a solution in train. He found the bushy-bearded West Pointer, John Cleveland Robinson, riding behind his division, encouraging the men as they slowly beat down the fire of the Virginia regiments in the gap. Robinson was a veteran of the Seminole and Mexican Wars, the Mormon expedition, and frontier service. He had com-

manded Fort McHenry in April 1861 when Secessionist mobs had attacked the
6th Massachusetts on its way to Washington. He so thoroughly prepared the
fort for action that the mob was deterred from further action. He had risen
quickly and had proven himself a tough, unflinching fighter. The day before he
had held off five enemy brigades with just his two for four hours. He was a man
for desperate measures, and so were his troops. There was an iron-like resiliency
about the entire I Corps, and not just the Iron Brigade. Few corps could have
taken their punishment yesterday and still have such a reservoir of courage as
these men were showing now.

Hancock explained what he needed to Robinson and rode back to Hays. Just
as he arrived, a shout went up from the I Corps division, and their flags
advanced. Turning to Hays, he said, 'General, we have only a few moments
before they hit us. Be ready to throw Carroll forward around your right to catch
them in the flank and rear as soon as they come up.'

That moment was approaching quickly as Pender and Hill led the brigades
of Thomas and Lane up to the stone wall through a blaze of fire from Smyth's
Brigade and the six Napoleons of Battery I, 1st US Artillery on the right of the
line in Ziegler's Grove, commanded by First Lieutenant George A. Woodruff.
Lane's North Carolinians returned fire and advanced. This was Hill's old
brigade, and he had ridden off from Pender to see them into the fight. Thomas'
Georgians, led by Pender, were coming in behind Mahone. Captain Thomas B.
Hazar, commanding the 1st Delaware in Smyth's line, had a lot to prove.
Command had devolved upon him suddenly when Hancock had relieved his
commander for an unauthorized withdrawal from the skirmishing to the
division's front at the Bliss Farm. As the enemy's brigades advanced across the
valley and up the slope, all the while savaged by the guns and finally his
brigade's rifle fire, he took some small satisfaction from the fact that the enemy
must be feeling just what he had felt in that awful attack against Marye's
Heights at Fredericksburg only seven months before. On the right of the 1st
Delaware was Major Theodore Ellis' 14th Connecticut, which had already
proved quite a lot that afternoon. The genial Ellis could turn caustic when faced
with incompetence, but had earned the respect of his men. 'Cool, intrepid,
unshrinking in the severest contest, he caused the men he led to repose entire
confidence in his management.'[31] Ellis had succeeded where Hazar's former
commander had not, and had charged the Bliss Farm and cleared the enemy
from it and the adjoining orchard. He burned the farm when ordered to
withdraw and resumed his place on the left of the line, but with one-third fewer
of the 160 men he had charged with.

---

[31] *Minutes of the 19th Annual Meeting of 'The Society of the Fourteenth Connecticut'* (Bridgeport,
Connecticut, 1887), p.7; cited in Charles B. Hamblin, *Connecticut at Gettysburg* (The Kent State
University Press, Kent, Ohio, and London, 1993) p.90.

The rest of the Nutmeggers had not lost their edge and were rapidly firing over the stone wall, filling in the holes in the line that formed as men fell. Next in line, the Delaware men were equally intent on their work. Repeated charges by the Carolinians carried them to the stone wall but never over it, save for their dead. Such was the color-bearer of the 16th North Carolina, who led one gallant rush towards the wall. The officers and men behind him wilted one after the other in the steady fire as he, the single survivor, leapt onto the wall and jumped down onto the bayonets of the Connecticut men. Again and again the Carolinians came, until their dead and wounded heaped in front of the wall formed ghastly stiles over which their comrades climbed, only to be shot, stabbed, or bludgeoned in turn. Bodies blue and gray draped the wall as both sides hacked and clubbed at each other. Woodruff's battery had swiveled its guns to the left to enfilade whole front of Lane's Brigade, cutting red holes through its ranks.

Thomas' Georgians had come up on Lane's right ready to pass through Mahone, only to be surprised as the Virginians began stampeding back through their ranks. On their heels were the I Corps men, who slammed into the disorganized mass of Confederates, stabbing and shooting. Hancock waved his hat at Carroll, who, hidden from view behind Ziegler's Grove with his three regiments, was waiting for the signal; Carroll plunged through the northern arm of the grove and then wheeled through Emmanuel Trostle Farm and onto the flank and rear of the Carolinians. The 18th North Carolina, on the flank, was already reeling amid dead and wounded inflicted by Woodruff's rapid canister, and could only respond with drunken slowness. Carroll's first volley swept the regiment away and shredded the backs of its unsuspecting sister regiments. Caught front and rear, the brigade began to unravel. Hundreds threw down their rifles as the rest bolted to the rear. Hill rode among them, frantically trying to rally the men, seizing the flag of the 7th North Carolina and shouting at them what had saved the day at Frasyer's Farm: 'Damn you, if you will not follow me, I'll die alone!' [32] That he nearly did, as Carroll's next volley riddled his horse and sent him crashing into the grass with severe wounds in the shoulder and thigh. Pender too was shot from his horse moments later as the animal was hemmed about by the confused mass of men pressed back by Robinson's bayonet attack. The bullet that pierced his heart had gone through his wife's last letter in his coat pocket.

The Confederate attack had suddenly collapsed. Posey's Brigade had also been repulsed and streamed to the rear, uncovering the flank of the disorganized brigades of Mahone and Thomas. Through the smoke Thomas could

---

[32] *Richmond Times Dispatch*, 28th October 1862; cited in James I. Robertson, Jr., *General A.P. Hill, the Story of a Confederate Warrior* (Vintage Books, New York, 1987) p.92.

see Gibbon's regiments in pursuit. It was obvious the attack had failed, and now the Confederate flank was threatened. He ordered a retreat, managing to extricate the hopelessly mixed brigades with enough grudging defiance to keep Robinson at bay. Scales' Brigade had come up just as the attack had fallen apart and was only in time to form a rearguard into which the Union artillery sent a hail of fire. Mercifully, the last light of day was finally flickering out and darkness enfolded the retreat.

First Lieutenant Haskell of Gibbon's staff remembered the exultation of that heady moment. 'The Rebel cry has ceased, and the men of the Union begin to shout there, under the smoke, and their lines to advance. See the Rebels are breaking! They are in confusion in all our front! – The wave has rolled upon the rock, and the rock has smashed it. Let us shout too!'[33]

8:10 PM, Long Lane

In the deepening gloom, illuminated only by a rising moon, Rodes rushed his five brigades from east of Gettysburg town towards Long Lane, a sunken road paralleling the Emmitsburg Road about 500 yards away to the east. The men had just been told they were to take the hill at the point of the bayonet and to expect confusion in the darkness. To avoid another tragedy such as that which killed Jackson at Chancellorsville, the men of Brigadier Stephen D. Ramseur's Brigade were told the watchword was 'North Carolina to the rescue'.[34] Despite his orders to be as quiet as possible, enemy skirmishers had already fired upon them and withdrawn up the hill. Rodes had placed his brigades in two lines, with Ramseur's Brigade on the right of the first line. To Ramseur, Rodes then inexplicably surrendered control of the attack. Ramseur recalled that Rodes stated that the 'remaining brigades of the division would be governed by my movements.'[35] Accordingly, after the division had advanced several hundred yards past Long Lane, Ramseur's caution justifiably caused him to order a halt. Already several of his men had been hit by the enemy's skirmishers, who had receded into the dark. To save lives he ordered his brigade to lay down, and the command was passed through the whole division. He moved forward to make a personal reconnaissance.

8:10 PM, Cemetery Hill

The North Carolinians and Louisianans had broken through the center of Howard's thin line and came charging up towards the first battery above them. 'You will not limber up under any circumstances. Fight your battery as long as

[33] Frank A. Haskell, *The Battle of Gettysburg* (Wisconsin Historical Commission, Madison, Wisconsin, 1908).
[34] Raleigh *Semi-Weekly Standard*, 4th August 1863.
[35] *OR*, vol.XXVII, part II, p.587.

you can.' Wainwright's words had been running through Captain Rickett's mind all afternoon. The men had been firing non-stop for half-an-hour, and still the Rebels came. The case shot and canister smeared ragged red holes in their ranks that seemed to fill up automatically with more of the gallant, lean men in butternut and gray. They just kept coming. And now, having overwhelmed the thin line of infantry at the stone wall, they were running up toward him. Running! Where did they find such courage? His guns kept firing, double canister now, blowing away the leading wave in a spray of blood and body parts, but behind more were coming. The stone wall was breaking under the human wave sweeping over it. Ricketts pulled out his pistol and fired the whole cylinder into the oncoming enemy. They made the last yard through a lull in the firing and were among the guns with the bayonet howling like wolves. His gunners did not flinch and met them with ramrod and sponger, bare knuckles and swords.

A young rebel with a blue bandanna wrapped around his red hair jumped onto gun No.3 waving his regimental colors. Ricketts ran up the incline of the trail and thrust his sword up into the boy's belly. As the rebel folded over with a shriek and fell off the gun, a Union gunner grabbed the color and waved it until he was bayonetted. The fight for the flag left a heap of bodies around the gun, until a brawny, black-bearded Rebel officer rushed up to the gunner who had it last, pressed his pistol to the man's side and fired. Waving the color overhead, he shouted, 'Forward, the 6th!' Ricketts had every man in the fight; even the men at the caissons and limbers had grabbed what weapons they had and joined the fray, but he was losing the fight. The breach in the stone wall widened and more of the enemy poured over.

For Howard, everything rode on this action – the tattered honor of his corps, his own reputation, and above all the battle itself. He had resolved not to leave the field this day. He had shouted in joy as Schurz's brigades did not break but blazed away at the enemy as the distance closed. The canister whistling over their heads had stiffened their backbones as well. Even when the enemy had broken over the wall in two places, he still did not despair. The rest of the lines held. The 74th Pennsylvania was giving ground slowly back up the hill, and the 75th had died in place rather than run. He sent the Nutmeggers down to reinforce the 74th. They struck the enemy in the flank and stopped him cold. But the breakthrough in the center, that got among the guns, was critical. In the failing light he could barely make out another Confederate brigade descending into the low ground below the stone wall. He had only his own staff. As he drew his sword, an excited officer shouted, 'Look! Look! It's Smith's Brigade!' Behind them at the double-quick was the brigade Steinwehr had dispatched the moment he had seen Hill's attack break and fall back. Colonel Orlando Smith came running past waving his sword; his brigade was fresh; they had been dropped off to hold the hill on the first day as the rest of the corps had marched off to a savage beating. They were also out to avenge the injuries to the reputation of the Half-Moon corps.

Howard stuck his sword in his belt, grabbed his corps colors – the red number eleven centered on its white cross on a dark blue field – and ran forward with Smith, his staff racing to keep up. The head of the column double-quicked straight for the melee at Ricketts' Battery, not even taking time to come into line. With a shout the lead regiment plunged into the fight. Their shock shoved the fighting forward of the guns. The flanking batteries had kept the enemy from feeding too many men through the center by sweeping the breach with canister. Now the struggling mass heaved back down the hill step by step to the stone wall, trailing a carpet of bodies. Confederates on the other side of the wall were firing into the fight, but with little effect. Trapped against the wall, many of the North Carolinians and Louisianans finally gave up and surrendered. Others jumped over and escaped. Smith's other regiments spread out behind the wall, adding their fire to that of Schurz's regiments.

Early had taken a lesson from his failure to support Gordon's attack that very morning and was personally leading 'Extra Billy' Smith's Virginia regiments to support Hays and Hoke's Brigades. He had seen them go forward in a most gallant style through a perfect hell of artillery. As they descended into the valley at the base of Cemetery Hill, he had intercepted Major Tate's request for support of his breakthrough of the center by the 6th North Carolina and part of the 9th Louisiana. Early immediately directed Smith's Brigade to the center. As they began to ascend the slope, men began to drift back down the hill in ones and twos, then in clumps, and finally in whole companies and regiments. The last faint light sinking behind the horizon was going fast. The spreading gloom was illuminated only by the flash of the artillery on the hill. But even that was stopping as darkness' cloak settled over the death-strewn field. Early gave the order to the Virginians to fall back; the other brigades were doing that on their own. One of the figures that appeared out of the darkness was Major Tate. His bitter rage trampled down normal courtesies. 'My regiment is destroyed, General, destroyed! Ten G-d——d minutes, if only you had come ten minutes earlier. They were breaking. We were among the guns! We had them!' [36]

8:45 PM, east of Long Lane

Ramseur's senses were fully alive as he walked closer to the Union position on Cemetery Hill. The sounds of fighting had died away. In their place he could hear triumphant shouting and the noise of a military band lustily belting out a German march. He strained to hear the chant echoing from over the hill: '*Hoch, Hoch, Dreimal Hoch!*' [37] He wondered what that could mean. He had

---

[36]* Samuel Tate to Zebulon B. Vance, Governor of North Carolina, 10th July 1863.

[37] 'High, High, Three Times High!', a German acclamation for a victorious general.

approached within 200 yards, 'where batteries were discovered in position to pour upon our lines direct, cross, and enfilade fires. Two lines of infantry behind stone walls and breastworks were supporting these batteries.' [38] Adding to the sense of overpowering strength was the sight of Smyth's Brigade returning to its position after its counterattack. The enemy was actually reinforcing their already strong position, he thought. He had seen enough. Returning to the division he conferred with several of his fellow brigade commanders and sent a message to Rodes, who was not up front, that an attack would be most unwise. Rodes took his report at face value and ordered the division back to Long Lane where it spent the night. As they settled down for cold rations in the dark, Rodes' Division could hear the noise of jubilation on the hill slowly fade away.

[38] *OR*, vol.XXVII, part II, p.588.

CHAPTER 10

2nd July 1863
'I held you long enough'

'Cousins, move on; you are drawing the fire our way'

7:30 PM, the Bricker Farm

The collapse of Sweitzer's Brigade had unhinged the line that Colonel Vincent had established, with its right anchor on the Bricker Farm at the base of Little Round Top. Vincent had just barely held his line against the savage assaults of Robertson's Texas Brigade by feeding the small regiments of Tilton's Brigade into the fighting. With Tilton dead, he now commanded the two fused but decimated brigades. His own casualties had been crippling. The massed guns of Colonel Alexander's artillery had added their own iron fury to that of the Texans, reducing the Bricker and Group farms to burning ruins. With the 1st Texas swinging around his left, Vincent could not withdraw, but to stay meant being ground up and trampled down. Vincent ordered his command to uncoil to the right toward the hill, where he would make a stand in the trees, a living fortress in the enemy's rear. The odds were still long – to disengage from an aggressively attacking enemy was one of the hardest of all maneuvers, and against John Bell Hood it would be next to impossible.

Hood instantly sensed the slackening of fire to the front and ordered the Texans forward again. Through the shattered apple orchard they came, and past the burning farm buildings filled with dead and wounded, keening their war cry like the Furies. So fast were they that they caught Vincent's regiments that had been on the left even as they were trying to swing around toward the hill, and, like wolves, their blood was up; the Texans tore into them, shooting and stabbing. Vincent and Tilton's regiments were mixed together around their battle-flags, trying to keep together and fend off the Texans. Alexander had been quick off the mark and sent in two batteries to torment the dwindling blue regiments with canister. Only Vincent's regiments that had been at the Bricker Farm – the 44th New York and 83rd Pennsylvania – and Tilton's regiments that had reinforced them, made it to the safety of the woods on the hill. The rest were driven north up to the saddle just below Little Round Top. The remnants of the 16th Michigan and its attached Michigan company of sharpshooters found refuge in a jumble of boulders, a natural redoubt, just behind the Bricker Farm and a hundred yards or so up the road north of the hill. The survivors of the other regiments clustered to either side. Entrusting Colonel Rice of the 44th with command of the survivors in the woods, Vincent ran down to the forlorn hope amid the boulders. Robertson was in a perfect rage at the cost of Vincent's resistance and was hell-bent on smashing this last small remnant. But the Michiganders were holding on as if they had just bought title to their rocky patch, with Vincent prowling among them, encouraging them to hold on. Attack after attack flowed forward and receded again, every repulse leaving more bodies in butternut and gray heaped around the rocks. Private Fletcher of the 4th Texas and his squad found a fold of ground for protection after the last attempt on the rocks. Just then a field officer walked up behind them, urging, 'Boys, aim well.'

Fletcher coolly replied, 'Cousins, move on; you are drawing the fire our way.' The officer was even cooler and paused to stare with great determination towards the enemy, an act Fletcher was to describe as the bravest he had ever seen.[1] Brave it was, for the Michigan sharpshooters were dropping men left and right, especially the officers, who, among the Texans, were always up front.

Hood himself rode through the men, waving his hat as he urged them on for one more attack. It was an act of leadership that attracted a sharpshooter to his golden hair and beard, glinting in the sun. He squeezed off a shot. The golden officer pulled up short on the reins of his horse, pulling its neck around sharply, and he slid slowly out of the saddle, still clutching the reins taut. He was caught by a dozen hands of the shocked men around him. The attack he had urged now spontaneously erupted.

While the 16th Michigan and the others fought it out amid the boulders, Kershaw's Brigade was scrambling up the undefended shelf of rock above Plum Run directly behind them. The South Carolinians had a clear view of the open ground to their front, the dip at the end of Cemetery Ridge at the northern base of Little Round Top. Their lines moved forward quickly but warily, unable to believe the obvious – that there was not a single Yankee facing their way. The noise of a desperate fight just ahead of them and the singing of bullets well overhead told them that there were still plenty of Yankees on the other side of the slight ridge.

Their skirmishers soon topped the ridge and looked down on the desperate fight for the rocks. They began firing into the backs of the Michiganders from their slight elevation and were quickly joined by the 8th and 15th South Carolina. One good volley and the Blue bodies sprawled in heaps amid the boulders as the Texans crossed the last few yards to capture the few survivors, whose hands were now in the air. It was only then that the two brigades realized what they had accomplished – they had severed the Cemetery Ridge backbone

---

[1] William A. Fletcher, *Rebel Private: Front and Rear, Memoirs of a Confederate Soldier* (Dutton Books, New York, 1995) p.79.

of the Army of the Potomac: in this war, the average soldier had a good eye for the ground and could think for himself. Kershaw and Robertson embraced amid the cheers of their men. An officer came up to Robertson and told him that the enemy commander wanted to see him. He pushed through the prisoners being escorted out, to find Vincent in the arms of an aide, the blood welling up from a jagged wound in the left breast. Robertson knelt down and took off his hat. Vincent reached up and took him by the shoulder, 'I held you long enough!' There was a proud glint in his eyes. 'Long enough.'

Robertson replied, 'You damned may well have, sir. A gallant fight. Your people have never been more formidable.' The aide was frantically trying to staunch the flow of blood as Vincent coughed and shook. 'I will send for a surgeon immediately. My compliments on a gallant action, sir.' Vincent was beyond hearing then. Robertson walked away, momentarily lost in thought. To a staff officer, he mumbled, 'He damned may well have.'

Longstreet appeared at that moment and put an end to the budding euphoria in the ranks. To his brigadiers, he said, 'Gentlemen, the enemy is still on this field. Celebrate when he has left it.' From Kershaw he learned that McLaws had been attacking to the left of the South Carolinians. He was pleased that he had his corps back in the same harness again, but the Yankees were fighting damned hard. It was not enough to kill them, you had to knock them down too. Smash up one brigade and another appeared. He put Robertson and Kershaw on line and ordered them to attack due north through the woods which paralleled the Taneytown Road. If he could roll through the woods along the ridge at the same time as McLaws was striking the ridge head-on, he would unravel both the defenders on the ridge and those on the road at the same time. He did not have much choice. The brigades of Law and Benning were locked into a slugging match with the two tough regular brigades of V Corps and getting nowhere. His reserve was Anderson's Brigade, which he would commit as soon as Robertson and Kershaw got rolling. Right now he was commanding Hood's Division himself until he could transfer its command to the senior brigadier, Law. He could feel the enemy reeling. At all costs, he had to keep pushing. The daylight was racing away. He estimated there was an hour's worth of light at the very best before night shut down the fighting.

7:30 PM, the Taneytown Road, south of Big Round Top

As a Federal courier had given the first warning of Longstreet's appearance in the Union rear, now it was a Confederate rider who whipped his lathered horse to bring word to Longstreet that the enemy was now in *his* rear – and coming fast.

Buford's brigades had pressed hard on the retreat of Fitzhugh's command. The Confederate cavalry reformed again and again to contest every advance. But every stand could only last for minutes before the swaying forest of

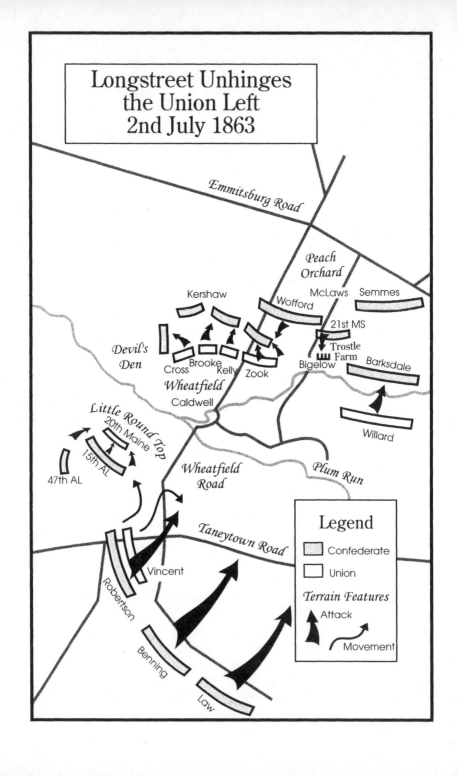

Longstreet Unhinges the Union Left 2nd July 1863

Emmitsburg Road

Peach Orchard

Kershaw

Wofford

McLaws   Semmes

21st MS

Devil's Den

Trostle Farm

Bigelow

Cross   Brooke   Kelly   Zook

Barksdale

Wheatfield

Caldwell

Willard

Little Round Top

20th Maine

15th AL

47th AL

Wheatfield Road

Plum Run

Taneytown Road

Vincent

Robertson

Legend

Confederate

Union

Terrain Features

Attack

Movement

Benning

Law

advancing bayonets of VI Corps' van, the 'Vermont' Brigade, appeared and began to deploy. Against the determined advance of infantry, the gray cavalry could not stand. Still, every time they hung on until the Vermonters began to deploy ate up the minutes that might give Longstreet a fighting chance.

That is all he would have. The trap he had planned for Meade was now turned on him. Vincent's stand at the Bricker Farm had been all the margin Meade had needed. He had not panicked but had calmly begun to funnel reserves towards the fighting. Barnes' 1st Division of V Corps had been consumed, but Ayres' 2nd Division with its Regular Army brigades had stopped Hood's flanking movement. Brigadier General Samuel W. Crawford's 3rd Division was ready to plug the gap caused by the collapse of Barnes' brigades. Meade now had a strong line, with the rest of V Corps and the Reserve Artillery to oppose Longstreet. Also, somewhere between the V Corps firing line and their old positions on Culp's Hill, Williams' Division of XII Corps was supposed to be on its way. Finally, he had also ordered one of the brigades from Brigadier General Gregg's 2nd Cavalry Division on the northern flank to counter Hampton's cavalry. Meade had also ruthlessly delegated the other half of the battle, facing west, to Hancock's direction, recognising that no one man could command a battle, bent at a right-angle, fighting in two different directions. At least each of them would have that one sector under direct observation, despite all the powder smoke that seemed to hang in the still, humid air, obscuring half of what was going on.

But Meade was anything but assured of his situation. He was highly disturbed by the continued absence of VI Corps, which appeared to have disappeared from off the face of the planet. He had expected them hours ago and could only presume that Longstreet had somehow defeated Sedgwick. Worst of all, the right-angled shape of the battle-line was broken at the very angle itself. McLaws had rushed his division into the gap at the base of Little Round Top and reunited Longstreet's Corps. With Kershaw linked up with Robertson, that left Semmes and Wofford's Brigades at the right place to pry apart the Union defenses. For Meade, all seemed threatened once more. Again and again he would patch up a defense, only to see it consumed by the ferocity of the Southern infantry.

Longstreet was just beginning to piece this picture together from the fragmentary reports brought to him in the minutes after his two divisions had linked up. He immediately recognized this as the decisive moment of the battle. He ordered up Anderson's Brigade, his only reserve, to throw it in to support McLaws' attack. At the same time, he sent to Hampton to try to cut the Baltimore Pike over Rock Creek. At best he could cut off the enemy's last escape route, and at worst panic Meade sufficiently to divert forces to holding it while Longstreet attacked hard elsewhere. He was also confident that Hill was pressing a strong attack on Cemetery Ridge. What he did not like was the absence of any tell-tale smoke from Culp's Hill to the north, telling him that Ewell had failed to begin his attack. It was then that the cavalryman rode up, caked with dirt and sweat, to gasp out the news that the enemy was in the rear in great strength – horse, foot, and artillery.

For Meade and Longstreet this was the defining moment of the day. Catastrophe had shared her gifts equally between them. How each of them rose to the occasion would be decisive. Longstreet, at least, had the priceless knowledge that McLaws was pressing his attack over the ridge into a gap. Meade was still in the dark about the whereabouts of Sedgwick, much less that he was about to strike Longstreet from the rear. Still, this was a test of the fortitude and resourcefulness of two very tough men.

'There they are, General!'
7:45 PM, Granite Schoolhouse Lane

Meade's crisis was the more immediate. Semmes and Wofford's Georgia Brigades had entered the woods just west of the Taneytown Road bound by the Fray, Swisher, and Patterson farms. In moments they would burst into the open and into V Corps' rear. Meade had ordered up Ayre's 3rd Brigade, but it was at the western end of the division line and could not arrive in time.

But Lockwood's Brigade just might. It was in the van of Williams' Division and approaching fast on Granite Schoolhouse Lane, just south of Power's Hill. Captain George Meade, the General's son and staff officer, was with his father at this moment.

> At this gap ... surrounded by only a few of his aides and orderlies, stands MEADE. The crash of musketry and the shouts of the contending troops resound on all sides, and the air seemed filled with shot and shell. At this moment MEADE sees at a short distance off a line of the enemy making straight for the gap. Will nothing stop these people? He glances anxiously in the direction ... whence succor should come. It will be a disaster unless something can stop these troops ... The general realizes the situation but too well. He straightens himself in his stirrups, as do also the aides who now ride closer to him, bracing themselves up to meet the crisis. It is in the minds of those who follow him that he is going to throw himself into the breach – anything to gain a few moments' time. Suddenly someone cries out, 'There they are, General!' [2]

The column was rushing down the road at the double-quick. Meade was lucky they had made it. For once, the staff work of the Army of the Potomac had failed completely. Williams had been ordered to the southern part of the field

[2] George Gordon Meade, *The Battle of Gettysburg* (George Gordon Meade, Ambler, Pennsylvania, 1924) p.78.

but with no specific orders where to go and no-one to guide him in the sinking light. Instead, he substituted good judgement and initiative to find the fastest route to the sound of the guns. He also had more than a good measure of luck. Gregg's cavalry had fought a desperate action to stop Hampton from capturing the bridge over Rock Creek, which had left the intersection of the Pike and Granite Schoolhouse Lane littered with dead horses and men. The column just tramped over and around the dead and followed the noise of war. The lane was crowded with walking wounded and fugitives who parted quickly for the rapidly moving head of the column, officers at the front with drawn swords and colors flying. Some of the stragglers recognized the 150th New York in Lockwood's Brigade and shouted encouragement: 'Go in, Dutchess County! Give it to them, boys! Give it to them!'

It was hot marching, and the men of Lockwood's Brigade quickly began to toss away their blanket rolls in the excitement of imminent action. As the column turned onto the Taneytown Road, the first Confederate infantry – Semmes' 10th Georgia, which had glided out of the woods along the same road only a few hundred feet from the XII Corps men – began to advance. They did not see the column quick-timing toward them on their left as they formed up on the road. It was against this open flank that Williams ordered Lockwood in.

So near was the enemy that the lead regiment, the 1st Maryland Home Brigade, did not even deploy in line but continued in column, ploughing straight through the flank of the surprised Georgians with the bayonet. It had been a fluke of time and place. Line against line and without the advantage of surprise, the Georgians would have taught the green Marylanders a hard lesson. But now they were practically spent, and the shock of the bayonet attack in the flank did the rest. The Georgians recoiled into the woods or threw down their weapons. Semmes' other regiments emerged from the woods to a scene of confusion and an onrushing blue column slicing through them from the left. From their front, in line of battle, came Ayres' 3rd Brigade of New York and Pennsylvania regiments, commanded by Colonel Stephen H. Weed.

'We're in no hurry, Uncle John'

7:45 PM, Taneytown Road east of Little Round Top

Brigadier General George T. Anderson had chafed for more than two hours as his big Georgia brigade of almost 1900 men had cooled its heels in the shade of the hills. The battle had raged just to the north then moved suddenly away, and still he had waited for orders. There was still heavy firing going on from the top of the small hill nearby, but Longstreet had led him to believe that it was a flanking operation. To his stunned surprise, his orders had come up from the south in the excited words of fugitives from Fitzhugh Lee's Cavalry Brigade. He had thrown a company across the road with fixed bayonets to stop the next group and quickly pieced together what had happened from their frightened accounts as the sounds of fighting grew closer.

More and more cavalry began coming up the road. He ordered them to concentrate in his rear and decided to throw his brigade in line of battle along the stream that ran off the Little Round Top near the J. Weikert Farm. He notified Colonel Alexander, whose artillery was limbering up, to move north. Alexander turned several batteries around immediately to reinforce his line. It was only minutes after the artillery rode into place that most of the cavalry came riding down the road in a big hurry. Buford's men were hot on their heels. This time it was their turn to be surprised. Anderson's riflemen slammed the head of the column into the ground, sending men and horses sprawling. The rest pulled back.

John Buford realized that now that he had finally come up against infantry his direct job of forcing the road was over. Now it was up to the infantry following just behind. He could still work around the flank and threaten the enemy, which would be the best thing he could do for Sedgwick's brigades, stacked up in front of the enemy blocking the road. Devin's Brigade was already moving off in that direction when Colonel Lewis Grant rode up with his staff. Behind him the Vermont Brigade had already deployed in line of battle and was advancing at a rapid clip. 'Well, Colonel, they're all yours. Looks like a strong infantry brigade and plenty of artillery.'

Grant was all Yankee business. 'You can recall your skirmishers, General; Vermont is on the field. I'm going to pitch right into them.' With a salute that brought his riding crop to his cap brim, he rode up to look over the ground, a wide expanse of open meadow, as bugles were sounding to recall Gamble's dismounted cavalry skirmishers. Buford's artillery battery was the last of his division to pull out, and not until after several of VI Corps' batteries accompanying the Vermont Brigade had arrived to pull into line in support of the attack. Alexander's gunners almost immediately shifted their fire from the retiring cavalry to the Union batteries, which went right into action themselves.

Amid the drifting smoke around the batteries, Sedgwick rode up with his trailing staff to confer with Grant. 'Go right in, Colonel. Break through. The rest of the corps will go in on your right and swing around or be in immediate support. We must get through to the army at all costs!' That had been Grant's intention all along, but to have the commander fully in tune with the spirit of the attack was heartening. That was simply 'Uncle' John Sedgwick's nature. The big, barrel-chested general was like the proverbial boxer with an iron right punch and a granite jaw. At the same time, he was careful with the lives of his men and was personally fearless. The Vermonters were sweeping by, and he stood up in the stirrups, waved his hat, and shouted, 'Give 'em hell, Vermont!' A cheer rippled from the line. Behind the 3rd Vermont, Drummer Boy Willie Johnson saw Sedgwick sitting his horse, Cornwall, as the regiment passed. The boy called out, 'Get another horse and come on; we'll wait for you, Uncle John; we're in no hurry, Uncle John!' Sedgwick beamed and tipped his hat.

Alexander's gunners had redoubled their efforts, seeing the corps commander's flag and the knot of horsemen behind the guns. The shells were well-directed. A limber was shattered, spewing smouldering ammunition; its horse-team, out of control, dragged the wreckage to the rear. Wounded gunners began drifting back from the guns. Colonel Martin T. McMahon, the corps Assistant Adjutant, urged Sedgwick to move to the rear. 'Uncle John', thoroughly unperturbed, replied, 'They can't hit me; I've got too much to do today.' As if to mock him, a Confederate case shot exploded in front of the command group, its load of small iron balls plunging forward into men and horses. Cornwall collapsed in a spray of blood, carrying Sedgwick to the ground. McMahon, one of the few left unhurt, leapt off his horse to rush to the side of his stricken chief. Cornwall was dead, pinning Sedgwick, who was trying to free his leg of the dead weight. McMahon shouted to some of the Redlegs for help. A half-dozen artillerymen ran over and heaved the dead horse off as McMahon pulled Sedgwick away. The general struggled to his feet as the surviving staff rushed over to him. 'Get me a horse, damn it! I've got work to do!'

Up ahead, the Vermonters had passed the line of guns and entered cornfields on both sides of the road. Colonel Grant halted them for a few minutes to catch their breath before the charge. Then, cheering the men forward, he rode down the brigade front shouting, 'Up now, my brave boys, and give it to them!' With a collective growl the brigade stepped forward, trampling the corn. The moment they emerged from the field, the Confederate infantry fired from behind the creek near the Weikert Farm. The range was short, seventy yards across a grassy field. It was also well-aimed, scything through the front rank of the Vermonters, tossing bodies in blue back into the corn or forward onto the grass. The brigade staggered at the blow. The word retreat was shouted, but other men shouted louder, 'Forward! Don't go back! We shan't get so close again.' Grant was riding through the corn rallying his men. Their eagerness was still alive as they shook off the blow and came forward again.

'You die a sergeant'

7:30 PM, Little Round Top

For Colonel Oates of the 15th Alabama, the Union troops on the crest above him had proved uncommonly tough. Again and again his Alabamians had dashed themselves against the stone and log breastwork. Even when they had fought their way over the barrier, the enemy had ejected them in savage hand-to-hand fighting. He had tried to flank them with his own regiment to the right and with the 47th Alabama to the left. But always the enemy seemed to have a few more men to extend the line just long enough.

A steady stream of his wounded staggered past him down the hill. The men had emptied their canteens, thankfully refilled before the attack, and had already had them refilled twice by a detail from the creek at the base of the hill. Thirst was one of the great unspoken torments of the battle-line, especially on a hot, sultry day, with mouths full of salty gunpowder from tearing the ends off paper cartridges. As the men gulped down the water from their newly filled canteens, Oates readied for one more push. The battle behind him was forgotten in the lonely contest between the sons of Alabama and Maine; the whole war was right in front of him, as any soldier in the firing line of any war can attest.

Above Oates on the crest, Colonel Chamberlain was equally impressed with his opponents. Hammer blows to his front and envelopments of his flanks had been beaten off with the greatest difficulty, and now his line was stretched to breaking-point; his dead and wounded were thickly spread a few yards behind the 20th Maine, where they had been carried to clear the firing line. Among the wounded was a former sergeant, George Washington Buck, who had served gallantly at Antietam and Fredericksburg until reduced to private by the vindictive charges of a quartermaster and the carelessness of his commander. Chamberlain had marked his case for correction, but now the young man lay stricken with a

> great bullet-hole in the middle of his breast, from which he had loosened the clothing, to ease his breathing, and the rich blood was pouring in a stream. I bent down over him. His face lightened; his lips moved. But I spoke first, 'My dear boy, it has gone hard with you. You shall be cared for!' He whispered, 'Tell my mother I did not die a coward!' It was the prayer of home-bred manhood poured out with his life blood. I knew and answered him, 'You die a sergeant. I promote you for faithful service and noble courage on the field of Gettysburg!' This was all he wanted. No word more. I had him borne from the field, but his high spirit had passed to its place.[3]

Another Maine man had been attracted to the noise of the 20th Maine's struggle. From its bloody encounter in the Wheatfield, Brigadier General John Caldwell, a former school principal from Machias, Maine, had just led his 1st Division, II Corps, up the western face of Little Round Top, to avoid being cut off by the charge of McLaws' Division over Cemetery Ridge. Three of his four small brigades had lost their commanders, and the ranks had been sadly thinned by Kershaw's men, but the division had held up well and retreated in good order. Caldwell's chief concern was to get them back into the fight. The

---

[3] Joshua Lawrence Chamberlain, *'Bayonet! Forward!' My Civil War Reminiscences* (Stan Clark Military Books, Gettysburg, Pennsylvania, 1994) p.31.

heavy gunfire and the smoke slowly rising up from the other side of the hill told him that he did not have far to go.

That same smoke was still drifting up through the trees where the Alabamians had pulled back to get their breath. It had been so hot that they drained their newly-filled canteens almost as soon as they arrived with the watering detail. Seeing his men revive, Oates determined on another attack, attempting once more to outflank the enemy on both sides. His companies extended to the left and right, reaching out to gather the enemy into a crushing embrace. The lines rustled with the soft clink of their accoutrements and the crunch of last year's leaves as they ascended the hill once again. Chamberlain gathered in the danger in a moment:

> The silence and the doubt of the momentary lull were quickly dispelled. The formidable Fifteenth Alabama, repulsed and as we hoped dispersed, now in solid and orderly array – still more than twice our numbers – came rolling through the fringe of chaparral on our left. No dash; no yells; no demonstration for effect; but settled purpose and determination! We opened on them as best we could. The fire was returned, cutting us to the quick.

The 47th Alabama was also coming. 'We were enveloped in fire, and sure to be overwhelmed in fact when the great surge struck us.'[4] Still the Maine men blazed away, fingers groping through their pouches for the diminishing number of paper cartridges. As long as the cartridges lasted, their fire was rapid and destructive. Oates flinched at the storm: 'My men obeyed and advanced about half way to the enemy's position, but the fire was so destructive that my line wavered like a man trying to walk against a strong wind.' One of the bravest and most admired officers in the regiment, Captain Brainhard, had just fallen at the head of his company, exclaiming, 'O God! that I could see my mother.' Oates' own brother succeeded in command, and promptly fell mortally wounded. His officers had been shot down all at once, it seemed, 'and the carnage in the ranks was appalling. I passed through the line waving my sword, shouting, "Forward, men, to the ledge!" and was promptly followed by the command in splendid style... It was our time now to deal death and destruction to a gallant foe, and the account was speedily settled.'[5]

In the face of the heavy Confederate fire, that of the 20th Maine suddenly slackened. Their ammunition was exhausted. The men began to look down the line at their tall colonel, sweat streaming down his face, sword in his hand. Then

---

[4] Joshua Lawrence Chamberlain, 'Through Blood and Fire at Gettysburg', *Hearst's Magazine* (June 1913).
[5] Colonel William C. Oates, *The War Between the Union and the Confederacy* (The Neale Co., New York, 1905) pp.97–8.

they faced front again and steeled themselves to take whatever came from that direction rather than seek shameful safety in flight. They had taken courage from the sight of him; now he took courage in turn from them, seeing the squared shoulders of his 200 survivors. He made his decision instantly:

> I stepped to the colors. The men turned towards me. One word was enough, – 'BAYONET!' – It caught like fire, and swept along the ranks. The men took it up with a shout . . . It was vain to order 'Forward.' No mortal could have heard it in the mighty hosanna that was winging the sky . . . The grating clash of steel in fixing bayonets told its own story; the color rose in front; the whole line quivered for the start; the edge of the left-wing rippled, swung, tossed among the rocks, straightened, changed course from scimitar to sickle-shape; and the bristling archers swooped down upon the serried host – down into the face of a half a thousand! Two hundred men![6]

In those few seconds between the slackening of the 20th's fire and Chamberlain's command, 'Forward', Oates' hopes of breaking the Maine regiment leapt. His flanks were within seconds of wrapping around the enemy. Then every pair of eyes turned upward, lead by the sound of that great shout. Bayonets at the level, the enemy was running downhill, bounding over the rocks and dodging the trees, but gaining in speed and momentum, roaring like devils. The Alabamians hesitated, the line wavered like wheat in a storm. It is rare for two lines of bayonets to crash into each other. The attacker either stops before he closes or the defender turns and runs. This time was the exception.

The Alabamians began to recoil; every muscle screamed flight. Then Oates ran out along the front of the 15th, shouting, 'Forward, boys! Forward!' The 15th coalesced in that moment from hundreds of fear-stricken individuals back into a regiment. A howl born in their bellies split the air as the line surged up the hill. The Maine men were going too fast downhill to stop even if they had wanted to. The two masses of American manhood crashed into each other in a killing frenzy unparalleled in two years of war. The Maine men crashed into the Alabamians with the power of gravity, the impact driving the now mixed mass of blue and gray several yards back down the hill. Oates and Chamberlain were in the middle of the fighting. Oates saw that a 'Maine man reached to grasp the staff of the colors when Ensign Archibald stepped back and Sergeant Pat O'Connor stove his bayonet through the head of the Yankee, who fell dead.' The sight was indelibly impressed into Oates' memory and years later still evoked a manly admiration for the foe. 'There never were harder fighters than the Twentieth Maine men and their gallant colonel.'[7]

---

[6] Chamberlain, *'Bayonet! Forward!' My Civil War Reminiscences*, p.33.
[7] Oates, op.cit.

They were selling out dearly. Once the 15th had stood to take the bayonet charge and had absorbed its impact, the advantage of the 20th was gone. Now it was numbers that counted in the melee of bayonets, rifle butts, knives, and pistols – and Oates still had almost two men to every one of Chamberlain's. The brave scholar-colonel took back seat to no man of his regiment in the combat. The shock of the attack had brought him face to face with one of Oates' company commanders with a sword in one hand and a pistol in the other. With a snarl the man had fired his big Navy revolver into Chamberlain's face; it misfired. A blank look of astonishment overcame him. Chamberlain gave him no second chance and drove his own sword into the enemy's chest. The color-bearer, Sergeant Tozier, and the few surviving color guards had followed the colonel and were now beset by a ring of Confederates, stabbing and grabbing for the 20th's blue banner. Chamberlain drove into the ring hacking and shooting until he had fought his way to Tozier's side, but the color-sergeant was by now wounded, and slumped to the ground. He handed the color to the only member of the 20th within reach. Chamberlain threw away his empty pistol and took the staff. His back to a rock, he was alone, the color guards having gone down with Tozier. In that brief instant, he saw everything around him with the slow-motion clarity of a dream. The fight was lost; the enemy too many.

He was right. The flanking companies of the 15th and 47th had been extended so far that the 20th's charge did not affect them. They loped through the open forest, through the line of the 20th's dead and wounded, and to the breastwork a few yards below. Chamberlain and his dwindling band of heroes were trapped. The Confederates lined the breastwork, splattered with puddles and splotches of dark, sticky blood. The encirclement was complete – but only for the briefest of moments. Masses of Union troops suddenly materialized behind them, green flags thick among them. Caldwell's Division had arrived. Their volley swept the breastwork, sprawling bodies and staining the stones afresh. Then they charged.

From the moment he became aware of the fighting on the east side of the hill Caldwell had wasted little time in reorganising his command, sending the regiments up and over the hill as they appeared. It was the Irish Brigade that had come up directly behind the 20th Maine's breastworks. The Irish Brigade had been small before its fight in the Wheatfield, but afterwards it was no bigger than most of the regiments in the field, so that its five colors stood almost in a cluster. The Irishmen surged forward and took the breastwork in a step. Below, the fighting paused almost as if on command as the Celtic battle cries, so like the Rebel yell, turned every head uphill. To the right more blue masses were coming down the hill flanking the 15th. Bullets were whizzing through the trees, bringing down Oates' men. Near him, one man was shot in the face and another in the side while a third fell with a bullet in the back. The men were turning to run down the hill. A soldier named Keils, of Company H, ran past Oates to his right and rear, spewing foam-flecked blood from a severed windpipe. Oates turned and ran with his men, the Maine men hard on their heels with Chamberlain and his color in the lead and the Irishmen just behind them.

Caldwell was trying to organize a great wheel to the left to scoop up the enemy. He was completely unaware of the desperate rearguard action being fought by Anderson's Georgians at the base of the hill. Oates' survivors were heading straight in that direction and Caldwell was following them. But darkness was slowing him. The last glimmers showed above the horizon, throwing the faintest of light, little of which penetrated into the woods. The great wheel was creeping along hesitantly.

There was nothing hesitant in the flight of Oates' two regiments. Darkness was more an ally than a foe as they streamed back down the slope, through the rocks, and into the grassy meadows at the base of the hill. Their flight took them to the rear of Anderson's firing line. Anderson was in the middle of trying to pull back his brigade; the enemy had sent another infantry brigade with cavalry to turn his open flank. The Bricker and Group farms still smouldered, casting a ruddy glow which, aided by a newly rising moon, illuminated a scene of growing chaos. Anderson's regiments were retiring behind an increasingly ragged line of rifle fire while a few of Alexander's batteries were interspersed among them, firing by prolonge to keep pace with the infantry. In the growing darkness, the trace of Anderson's withdrawing line was marked by sudden sheets of flame from the riflemen and great gusts of it from the guns. Behind them, the leading edge of their pursuers in the Vermont Brigade was visible in its own advancing line of fire, winking fiercely into the darkness. The wild appearance of Oates' men coming out of the twilight and shouting about thousands of Yankees behind them threw Anderson's careful, stubborn retreat into confusion. Terror runs faster through the night, and now worked its way along the rear of Anderson's regiments. Men began to slip out of the ranks as the cohesion of the regiments, tenuous at best under these conditions, began to unravel completely. In minutes, Anderson's carefully controlled fighting retreat had dissolved into a stampede for the rear.

8:20 PM, intersection of the Taneytown and Millerstown roads

However, there was not much rear left. Anderson's Brigade, Hampton and Fitzhugh Lee's cavalry, and the rest of Alexander's artillery, were being rapidly compressed toward the rear of Hood's stalled brigades facing north. Hampton had just ridden up to report that at least an enemy corps was coming up from the south, most likely VI Corps. The battle had come apart for Longstreet in the last half-hour. McLaws' sudden link-up over Cemetery Ridge had seemed finally to put the battle into his hands, but with the appearance of VI Corps in his rear, and Meade's skillful assembling of reserves from V and XII Corps, it was too little too late. The flashes of heavy fighting had come from the direction of Hill and Ewell's Corps. If either had succeeded, the accelerating sound of disaster and pursuit would be rolling towards him. In fact, the noise had begun to recede and the flashes to dim. Only minutes were left of his last hour of usable light, before darkness – despite the rising moon – would render any continuance of the fight against strong enemy forces extremely difficult. And he did not have a single fresh regiment, much less a brigade, to throw into the balance.

His conclusion was as bitter as it was inescapable. Every minute he continued the fight would be tantamount to the murder of his own men. Savage in combat, Longstreet could not countenance the sacrifice of life when military necessity and the hope of a successful outcome no longer justified it. He had opposed Lee's frontal attack for the same reason. Now he must save as many lives as possible, to fight again another day. His pride rankled at the thought of failure. They had been so close, so close. But he saw the situation with crystal clarity, not the blood-hued haze which seized Lee in battle.

'Major Sorrel,' he said to his chief of staff, sitting his horse at his side. 'Inform Generals Law and McLaws that the corps will retreat. McLaws will hold the ridge while Law passes through him. General Hampton, you will assume command of the rearguard with your cavalry.' Longstreet had begun giving the details of the orders when infantrymen started running past from the south, yelling about Yankees behind them. Cavalry thundered past in better order, and came to a halt when the order 'Halt' boomed out from Longstreet. An officer rode up to him. 'General, the enemy is coming up fast from the south. Anderson's Brigade has broken, and I've lost track of half of my own men in the confusion, and . . .'

Longstreet held up his hand for silence. 'Put your cavalry on line here and stop everyone running past. Reform them on their colors and hold this line at all costs, colonel!' Pulling his horse around, he said, 'Major Sorrel, carry out your orders, and I will hold our bolt hole open. Order Robertson up. Now ride!' Hampton, Sorrel, and their staffs disappeared into the darkness while Long-street, with only his color-bearer, rode up and down the line of deploying cavalry to help intercept the fugitives from Anderson's Brigade. 'Stop, men, form on your colors,' he shouted. One color-bearer kept going, and the corps commander rode him down, leaned over, and tore the color from his hand. Waving it aloft, he rode from group to group as they emerged from the dark. 'Georgians, stand fast! Remember your duty!' His other staff officers who had not accompanied Sorrel were riding through the night as well, stopping group after group. The line of horsemen, sabers drawn, stopped many, and as soon as they had stopped, their terrors fell away. The sight of the great Longstreet riding up and down in front of the cavalry, banner in hand, cheered them. Here was the pride of Georgia, Lee's mighty warhorse! Soon the regiments began to gather around their colors as men shouted out their numbers to those out of sight: '59th Georgia! Rally, 59th Georgia!' '8th Georgia, 8th Georgia!' One of the last men to come out of the darkness was Anderson himself, wounded and barely sitting his horse, held up by an aide. The last to appear, with a roar, were Alexander's guns, heaving themselves back as they retired by prolonge.

Behind them came the serried dark masses of the enemy. Bayonets and accoutrements glinted darkly and the glow of the burning farms. 'Time, I need time,' Longstreet thought. Still holding the colors, he rode up and down in front of the reformed brigade, encouraging the men for one more effort. 'Forward, Georgia, forward! Let them hear you, Georgians!' A shout rose from the ragged regiments, rising to the soul-shivering Rebel yell. He turned his horse to the enemy and spurred it forward. The regiments stepped out behind him. Time.

As Longstreet led the Georgians back into the night battle, he picked out of the noise of war the particularly fine drumming coming from the enemy ahead. In the midst of the 3rd Vermont, Willie Johnson was giving it his best, beating out *Yankee Doodle*, with twelve-year-old Joe Miller on the fife. A pang of remorse shot through Longstreet as he picked out the music, the same as had thrilled him as a young officer in the US Army. They had played *Yankee Doodle* as his regiment had charged up Chapultepec Hill so long ago. Sam Grant, his best friend at West Point and after, had remarked that Longstreet recognized only two pieces of music: one was *Yankee Doodle*, and the other wasn't. The past came elbowing its way up to him. Even in the heat of action, they would not be denied; memories and ghosts struck at his regrets and pain. Memories of loyalties renounced and ghosts of his dead children and countless bodies in blue. That terrifying thought came back. Had God Almighty taken his children in punishment for denying his oath to the United States in the cause of the subjugation of other men? The sudden stab of that familiar heartache almost doubled him over. The ghosts then fled as quickly as they had come, the battle driving them away. He was James Longstreet again, the commander of 1st Corps of the Army of Northern Virginia.

As Longstreet bought time, Sorrel reached Law on the right with the orders to retreat; at almost the same time, Captain T.J. Goree was desperately searching for McLaws on the Ridge. He had first found Robertson and delivered his orders, and then sped on to find McLaws. That was easier said than done. Even with the light of the rising moon, he was risking his life even to search for McLaws. No-one wanted to be another Jackson, shot by his own men in the dark; at night every uniform seemed dark blue and every noise the enemy. The air was still whistling with bullets as he came across small groups of men here, part of a firing line there, an occasional senior officer; but none could tell him where McLaws was.

9:30 PM, the Granite School House

The night that threatened Captain Goree had covered 1st Corps with a shield of invisibility. Only Sedgwick to the south pressed bravely into it, but Meade, ever prudent, hung back. He had set up a temporary headquarters in the Granite School House just west of Power's Hill. Although the firing continued sporadically, all forward movement stopped. Williams' counterattack came to a halt in woods still shared with Semmes and Wofford's men. Meade had come within a hair of being crushed and was not about to risk God-knew-what dangers against an enemy that he still thought heavily outnumbered him. He was now pretty sure it was VI Corps coming up from the south. Every man in the Army of the Potomac had also heard of Jackson's fate, and Meade did not want to risk blundering into VI Corps in the dark, with the inevitable fratricide that would ensue from such an encounter. Let VI Corps continue its drive, he thought; if successful, Sedgwick would hammer the enemy onto Meade's anvil. As the firing died down, a sense of immense relief washed through the Union ranks in this part of the field. No-one was too eager to maintain close contact with the enemy, who also seemed to have lost his usual taste for combat.

The only man in the army who did not believe that was Meade, but in the darkness he entirely missed the peril that had pressed in on Longstreet's brigades. With the recoil of Anderson's Brigade and the cavalry, most of Hood's Division and the cavalry brigades were compressed into a long pocket barely 500 yards wide in some places and almost a mile long, stretching from Little Round Top to Rock Creek. The two surviving divisions of V Corps that faced south onto this pocket now kept to their arms, alert and prepared to resist a night attack from the enemy. Confirmation of such a possibility came from the unmistakable sounds of hurried movement in their front as the enemy seemed to be repositioning himself for another attack in the morning or even that night. They could hear the shuffle of feet, the rattle of accoutrements, the shouts of officers, the clatter and noise of thousands of horses, and the creak of dozens of guns and limbers traversing their front.

Meade spent the early evening carefully repositioning guns and brigades to brace for the morning onslaught. He also ordered Butterfield, his chief of staff, to brief him on the withdrawal plans he had been preparing all morning and afternoon. He bitterly reflected on the conclusion that late this night he would be making the most fateful decision of his career – whether or not to withdraw the army to fight elsewhere. With the enemy sitting on the Taneytown Road, only the Baltimore Pike remained open as an escape route. As good a road as it was, he would have to make his decision whether to withdraw or not by at least midnight in order to get most of the army and its trains out by morning, covered by a strong rearguard. It takes time to move so many men by one road. He was not sure that the army could take another pounding such as it had endured these last two days. It had been so close today; how many times had the army been dragged to the brink of disaster, all in one dreadful afternoon?

For Longstreet the problem of extricating his corps consumed all his attention for the next several hours. The key had been his own effort to lead Anderson's Brigade back into the fight; the Vermonters had been hard to discourage, but night with its uncertainties was a great ally. The arrival of Robertson's Brigade was the clincher that caused Sedgwick to hold off any further action, and with that the fighting of 2nd July trailed off. The exhausted pause in the battle was only broken when stray bands of lost troops wandered into each other, provoking sudden but brief firefights. This was enough to keep the Union side in continued expectation of Rebel attack, and Longstreet did his best to feed this delusion. To avoid the enemy detecting movement only in a western direction, he had a few of Alexander's batteries and Hampton's regiments make a noisy transit east before turning around to join the escape. It also helped to have men shouting commands to various regiments that had already departed. Longstreet made a special effort to collect the wounded and move them out by captured wagons. Their agony rent the night, a Golgotha traveling west. It did much to cover the noise of the rest of the corps moving in the same direction. North and south of the emptying pocket thousands of ears strained to hear every noise and magnify them a dozen-fold.

Longstreet was standing on Cemetery Ridge, amid the boulders where Vincent had made his last stand, as the stream of the exhausted 1st Corps trudged, rumbled, and rode past and down into the valley. A beautiful full moon now hung in the sky, its pale light reflecting off the boulders and throwing its ghostly sheen over the indomitable Georgian. Only once did he leave his place atop the rocks – when the ambulance carrying Stuart came by with its escort of anxious cavalrymen. He paused only long enough to be told that Stuart might not survive the ride back to their own lines. 'It's in God's hands, then,' he said.

At last, when the torrent of the great 1st Corps had passed, Colonel Hampton rode up with a few men. 'That's the last, General. You and I are the rearguard.'

Longstreet climbed down from his rock and slowly mounted. Just then a few figures were seen coming up the road from the intersection of the Taneytown Road and the Wheatfield Road. One man leaned heavily on another. Longstreet waited a moment as the two soldiers came up. The stronger of them was supporting a wounded comrade, and let him down by the side of the road. 'Gotta wait to let Joe rest, General.'

'Help him onto a horse,' Longstreet ordered. As several of the cavalrymen came forward, the other soldier came up to the lieutenant-general with the proud easiness of the Southern fighting man, that respect between those who have carried a man's burden, whether man or master.

'Don't worry none, General. We'll get 'em tomorrow; we've skeered 'em half to death today. The Yankees have heard from Georgia today, by Gawd!' He saluted and followed his friend, who was sitting behind a cavalryman and clinging on for dear life. Then he turned back to say, 'Thanks for helping Joe, General.' In a second he was running down the road after the cavalrymen, shouting, 'Hey, there, we're trying to find Benning's Brigade.'

Longstreet stared after them for a moment, then turning to Hampton, he said, 'That's just the problem, Colonel, that private and so many others need not have shed a drop of blood to have driven the whole Union Army out of this position.'

In silence they rode over the ridge.

CHAPTER 11

2nd–3rd July 1863
'General, we have got them nicked'

Midnight, across the battlefield

The cessation of battle did not mean the end of the day's activity, merely a shift to a different level as men struggled to repair the damage done to their armies, to succor the wounded, and, above all, to prepare for the next day's slaughter.

Porter Alexander wrote: 'The fighting gradually ceased as night compelled it. And then how much there was to do! The first thing was to care for the wounded of both sides.' The Army of Northern Virginia strictly adhered to Lee's standing orders to pick up the wounded as they were found irrespective of uniform. The many hundreds of 1st Corps wounded that had been carted from behind Cemetery Ridge were sent to the already crowded field hospitals; thousands more were picked up in the valley between the ridges along the course that marked the advance of McLaws' Division. The Confederates buried their own dead and left the enemy where they lay. On the other side of Cemetery Ridge, thousands more wounded were being gathered by the Union into makeshift field hospitals. Over 650 medical officers struggled ceaselessly through the night and the early hours of the morning to save as many lives as they could. Every available building had been turned into a field-hospital, but they were hardly enough. Thousands more wounded lay in open hospitals lacking even the most basic amenities, all of which were sitting safely packed in their wagons at Westminster. Even worse was the lack of food for the wounded; that, too, was sitting at Westminster. The men in their regiments still had a hardtack or two left in their haversacks, but the wounded had lost even this and needed more intense nourishment. Army quartermasters were combing the area for supplies, and many civilians opened their larders and barns for the suffering, just as they had already opened their homes. The Confederates, for once, were in much better condition; trains, stuffed with the loot of Pennsylvania's rich farms, were concentrated behind Gettysburg. Major Jonathan Letterman, the medical director of the Army of the Potomac, was beside himself in frustration. He had created the most efficient military medical organization in history, and now he could not properly use it. The effect of Meade's order for the army's trains to be sent to Westminster for safety 'was to deprive this department of the appliances necessary for the proper care of the wounded, without which it is as impossible to have them properly attended to as it is to fight a battle without ammunition.'[1]

Repair of wounded military organizations was as frantically pursued that night as the repair of wounded bodies. Alexander was busier than most, with the complexities of putting a hard-fought artillery brigade back into shape for the next day's battle:

> Then our poor horses needed to be taken off somewhere & watered & brought back & fed, the crippled ones killed, & harness taken from the dead, & fresh ones scuffled from with the quartermasters. The limbers & caissons of all guns must rendezvous with ordnance wagons containing the particular kind & calibre of ammunition which its gun needs, & the boxes must be opened & cartridges, shell, fuses, primers, & c. be packed in the ammunition chests replacing all expenditures of the afternoon. The men must get something to eat – not only for tonight but tomorrow too. And then the scattered batteries & battalions must all be gotten together & in hand. And when it is sure that all are fit & ready to resume action at dawn, they must be put near their probable positions, & some chance given the men to get a little sleep.[2]

Alexander was immensely relieved at the arrival of his slave, Charley, looking for his master with food. Slaves searching for their masters were not an uncommon feature of that exhausted night.

On the other side of the field, another officer was equally busy ensuring that the guns would be well-fed the next day. Brigadier General Hunt spent a ceaseless night and morning assisted by the Chief of the Artillery Reserve, Brigadier General Tyler, in reducing and reorganising the many batteries that had lost so many men and horses that they could no longer fight their full complement of guns. By morning the repair of many of these batteries had still not been completed, and Hunt ordered batteries from the Artillery Reserve to replace them. He was becoming worried. The Artillery Reserve had nearly been used to the hilt in the second day's fighting. Almost every battery had been deployed into action, either on Cemetery Ridge, Cemetery Hill, or along the Taneytown Road. Over 400 artillerymen had become casualties. The replaced batteries would, at least, have part of the day to be put back together. They would become the Artillery Reserve, so fully had Hunt's guns been employed.

Luckily, the placement of the Artillery Reserve and the ordnance trains just south of Power's Hill had been the salvation of the second day. Had they still been behind the Round Tops as they had been earlier in the day, shortly after

---

[1] *OR*, vol.XXVII, part I, pp.196–7.
[2] Edward Porter Alexander, *Fighting for the Confederacy: The Personal Recollections of General Edward Porter Alexander*, ed. Gary W. Gallagher (The University of North Carolina Press, Chapel Hill and London, 1987) p.243.

they had arrived, they would have been overrun piecemeal. Instead, they had been just at the outer edge of the enemy cavalry's advance. Even so, one brigade had been badly cut up by the 1st North Carolina Cavalry even before it had gone into action. Vincent's grim stand had saved them from being overrun by Hood's infantry as well. But Hunt's careful organization and deft handling of his guns and their supporting elements had paid off that day. The guns had been the army's critical edge in almost every part of the field, and Hunt was determined that they should play an even greater part on the third day. He, like every other officer in the field, was elated by the army's success during the second day, but was also thoroughly aware that the contest was yet to be decided by another day's carnage. By the early morning, he had 175 guns in position along the length of the Federal line, of which 132 stretched from Little Round Top to Cemetery Hill. Another 95 were in reserve, centrally located behind the ridge. He arranged the guns in three great Napoleonic concentrations. The first, commanded by Colonel Wainwright, commander of the I Corps Artillery, was on Cemetery Hill. The second was the Cemetery Ridge Line, extending from Ziegler's Grove south of the Copse of Trees. The third was the McGilvery Line, running almost 700 yards to the southern end of the Ridge and dominating Plum Run. Hunt spent the rest of the morning briefing his officers on exactly what to expect and how he wanted their guns employed.[3]

And now Hunt's machine was being rapidly fed and repaired in order to fight again on the morrow. Second Lieutenant Cornelius Gillett commanded the ordnance train of the Artillery Reserve, which Hunt had ensured would be carrying twice its normal supply of ammunition, to bring up the average number of rounds carried per gun to 270. His small command was kept busy the entire night, passing out ammunition to the batteries of the Artillery Reserve and to II, III, and XI Corps, whose commanders, inexplicably, had sent their corps artillery trains to the rear when Meade had ordered everything but ammunition to be sent to Westminster. Hunt's prescience in bringing twice the normal ammunition allowance was justified by the fact that these corps had left their own reserve artillery ordnance trains behind. Seventy wagons were emptied and sent back to Westminster. That night Gillett supervised the distribution of 19,189 rounds of ammunition. Almost 7500 rounds were packed into caissons before leaving the park. All in all, it was an immense achievement of efficient logistics. By the morning all that remained in the trains was 4700 rounds, 'nearly all of which, though not in the best possible condition, could have been used to advantage had occasion required.'[4] For his part, Porter Alexander, was much less confident in the ammunition supply for his guns. The

---

[3] David Schultz, *'Double Canister At Ten Yards': The Federal Artillery and the Repulse of Pickett's Charge* (Rank and File Publications, Redondo Beach, California, 1995) pp.3–4.
[4] *OR*, vol.XXVII, part I, pp.241, 873, 878–9.

artillery of the Army of Northern Virginia had begun the campaign with at most 200 rounds per gun, 125 carried with the batteries and the rest in the trains. During the actions of 2nd July, his brigade had exhausted the ammunition in its caissons and limbers and had to replenish them once already from the trains which, he thought, were almost empty of everything except canister. Whatever happened the next day, the reserve of artillery ammunition was almost non-existent.[5]

Another staff element had also been busy. Colonel Sharpe's Office of Military Information had been interrogating the almost 1500 prisoners brought in during the day's fighting, as well as those taken yesterday. By early evening, the contractor John Babcock, Sharpe's deputy, had written Butterfield a note of critical importance. 'Prisoners have been taken today, and last evening, from every brigade in Lee's Army excepting the four brigades of Pickett's Division. Every division has been represented except Pickett's from which we have not had a prisoner. They are from nearly one hundred different regiments.'[6]

'Don't you think Sharpe deserves a cracker and a drink?'

10 PM, the Widow Leister's house

That evening Meade summoned Sharpe to his headquarters to discuss the report. On the table Sharpe noticed a pint of whiskey and a few hardtack, apparently Meade's supper. He himself had not eaten for some time and was faint with hunger, but he dared not ask for part of the army commander's Spartan meal. Hancock and Slocum were also in the room, lounging on a small bed, as Meade asked him for a few more details on Babcock's report. Sharpe left to track them down, and when he returned a few minutes later, he noticed the whiskey and hardtack still on the table. He added to his report that three small cavalry units had not been in action, and that 'Pickett's division has come up and is now in bivouac, and will be ready to go into action fresh tomorrow morning.' Hancock sat up straight, raised his arm into the air, and said, 'General, we have got them nicked!' Slocum also got up as a heavy silence fell upon the room. Then Hancock said, 'General Meade, don't you think Sharpe deserves a cracker and a drink?'[7]

Shortly after eleven, Meade assembled his senior officers. Sharpe's information had been priceless; Lee had shot his bolt except for Pickett's Division. There was a genuine opportunity here. That was on the credit side of the ledger. The red ink on the debit side loomed larger. The army was in a perilous position with only one route of retreat. That route could not be employed in the midst of

[5] Alexander, op.cit. p.246.
[6] Edwin C. Fishel, *The Secret War for the Union: The Untold Story of Military Intelligence in the Civil War* (Houghton Mifflin Co., Boston and New York, 1996) p.527.
[7] Fishel, ibid, p.528.

crisis; it would clog quickly with the mass of panicking troops and hundreds of guns, caissons, and wagons. When Sedgwick's patrols made contact with V Corps, Meade realized Longstreet had slipped away. The great weight that had been pressing down on him suddenly disappeared. He even allowed himself a few moments of uncharacteristic celebration. The ever-present thought of retreat receded momentarily as Sedgwick dismounted at the Widow Leister's house for the council of war. Sedgwick's arrival solved a number of his problems. Here was his strong reserve. The Taneytown Road, which could be used either for resupply or retreat, had also been reopened, at least temporarily. The red ink seemed to be fading. Meade had made up his mind.

Now crowded into that hot, stuffy room, barely ten by twelve feet, were Meade; his two wing commanders, Slocum and Hancock; seven corps commanders, Newton, Gibbon, Birney, Sykes, Sedgwick, Howard, and Williams; and his senior staff, Butterfield, Warren, Hunt, and Tyler. Meade had not convened a formal council of war. Rather, he was a believer in sharing information among his senior officers and 'as opportunities to discuss army affairs with his generals in a more or less relaxed manner.' [8] For a while the talk was informal and excited – excited because, despite the exhaustion of the day's fighting, the army had repelled every one of Lee's assaults and had even turned the tables on Longstreet's surprise flanking attack.

Meade took very little part in the banter, more willing to listen and learn than be heard. He took the opportunity to evaluate the men around him. Who would he trust in his place? Newton, Birney, Williams, and Gibbon were all fine division commanders who over the last two days had succeeded to the command of corps, but they were just too untested at that level.[9] Slocum and Sykes were solid and reliable but not much more. That left Sedgwick and Hancock. Sedgwick ranked Meade and was intelligent, aggressive, and professional. He had done a brilliant job in storming Marye's Heights at Fredericksburg while Hooker had bungled the rest of the Chancellorsville battle. But Hancock had shone the last two days. He had saved the army both on the first and second days of the battle. Professional and yet a natural soldier; charismatic in a genuine way that made the fraud McClellan pale with all his contrived cheering from the ranks; and no man in the army had demonstrated that finger-tip feel for the ebb and flow of a battle, for the morale of the men, and, above all, for the main chance.

Finally Newton put a skunk up on the table, silencing the banter, when he

---

[8] Edwin B. Coddington, *The Gettysburg Campaign: A Study in Command* (Charles Scribner's Sons, New York, 1968) p.451.
[9] Gibbon had assumed temporary command of II Corps that afternoon when Meade had given Hancock command of all the forces along Cemetery Ridge, including his own corps and III Corps.

said that 'this is no place to fight a battle in.' As he was a distinguished engineer, the others paid attention, but when he was pressed for details, his objections were just that – a few minor details of the line. The rest of the group, having fought over those details, brushed them aside. They were unanimous in wanting to fight it out. With Meade's assent, Butterfield formalized the meeting by summarising the issue in three questions and asking each officer his opinion, from junior to senior, just as was done in announcing the verdict of a court-martial.

The first question was: 'Should the army remain in its present position or take up some other?' Gibbon, as the junior officer present, voted first. 'Remain here, and make such correction in our position as may be deemed necessary, but take no step which even looks like a retreat.' The rest were in agreement. Hancock added grimly that the Army of the Potomac retreated too much as it was. The second question: 'Should the army attack or wait the attack of the enemy?' Again the reply was unanimous all around – await Lee's attack. The third question: 'How long shall we wait?' received more varied responses. Gibbon, aware of setting the tone to each answer, replied, 'Until Lee moves.' The others fell into agreement. Howard added that if Lee did not attack, the army should then assume the offensive. Hancock was sure that by waiting the army would invite the enemy to mass and attack. That would be a splendid opportunity. He did not want to wait long before shifting to the attack, sensing that the operational dynamic would shift and that the army should be ready to take advantage of it. 'We can't be idle,' he concluded. Sedgwick was more patient and suggested that the army wait one day before attacking. Old Slocum, the senior of Meade's generals, just said, 'Stay and fight it out.' [10] Hunt and Tyler were adamant that the artillery was willing and eager for another fight, and emphasized that there was enough ammunition for any option.

The results were gratifying to Meade, who had come to the same conclusion just before the meeting had begun. Meade, in the end, had not so much relied upon the opinion of his assembled subordinates as he had taken an official poll of their fighting spirit. He had been impressed with them over the last two days, with the exception of Sickles. They worked well together and were exercising a higher level of initiative than the Army of the Potomac had ever seen before with any combination of their predecessors. And it was that initiative which had repeatedly saved the day from Southern valor. He knew that they would 'stay and fight it out.' As he rose to dismiss the meeting, he said quietly but decidedly, 'Such then is the decision.' As the meeting was breaking up, Meade took Gibbon by the arm as the younger man was about to leave and said, 'If Lee attacks to-morrow, it will be upon your front.' Taken aback,

---

[10] John Gibbon, 'The Council of War on the Second Day', *Battles and Leaders of the Civil War*, vol.III, pp.313–14.

Gibbon asked why. 'Because he has made attacks on both our flanks and failed, and if he concludes to try it again it will be on our center.' [11]

As the room was about to empty, Colonel Sharpe entered with a fair-haired young captain in tow. 'General Meade, I think you should read these.' Meade looked at him for an explanation. Sharpe, perhaps, was milking the moment for every drop of drama. After all, he was presenting the coup of a lifetime for an intelligence officer. 'Captain Dahlgren has captured dispatches from Jefferson Davis to Lee at Greencastle this very morning.' You could hear a pin drop. As Meade opened the letters handed to him, Sharpe summarized them and concluded, 'There will be no reinforcements for Lee; what we have already identified is what he will fight us with tomorrow. There is also no new army assembled in Northern Virginia to threaten Washington.'

Meade read on, then passed the letters around to eager eyes. 'This has confirmed the strength of the enemy.' He allowed himself a small smile as he said, 'This will undoubtedly be of even\ greater value to the President and Mr Stanton, gentlemen, to know that they have not stripped the defenses of Washington to reinforce the army in the face of a genuine threat.' To himself he thought, 'And they will get off my back for a day or two, if I am lucky.' Then he gravely reached out to shake Dahlgren's hand. 'You have done your country a great service, Captain. What may I do for you?'

Meade noticed how the captain was all whipcord leanness and that his blue eyes were like gas flames. 'Send me out again tonight, Sir – with more men!'

'You will attack in the morning'

11 PM, the Seminary

A similar conference was underway across the valley littered with the dark forms of thousands of dead and wounded. But this one had none of the collegial nature of Meade's. That fact that it was happening at all was a sign of Lee's disquiet. For two days the Army of Northern Virginia had hammered the Army of the Potomac with blows of even greater fury than had driven its Northern opponent from many other fields. And for all that, victory eluded the Southern host. Yet the cost had been staggering. Not one brigade had avoided heavy loss in the past two days, save those in Pickett's Division, which had arrived this afternoon exhausted from their long march. Jenkins and Corse's Brigades had marched into sight from the south only an hour after Pickett's main body had halted behind Seminary Ridge. Pickett personally rode over to give his prodigal 'boys' a hearty welcome. Jones and Robertson's Brigades of cavalry were not expected until tomorrow. Lee was immensely relieved to hear from Pickett, whose arrival now placed a vital fresh reserve in his hands. Despite the fact 'his

---

[11] Gibbon, ibid, p.314.

poor men were almost exhausted by the march in the intense heat,' Pickett had felt the situation demanded that he assure 'Marse Robert' that 'with a few hours' rest, my men would be equal to anything he might require of them.' Pickett was gratified to hear from Lee. 'Tell Pickett I'm glad that he has come, that I can always depend upon him and his men, but that I shall not want him this evening.' [12]

The cost of the day's fighting also included an unprecedented loss among Lee's senior officers. Of his four main subordinates, Hill and Stuart had both been wounded. Of his eight division commanders, Heth, Hood, and Pender had also been wounded and Anderson killed. Hill's Corps was the most cruelly hurt, with the loss of its corps commander and all three division commanders. The wounding of Stuart at Barlow had been the most personally painful of all. The sharpness of his words to Stuart upon his arrival the previous evening had wounded himself possibly even more than Stuart. He had said what needed to be said between men, between a commander and his subordinate, but that had only masked his great affection and admiration for the young cavalier who came close to being a son. Word having reached him that Stuart had been wounded and brought safely back through the lines, he had ridden over to the field hospital to see him. After the surgeons appraised him of the seriousness of Stuart's wounds, Lee pulled up a stool next to the young man's cot and sat quietly in prayer for ten minutes. The laudanum they had administered before surgery had given the balm of sleep. Stuart's aides clustered outside the tent at a respectful distance with Lee's own staff, all in open grief. Stuart was beloved, even more so by those who followed the plume.

Presently Lee arose and walked out of the tent and over to the young officers around Stuart's division standard. No words were necessary to those who saw the pain in Lee's brown eyes. To Stuart's chief of staff, Major McClellan, Lee said, 'It is in God's hands now. I pray the Almighty will not deprive this army of such a valuable officer.' A few men sobbed openly. Lee's own eyes glistened, but he pulled himself back to duty. 'Major McClellan, be so good as to notify General Hampton that he will succeed to command of the Cavalry Division. Have him report to me at once.'

As Lee rode back to the Seminary, he analysed what had gone wrong in the last two days. Again and again he came back to the lack of co-ordination and the uneven performance of his senior subordinates. Both Ewell and Longstreet had been unaccountably difficult to propel speedily into combat, and Hill had essentially lost control of the first day's fighting. What struck him the most was Longstreet's stubborn resistance to his intentions. So much had his Old War-horse balked at Lee's direction that, for the first time, he had had to pull sharply

---

[12] Arthur Vrew Inman, ed., *Soldier of the South: General Pickett's War Letters to His Wife* (Books for Libraries Press, Freeport, New York, 1971) pp. 60–2.

on the bridle to establish who was master. He had yet to see Longstreet following the narrow escape of his corps, to ascertain what exactly had happened. But he had concluded that had Longstreet not dug in his heels and frittered away the morning, either Lee's original plan of attack or even Longstreet's modified plan of envelopment would have worked. And Ewell had been even harder to coax into action. Lee's normally perfect posture slumped ever so briefly as he reflected that Jackson was indeed dead.

By eleven Longstreet, Ewell, Trimble, and Hampton had arrived at the Seminary. Camp-chairs had been found for all of them and placed around a fire. Trimble was all eyes and ears; only yesterday morning he had been an unemployed major-general. Now he stood with Longstreet as the new 3rd Corps commander. It had been a dizzying ascent, but the old man was as unafraid of responsibility as he was of aggressive action. Lee came out of his tent and walked over to the fire as the others stood. 'Be seated, Gentlemen,' he motioned to them. 'I wish to hear from you what occurred today.' Unlike Meade's subordinates across the valley, the four Confederate officers were somber. They had been raised on success in this war, and were bewildered when the enemy proved uncooperative. Lee had to coax their explanations from them. None proved to be particularly edifying except that the enemy had been uncommonly tough and resilient and even more uncommonly lucky.

He had heard enough. He was about to pull hard on the bit, but first there would be a lump of sugar. 'Gentlemen, the fault for the lack of co-ordination on this field lays where it always does – with me. I ask your assistance in tomorrow's fight, and I know I can count on your utmost efforts.' In the middle of a prolonged battle was not the time to assign blame, something to which he was averse even under the best of circumstances. 'We have struck on their right and their left, and neither approach bears a repetition as the enemy is sure to have strengthened just those flanks. I believe he has strengthened the flanks by weakening the center of his line along the ridge. That is the point we will attack tomorrow morning. General Longstreet, I want you to attack with your whole corps tomorrow, which should be strong enough with Pickett's arrival.' [13]

Longstreet was on his feet. 'Great God! Look, General Lee, at the insurmountable difficulties between our line and that of the Yankees – the steep hills – the tiers of artillery – the fences – the heavy skirmish line – And then we'll have to fight our infantry against their batteries. Look at the ground we'll have to charge over, nearly a mile of that open ground there under the rain of their canister and shrapnel.'

Lee's voice was firm, quiet, and determined. 'The enemy is there, General Longstreet, and I am going to strike him.' [14]

---

[13]* Charles Marshall, 'The Last Council of War', *MAC*, vol.XV (1880), p.39.
[14] Inman, op.cit.

'Sir, my two divisions were badly cut up today and are required to guard the army's flank.' Longstreet was clutching at straws; he had come close to open insubordination, which only seemed to make Lee more obdurate.[15]

'Just so, General,' Lee replied coolly. Turning to Ewell, he said, 'General Ewell, your corps has attacked twice up these hills and has been unable to overcome the advantages nature has placed at the enemy's disposal. It is too bad I did not take the advice offered to me yesterday to side-step your corps to the right flank. I will rectify that error. General, you will withdraw your troops opposite those hills and direct Johnson's Division to march to the army's right flank where it will be placed under General Longstreet's command. With Early's Division you will prevent the enemy from descending from the hills and attacking into the town or turning our flank, though I doubt he has the stomach for the attack after the last two days.' [16]

He paused for a moment to let the import of what he had been saying sink in. Longstreet's explanation of the afternoon's events had convinced him that his original determination not to divide the army in the face of the enemy had been correct. Nevertheless, his 'Old Warhorse' had nearly pulled it off. He had come within an ace of a turning movement that would have eclipsed Jackson at Chancellorsville. The flaw had been the unexpected appearance of VI Corps, the very occurrence he had dreaded in dividing the army. Ewell and Trimble were not the men to do what had to be done. No-one but Longstreet had the wild-bull strength, the will, and the ability to organize and command what had to come next. The commander would be the vital element. Perhaps if Hill had not been wounded, he might have had an alternative, but it was Longstreet or no-one. Of the troops he had no doubt, even those whose brigades had been bled white in the last two days. They were invincible.

'Gentlemen, the fate of the Confederacy rides on our attack tomorrow. That is why I am committing all but Anderson's, Johnson's, and Early's Divisions to the attack tomorrow.' The four men sitting around the fire visibly stirred. 'Anderson's Division will form my only infantry reserve should we suffer a reverse and require a rearguard to hold open our route through the mountains.' [17] 'General Hampton, I must wield more than one fist in tomorrow's attack, and your division will be my left as Longstreet will be my right.' A quick conversation established that of Hampton's four cavalry brigades on the field, two had been fought out that day on top of their exhausting march of the last two weeks. Lee was far more sympathetic to the frailties of horseflesh. A horse can only be ridden so far, and then it just stops. A man always seems to have that something extra that keeps him going, but in the case of the cavalry the

---

[15]* James Longstreet, *From Manassas to Gettysburg* (J.B. Lippincott, Philadelphia, 1896), p.396.
[16] Marshall, op.cit.
[17]* Longstreet, op.cit. p.397.

two came as a set. Hampton's own brigade and that of Fitzhugh Lee would remain on the army's right to protect that flank. Which left only Jenkins and Chambliss' Brigades, with barely 2300 men altogether. Here Lee's determination paused in front of the small size of the fist. 'I fear your small command may not be able to land a strong blow, but their presence could be enough to unbalance Meade, which will be of inestimable value.' Now with some trace of regret, he went on, 'It is a pity that I did not order up Robertson and Jones' Brigades a day sooner. They should arrive sometime about noon tomorrow, too late for what we must do by then.'[18]

Longstreet's thoughts had been racing ahead of Lee's words to their ramifications. The old man was determined on driving his forehead through the enemy's defenses. His combativeness had not been sated by this afternoon's bloodletting but only aroused further. The images that raced through Longstreet's mind were washed with the blood of Malvern Hill and Fredericksburg. The thought was a twisting knot in his stomach. Yet, everything hung on this supreme risk, and here too everything in his nature and experience rebelled. He almost physically flinched at the thought of another frontal attack against that ridge at the foot of which the dead and wounded lay in heaps. At the same time, he recognized that Lee had allowed him the opportunity to exercize his own plan, despite a major modification – and it had failed, and not only failed but almost resulted in the loss of his whole corps in the very trap he was attempting to spring on the enemy. His troops had fought brilliantly, but he had nearly led them to disaster. It was a dispiriting thought, and for a moment, his supreme confidence in his own judgement slipped. Perhaps the old man was right. This time the direct method might just work if properly organized and supported. This time the deadly equation of modern rifled muskets and artillery just might be overcome. He was already thinking ahead of just how to do it. It would indeed be a bloodbath, everything he had feared, but it just might succeed, and in succeeding end the greater bloodbath that had gaped endlessly ahead of them as the war went on and on. In that moment, he made his decision. He had to do it. There was no one else.

He was pulled out of his thoughts by the realization that everyone was staring at him, especially Lee. 'General Longstreet, I am placing you in command of this attack. You will attack in the morning as soon as practicable.'[19]

1:15 AM, the Peach Orchard

Porter Alexander had just drifted into an exhausted sleep on the softest pillows he could find in the shattered Peach Orchard – two fence rails. He was jolted

---

[18] Wade Hampton, *For the Glory of South Carolina* (D. Appleton, New York, 1881) p.328.
[19]* Longstreet, op.cit.

awake by a young aide of Longstreet, ordering him to headquarters. As he stumbled, still groggy, into Longstreet's tent, the corps commander looked up from the map long enough to send several more aides off into the night. 'Porter, what kept you?' The dazed look on the young man's face told him. He waved his hand. 'Never mind. Sit down.'

He pushed a cup of coffee into Alexander's hands as he smiled to himself that he was getting into the habit of trying to keep young men awake while he himself never seemed to tire. He waited a few moments as the coffee took effect. 'Porter, we are going to attack tomorrow with six divisions straight into the enemy's center. You will co-ordinate the artillery including Hill's and Ewell's Corps.' Pointing to the map, he indicated the front of the attack so the young artilleryman could decide where best to position his guns. Alexander's powers of concentration sharpened with stunning speed. Longstreet thought he could almost hear the gears grinding in his head. Longstreet looked up and suddenly walked out of the tent, saying, 'Don't go away.'

He advanced to meet his three division commanders – McLaws, Law, and Pickett – who had just arrived. 'Major Sorrel, bring us a few chairs.' He allowed himself one of his few smiles as he reached out to shake Pickett's hand. 'George, am I glad to see you.' Pickett, ever hungry for recognition, beamed. McLaws and Law were much less animated, considering the first-class fighting they had been through less than twenty-four hours ago. In their grimy clothes and fatigue, they made a bedraggled contrast to Pickett, in his finery and long oily locks. McLaws sniffed as he joined the group. The only thing he had smelled for a long time had been gunpowder and blood, but something else seemed to be wafting from George. What was it? Too tired to care, he grumped, 'Good God, George, what are you wearing, perfume?'

Feigning shock, Pickett laughed. 'Why, Sir, I will have you know that the delightful fragrance is none other than a gift from Miss Sallie Corbell, my intended. A French cologne, Lilac, I believe.' McLaws just groaned and gratefully settled into one of the chairs.

Longstreet cut to business. 'Gentlemen, we attack tomorrow, with almost the entire army. The 1st Corps, with George's fresh division, will lead the attack.' He could see the consternation and surprise on the faces of McLaws and Law. 'I know, your divisions had a rough time yesterday, but this time the whole corps will go in with three more divisions attacking on our left – Heth, Pender, and Rodes. General Lee is concentrating everything for this attack.' Looking at McLaws and Law, he traced their new positions on the map. 'You will concentrate in and behind the woods that run on either side of the Millerstown Road. I want your men out of that exposed Peach Orchard here and out of that jumble of rocks, what are they called – the Devil's Den, hah! good name for this place, glad we didn't have to fight in it – here at first light. I want the Yankees to see Johnson's Division move in after first light. They should think we are reinforcing the right wing for another attack and hopefully will shift reserves that way.' He went on to explain that General Lee expected the attack to begin at first light. 'We will do our best to be ready by then, but I frankly do not believe Ewell's artillery and infantry can move around the flank fast enough to be ready by then. Ewell has the same problem with daylight. He must finish pulling Johnson off those hills before there's enough light for the Yankees to see him. He's leaving just enough men up there to keep the Yankees thinking the whole division is still there.'

He stood up, putting his fist on the map table. 'Gentlemen, I want it understood that I fully support this attack. Perhaps yesterday or the day before this army had a better chance to maneuver the enemy out of this position, but that chance is gone. If we withdraw now, we will have achieved nothing more on this field than the same bloody draw as Sharpsburg.' He let the words sink in. 'I believe that a strongly supported attack will break through right here. I say strongly supported, Colonel Alexander. This must not be Malvern Hill again. You must silence the enemy's artillery before the infantry begin the assault, and then you must drive the enemy infantry from the crest before our troops arrive.' Looking at his division commanders, he said, 'Your assault must be in depth. I believe that silencing the artillery will only be the first step. The next will be a race of reserves into that breach. That is where the battle will be decided. Whoever holds the crest in strength will win.' [20]

Pickett was all eagerness as Longstreet continued. His division had missed too many of the army's recent victories, and he was as jealous of its honor as of his own. The two other division commanders, once they had got over their initial shock, had just sat there, the set of their jaws and the tired look in their eyes announcing their aversion to more grim business so soon on the heels of yesterday's savagery. Their men had bled away more than life's blood that day; those who had come away unharmed had bled away much of their physical and spiritual store of courage. This took days if not weeks to restore. Still, as Longstreet went on they exchanged glances in growing surprise. Longstreet was not showing any of the obvious reluctance he had demonstrated to a frontal attack just a day ago. If anything, he was resolved in his own powerful, implacable way. It was not enthusiasm; they and he knew what a grim business it would be. Enthusiasm was simply too effervescent and airy a word to describe James Longstreet when this resolve turned into the relentless power of a granite-crushing glacier. This resolve jumped to them like a spark into tinder. As he spun his plan, they were also impressed by its professional thoroughness, which increased their confidence even more. When he finally dismissed them, they hastened to their commands. There was little of the night left, perhaps less than three hours, to cover their concentration. They had to hurry.

---

[20]* Longstreet, op.cit. p.388.

1:30 AM, behind the Fishhook

So much had been done in the frenzied hours since the fighting had died away. Meade had been busy putting the pieces back in place as much as he could before sleep countermanded even the most stern order. The southern end of Cemetery Ridge and Little Round Top were reoccupied. Buford's 1st Cavalry Division was posted on the army's left below Big Round Top to prevent a repetition of Longstreet's near-lethal envelopment. Gregg's 2nd Cavalry Division was posted on the right flank, on the east bank of Rock Creek. Kilpatrick had ridden his 3rd Cavalry Division across country to the sound of the guns and arrived in time to fill in on the right flank, which Gregg had partially abandoned to stop Hampton on the Baltimore Pike. The noise of so many moving men, wagons, and guns had been clearly heard by Johnson's pickets on the other side of Culp's Hill. To many the wish was father to the thought that the noise was all moving in the direction of the Baltimore Pike, signifying a retreat. Ewell's men would not have been comforted had they known that the activity on the Baltimore Pike was, instead, the concentration of reserves. Activity ceased by the early morning hours, as even the most energetic officers sank naturally into sleep. Hancock, Gibbon, and Newton shared the rough floorboards of Gibbon's headquarters ambulance and the tireless Hunt had curled up beside one of his guns. Meade alone of the generals could not sleep, but remained deep in his own thoughts as the early morning hours slipped away. This would be the fifth night, since assuming command, in which he had not surrendered his duties to the demands of his body. Around him and across the valley over a hundred thousand less-burdened men surrendered to the drug of exhaustion. Captain Elisha Hunt Rhodes, with the 2nd Rhode Island, had arrived on the field with the rest of VI Corps, and said it as well as anyone: 'The men threw themselves upon the ground, and oblivious to the dead and dying around us slept the sleep of the weary.' [21]

For thousands on the other side, that sleep was now being broken. The staff officers and aides who had stayed awake as their commanders deliberated now fanned out to the brigades to begin breaking the chain of sleep that would finally lead to hundreds of sergeants and corporals shaking thousands of riflemen from their dreams. It was not too long before the Union pickets on Culp's Hill and Little Round Top began to hear the noise of men and guns in motion.

---

[21] Elisha Hunt Rhodes, *All For the Union: The Civil War Diary of Elisha Hunt Rhodes*, ed. Robert Hunt Rhodes (Orion Press, New York, 1985) p.116.

CHAPTER 12

3rd July 1863
'My men will stay!'

4:36 AM, the Peach Orchard

Longstreet had been right. It was a characteristic which earned him enemies. He had risen thoroughly refreshed after barely an hour's sleep and had begun to pick up the reins of the coming fight even before dawn. Now her blood-red fingers, beginning to streak up the eastern sky, found him in the almost deserted Peach Orchard checking to make sure that his orders had been carried out. Aides brought him the news that Ewell had been late again, just as Longstreet had predicted. Not that the fault was Ewell's, or Johnson's either; it was one of miscalculation. Lee had been far too optimistic in his estimate of how long it would take to pull Johnson's Division off Culp's Hill and move it to the opposite flank. The moon had waned as Johnson tried to bring his men down the hill in the last hour or so of darkness, slowing down the entire process. The movement of the corps' artillery brigade was equally difficult; the absence of the dead Latimer was sorely felt in this move. The army's chief of artillery had done little to assist the transfer of these eighty guns to their new positions.

Shortly after five, General Lee rode out from Spangler's Woods to the shattered Peach Orchard, to find Longstreet conferring with his commanders. He returned their salutes and dismounted. Walking up to the group, he said, 'General Longstreet, pray continue.' Old Peter resumed issuing his orders. Motioning to McLaws and Law, he said, 'You gentlemen will form the flank of the attack, but your own right flank will be protected by Anderson's Division.' Here he paused to look at Lee. 'I expect General Anderson will arrive shortly.' Then turning back to the others, he went on. 'I want you to attack in two lines of two brigades. George, because you will be the center of the entire army's attack, I want you to attack in three waves of two, one, and two brigades. General Trimble will form 3rd Corps on our left and guide on you, George. Those divisions will be as deeply arrayed as ours in order to power this attack until the enemy breaks. You see, gentlemen, the attacking divisions will advance along almost the entire length of the ridge. Anderson will protect one flank anchored on the Devil's Den and Early the other in the town itself. There will be very little scope for the enemy to strike us in the flank with a counterattack. I cannot say the same for his artillery. From what we can see already, his guns will be able to enfilade much of the attack.' And again he returned to a subject that was fast becoming an obsession. 'Which is why, Colonel Alexander, you must clear them away.' [1]

All this time Lee remained silent. McLaws was sensitive to the tension he had seen openly expressed between Lee and Longstreet yesterday morning and looked with some apprehension from one to the other. But now Lee merely listened intently as Longstreet confidently continued. He had no reason to interfere, and in fact was heartened by Old Peter's powerful advocacy of the attack.

When Longstreet had finished, he asked for questions and clearly answered the few that were asked. Then Lee finally spoke. 'Will you excuse us, gentlemen?'

'You have your orders, gentlemen,' said Longstreet. They saluted and departed.

'General, please walk with me,' said Lee. They walked into the low ground east of the Peach Orchard and through a picket line of the 18th Mississippi. The pickets had had the good sense to find sheltered spots wherever the ground offered them, but they were still exposed enough to attract the fire of their counterparts. So they were more than a little amazed to see Lee and Longstreet wander nonchalantly over the same ground being swept by the enemy's bullets. At least they had had the common sense not to walk side by side and stayed about twenty steps apart. One of the pickets more bold than the others spoke up: 'General Lee, you are running a very great risk.' Private Garth Johnson remembered that Lee did not reply but appeared 'calm and serene as if viewing a landscape.' Mesmerized by the presence of the demigods, he remembered clearly Lee's words to Longstreet: 'Mass your artillery behind that hill, and at the signal bring your guns to the top of the ridge and turn them loose.' [2]

More men along the entire front of the planned assault would see the two generals inspecting the ground and refining the details of the attack. Lee, for all his determination and his faith in the invincibility of his infantry, was not blind to the dangers. He closely questioned Brigadier General Wofford, whose brigade had crossed the ridge the day before, as to whether he could do it again. 'No, general, I think not.'

'Why not?'

'Because, General, the enemy have had all night to entrench and reinforce.' [3]

If Wofford's reply took Lee aback, he did not show it. His concern grew, though, as Longstreet and he continued north up Seminary Ridge. As Trimble escorted him past Scales' Brigade, so badly savaged on the first day and which

[1]* James Longstreet, *From Manassas to Gettysburg* (J.B. Lippincott, Philadelphia, 1896), p.388.

[2] George R. Stewart, *Pickett's Charge: A Microhistory of the Final Attack at Gettysburg, July 3, 1863* (Houghton Mifflin Co., Boston, 1987) pp.30–1.

[3] Stewart, ibid, p.31.

had lost more men covering the retreat of 3rd Corps yesterday, he noticed how many of the men in the shrunken ranks had bandaged heads. To Trimble he said, 'Many of those poor boys should go to the rear, they are not fit for duty.' He turned to Trimble, his voice full of sadness, 'I miss in this brigade the faces of many dear friends.' Then riding on, he muttered more to himself than to Trimble, 'The attack must succeed.'[4]

He would have been heartened and immeasurably proud of his Virginians in Pickett's Division. As his doubts and fears grew, their faith was on the level of Constantine's vision of 'By This Sign We Conquer', for Lee was their talisman of victory and their faith in him was utter and absolute. They looked over the long empty space between the ridges and the rising enemy position, bristling with men and guns, and concluded that if General Lee thought this attack was necessary, then they would just have to do it, despite the evidence of common sense and experience. Lieutenant Colonel Rawley Martin, 53rd Virginia, in Armistead's Brigade, was able to put his finger on the magic of that moment:

I believe that if those men had been told: 'This day your lives will pay the penalty of your attack upon the Federal lines,' they would have made the charge just as it was made. There was no straggling, no feigned sickness, no pretence of being overcome by the intense heat; every man felt that it was his duty to make that fight; that he was his own commander, and they would have made the charge without an officer of any description; they only needed to be told what they were expected to do ... They knew their own power, and they knew the temper of their adversary; they had often met before, and they knew the meeting before them would be desperate and bloody.[5]

That sentiment was echoed from the ranks as well. The private soldiers in this war, north and south, were literate and politically aware to a degree unprecedented in history. Sergeant-Major David Johnson of the 7th Virginia, in Kemper's Brigade, remembered:

On our way to the battle field the men were cheerful and seemed to realize their weighty responsibilities and the importance – in fact, the imperative necessity of success, and that probably in their hands rested the destiny of the Republic. If the enemy could be beaten here in his own country, with the political and other troubles North growing out of the draft, etc., it seemed reasonable to suppose that subjugated, down-trodden Maryland would be free, and with her the Confederacy also. These matters were freely discussed by the men in the ranks who seemed fully aware of the gravity of the situation and the absolute

[4] W.H. Swallow, 'The Third Day at Gettysburg', *Southern Bivouac*, 4th February 1886, p.565.
[5] Rawley Martin, 'Rawley Martin's Account', *SHSP*, vol.XXXIX (1911), p.194.

importance of victory, and perfect confidence was expressed in our ability to beat the enemy, if we could meet him on anything like equal terms. Southern prowess, individuality and self-reliance had accomplished wonders in the past, and had become the admiration even of our enemies.[6]

But even amid such resolve, there were doubts. Colonel Joseph Mayo, commander of the 3rd Virginia, remarked to the commander of his sister regiment, the 7th Virginia's Colonel W.T. ('Taz') Patton, that the men had become as 'still and thoughtful as Quakers at a love feast' upon hearing that 'the commanding general had assigned our division the post of honor that day.' 'This news has brought about an awful seriousness with our fellows, Taz.'

Patton replied, 'Yes, and well they may be serious if they really know what is in store for them. I have been up yonder where Dearing is, and looked across at the Yankees.'[7]

If this was the opinion of an experienced officer commanding a fresh regiment, that of men in regiments already savaged in the preceding two days was indicated by a conversation overheard by Captain Robert Bright, one of Pickett's aides, during the cannonade. A Colonel Gordon, an Englishman in Confederate service, who Bright thought was from Pettigrew's neighboring brigade, had come over to visit Pickett. They apparently had met on opposing sides in the San Juan Affair just before the war, when Pickett with one company of infantry had occupied San Juan Island which the British claimed, and defied them to take it. He had for the second time become a national hero. Now Gordon was very emphatically telling his old friend, 'Pickett, my men are not going up to-day.'

Pickett seemed incredulous. 'But, Gordon, they must go up; you must make them go up.'

'You know, Pickett, I will go as far with you as any other man, if only for old acquaintance sake, but my men have until lately been down at the seashore, only under the fire of heavy guns from ships, but for the last day or two they have lost heavily under infantry fire and are very sore, and they will not go up to-day.' Lee may have thought his men were invincible, but enough of them had had their store of courage drained in the last two days to provoke a scene like this. They had seen the field across which they must attack, and thought little of the odds, their own experience of the last two days still painfully fresh.[8]

Longstreet was bending every effort to provide his men an even chance of success. Besides the necessity of throwing every possible man into the attack, he

[6] David E. Johnston, *Four Years a Soldier* (n.p., Princeton, West Virginia, 1887) pp.249–72.

[7] Joseph C. Mayo, 'Pickett's Charge at Gettysburg', *SHSP*, vol. XXXIV (1906) pp.328–35.

[8] Robert A. Bright, 'Pickett's Charge at Gettysburg', *Confederate Volunteer*, vol.XXXI (1903), pp.263–6. Despite his inquiries, Bright could never identify Colonel Gordon or his command.

was equally insistent on bringing every possible gun to bear. He had given Alexander the order to co-ordinate the use of the artillery to support the attack, but that young officer, brilliant as he was, did not have the authority to give orders to the artillery brigades of the other two corps, nor the staff to co-ordinate that support. The army's Chief of Artillery theoretically did. Brigadier General Pendleton was, in fact, doing little to organize the combined fire support from the guns of all three corps for Lee's great attack. Lee had reorganized the army's artillery early that year partly in order to mask Pendleton's patent lack of ability, rather than simply sack him. The organization of the artillery into battalions and brigades subordinated directly to the corps had worked very well, especially since Lee's battles had allowed his corps commanders to fight independently. But here at Gettysburg, for the first time, all the guns would have to be bent to a single effort, and here the army's Chief of Artillery would have to exert an organizing and controlling presence. That is exactly the criticism that Alexander would make:

> There is where the use of a chief of artillery for the army comes in. He visits & views the entire field & should recognize & know how to utilize his opportunities. The chief of each corps only sees his own ground. I never had an idea of the possibility of this being done at the time, for I had but the vaguest notion of where Ewell's Corps was. And Ewell's chief doubtless had as vague ideas of my situation & necessities. But Gen. Lee's chief should have known, & given every possible energy to improve the rare & great chance to the very utmost.[9]

Instead, Pendleton seemed to ride amiably along the field, limiting his efforts to inspecting artillery positions and approving everything that had been done. He had given only the vaguest suggestions to the commander of Ewell's reserve artillery brigade on setting up his thirty guns on the right of the line. He did not even visit Johnson's Division, as it finally moved into position, to see to the placement of its artillery brigade, so badly battered on Benner's Hill the day before. Early's guns remained with him, and Rodes' were already in place. He did, however, surprise Alexander with the offer of nine light field-howitzers that the 2nd Corps' artillery was unable to employ. Alexander jumped at the chance. He ordered the guns placed behind the woods on Seminary Ridge in the safest place he could find to preserve them through the initial bombardment and then produce them to follow the infantry and support them once they had made a lodgement on the enemy ridge. Every one of his seventy-five pieces in direct support of the attack would be needed on the gun line, leaving none mounted with full limbers and caissons to immediately dash across the field.

---

[9] Edward Porter Alexander, *Fighting for the Confederacy: The Personal Recollections of General Edward Porter Alexander* (The University of North Carolina Press, Chapel Hill and London, 1987) p.251.

'I think we can run the machine'

4:00 AM, Cemetery Ridge

Responding to an internal mechanism, or, more likely, depending upon faithful servants, the generals were some of the first to rise just before dawn. Hancock, Newton, and Gibbon climbed out of the ambulance wagon where they had spent the night, stretching to work off the stiffness inflicted by such a hard bed. All three went looking for their staffs in the dark. Hancock and Gibbon picked up speed as the sound of firing swept up over the ridge. Gibbon found Lieutenant Haskell so deep in the arms of Orpheus that he had to grab his foot and shake it violently to wake him up. Haskell looked up through blurry eyes to hear his commander shout, 'Come, don't you hear that?' Haskell was on his feet instantly, pulling on his boots, and then ran over to his horse buckling on his sword and pistol. In moments he had spurred over the ridge. The last of the darkness was being dispelled: 'The serene splendor of the morning now breaking through rifted clouds, and spreading over all the landscape, soon reassured me. Come day of battle, up Rebel hosts, and thunder with your arms; – we are all ready to do and die for the Republic!' [10]

Haskell's enthusiasm was premature. The new light quickly revealed that all the racket was caused by the aggressiveness of the two picket lines on the right front of II Corps. The thousands of Union troops along the ridge were not the least distracted by the bluster along the picket line. They were too long in uniform to be disturbed by minor things and were concentrating on the one big thing dear to the infantry – sleep. Haskell looked across the valley between the ridges and could detect no activity on the Rebel side either. But in the valley itself 'the wounded horses were limping about the field; the ravages of the conflict were still fearfully visible, – the scattered arms and the ground thickly dotted with the dead, – but no hostile foe.' But the chain of command was already active:

> The men were roused early, in order that their morning meal might be out of the way in time for whatever should occur. Then ensued the hum of an army, not in ranks, chatting in low tones, and running about and jostling among each other, rolling and packing their blankets and tents. They looked like an army of rag-gatherers, while shaking these very useful articles of the soldier's outfit, – for you must know that rain and mud in conjunction have not had the effect to make them very clean; and the wear and tear of service have not left them entirely whole. But one could not have told by the appearance of the men, that they were in battle yesterday, and were likely to be again to-day. They packed their knapsacks, boiled their coffee, and munched their hard bread, just as usual, –

---

[10] Frank A. Haskell, *The Battle of Gettysburg* (Wisconsin Historical Commission, Madison, Wisconsin, 1908).

just like old soldiers, who know what campaigning is; and their talk is far more concerning their present employment, – some joke or drollery, – than concerning what they saw or did yesterday.[11]

Senior officers, seeing the easy confidence of the men after two days of the grimmest fighting, took courage from their example, and more than one must have said to himself, with pleased amazement that, finally, after two defeat-ridden years, 'I think we can run the machine.'

Meade's tactical problem was considerably easier than Lee's at that moment. He had only to await an attack from a position of great strength. That did not mean, though, that he and his army had less to do than Lee and his. The day's fighting had thoroughly mixed up the corps of the Army of the Potomac. Parts of each corps seemed to be intermingled with those of all the others due to the necessity of plugging reserves into the holes the Army of Northern Virginia had been punching throughout the afternoon and early evening of the previous day. So the Taneytown Road and the area between the front and Rock Creek had been clogged with troops marching in all directions through the moonlight.

Meade had been entirely serious when he told Gibbon he thought Lee would strike at his center in the morning. That was the key to the realignment of his corps. Williams' Division returned to its positions on Culp's Hill, to hear from Geary's men, as they relieved them, that the last Rebel attack had been a tame affair. XII Corps was now strongly situated. XI Corps was also firmly entrenched on Cemetery Hill, its morale restored by the successful repulse of Early's attack. But, just in case, Meade returned Robinson's Division of I Corps to a position in reserve just behind the hill. Caldwell's Division returned to its place on the left of II Corps along Cemetery Ridge. Meade was about to put in a division of VI Corps on Caldwell's left when he was thoroughly surprised to learn that Ward's Brigade, under the command of its senior regimental commander, had returned to the army by taking a wide circuit south of the fighting. The brigade had taken a heavy loss in the deaths of both Brigadier General Ward and Colonel Berdan. It seemed ironic that Berdan, who had founded the Sharpshooters, should himself have been shot by a Rebel sharpshooter a half-hour after he had disengaged the brigade. The arrival of this intact brigade allowed him to give the fought-out III Corps more of a role than he had originally intended. Meade put the brigade and the rest of Birney's Division in line on the Ridge to the left of Caldwell. Humphreys' Divisions he placed in reserve behind the Ridge. III Corps now occupied some of the same ground Meade had intended it to before Sickles had charged off. Its left brushed the bottom of Little Round Top. To strengthen the lower half of the Ridge line, Hunt had also stationed eight batteries of the Reserve Artillery under Major McGilvery in a grand battery. Finally, the army's left was held by the two surviving divisions of V Corps, stretching over the two Round Tops.

Having told Gibbon where he thought Lee would strike, Meade planned to take advantage of it. He kept VI Corps out of the line as a reserve for just such a purpose. He placed Brigadier General Horatio Wright's 1st Division behind III Corps, Brigadier General Albion Howe's 2nd Division behind II Corps, and Brigadier General Frank Wheaton's 3rd Division along the Baltimore Pike, from where it could support either II, XI or XII Corps. The advantage of this deployment was that the corps could be pulled together quickly or used to plug holes in the line. Crowded together with them were Hunt's batteries of the Reserve Artillery about a half-mile behind Cemetery Hill. Rarely had a commander such a powerful reserve so perfectly positioned behind such a strong position.

4:30 AM, Cemetery Ridge

Brigadier General Hunt awoke just as Longstreet was inspecting the Peach Orchard position. Someone handed him a tin cup of strong army coffee. In moments he could feel the energy coursing through his body and was ready to begin the day. Although the artillery had been put back into fighting shape by the early hours of morning, there was still much to see to. He was determined to control the army's artillery as a single weapon during the day's fighting. Hunt was the type of man who seized as much initiative as he considered necessary to do his job and as much as he could get away with by acting brazenly, as if it had already been granted. The fact that most senior officers had come to recognize that he was the finest artilleryman in North America prepared the way for him. They were eager for his assistance. He had also trained almost all the artillery commanders in the army and had placed loyal but competent men in the corps artillery brigades. There was not one who would not respond immediately and with professional skill to his direction, and they fully expected him to be continuously inspecting their batteries to ensure they knew exactly what was expected. He was a stickler for the accurate but frugal use of ammunition, his 'Ghost Train' notwithstanding. He believed fundamentally that carefully aimed shots, although slower, were infinitely more effective than rapid, poorly aimed fire. He also believed, almost as a religious tenet, in conserving fire for the supreme moment. He put it succinctly:

> It was of the first importance to have our line in the best possible condition to meet the assault, to which the cannonade would be a mere subordinate preliminary; and with that view to subject his troops from the first moment of their advance and whilst beyond musketry range to a heavy concentrated cross fire of

artillery in order to break their formation, check their impulse and bring them in as disordered a condition and with as much loss as possible to the point of attack, and my orders were given specially with this view.[12]

By ten o'clock Hunt and his senior aide were riding up Culp's Hill to inspect the situation, beginning an inspection of the entire Federal line, ascertaining that all the batteries were 'in good condition and well-supplied with ammunition.' Finding little amiss in the guns supporting XII Corps, they rode back down onto the Baltimore Pike and then to Cemetery Hill. The strong batteries posted on East Cemetery Hill the day before still faced north in the direction of Early's two failed assaults. There he met Colonel Wainwright, and after a brief conversation in which both men agreed that a third assault was unlikely from that direction, ordered all but five batteries returned to the Artillery Reserve. On the western side of the hill, he inspected the seven batteries of Major Thomas Osborn's XI Corps artillery brigade. Among the rows of guns facing west towards Seminary Ridge, he stood to examine the opposing treeline, still in deep shadows. It remained silent and still. As he moved further south along the line, he could plainly see the massing of Ewell's guns opposite the Union left. Hunt began to give orders

to the batteries and to the chiefs of artillery not to fire at small bodies, nor to allow their fire to be drawn without promise of adequate results; to watch the enemy closely, and when he opened to concentrate the fire of all their guns on one battery at a time until it was silenced; under all circumstances to fire deliberately, and to husband their ammunition as much as possible.[13]

'The trouble is to *stay* there'

11:00 AM, Seminary Ridge

At just that same moment Porter Alexander was also worrying about ammunition. As he tallied the guns that would be directed against the enemy, the calculations of ammunition consumption were frightening. In addition to his own seventy-five guns, 3rd Corps had wheeled sixty-three into line on his left, to which were added Rodes' sixteen. On his right were Colonel Thompson Brown's thirty guns and the nine light howitzers from 2nd Corps, giving a total of 193 guns. He had received a note from Longstreet instructing him to determine the right moment for the assault and to give Pickett the instructions accordingly. Pickett's advance would be the signal for the divisions on his right and left to advance at the same time. Alexander felt the weight of the world crashing onto his shoulders. As he put it, 'If the assault was to be made on

---

[12] Henry Hunt to Bachelder, 20th January 1873, *Bachelder Papers*, vol.I, pp.428–9.
[13] *OR*, vol.XXVII, part I, p.238.

General Lee's judgement it was all right, but I did not want it made on mine.'
He wrote back to Longstreet laying out his dilemma.

> GENERAL: I will only be able to judge of the effect of our fire on the enemy by
> his return fire, for his infantry is but little exposed to view and the smoke will
> obscure the whole field. If . . . there is any alternative to this attack, it should be
> carefully considered before opening our fire, for it will take all the artillery
> ammunition we have left to test this one thoroughly, and, if the result is
> unfavorable, we will have none left for another effort. And even if this is entirely
> successful, it can only be so at a very bloody cost.

Longstreet's reply glossed over Alexander's concerns and simply reiterated his
instructions to advise Pickett when 'the moment arrives'. This merely deepened
Alexander's anxieties. He discussed them with Brigadier General A.R. Wright,
who was with him when Longstreet's note arrived. Wright, whose brigade had
broken over the ridge only to be thrown back by the enemy's reserves, was not
encouraging. 'It is not so hard to *go* there as it looks; I was nearly there with my
brigade yesterday. The trouble is to *stay* there. The whole damn Yankee army is
there in a bunch.' This determined Alexander to send the nine howitzers he had
in reserve ahead of Pickett, to help clear the way rather than trail behind him,
despite the vastly increased risk to the guns. To his consternation, his courier
was unable to find the guns were they had been left. Only after the battle would
he discover that Pendleton, having given the howitzers to Alexander, had
decided to use them elsewhere. He had not given a thought to informing
Alexander of the change.[14]

The lack of a single controlling hand became more and more evident to
Alexander as the morning wore on. At about eleven o'clock a furious artillery
duel started between Hill's massed batteries and the Union guns on Cemetery
Hill, begun by the aggressive contest between the pickets over possession of the
Bliss Farm buildings and especially the barn in the valley between the ridges.
Alexander shook his head in disbelief at the complete waste of ammunition.
The firing lasted a full hour and only died away around noon after General
Gibbon sent a detachment to burn the barn. It further occurred to Alexander
that the transfer of 2nd Corps' artillery to his right deprived the attack of the
ability to enfilade the Union artillery massed on Cemetery Hill. Although
Latimer's Battalion had been roughly handled attempting to slug it out with
that same concentration the day before, enfilade fire was potentially far more
effective because it ploughed through the length of the formation. The guns on
Seminary Ridge, on the other hand, could at best only strike their opposing line,

---

[14] E. Porter Alexander, 'The Great Charge and Artillery Fighting at Gettysburg', vol.III (*The
Century Magazine*, 1888) pp.362–3.

nowhere more than one gun deep. In disgust at the undisciplined expenditure of scarce ammunition, Alexander sent the order quickly up and down his gun line forbidding anyone to take part in the duel.

12:00 noon, from Emmitsburg to Cashtown

To the south of Gettysburg, along a line running from Cashtown in Pennsylvania to Emmitsburg in Maryland, cavalry forces of both armies were already in action. Lee had ordered Robertson, who had just arrived in Cashtown with both brigades, to detach Jones' command to guard the army's rear, the cavalry division's trains, and the approaches to the passes through the Catoctin Mountains, the army's escape route in case of a reverse. Jones was ordered to the small village of Fairfield, half-way between Emmitsburg and Gettysburg. Founded by English colonists and named for their departed village, Fairfield was a charming dot in the lush foothills of the Catoctins that spilled over the Maryland line barely a few miles to the north. It boasted an imposing stone inn built a hundred years before and a new red brick Lutheran church next door.

Fairfield was also the destination of the 600 men of the 6th US Cavalry of Colonel Wesley Merritt's Reserve Cavalry Brigade of Buford's 1st Cavalry Division. Around noon Merritt had been ordered from Emmitsburg to attack and annoy the enemy's rear. He detached the 6th under the command of Major Samuel Starr to drive north through Fairfield to intercept an enemy wagon train while he took the rest of his brigade up the Taneytown Road. Also detached from his command were a hundred troopers of the 6th Pennsylvania Cavalry, much to the reluctance of its commander. But the orders from General Meade were clear: 'You will detach a body of one hundred cavalrymen to operate under the independent command of Captain Ulric Dahlgren.' [15] Young Dahlgren was already known to the 6th Pennsylvania; he had rallied them to lead a charge at Brandy Station where they had distinguished themselves. He had suggested to Merritt that his detail come from this regiment. As soon as Merritt agreed, he was gone with them in a cloud of dust in the direction of Waynesboro.

Starr's scouts rode through Fairfield shortly before one in the afternoon and found its citizens strangely uninformative about the presence of the enemy in the area. When the 6th rode through the village, Starr got to the bottom of their silence by reaching down and grabbing a worthy-looking individual by the lapels, and raising him off the ground to eye-level. Starr shook him enough to rattle his teeth, which produced a flood of information. Yes, the Rebels had been through here yesterday, but they promised to kill anyone who passed information to the Federal troops. They also had foraging wagons in the valley between Fairfield and Cashtown; some had been in the village only an hour

---

[15]* *OR*, vol.XXVII, part I, p.1072.

before and headed back toward Cashtown. With a growl of disgust, Starr tossed the man into the mud of the street and hurried his regiment forward. Just north of the town, the roads from Gettysburg and Cashtown joined. Starr sent scouts in both directions. Those from the direction of Cashtown were back in fifteen minutes with a tow-headed farm boy riding a buggy horse. He babbled about how his papa had sent him off when a neighbor had brought the news that Rebel cavalry were coming up the road.

The boy had been right. Jones' Brigade was approaching the intersection with the 7th Virginia in the lead followed by the 6th and 11th. The Faulkner brothers were in the middle of the column, and, as farmers, were admiring the lush but narrow valley with its high hills and its tidy, rich farms lining the sides. They particularly admired the mile after mile of post and plank fences which lined the road and intersecting lanes. For one thing, the fences were intact; there were not a lot of surviving fences left in the upper half of Virginia after two years of war. The more common Virginia or snake fence, which zigzagged around farmers fields, had simply disappeared. The post and plank fences were now just strings of lonely posts, their planks long since stripped away for firewood by the troops of both sides. Up ahead, along those intact Pennsylvania fences, Starr's dismounted cavalry lay in hiding, their carbines cradled in their arms. Another large group were mounted further back down the road. As the Confederates approached, Starr sent men through gates on the left and right that allowed them to strongly secure their flanks along another fence and in a peach orchard. Starr was outnumbered at least three to one but had no way of knowing. In any case, he was confident he held the advantage of surprise and that the enemy could not easily or quickly deploy superior numbers because of the fences.

He was immediately proved right. On seeing the enemy, 'Grumble' Jones ordered the 7th Virginia in the lead to charge straight down the road, hoping that dash and momentum would bounce him out of his stronger position. The 7th was met with the concentrated fire of several hundred carbines, and the head of the column crumbled as horses and men went down in a flailing jumble. The road was clogged with the dead and dying. Unable to maneuver, the rest panicked and stampeded to the rear, leaving behind thirty dead, wounded, and captured. Jones was beside himself in rage as they thundered past him, deaf to his curses. Turning to the 6th Virginia behind him, he shouted, 'Shall one —————— regiment of Yankees whip my whole brigade?'

The men of the 6th Virginia cried, 'Let *us* try them!'[16] Colonel Flournoy drew his saber, and with a roar the Bloody Sixth in turn charged down the road into the deadly crossfire. Their charge was so impetuous that the 6th US barely

[16] William N. McDonald, *A History of the Laurel Brigade*, ed. Bushrod C. Washington (Mrs Kate S. McDonald, Baltimore, 1907) pp.155–6.

had time to fire, though when they did it was to deadly effect. Adjutant John Allen at the head Virginians went down, but his men never slackened their pace as they galloped by, shooting at the enemy along the fences with their pistols and slashing down with their sabers. Elements of the 7th also charged again on both field sides of the road. The head of the 6th Virginia's column leapt the few horses that went down in the road and crashed into Starr's mounted force. Lieutenant R.R. Duncan, Company B, charged at Starr and crushed his skull with a saber blow. Then the Federal second-in-command went down. Duncan sabered his way through the blue ranks in frenzy, hacking down four more troopers, twisting the last out of his saddle.[17]

For a moment the Union troopers held and fought back. Private Patrick Kelly, Company H, spurred his horse towards the colors of the 6th Virginia. He shot down two of the enemy who barred his way, but his pistol misfired as he pulled the trigger point-blank on the color-bearer. In a rage, he struck the man across the face with the pistol and then grabbed the color staff, but the Rebel would not let go. For a few seconds they struggled over the staff, even as the three Faulkner brothers rode up shooting at Kelly or swinging their sabers. They should have killed him; all were crack shots and handy with the saber, but neither lead nor steel so much as touched him. However, one of Tom Faulkner's slashes cut his reins through, and Sam's bullet hit Kelly's horse, which bolted away tearing the staff from his grip.[18] As Kelly escaped, the rest of the 6th US was breaking and racing to the rear down the road. Elsewhere Confederate troopers jumped the fences to get at their dismounted foes with saber and pistol. Many of these were running across the road, but more just threw down their carbines and raised their arms. Jones rode up with the 11th Virginia as Flournoy led the pursuit. Dead men and horses clogged the road and others lay crumpled along both sides of the fences. Jones' men were chasing surviving blue troopers across the fields. He laughed out loud that the enemy were behaving normally. Besides thirty-four dead and wounded 184 had been taken prisoner, in a victory reaped mostly by the hands of the 'Bloody Sixth'.[19]

The citizens of Fairfield had mingled in the streets whispering at the sound of the gunfire to the north. They retreated to their homes as this time ambulances instead of foraging wagons began driving into town. The Rebels commandeered the Lutheran church as a hospital, filling it with the wounded of the 6th US and 6th and 7th Virginia Cavalry.

---

[17] *OR*, vol.XXVII, part II, p.756.

[18] *OR*, vol.XXVII, part I, p.949.

[19] *OR*, vol.XXVII, part I, p.185; part II, p.752; in part I, the Official Returns of the battle list 242 missing and captured against the 184 claimed by Jones.

12:00 noon, Spangler's Woods

Lee and Longstreet had been seen by thousands of men already that morning as they made two complete inspections of the entire line. To many of them, Lee had seemed far more apprehensive than usual, but they expected their generals to worry. Now he and Longstreet were going over the plan of attack for the last time with the division commanders. Pickett, McLaws, and Law of Longstreet's own corps were on hand, as was Trimble, who would be commanding the other three divisions, represented by Pettigrew, Lane, and Rodes. These seven men and Longstreet would make the charge and four of them were battlefield replacements. All four were able men who could be relied upon to press the attack home. Lee had insisted that Longstreet not expose himself, but the Georgian had put his cards on the table. 'General Lee, if this charge does not succeed, it will not make a whit of difference if I survive or not. It must succeed, and the only way I can make sure it does is to be with it and not at my headquarters.'

Lee relented. Longstreet was simply stating the obvious truth – that Lee had staked the survival of the army and the Confederacy on this charge. That truth with its awful weight was settling on his shoulders. Lee was mentally tough enough to bear it despite the pain that been running up his left arm and through his jaw all morning. The vitality he had found the day before seemed to have entirely drained away, and now the dullness had returned, dragging at every thought and step. Longstreet, at last, had stopped balking and was his old self again, throwing his titan-like energy into Lee's plan and making it happen. It did much to lessen the stress he had been under. He let him take charge of the briefing.

'Gentlemen, let no-one mistake the importance of this attack. We are throwing six divisions against the Army of the Potomac on the high ground. The fate of our country rests on this day. The men know that Baltimore and Washington and home lay just over the crest of that ridge.' Longstreet paused for a moment. The entire group was utterly focused, yet strangely each man's thoughts were flying across the valley, flaring in crimson on the crest, then sailing in victorious exultation beyond, into Northern cities, and then back down Southern roads, and finally racing through a gate in a picket fence, up steps, and through a front door, and into the arms of a woman, face wet with tears.

He began again, and their far-away thoughts evaporated suddenly, leaving only a small ache that each man tucked away as he concentrated on the work ahead. 'The signal to begin the attack will be two cannon shots in rapid succession. Pickett will lead off the attack, and the divisions on either flank will guide on him. You will guide on that clump of trees directly across from us.' Gentlemen, I want to be perfectly clear on the timing of the attack. We cannot afford to hit the enemy piecemeal. Hancock will just shift his reserves around like he did yesterday, and his II Corps is tough enough as it is. Everyone will strike the enemy at the same time.' He went on to explain that McLaws and Law's Divisions would begin as soon as Pickett's brigades were half-way to the red barn[20] in the center of the valley. Their divisions would wheel out of the woods and hook onto Pickett's right just as they passed on either side of the red barn. Since Law was on the left, he would wheel out from behind the woods west of the Wheatfield, to be followed by McLaws coming out of the Trostle Woods. Pickett's Division would do a series of left obliques that would center it on the aiming point of the attack, the Copse of Trees on Cemetery Ridge directly opposite from where they were all standing. Pettigrew and Lane would align themselves with Pickett and strike just north of the Copse of Trees, into the angle formed by the low stone walls on the ridge. Rodes would wait for Lane's Division to come up to where his brigades were already positioned in a sunken road and then step out to attack Cemetery Hill. 'With luck and a tight rein held by each of you and your brigade commanders, we will strike them all at once – over thirty thousand men in twenty-seven brigades supported by almost two hundred guns.[21] Gentlemen, no such single attack has ever been attempted on this continent.' He did not draw any parallels to Malvern Hill and Fredericksburg.

'Almost the whole army will be in this attack. Early and Johnson's Divisions on either flank will demonstrate in front of the hills to draw attention away from the main attack. General Hampton will strike the enemy in the rear from the north-west. Hopefully, these efforts will confuse Meade just long enough to distract him from our attack on his center and draw his reserves to the flanks and rear. Anderson's Division, now commanded by Wilcox, will be the army reserve under General Lee's direct control and will be in support of this attack.'

Again he paused. 'Gentlemen, it is an honor to be with you on this field today.' One or two of them detected a faint catch in his voice, but he simply stood back, leaving the stage for Lee.

'We have been on many fields together, you and I, gentlemen,' began Lee. 'And now we are on what I hope is the final field, the one that will justify the

---

[20] The Codori Farm.

[21] Approximate strengths of the divisions in Longstreet's Charge on 3rd July 1863:

Divisions/Bdes	Strengths	No. of Bdes
Law (Hood)	5,000	4
McLaws	4,900	4
Pickett	9,700	5
Pettigrew (Heth)	4,500	4
Lane (Pender)	4,800	4
Rodes	4,700	5
Sanders	1,500	1 (Brigade only)
Totals	35,100	27

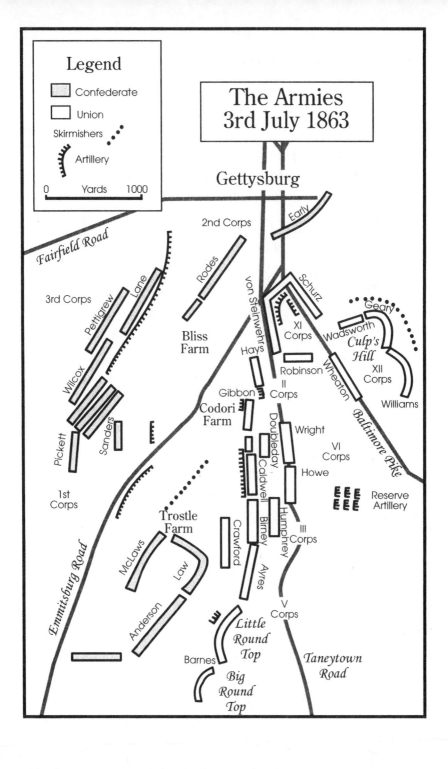

sacrifices on so many others. Once again, as always, we must do our duty. We can do no more.' His words had held them for that magic moment and more than one struggled to hold back a tear. Then he stepped forward, 'I want to shake each man's hand here.' First he shook Isaac Trimble's hand, and the gruff old soldier rasped out, 'Thank you, Sir, for this opportunity.' He stood back and saluted. Lee passed from man to man, looking each in the eye with that immense dignity and manliness, and above all that genuine humanity, that had made him an object of worship for untold thousands. Every man was humbled. Even Longstreet fought down his lingering inner aversion to this attack and eagerly grasped Lee's hand. Only Pickett retained his jaunty disposition, snapping as gracious a salute as any cavalier at the Restoration court of Charles II. But as they walked away, Lee's heart was pounding in his chest as he felt an overwhelming sense of doom.

12:00 noon, Cemetery Ridge

Meade dismounted slowly from his horse Baldy at his headquarters in Widow Leister's house. He had hardly slept and had not eaten more than a cracker for twenty-four hours or more. He had just returned from the right of the line, where he had gone to observe the fight for the Bliss Farm and to ensure that positions were strengthened and the troops reformed properly. In riding down the line he had found Hancock and discussed the 'probability of an attack by the enemy on the center of the Union line, and decided, in the event of such an attack being made and repulsed, to advance the Fifth and Sixth Corps against the enemy's flank.' [22] Hancock had emphatically agreed, but now Meade was having second thoughts. Perhaps the left was more threatened; after all, it was the left which had been turned the day before, and the saddle at the end of the ridge on the left had been the only point on the ridge which the enemy had overrun. He was chewing on this thought when Gibbon entered in search of him. He gathered that the army commander had neither slept nor breakfasted and urged him to join him at his headquarters for lunch. Meade demurred, saying that he should stay close to his headquarters in case of an emergency. Gibbon would not relent and suggested that it was Meade's duty to eat to maintain his strength, and besides, Gibbon's own headquarters was only a few hundred feet away. Meade's staff would know where to find him. Finally he added that there was chicken stew simmering in the pot, boiled potatoes, and bread – and with a smile Meade was convinced. As they left the house, Gibbon joked that he was sure no money had changed hands in his orderly's acquisition of these birds.

It was a relaxed company that rose when Meade and Gibbon arrived.

---

[22] George Gordon Meade, *The Battle of Gettysburg* (George Gordon Meade, Ambler, Pennsylvania, 1924) p.89.

Hancock was there, as was Gibbon's staff, including Lieutenant Haskell. The only two stools available had been allotted to Hancock and Gibbon, but the headquarters cook, always handy, promptly provided a cracker box for the army commander to sit on. The cook served an enormous pan of stewed chicken accompanied by boiled potatoes, butter, and a gargantuan loaf of bread acquired from a soldier too tired to carry it further. It was a perfect moment, as the party ate its first good meal in twenty-four or more hours with relish. Many would remember the meal and the good company forever. And, of course, when good food is served in the field, guests seemed to automatically arrive. Generals Newton and Pleasanton with their aides rode up and were promptly invited to join the party. The sun was hot overhead and the air still and sultry, adding to the sense of almost sleepy relaxation as the generals squeezed under the shade of a particularly small tree to enjoy their cigars and talk about the day's prospects. The talk was good-natured. Newton pulled Gibbon's leg by saying how 'this young North-Carolinian' was becoming 'arrogant and above his position because he commanded a corps.' Gibbon retorted with a laugh that Newton had not been a corps commander himself long enough to judge Gibbon's condition. Meade added that he would save Gibbon from a swelled head by allowing Hancock to resume command of his corps and Gibbon his division. He mused that he now thought that the enemy would strike the left of the ridge rather than the center as he had predicted the night before to Gibbon and only this morning to Hancock. He cited the arrival of an enemy division on the left that morning. Hancock, for his part, continued to maintain that they would strike II Corps' line.[23]

'Go to Hell, General!'
1:00 PM, Little Round Top

Hunt had been too busy on his rounds of inspection to stop for a leisurely lunch. As he rode his horse Bill over the ridge,

> a magnificent display greeted my eyes. Our whole front for two miles was covered by batteries already in line or going into position. They stretched – apparently in one unbroken mass – from opposite the town to the Peach Orchard, which bounded the view to the left, the ridges of which were planted thick with cannon. Never before had such a sight been witnessed on this continent, and rarely, if ever, abroad.

It was obvious that the enemy was preparing a single great effort that would be preceded by a long and deadly cannonade. Hunt was convinced that all the

---

[23] Haskell, op.cit.

Union artillery facing west, whether of the corps or the Artillery Reserve, should respond under a similar single direction. 'It was of the first importance to subject the enemy's infantry, from the first moment of their advance, to such a cross-fire of our artillery as would break their formation, check their impulse, and drive them back, or at least bring them to our lines in such condition as to make them an easy prey.'[24] Since time would not permit him to consult Meade, as he rode down the line he instructed the chiefs of artillery and battery commanders to hold their fire for the first fifteen or twenty minutes of the enemy's cannonade. They were then to concentrate their fire against the most effective of the enemy's batteries. They were to fire with the most slow and careful aim in order to have enough ammunition left after the enemy had exhausted his to then concentrate on breaking the infantry assault.

As he rode Bill up Little Round Top, he glanced at his pocket-watch. It was almost one o'clock. He dismounted and walked among the six 10-pounder parrot rifles of Lieutenant Charles E. Hazlett's Battery D, 5th US Artillery. From that vantage point, he could see the massed Confederate infantry lying prone in a swale near the Staub Farm west of the Emmitsburg Road, and movement behind the woods north of the Wheatfield, and the glint of bayonets. As he and Hazlett were discussing when the enemy would act they heard the sharp report of two cannons in quick succession. One, two, three seconds, and the entire Confederate artillery exploded in unison. The fire had been delivered with such precision that it sent a single rolling shock wave over the entire Union line. Hunt and Hazlett felt it even on Little Round Top.

The shock wave was felt in Gettysburg as well. The wounded Union prisoners held in the Gettysburg train depot there were kept informed of the battle by a lookout in the cupola, who came down to announce that the 'The Johnnies were moving.' Sergeant James P. Sullivan of the 6th Wisconsin remembered that the double report of the two Confederate guns had come then, followed by 'such a roar of artillery as I have ever heard before or since. Bull Run was not a patching; the ground shook, and the depot building fairly trembled. Our fellows answered just as loud, and it seemed as if the last day had come.'[25]

On Cemetery Ridge itself, the luncheon party at Gibbon's headquarters was shaken out of its sense of well-being by the crack of the two Confederate shots as every eye turned in the direction of the sound. Lieutenant Haskell remembered that every sense became instantly alert.

[24] Henry J. Hunt, 'The Third Day at Gettysburg', *Battles and Leaders of the Civil War: Retreat From Gettysburg*, ed. Robert Underwood Johnson and Clarence Clough Buel (*The Century Magazine*, 1888) pp.371–2.
[25] William J.K. Beaudot and Lance J. Herdegen, eds., *An Irishman in the Iron Brigade: The Civil War Memoirs of James P. Sullivan, Sergt., Company K, 6th Wisconsin Volunteers* (Fordham University Press, New York, 1993) p.100.

In an instant, before a word was spoken, as if that was the signal gun for general work, loud, startling, booming, the report of gun after gun, in rapid succession, smote our ears, and their shells plunged down and exploded all around us. – We sprang to our feet. – In briefest time the whole Rebel line to the West, was pouring out its thunder and its iron upon our devoted crest. The wildest confusion for a few moments obtained among us. The shells came bursting all about. – The servants ran terror-stricken for dear life and disappeared. – The horses, hitched to the trees or held by the slack hands of orderlies, neighed out in fright, and broke away and plunged riderless through the fields. . . . I had time to see one of the horses of our mess wagon struck and torn by shell ; – the pair plunge, – the driver has lost the rein, – horse, driver, and wagon go into a heap by a tree. – Two mules close at hand, packed with boxes of ammunition, are knocked all to pieces by a shell. – Gnl. Gibbon's groom has just mounted his horse, and is starting to take the General's to him, when the flying iron meets him and tears open his breast, – he drops dead, and the horses gallop away.

The only calm creature was Haskell's horse, tied to a tree and coolly munching its oats.[26] Hancock's assistant-adjutant watched as the

air shrieked with flying shot, the bursting shells sent their deadly fragments down in showers upon the rocky ridge and over the plain behind; the earth was thrown up in clouds of dust as the monstrous missiles buried themselves in the ground, or glanced from the surface to take a new and, perchance, more fatal flight; on every hand caissons exploded, struck by iron balls, which but a half-minute before had lain in the limber-chests of batteries a mile away. All that is hideous in war seemed to have gathered itself together, to burst in one fell tornado upon Cemetery Ridge.

The effects of this unparalleled cannonade, as seen by the staff galloping along the line, were, on one side, very great, on the other, comparatively slight. The plain behind the ridge was almost immediately swept of all camp followers and the unordered attendants of an army. Headquarters and ammunition wagons went to the rear with prodigious zeal; a body of stragglers and men casually absent from their regiments poured down the Baltimore road to the rear; even General Meade's headquarters were broken up by the intolerable bombardment as the non-combatants sought safety in flight, while the commander and staff mounted their horses in haste and sought safety nearer the line of battle. On the contrary, looking to the front, one saw only thin lines of infantry crouching behind the stone walls or clinging prone to the ground, the musket clutched tightly in each soldier's hand as he waited for the great charge which he well knew was to follow.[27]

---

[26] Haskell, op.cit.

[27] Francis A. Walker, *History of the Second Army Corps in the Army of the Potomac* (Charles Scribner's Sons, New York, 1886) p.292.

John Gibbon with his aide, Lieutenant Haskell, walked through his division positions with an air of total calm. The smoke from the II Corps batteries, rapidly returning the enemy's fire, hovered just above the ground so thickly that they could only see the legs of the gunners rushing to serve their pieces. As he reached the line just to the left of Cushing's Battery, he found Colonel Webb sitting on the ground coolly observing the enemy's fire. He asked the question that was praying on everyone's mind. 'What does this mean?' Webb just shook his head in silence. As they watched, one of Hancock's aides rode up to ask them, for the corps commander, what they thought was the meaning of this terrific cannonade. Gibbon replied that it was a 'prelude either to an attack or a retreat.' [28]

In one of the most evocative moments of the battle, Hancock was riding behind the line at this time, when he was presented with probably the most incredible scene of the entire war. He had come upon a six-year-old girl, all alone, barely able to carry the heavy rifle in her little arms. He stopped as she tried and failed to lift the heavy piece, and quickly dismounted to catch her as she fell in tears into his arms. She choked out the words, 'My papa's dead, but here's my papa's gun.'

This child had stumbled upon the field to offer what she could to the Republic. Hancock was in tears in later years as he described the moment: 'I never recall that brave chit of a child's offering to our cause without feelings of the deepest reverence.' [29]

Despite Hunt's instructions, enough Federal guns were replying to make life hell for the gray infantry as they waited flat on their bellies in the woods or just behind, laying in the heat of the open fields. Although the Union artillery was more accurate, still a large number of shells had struck the woods or the fields behind, as they engaged the Confederate guns in the greatest artillery duel of the war. Splintered limbs and trunks sent jagged wooden canister into their packed ranks along with the pieces of shell and round shot. Sergeant-Major David Johnston, 7th Virginia, Kemper's Brigade, was experiencing flat on his face in an open field what Sergeant Sullivan of the 6th Wisconsin was only feeling in the Gettysburg train depot:

The very atmosphere seemed broken by the rush and crash of projectiles, solid shot, shrieking, bursting shells. The sun, but a moment before so brilliant, was now almost darkened by smoke and mist enveloping and shadowing the earth,

[28] John Gibbon, *Personal Recollections of the Civil War* (G.P. Putnam's Sons, New York, 1928) pp.146–53.
[29] *Grand Army Review*, February 1886, scrapbook of newspaper clippings about Winfield Scott Hancock, Pennsylvania State Library, Harrisburg; cited in Glenn Tucker, *Hancock the Superb* (Morningside Press, Dayton, Ohio, 1980) p.148.

and through which came hissing and shrieking, fiery fuses and messengers of death, sweeping, plunging, cutting, ploughing through our ranks, carrying mutilation, destruction, pain, suffering and death in every direction. Turn your eyes whithersoever you would, and there was to be seen at almost every moment of time, guns, swords, haversacks, human flesh and bone, flying and dangling in the air, or bouncing above the earth, which now trembled beneath us as if shaken by an earthquake.[30]

Back on Little Round Top, Hunt had a magnificent view of the spectacle. The entire Confederate firing line was obscured by smoke, 'through which the flashes were incessant, whist the air seemed filled with shells, whose sharp explosion, with the hurtling of their fragments, formed a running accompaniment to the deep roar of the guns.' Hunt watched the Rebel gunners walking out ahead of their guns and the thick stationary clouds of smoke to watch the effect of their shots. He quickly mounted Bill and road down the hill and over the ridge to the Reserve Artillery to order up fresh batteries and ammunition once the enemy's cannonade had ceased. To his surprise he found most of the enemy's shells were sailing forty feet overhead to land on the crest or just behind the ridge, well out of the way of his batteries which he had hidden on the forward slope. On the other side of the ridge where he expected to find the reserve guns and trains, there were only a few messengers, dead animals, and the smoking remains of a dozen caissons. The mass of batteries and ammunition wagons had been the recipient of enough of the enemy fire coming 100 feet over the ridge to create pandemonium among the densely-packed batteries and trains. Brigadier General Tyler had just returned from the ridge himself when his own horse was killed. He got to his feet and ordered the command moved far enough to the east to get out of the enemy's fire, then collapsed from sunstroke. Under the command of Captain James M. Robertson, the guns and trains quickly 'decamped' to safety just of range.[31]

Convinced that the Reserve was safe and still at hand, Hunt spurred Bill back over the ridge, where he joined McGilvery's guns. On the way he saw the infantry lying on the reverse slope near the crest, for the most part but not entirely protected from the enemy's fire. 'As I passed along, a bolt from a rifle-gun struck the ground just in front of a man of the front rank, penetrated the surface and passed under him, throwing him "over and over." He fell behind the rear rank, apparently dead'.[32] All along the ridge, the infantry lay in open ranks under arms 'behind their works, behind every rock, in every ditch,

[30] Johnston, op.cit. pp.249–72.
[31] OR, vol.XXVII, part I, p.1021.
[32] Hunt, op.cit. p.374.

wherever there is any shelter, they hug the ground, silent, quiet, unterrified, little harmed.'[33]

Hunt was pleased that McGilvery's guns had coolly kept silent for a full fifteen minutes before slowly and deliberately returning fire. To have engaged the enemy with a similar cannonade would have done nothing but reveal the hidden positions of his batteries, but the careful fire of individual guns masked their concentration. On II Corps' front, Hancock was having nothing to do with such technical calculation. Probably the finest battlefield commander in the Union Army, Hancock had his fingers constantly on the pulse of the fighting man's morale. And that reading told him that the infantry must feel they are not being left alone to face the cannonade; that the artillery is there actively supporting them. He had already countermanded Hunt's order to hold their fire to his own II Corps batteries, and now rode up to McGilvery's right flank batteries and ordered them to begin firing. When several battery commanders objected, he unleashed a stream of profanity, promising to arrest them all. The report of their guns now attracted McGilvery, who had the showdown of showdowns with Hancock. McGilvery, an old sea captain and no stranger to strong language, which he now proceeded to use, told Hancock that he had no authority over the Reserve Artillery, and ended his tirade with a sure-to-infuriate 'Go to hell, General!' The confrontation must have ended in McGilvery's favor, because the guns remained silent until Hancock rode away. But it was a case of bolting the barn door; their positions had already been revealed and now attracted a storm of fire that quickly disabled guns and began wreaking havoc with the caissons and limbers behind. Only then did McGilvery authorize the batteries to begin a slow and careful counter-battery fire.[34]

On Cemetery Hill a more civil and fruitful conversation was taking place. Hunt had been in conversation with the XI Corps commander when Major Osborn, the corps chief of artillery, suggested that they slacken their artillery fire to give the enemy the impression they had been silenced in order to lure the enemy into the attack. Hunt then asked Osborn, gunner to gunner, 'If you stopped your fire, would your men stay here?' Osborn replied that they would if the infantry would, to which Hunt expressed doubts. Howard cut in. He had had enough of criticism of his corps, especially after last night's action. 'I support Major Osborn's idea of stopping the artillery fire, and my men will stay!'[35]

Hunt wasted no time, and, riding down the line, ordered the batteries to

---

[33] Byrne and Weaver, op.cit. p.149.

[34] David Schultz, 'Double Canister At Ten Yards': The Federal Artillery and the Repulse of Pickett's Charge (Rank and File Publications, Redondo Beach, California, 1995) p.28.

[35] Thomas W. Osborn, The Eleventh Corps Artillery At Gettysburg: The Papers of Maj. Thomas W. Osborn, ed. Herb S. Crumb (Emdmonston Publishing, Hamilton, New York, 1990) pp.37, 72–3; cited in Schultz, op.cit. pp.29–30.

cease fire and fresh batteries to replace those out of ammunition or fought-out. The whole front was quickly alive with batteries pulling off the ridge.

As the cannonade seemed to reach a crescendo, Hancock was on the left of his corps line. As a regimental band began to play *Star Spangled Banner*, he found something so stirring in the music that he lifted his hat in admiration. He then began to ride down the line, according to a staff officer, to show every man that 'his general was behind them in the storm,' just as he had sought to overrule Hunt to encourage them. The men were more than encouraged as they watched him ride with total unconcern through the shot and shell that had caused each of them to burrow into the thin soil with their buttons. It was a scene none of them would forget, each one thinking that at any moment the general would be struck down. But on he rode in complete safety like a modern Achilles, despite his large size and conspicuous action. Even his white shirt seemed to attract attention; he wore his sword-belt under his coat which he kept unbuttoned almost to the top. At first his staff accompanied him, but he soon sent each off on various missions until only he and Private James Wells, that 'short, stout Irishman', the bearer of the II Corps flag, were left. At one point when the enemy's fire was at its most intense, Hancock's sorrel, normally one of the calmest animals, was simply overcome and became unmanageable, despite the general's spurs. He quickly changed mounts and continued his ride. One of his brigadiers told him, 'General, the corps commander ought not to risk his life that way.'

Hancock replied in words that made him immortal: 'There are times when a corps commander's life does not count.' [36]

General Doubleday, an observer of the scene, would say years later, 'I can almost fancy I can see Hancock again as he rode past the front of his command, just previous to the assault, followed by a single orderly displaying his corps flag, while the missiles from a hundred pieces of artillery tore up the ground around him.' [37]

At about 2:30 he rode back to the left of the line and went with his staff to a farmhouse about 200 yards below the Federal position to observe the effect of the artillery on the enemy. He turned his horse to face the men who had served him most closely. He felt the need, as this climatic event rolled towards them, to balance his ledger as a man and a leader. 'Gentlemen, after this artillery fire is over it will be followed by an infantry attack upon our lines. This battle is the turning point of the war; if we win this fight the war is practically over ... We cannot tell where any of us may be before this day is over; before leaving you I wish to say I speak harshly sometimes. If I have at any time ever said anything

[36] Tucker, op.cit. pp.150–1.
[37] Elmira Hancock, *Reminiscences of Winfield Scott Hancock* (Charles L. Webster & Co., New York, 1887) p.270.

to offend or hurt the feelings of any one of you I wish now to offer an apology.'[38]

As the fresh batteries moved over the crest to take their positions, the Union reserves were also in motion. Meade was fulfilling one of the chief functions of an army commander – he was preparing to commit his reserve. His son and namesake, Captain George Gordon Meade, serving on his staff, recorded the galloping of staff officers bearing the orders to assemble the reserve: 'During all the time of the cannonade orders were being sent from headquarters to take troops from every part of the line from which they could be spared and to place them in reserve for the support of that part of the line which the enemy's artillery fire indicated was about to be assaulted.'[39] That part of the line most clearly the object of the assault was II Corps. It was all too clear that his original calculation had been correct. In addition to Newton's two small divisions already there, he had ordered Slocum to send Williams' Division and Sedgwick to assemble his entire corps. Lieutenant Elisha Hunt Rhodes, 2nd Rhode Island, was in the VI Corps reserve massed behind the ridge:

> The firing began, and our Brigade was hurried to the right of the line to reinforce it. While not in the front line yet we were constantly exposed to the fire of the Rebel Artillery, while bullets fell around us. We moved from point to point, wherever danger seemed to be imminent until noon when we were ordered to report to the line held by Gen. Birney. Our Brigade marched down the road until we reached the house used by General Meade as Headquarters. The road ran between ledges of rocks while the fields were strewn with boulders. To our left was a hill on which we had many Batteries posted. Just as we reached Gen. Meade's Headquarters, a shell burst over our heads, and it was immediately followed by showers of iron. More than two hundred guns were belching forth their thunder, and most of the shells that came over the hill struck in the road on which our Brigade was forming. Solid shot would strike the large rocks and split them as if exploded by gunpowder. The flying iron and pieces of stone struck men down in every direction.[40]

---

[38] Tucker, op.cit. p.153.
[39] Meade, op.cit. p.91.
[40] Elisha Hunt Rhodes, *All For the Union: The Civil War Diary of Elisha Hunt Rhodes*, ed. Robert Hunt Rhodes (Orion Press, New York, 1985) p.116.

CHAPTER 13

3rd July 1863
Longstreet's Charge

2:45 PM, Seminary Ridge

Colonel Alexander's morbid fear of personally being the cause of wasted time in a military operation was preying upon him strongly as he watched Longstreet ride up. He was all impatience now that the fire of his guns was slackening. He had given no such order, and wondered whether it resulted from an exhaustion or ammunition or because the enemy had ceased fire. In either case, the infantry must move quickly. As soon as Longstreet arrived, Alexander informed him that the enemy's batteries had ceased fire and that this would be the best time to commence the attack. He also informed him that the howitzers he had been expecting to accompany the attack had been withdrawn by the army's Chief of Artillery and that consequently the support to the attack was not all he had wished for. That was the first Longstreet had heard of the guns, and he immediately said, 'Then replenish your ammunition while I delay the attack.' [1]

'General, we can't do that. We nearly emptied the trains last night. Even if we had it, it would take an hour or two, and meanwhile the enemy would recover from the pressure he is now under. Our only chance is to follow it up now – to strike while the iron is hot.' [2]

'Damn!' Longstreet's faced tightened in barely controlled anger. Then, through clenched teeth, he growled, 'Then we will just have to go. Porter, just give us everything you can.' [3]

Their attention was soon fixed on Pickett's Division as it moved into position. Alexander rode up to shake hands with Dick Garnett, with whom he had crossed the plains in the Old Army, and with Armistead, too. He rode ahead for a few yards with Garnett, and then turned off to ride along the line of his batteries. He ordered every gun with more than fifteen long-range projectiles to be prepared to limber up and follow the assaulting infantry; this amounted to about two guns in every five. If necessary they were to take horses from other

---

[1] * James Longstreet, *From Manassas to Gettysburg* (J.B. Lippincott, Philadelphia, 1896) p.392.

[2] Edward Porter Alexander, *Fighting For the Confederacy: The Personal Recollections of General Edward Porter Alexander*, ed. Gary W. Gallagher (University of North Carolina Press, Chapel Hill and London, 1989) p.261.

[3] * Longstreet, op.cit.

teams to compensate for the large numbers lost to the enemy's fire. The remaining guns were to wait until the infantry had begun to advance and then take under fire the enemy's batteries firing at the storming column.

Perhaps 800 infantrymen had been killed and wounded by the enemy's artillery. One of those injured, Sergeant-Major David Johnston, 7th Virginia, was tending his wound as the officers were shouting to fall in. As the ranks assembled in that seemingly automatic fashion of a living thing, Pickett rode up. Longstreet would describe him as 'a graceful horseman,' who 'sat lightly in the saddle, his brown locks flowing quite over his shoulders.'[4] Johnston watched as this flower of chivalry called out to the men:

> 'Up, men, and to your posts! Don't forget today that you are from Old Virginia!' The effect of his word upon the men was electrical. The regiments were quickly in line, closing to the left over the dead and wounded... The advance now began, the men calling out to the wounded and others: 'Goodbye, boys! Goodbye!'[5]

The commander of the 3rd Virginia, Colonel Joseph Mayo, was already grief-stricken to see so many casualties before the charge had even begun,

> especially ... our color-bearer, Murden, as fine a type of true soldiership as ever stepped beneath the folds of the spotless stars and bars, now lying there stark and stiff, a hideous hole sheer through his stalwart body, and his right hand closed in a death grip around the staff of that beautiful new flag.[6]

Behind Garnett's Brigade, Armistead was pacing up and down in front of the 53rd Virginia, his battalion of direction, when a courier rode up bearing Pickett's order to advance. Lieutenant Colonel Rawley Martin, commanding the 53rd, remembered that

> At once the command 'Attention, battalion!' rang out clear and distinct. Instantly every man was on his feet and in his place; the alignment was made with such coolness and precision as if preparing for dress parade. Then Armistead went up to the color sergeant of the 53rd Virginia Regiment and said 'Sergeant, are you going to put those colors on the enemy's works to-day?' The gallant fellow replied: 'I will try, sir, and if mortal man can do it, it shall be done.'

---

[4]* Longstreet, op.cit. pp.392–3.

[5] David Johnston, *The Story of a Confederate Boy in the Civil War* (David Johnston, Radford, Virginia, 1914) pp.203–8.

[6] Joseph C. Mayo, 'Pickett's Charge at Gettysburg', *SHSP*, vol.XXXIV (1906), pp.328–35.

Then to the 53rd itself and the regiments on either side, Armistead shouted, 'Men, remember your wives, your mothers, your sisters and your sweethearts.' [7]

Behind Armistead's Brigade, young Micah Jenkins had roused his six South Carolina regiments from their baking in the hot sun, as he strode along the line putting it in motion. 'Forward, my men! Forward!' his clear, tenor voice carried down the line as his 2300 men stepped off. Colonel John R. Hagwood, commanding the 1st South Carolina, wrote of that moment:

> I cannot forget the grand appearance of General Jenkins on this morning. Elegantly dressed (as he always was), superbly mounted and his face lit up with a martial fire such as I have never seen in anyone else, he realized all that I had ever dreamed of in the true soldier. His words shot life into the hearts of everyone.[8]

Sergeant Robert Jennings of Jenkins' old 5th South Carolina Volunteers never forgot the 'look of pure manly beauty on the young colonel's face and the innocent, almost radiant, light in his blue eyes. We all loved him and would follow him to hell.' [9] Another man remembered that 'Jenkins came down our lines, with a smile on his face, saying, "now, my boys, don't get scared before you are hurt." ' [10]

To Jenkins' right, Corse's smaller Virginia Brigade stepped off as well. For the 17th Virginia in Corse's line, more than any other regiment in the army, this attack was the way home. Raised in Alexandria on the Potomac, just below Washington, the regiment had assembled in front of the courthouse and marched off to join the army only hours before Union troops had occupied the town. For them, the way home truly was by way of Cemetery Ridge. Now in its tens of thousands, the fighting strength of the Army of Northern Virginia was moving forward for the assault.

3:00 PM, Gettysburg

The impression of those thousands emerging from the sunken road in front of Cemetery Hill, the woods and swales along Seminary Ridge, and from the Trostle Woods, was stunning. No man who gazed upon it and wore the blue ever forgot it. From Union prisoners in Gettysburg itself, to the troops stretching from Cemetery Hill to Little Round Top, the supreme moment of the war had come. Sergeant Sullivan in Gettysburg railroad depot had another

[7] Rawley Martin, 'Rawley Martin's Account', *SHSP*, vol.XXXIX (1911), pp.184–94.

[8] James J. Baldwin III, *A Biography of The Struck Eagle: Brigadier General Micah Jenkins* (The Burd Street Press, Shippensburg, Pennsylvania, 1996) p.274.

[9]* Jonathan Miller, ed., *The Civil War Letters of Sergeant Robert Jennings, 5th South Carolina Volunteers* (High Water Mark Press, Gettysburg, Pennsylvania, 1979) p.119.

[10] Baldwin, op.cit. p.275.

prisoner help him climb up the steep cupola steps to get a look at what all the artillery was about:

> Looking over towards the right of the town (south) I saw what appeared like a whole rebel army in a chunk start for our lines with their infernal squealing yell. It seemed as if everything stood still inside of me for a second or two, and then I began to pray. Now I never was and am not yet, noted for the frequency and fervency of my prayers, but that time I prayed from the bottom of my heart that they would catch h–l, and they did.[11]

3:00 PM, Cemetery Ridge

Gibbon and Haskell were on the reverse slope of the ridge when they noticed Hunt on the crest, excitedly riding back and forth giving orders to Woodruff's Battery. The orderlies drifted back from the crest with the command group's horses. Captain Wessel was among them. He was pale and excited. 'General, they say the enemy's Infantry is advancing.'

In an instant they were in the saddle and riding the short distance to the crest, where they heard men shout, 'Here they come, here come the Johnnies.' Haskell was awe-struck.

> To say that none grew pale and held their breath at what we and they there saw, would not be true. Might not six thousand men be brave and without shade of fear, and yet, before a hostile eighteen thousand, armed, and not five minutes' march away, turn ashy white? None on that crest now need be told that *the enemy is advancing*. Every eye could see his legions, an overwhelming, resistless tide of an ocean of armed men, sweeping upon us! Regiment after Regiment, and Brigade after Brigade, move from the woods, and rapidly take their places in the lines forming the assault ... the dull gray masses deploy, man touching man, rank pressing rank, and line supporting line. Their red flags wave; their horsemen gallop up and down; the arms of eighteen thousand men, barrel and bayonet, gleam in the sun, a sloping forrest of flashing steel. Right on they move, as with one soul, in perfect order, without impediment of ditch, or wall, or stream, over ridge and slope, through orchard, and meadow, and cornfield, magnificent, grim, irresistible.[12]

The II Corps men were remarkably self-possessed, and went about the business of preparing to repel the irresistible advance just as would men who had fought on a score of fields. The artillery had momentarily abated on both sides, leaving

---

[11] Beaudot and Herdegen, op.cit. p.101.

[12] Frank A. Haskell, *The Battle of Gettysburg* (Wisconsin Historical Society, Madison, Wisconsin, 1908). *In one of Haskell's rare understatements, his estimate for the size of the attacking force was off by almost half – 18,000, compared to the 35,000 that actually took part in the attack.

a strange silence. The clicks of locks as thousands of hammers were raised rippled down the front, accompanied by the squeak of iron axles as the guns were run back into position. The faint sound of leather was next as cap boxes were slid around to the front of the body, cartridge boxes opened, and officers' holsters opened in readiness. The unit colors retired behind their troops, but the Stars and Stripes were advanced everywhere to the front ranks, 'and the west wind kissed it as the sergeants sloped its lance towards the enemy.' Behind the lines, Gibbon rode slowly, and in a calm voice spoke to the men. 'Do not hurry, men, and fire too fast; – let them come up close before you fire, and then aim low, and steadily.' [13] Similar scenes were being enacted along the entire front, from Cemetery Hill to the base of Little Round Top.

Informed by General Hays that the attack had begun in great force, Meade arrived on the crest with his staff trailing behind after dispatching two aides to hurry up VI Corps' brigades. Hays, Hunt, and Hancock rode over to him to confer. Even then they took a moment or two to admire probably the single greatest military display of the war. They all gave the enemy the highest professional marks for the order and control of the heavy formations advancing across the valley. Three miles away on Oak Hill, the Alabama gunners of Captain W.B. Hurt's Hardaway Battery slammed the hexagonal 2.75-inch shells in the breeches of the only two breech-loading cannon on the field, British Whitworth 12-pounder rifles of great range and accuracy. All during the cannonade their bolts and shells had sailed the great distance from Oak Hill to strike the whole length of the Union line and unnerve the Union troops with their eerie screech. Although the firing along Seminary Ridge had ceased to allow the infantry to pass through the guns, Hurt's guns had no such reason to cease fire. Through his field glasses Hurt saw the large group of mounted men with flags on the crest of Cemetery Ridge and personally sighted the guns. Meade was pointing towards Seminary Ridge when a screech rent the air, then another, turning thousands of heads. Two quick explosions – then the group of horsemen blossomed like a red flower, peeling off in every direction, leaving several horses kicking and several bodies in blue on the ground.

Hancock's hand steadied his horse immediately. A man was shouting, 'General Meade is down! General Meade is down!' Hancock looked down to see Meade cradled in the arms of his son and aide, a gash in his forehead spilling blood down his face. He leapt down and knelt by the army commander. Young Meade was now more the son than the soldier, saying, 'Papa, Papa, do you hear me? Papa!' A surgeon pushed both of them aside and laid Meade on the ground. He stirred, opened his eyes, and tried to get up, but helpful hands kept him down. The surgeon deftly examined the wound and, announcing 'It's a bad gash, but there is no serious injury', began to clean and bandage it. Meade was

---

[13] Haskell, ibid.

awake as the doctor worked, murmuring something about the battle. As the stretcher-bearers were about to lift him into an ambulance, Hancock spoke to one of the aides. 'Ride to General Slocum and inform him that he is now in command of the army.'

From the stretcher came a faint voice, 'Wait, Hancock, wait.' Hancock rushed over to him as Meade's hand reached up. Hancock took it and felt it squeeze his fingers. 'No, Hancock, you must command on this field.'

'But General Slocum is senior, Sir.'

With an effort, Meade raised his voice for the audience he knew was listening. 'I know that, Hancock, but the Congress and the President have given me the power to make my own appointments. Slocum and Sedgwick are not here. You are and so is the fight. I appoint *you* my second-in-command.' The effort exhausted him, and he fell back onto the stretcher, his voice again almost a murmur, 'Now, General, the enemy is upon you.'

3:00 PM, Spangler's Woods

Lee sat Traveler, his staff behind him, in the open glade that opened into the eastern side of Spangler's Woods. He had never seen the Army of Northern Virginia step more lively into an attack and in such splendid alignment, not even in parade. They covered the valley from end to end, a forest of bayonets glittering at the same angle. Major Marshall was noticing again how Lee was rubbing his shoulder, something he had only begun to do in the last few days. Lee had seemed like his old self the day before, suffused with vigor, but today he did not look well. Nor did he feel well. Only with the greatest self-control was he fighting off the nausea and dizziness that were hitting him in waves as a rushing sound filled his ears. Traveler could feel his distress and grew nervous.

Terrible as an army with banners

3:00 PM, the valley between the Ridges

Lee's growing incapacitation would not affect Longstreet. He would be riding between Pickett's second and third lines in order to see and control the main attack, as the men advanced at a steady 110 steps a minute, or a little less than a hundred yards. He had planned for the three center divisions – those of Pickett, Pettigrew, and Lane – with their thirteen brigades, to converge on a single point, the Copse of Trees on Cemetery Ridge. The path of the attack would assume the form of a blunt triangle with its base beginning along Seminary Ridge and its blunt apex striking the trees. Pickett on the right and Pettigrew and Lane on the left each formed one long side of the triangle. Between Pickett's and Pettigrew's Divisions at the base was an open distance of about 350 yards, in the center of which stood Lee and his staff. Trimble's two divisions were directly across from the aiming point and would only have to march directly east to reach it. Pickett's Division, on the other hand, would impact significantly south of the trees if it marched directly east, therefore necessitating a series of sharp left-oblique turns as they closed the distance to the apex of the triangle. Since the object was to have all three divisions strike the ridge at the same time, Trimble's divisions would allow Pickett's a short head start, because otherwise the left oblique maneuvers would slow down his brigades enough to disrupt the synchronization of the final assault.

Pickett's Division was deployed on a front of 825 yards, with Kemper on the right and Garnett on the left in the first wave. Armistead's Brigade formed the second wave midway behind the first two brigades. Corse's and Jenkins' Brigades formed the third line, with Corse on the right and Jenkins on the left. Longstreet had directed Pickett to place Jenkins in just this position. His crack brigade of 2300 men was just what would be needed for the last surge over the ridge.

On Pickett's left, Pettigrew's Division was formed in two waves of two brigades each, the square formation, two up and two back, that the Confederates liked so much.[14] Archer's Brigade was on the right and Pettigrew's old brigade under Colonel J.K. Marshall (52nd North Carolina) on the left in the first wave, followed by Davis' and Brockenbrough's Brigades in the same order in the second wave. The formation of the divisions of Lane and Rodes was determined largely by their positions held at the close of the second day's fighting. Of the four brigades in Lane's Division, Scales' and Lane's old brigade, under Colonel C.M. Avery (33rd North Carolina), had returned to Seminary Ridge. Perrin's and Thomas' were in the sunken road to which most of Rodes' Division had fallen back after its aborted attack on Cemetery Hill the night before. Longstreet's solution was to place Lane and Scales on Pettigrew's left; they would advance until parallel with Perrin and Thomas when these brigades would join them to assemble the complete division, which would keep a tight hold on Pettigrew's left. At the same time, Rodes' Division would advance. Its five brigades in the sunken road were arranged in the first wave, from right to left, Ramseur, Iverson, and Doles, with Daniel and O'Neal forming the second wave. McLaws and Law's Divisions on the right flank would also be in the square formation. McLaws had Semmes and Wofford in the first wave followed by Kershaw. Barksdale's Brigade (now commanded by the 18th Mississippi's Colonel B.G. Humphreys) already formed a skirmish line north from the Trostle Farm. Law placed his old brigade, under Colonel James L. Sheffield, and Anderson's brigades in the first wave, followed by those of Robertson and Benning.

---

[14] Such a formation was natural, since most Confederate divisions were built on four brigades. Of the nine divisions at Gettysburg, only Anderson's, Rodes', and Pickett's had five brigades.

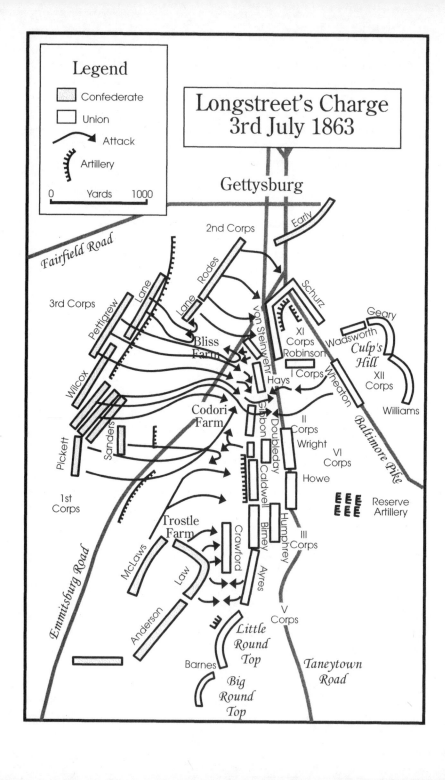

Legend

Confederate

Union

Attack

Artillery

0   Yards   1000

**Longstreet's Charge
3rd July 1863**

Gettysburg

Early

Fairfield Road

2nd Corps

Rodes

Lane

Lane

3rd Corps

Pettigrew

Schurz

Von Steinwehr

Geary

Wadsworth

Culp's Hill

XI Corps

Robinson

I Corps

Hays

Wheaton

XII Corps

Williams

Bliss Farm

Wilcox

Codori Farm

Gibbon

Doubleday

II Corps

Wright

VI Corps

Baltimore Pike

Pickett

Sanders

Caldwell

Howe

1st Corps

Humphrey

III Corps

Reserve Artillery

Trostle Farm

Crawford

Birney

McLaws

Law

Ayres

V Corps

Emmitsburg Road

Anderson

Barnes

Little Round Top

Taneytown Road

Big Round Top

Half of Lane's Division, and Rodes, McLaws, and Law's Divisions, would be timing their own attacks so as to impact the ridge at the same time in order to prevent the shift of Union reserves from one threatened point to another, in effect presenting every yard of the Yankee line with its own threat. Longstreet had closely questioned Pettigrew and the other commanders of yesterday's assault on the ridge and determined to check the almost miraculous appearance of enemy reserves at each breakthrough point. Spreading the attack along the entire front would also keep the enemy's artillery from concentrating its fire against any one part of the attacking formation. Since Rodes, McLaws, and Law's Divisions had a shorter distance to go, they would begin after the center attack. In addition, Longstreet had deployed Wilcox's old brigade, now commanded by the 11th Alabama's Colonel J.C.C. Sanders, strengthened with the survivors of Perry's Florida Brigade, to cover the gap that would form between Pickett and Laws. Here was the weakest part of the attack, but he thought it sufficient to keep the Yankee's from attempting to get onto the flanks of any of his attacking columns. Pickett and Pettigrew's nine brigades were in the center in the main attack; Pender and Rodes disposed another nine brigades on the left, while McLaws and Law deployed eight on the right, with one covering the gap between center and right.

Longstreet took up a position between Armistead's and Jenkins' Brigades on the left flank, putting him exactly in the rear of the two center attacking divisions, those of Pickett and Pettigrew. This would give him the best view of the overall situation as well as having Pickett's strong third line at hand for the final struggle for the ridge. He had ordered Pickett further forward than was normal for a division commander. 'George, I want you just behind your first line. This attack must be tightly controlled, and you must ensure that your brigades go in just where they are supposed to.' [15]

All in all, Longstreet would be throwing more than 120 regiments into the attack, in twenty-seven brigades totalling over 35,000 men and supported by almost 200 guns. To date no single attack of the war had concentrated so many men and so many guns. Nor had any other attack of the war gambled the fate of either the Union or the Confederacy on its success. The glory and drama of this host, advancing along a two-mile front with six-score battle flags, red and blue, waving above glittering forests of bayonets, was not lost on the participants on both sides. It was an echo of the age of Shakespeare and of Sir Walter Scott, and above all of the Bible, from which countless minds were turning to that line of dread and strife from the Song of Solomon – 'an army terrible with banners'.

---

[15]* Longstreet, op.cit. p.426.

'Before us lay bright fields and fair landscape'

3:05 PM, the Valley of Death

Despite starting after Pickett, it was Pettigrew's Division that first stepped into the view, no longer obscured by the smoke of the cannonade, of the men on Cemetery Ridge. One of them would write of these precious, peaceful moments, 'Before us lay bright fields and fair landscape.' But Pettigrew's lead brigades had not gone fifty yards from the woods before Osborn's gunners on Cemetery Hill fired. Pickett was luckier. His division had begun its advance from the bottom of a swale, but within minutes his lead brigades were spotted by the Union signal station on Little Round Top, which transmitted their coming to the whole Union line.

The first problem was Pettigrew's. He looked behind him in horror to see that his entire second line of brigades had not emerged from the woods as they should have by now. Just as he dispatched an aide to find out why, Davis' Brigade appeared, but not Brockenbrough's. At last even these way-ward Virginians finally came through the woods and rushed to catch up with Davis' line. Pettigrew could only shrug; he was already aware of their low morale from the beating they had taken on the first day of the battle. On the right flank, Armistead's Brigade had emerged from the swale about the same time with its commander on foot at its head. Here he took off his black hat and impaled it on the end of his sword to the delight of his men. Ahead of him Kemper and Garnett's Brigade's had already begun to feel the sting of the Union artillery.

All the artillery that could bear was now firing on Hunt's long awaited object – the Confederate infantry. Hazlett's six highly accurate 10-pounder Parrotts on Little Round Top were enfilading Kemper and Garnett's Brigades from an elevation. McGilvery's right-hand batteries were also joining in, as did almost the whole of Osborn's massed batteries on Cemetery Hill. Osborn's target was Pettigrew's Division. He observed:

> From the very first minute our guns created sad havoc in that line. Lee's line of battle had advanced about two hundred yards, after it came within sight, when another line in every way similar followed. These two lines of battle, nearly a mile distant, were then the sole object of fire of all the guns which could be made to bear upon them. The effects of this fire could very soon be seen. At first the distance was so great that only solid shot from the brass guns and percussion shells from the rifled guns could be effectively used. The artillerymen endeavored to roll the solid shot through the ranks and explode the percussion shells in front of the lines. This method was effective to a large degree, as we would see the ranks thinned at many points and here and there a wide gap made as from two to a dozen men were taken out by the men being shot down. All this made no

impression on the movement of the double line of battle. The men moved as steadily as if on dress parade.[16]

On the other flank, Pickett's two lead brigades were not suffering terribly except from the plunging, enfilade fire of Hazlett's Battery. The official report of Garnett's Brigade stated:

> Up to this time we had suffered but little from the enemy's batteries, which apparently had been much crippled previous to our advance, with the exception of one posted on the mountain, about 1 mile to our right, which enfiladed nearly our entire line with fearful effect, sometimes as many as 10 men being killed and wounded by the bursting of a single shell.[17]

Only the guns directly in the path of the attack, II Corps', were silent. On Hancock's orders they had kept up a hot fire during the enemy's cannonade and had consequently suffered heavy casualties and exhausted all their long-range ammunition. Consequently, the surviving gun teams stood silently by their guns, canister stacked next to each piece, waiting. The only artillery left to II Corps were Lieutenant George Woodruff's six 12-pounder Napoleons supporting Hays' Division around Ziegler's Grove, three of Cushing's 3-inch rifles, and two of Captain James Rorty's 10-pounder Parrotts. Alexander Webb saw what was coming straight for his brigade by the clump of trees and desperately sent for a battery to replace one that had retired. He sent to Captain Andrew Cowan's Battery from VI Corps, which had been put in support of Doubleday. Cowan hesitated for only a moment until he saw Webb frantically waving his hat at him from the Copse of Trees. 'Limber to the right, forward!' he shouted, and the battery shot forward the 300 yards to the trees, and so impetuously did they drive that the first gun crashed into the trees on the north side. It was retrieved and stationed near Cushing's two guns while the other five 3-inch rifles were placed south of the trees. Cowan rode up to Cushing's guns to see to his wayward piece and asked Cushing, 'Is my piece crowding you, sir?' Cowan was appalled by the shattered state of the battery and of its lieutenant, who, though bleeding from two wounds, was still eager to fight. 'Your piece is fine where it is,' Cushing answered, clutching the wound in his belly. As Cowan rode away he heard Cushing shout the command, 'Forward to the wall!'[18]

Hunt had been near Cowan's Battery when he had seen the young officer

---

[16] Herbert Crumb, ed., *The Papers of Major Thomas Osborn: The Eleventh Corps Artillery at Gettysburg* (Edmonston Publishers, Hamilton, New York, 1992) pp.29–45.

[17] *OR*, vol.XXVII, part II, p.386.

[18] Cowan to Bachelder, 2nd December 1885, Bachelder Papers, vol.I, p.1157.

respond with such alacrity to Webb's frantic waving. He instantly understood, and began gathering every battery at hand and sending them after Cowan.

As the right flank of Kemper's Brigade approached the Emmitsburg Road, the command 'Left Oblique!' was given, to begin the series of 45-degree turns that were to unite Pickett's Division with Pettigrew's. As the lead brigades reached the half-way point, about 800 feet from their start point, they marched into the shelter of a swale which hid them from observation. Hazlett's guns merely switched their fire to the following three brigades. But the few minutes in the swale allowed Kemper and Garnet to redress their regiments and align them parallel to the enemy. Up to this time, losses had been relatively small and certainly not enough to affect the fighting ability of the division.

The same could not be said of Lane's two brigades on Pettigrew's left. They were walking into almost all of Osborn's fire. Both Lane's and Scales' Brigades had fought well but been severely handled in the first two days of fighting, and had left a growing trail of mangled bodies in their wake and a steady stream of wounded and skulkers stumbling to the rear. Now they were in range of not only Osborn's rifled guns but also his sixteen Napoleons as well. At this point, the fraying right of Scales' already small brigade came up to the end of Long Lane, where Perrin's and Thomas' Brigades emerged to join the division, with Rodes doing the same on their left. But Scales' Brigade was dissolving under the Napoleons' exploding shell and case shot, which wiped out so many files that the brigade resembled a skirmish line. Still they kept going, encouraged by the sight of their commander, Brigadier General Alfred Scales, sword in hand and seemingly impervious, at their head. But they were drifting harder right to keep that tight hold on Pettigrew's flank and instinctively to get away from the sheets of death coming from their left front. In doing so they never were able to hook onto Thomas' Brigade coming out of the sunken road. When they passed through the swale, many of them just stayed put.

As the shrinking band of steady men climbed back out into the fire of Osborn's guns, a new misery was added to their sufferings, in the form of Colonel Franklin Sawyer and the 160 men of the 8th Ohio on picket duty in front of XI Corps. They could have drifted out of the way of the oncoming Rebel tidal wave, but Sawyer was a tough literalist. He had been ordered to hold his position, but now he saw the opportunity to do more as Scales' Brigade wavered. 'I advanced my reserve to the picket front, and as the rebel line came within about 100 yards, we poured in a well-directed fire, which broke the rebel line, and it soon fled in the wildest confusion.' Both sides saw Sawyer's gallant advance from a distance. The Union observers thought he was suicidal; Longstreet was more impressed and immediately sent an aide to warn Lane, but it was too late. The volley not only broke the brigade but finally brought down Scales as well, with a bullet through the knee that left him helpless on the field.

The Ohioans just ran around him as he sat there clutching his shattered knee. Sawyer was not finished. Lane's Brigade was still advancing.

> Being relieved from this direction, I changed front forward on the left company, thus presenting our front to the left flank of the advancing rebel column. Our fire was poured into their flank with terrible effect for a few minutes ... but almost instantly on the fire from the front, together with the concentrated fire from our batteries, the whole mass gave way, some fleeing to the front, some to the rear, and some through our lines, until the whole plain was covered with unarmed rebels, waving coats, hats, and handkerchiefs in token of a wish to surrender.[19]

For the men on the flanks and those watching on Seminary Ridge, the sight of the two flying brigades was as stunning as it was demoralising. Never had the Army of Northern Virginia seen whole brigades on the run. There was an audible groan from the staff around Lee as they watched. Lee himself, struggling to maintain self-control of his body, murmured faintly to himself, 'Never let them see you run. Never.'[20]

Lane watched helplessly from behind Thomas' Brigade as half his division collapsed and fled. Trimble came riding up, laying about with the flat of his sword and shouting with all the fury of an Old Testament prophet to get the fleeing men to turn about. Under his direct gaze, they stopped in twos and threes, but drifted off as soon as he moved on. Lane had more than enough to worry about than the presence of his acting corps commander as Osborn redirected the fire of his guns on the brigades attacking from the sunken road. Osborn had already ordered up all but one of the remaining batteries on East Cemetery Hill, and these were just wheeling into position almost hub to hub along the crowded western face of the hill, which was wreathed in smoke and lit by spouting orange-red tongues. Great gaps were torn in the ranks of the advancing Georgians and Carolinians. Woodruff's Battery in front of Ziegler's grove added its weight as soon as the Rebels reached canister range. Whole companies were swept away. As they closed to half the 1000 feet between Long Lane and the hill, the guns switched to case shot and long-range canister. That was too much for Iverson's Brigade in the center of Rodes' first line. The brigade had suffered almost two-thirds casualties on the first day, and had brought fewer than 400 men into this attack. Half of them were down, and the rest broke to the rear, elbowing through the regiments in the second line. Ramseur's North Carolinians and Dole's Georgians on either side were steadier, having ridden out with far fewer casualties in the last winning phase of that fight. But

---

[19] *OR*, vol.XXVII, part I, p.462.
[20]* Charles Marshall, 'Lee at Gettysburg', *MAC*, vol.XIII (1878), p.47.

now Ramseur's Brigade guided left to fill the gap and almost instinctively so did Lane's brigades on its right. The last of Lane's Division was being dragged away from supporting the attack on the center, and straight into the fire of Osborn's massed batteries and, soon, the rifles of Steinwehr's infantry.

From the top of the hill, Howard was intently trying to peer through the thickening smoke from the batteries. He had already ordered up several of Schurz's regiments to thicken von Steinwehr's, part-way up the slope of the hill. That should put about 1800 rifles on the firing line, but left him with no reserve at all. Now was the time to call up Robinson's Division from I Corps, in reserve only a few hundred feet away at the base of the hill behind Ziegler's Grove. An aide spurred his horse away, its hooves flinging clods of earth in its wake.

On the far right flank, as Kemper and Garnett had made their first left oblique, Law's Division advanced from the protection of the woods north of the Wheatfield and came on line north of the Trostle Farm. Barksdale's Brigade had already been spread across this ground as skirmishers. It had suffered the cruellest losses of any brigade in 1st Corps – 50 per cent, 804 out of 1620 men. The 18th Mississippi had suffered badly – there were only 105 men left of 242 from yesterday's fighting, but the 17th had lost even more.[21] Still, they all rose from their wrinkles in the ground and advanced as Kemper's Brigade brushed by their left making its left obliques to the north-east. McGilvery's left-hand batteries almost immediately began to take Law's brigades under fire while the right-hand batteries continued to savage Kemper's flank. Hazlett, from his perch on Little Round Top, determined that the center attack was the more powerful and continued to concentrate on it.

For Law's Division, this was an especially painful route of attack, as much from the concentration of almost thirty guns throwing shot and percussion shell into them as it was the sight of so many dead comrades whose bloating bodies had been strewn over these same fields the day before. Nevertheless, they filled the gaps in their files and kept coming with a parade-ground precision that filled McGilvery's gunners and the V Corps infantry with soldierly admiration. As they advanced north beyond the Trostle Farm, McLaws' Division burst out of the Trostle Woods, wheeling to the left to bring itself in line with Law's Division.

Both divisions now found themselves in the soft ground around Plum Run. In particular, Law's brigades came up to the same brush-filled swale that had been the slaughter-pen for both Barksdale's and Willard's Brigades. The water in the run had backed up to form ponds in a few places, dammed by piles of bodies in blue and gray. This time, instead of rifle fire, the Confederate attackers were marching straight into the fire of over forty guns in McGilvery's line up

---

[21] John W. Busey and David G. Martin, *Regimental Strengths and Losses at Gettysburg* (Longstreet House, Hightstown, New Jersey, 1982) p.282.

the ridge. As they descended into the swale, they were slowed and disordered by the bodies and the brush. At the same time, the guns switched to canister. Semmes' and Wofford's Brigades seemed to melt away in sprays of blood and flesh.

McLaws hurried his men across Plum Run. All they had before them were enemy skirmishers which they rapidly pushed into the Weikert Woods. McLaws had closely questioned Kershaw about the approach to this piece of ground which he had penetrated so easily the day before. He was hopeful that the woods and poor fields of fire would limit the damage the artillery could do before he came to grips with the infantry.

That infantry, though, was thinking of coming to grips with him. The men of Brigadier General Samuel W. Crawford's 3rd Division, V Corps, were waiting in Weikert Woods. This was a Pennsylvania division, its two brigades present made up of nine regiments of the Pennsylvania Reserves, men fighting on home ground, especially the men of Company K, 1st Pennsylvania Reserves – whose home was the Gettysburg area – and they were fresh.[22] Crawford's 2800 men waited kneeling in the woods, quietly gripping their mostly older model .69 caliber rifled muskets, listening to the fire of the skirmish line crackle and sputter in the open space beyond.

In the center, the command 'Forward' brought Pickett's two lead brigades out of the swale with Pickett and his staff riding behind them, a ready target for Hazlett's guns. A shell had already brought down one of his aides, striking him full in the body and showering the others with his blood. From his polished boots to his long locks, the elegant Pickett now dripped with gore, but he kept his horse under no less control than he did himself. Captain Bright remembered the look of shock in the eyes of Armistead's men as Pickett continued to ride up and down the line; they were amazed that he was still able to keep his seat with what appeared to be such terrible wounds. If anything he would have enjoyed the thought that he appeared so sternly heroic, but his attention was fixed on Longstreet's orders to keep a tight hold on the attacking brigades, which had now covered half the distance to their objective, executing several difficult left obliques, dressing in the swale, and continuing on in good order. Despite the

---

[22] At one time, before its renovation by the Park Service, the Gettysburg Museum contained a newspaper cutting which celebrated the 100th birthday of the oldest surviving Union veteran of Gettysburg, possibly a member of Company K, 1st Pennsylvania Reserve. It was 1935, and President Franklin Roosevelt had sent his birthday greetings by the hand of the veteran's Representative in Congress, a Democrat. Asked by the assembled reporters to what he ascribed his longevity, the old soldier flatly stated, 'To voting a straight Republican ticket!' When the laughter had died down, he added proudly, 'I cast my first ballot for Abraham Lincoln and have voted a straight Republican ticket ever since.' This was certainly an example of the post-war exhortation to 'vote as you shot', but one can only envy the man who could say, 'I cast my first ballot for Abraham Lincoln.'

direct hit on a member of his own staff, he was also amazed that the enemy's artillery had not punished his brigades more severely. In fact, except for the few guns firing to his front, the enfilading fire from the flanks had slackened considerably to concentrate on Rodes, McLaws, and Law on the flanks. Old Pete was clever indeed, he thought to himself, to have given the Yankees too many targets for them to be able to concentrate on just one. Still, between McGilvery's right-hand batteries and Hazlett, the path of Pickett's Division was becoming increasingly stained with a reddened smear of mangled corpses and writhing wounded. To the rear the division was also unravelling, as hundreds of walking wounded and men whose courage had deserted them trudged back to the shelter of the swale behind the guns, or to the woods.

Pettigrew would not have been as optimistic as Pickett, because he continued to receive the fire of the left three or four batteries on Cemetery Hill. After the rout of Lane's two brigades, the flank of Brockenbrough's Brigade had taken one rending salvo from the all the guns on Cemetery Hill before most of them had switched to the direct threat from Lane's remaining brigades and Rodes' Division. What Pickett failed to appreciate was the play of miscalculation and chance. The center two divisions were moving forward in good order, but their immediate right and left flanks had been opened up. The collapse of Lane's two brigades had shown what a determined flank attack by even a small but determined unit could do. And now Sanders' Brigade on the right had got a late start, and even a casual observer would have recognized that here Longstreet had made a major error of calculation. The gap between Law and Pickett was too wide to be covered by a weak brigade such as Sanders', and the gap was yawning wider as Pickett continued to edge to the left.

'Don't shoot him!'
3:15 PM, Cemetery Ridge, the Copse of Trees

If anyone was aware of the failure to seriously impede the masses converging on his front it was John Gibbon, now acting II Corps commander again. The dozen or so guns on his front were not about to stop the almost 15,000 men crossing the valley to his front, especially since all but Cowan's six 3-inch rifles were out of action until the enemy got within canister range. He watched as his skirmish line engaged the advancing enemy's skirmishers and, to his shock, watched as a 'big man on a very tall light bay horse, in major-general's uniform, white shirt-front flashing in the sunlight' rode along the skirmish line. Captain Tom Hodges, 3rd Virginia, saw him too and pointed him out to Colonel Mayo, who described him as a 'splendid looking Federal officer, magnificently mounted, straining his horse at full speed along the crest of a hill a hundred yards in our front, and both of us calling to the skirmishers "Don't shoot him! Don't shoot him!"' Northern soldiers often derided the Confederates as 'The Chivalry,' but this day the Union cause had reason to honor Southern chivalry, which had just saved the life of its finest fighting general, Winfield Scott Hancock.[23]

Gibbon rode up to Hancock as the new army commander leapt his horse over the stone wall in front of Cushing's Battery. It was no time to chide Hancock for taking such a risk; that is what made him Hancock. Besides, it had worked. The skirmish line, in the face of a human tidal wave had stood its ground long enough, especially in front of Garnett's Brigade, to force it to halt, fire, reload, and come on again. Now, as Hancock rode up, the skirmishers were jumping over the stone wall to rejoin their regiments. If cautioning Hancock was useless, Gibbon could do the next best thing, and get the major-general out of the line of fire. Gibbon swung his arm to encompass his division's front, 'General, we're just too thin here; we can't hold without reserves. Get me reserves.'

'They're on the way, John, but you are right. They can't get here too soon.' His new army staff barely caught up with him before he sent a number of them off to hurry up Sedgwick's Brigades. Then the tall light bay seemed to leap forward almost from a standing start, and his staff had to spur after him again. Instead of riding off to summon the reserves, Hancock was racing back to the other end of Gibbon's line.

Gibbon's concern for the strength of his line was well-founded. His left flank was strong enough with Standard's Brigade of Vermonters from Doubleday's Division and Harrow and then Hall's Brigades fairly thickly positioned along the stone wall. A piece of rough ground in front of Hall's Brigade offered another obstacle to the enemy. But it was Webb's Brigade that was thin, dangerously thin, as the approaching enemy division seemed to be edging constantly to its own left and towards the section of the wall held by Webb, the section called the Angle because it dog-legged back where Gibbon's Division connected with Hays'. His 200-yard front was held by only three weak regiments totalling barely 375 men. From north to south, they were the 71st and 69th Pennsylvania and the 59th New York. On either side of the 69th there were large gaps through which Cushing and Cowan could fire. As a reserve, behind the Copse of Trees, was the 72nd Pennsylvania, a large regiment of 350 men reinforced by the 100 returned skirmishers from the 106th Pennsylvania who had fallen in on the initiative of their captain, who would say 'it was one of those actions in which every soldier felt that his duty was to be in the fight.'[24] A little to the south there were also fragments of the 42nd New York and 19th Massachusetts. If Gibbon had started the day with 2500 men he would have

[23] George R. Stewart, *Pickett's Charge: A Microhistory of the Final Attack at Gettysburg, July 3, 1863* (Houghton Mifflin Co., Boston, 1987) p.197; and Mayo, *SHSP*, vol.XXXIV (1906), pp.328–35.
[24] Stewart, ibid.

been lucky, but not lucky enough to face the more than 10,000 men that were now aiming at his front.

'A wild kaleidoscope whirl'

3:40 PM, the Emmitsburg Road

By now Kemper and Garnett were swarming across the Emmitsburg Road to the south and north of the Codori Farm. Kemper's left-oblique slide north had exposed his flank to more and more fire from batteries now using case shot – canister at a distance – batteries that Hunt had hurried into position further up the ridge behind the Union positions. The road itself had been lined on both sides with stout post and plank fences. Much of this had been knocked down in the previous day's fighting, but enough survived to prove a deadly obstacle as the case shot filled the sunken road with bodies. Rorty's two guns, now commanded by Lieutenant Robert Rogers, fired double canister – lethal shotgun blasts – as Kemper's men headed north, their heads down in a 'half stoop' as if bulling their way through a storm. Rorty's Battery had taken so many casualties that half the crew on one of the two surviving guns were volunteer infantrymen from surrounding regiments. To the north of the Codori Farm, Garnett's men were struck by double canister from Cowan's and Cushing's guns, tearing great holes in the ranks and throwing up a hail of blood, body parts, canteens, hats, bayonets, and bits of uniforms. The colors almost all went down, only to be snatched up again and surge forward. It was now that the parade-ground formations lost their cohesion and melted into clumps and masses. Canister was ripping holes in the regiments faster than any sense of order could repair them. Garnett was riding through the carnage, exhorting his men, 'Steady, men! Close up! A little faster; not too fast! Save your strength!' [25] Senior officers were falling everywhere. Among them was 'Taz' Patton of the 7th Virginia. Colonel Mayo remembered, 'After that everything was a wild kaleidoscope whirl.' [26]

The disorganized mass of Pickett's first line was careening to within 250 yards of the Copse of Trees, with most of Archer's Brigade of Pettigrew's Division coming in on their left. Nearby Lieutenant Haskell watched as Gibbon's front flared in a ferocious northward ripple of flame and smoke as brigade after brigade opened fire on the enemy. Half the battle-flags were flung to the ground by the lifeless hands of their bearers. The entire color guard of the 1st Virginia was cut down, and the Union front was shrouded by smoke through which continuous spurts of flame jabbed out. Archer's Tennesseans and Alabamians had the worst of it, if that was possible. They were caught trying to

---

[25] Stewart, ibid.
[26] Mayo, op.cit.

climb over the fences along the road; here these formidable obstacles were still intact, and the men were slaughtered by the canister and rifle fire. Colonel Birkett D. Fry of the 13th Alabama was cut down by a shot through the thigh as his other officers fell alongside him. But he was so confident of victory that as some of his men ran up to carry him off he shouted, 'Go on: it will not last five minutes longer!' [27] The Confederates, though hundreds had fallen, were still pugnacious, and returned their first heavy fire into the flame-specked powder clouds to their front. Haskell remembered:

> As if our bullets were the fire-coals that touched off their muskets, the enemy in front halts, and his countless level barrels blaze back upon us ... All along each hostile front, a thousand yards, with narrowest space between, the vollies blaze and roll; as thick the sound as when a summer hailstorm pelts the city roofs; as thick the fire as when the incessant lightning fringes a summer cloud. – When the Rebel Infantry had opened fire, our Batteries soon became silent; and this without their fault, for they were foul by long previous use, they were the targets of the concentrated Rebel bullets, and some of them had expended all their canister. [28]

Hays' Division was yet to fire, recessed as it was by the northern dog-leg of the Angle. To keep his men occupied and to impress the enemy, Hays had ordered the 1800 men in Smythe and Willard's brigades along the stone wall to perform the manual of arms. Carroll's Brigade of about 800 men was in a second line to the rear. But as the enemy had closed the distance, he ordered the first line to kneel behind the wall and keep low. But to Hays' surprise and amusement, the Rebel division advancing on him had split half away from his front. Only part of it would be coming at him on his left. He was further surprised as the brigade in the second line came apart and fled to the rear. Not too steady to begin with, Brockenbrough's Virginians had taken a good deal of the attention of Osborn's right-hand batteries. And finally, the redoubtable Colonel Sawyer and his still bloodthirsty 8th Ohio, now reinforced by 75 men of the 126th New York's skirmish line, had struck their flank and rear. That left only Pettigrew's old brigade, now much disorganized and diminished by its march on the flank, to face Hays' entire division. Here occurred one of those remarkable examples of initiative and co-operation that so marked the conduct of the battle by the Army of the Potomac. In a moment Hays had grasped the opportunity offered before him. To his right rear he could see Robinson's Division of I Corps moving up at Howard's request to counter Rodes' Division. Hays rode over immediately and in a few minutes excited conversation had won Robinson's hearty co-operation.

---

[27] B.D. Fry, 'Pettigrew's Charge at Gettysburg', *SHSP*, vol.VII (1879), p.93.
[28] Haskell, op.cit.

The race for reserves

3:45 PM, on the flanks

On the far right and far left, the two attacks upon which Lee and Longstreet had depended to hold down Union reserves had both failed in that purpose. So strongly had Meade stitched together his line after the second day's fighting that it seemed to be holding everywhere. Osborn's and McGilvery's grand batteries had effectively held off the divisions of both Rodes and Law on the right and left flanks of the Union line. Rodes' Division, with Lane's two remaining brigades, had crossed the 500 yards swept by the artillery on Cemetery Hill only to be stopped by the fire of von Steinwehr's and Schurz's now pugnaciously steady Germans as the guns continued to fire over them. It was here that Trimble fell as he urged his men on, a splendid target on horseback. Despite repeated attempts, Law could never get enough men to charge out of the corpse-stacked swale to threaten McGilvery's guns, and now they were threatened by the 1st and 2nd US Sharpshooters, sent forward by de Trobriand to enfilade their left flank. McLaws was locked in a death-struggle with the Pennsylvania Reserves in a seesaw fight that turned the marshy Plum Run and the Weikert Woods into slaughter-pens. Sykes was now ordering up the Regulars of his 2nd Division to throw into the fight.

Not a great deal of this was apparent to either Lee or Longstreet because of the north–south length of the battlefield and the blinding clouds of smoke. What Longstreet could see, though, was enough to panic a man with less nerve. On the right the continuous front had fallen apart as Sander's Brigade had failed to advance fast enough and Kemper's Brigade had edged to the center. On the left, the flight of three brigades had opened up another hole, which was being steadily widened by a handful of the enemy, Sawyer's 8th Ohio. 'So now,' he thought to himself, 'everything is riding on George – and on Pettigrew – four brigades in the second and third lines.' [29] It would all depend on what the enemy had behind that ridge. This was no time to stint. He sent an aide racing back to ask him to send up the rest of Wilcox's Division: Wright's Brigade of Georgians as well as Mahone's Virginians and Posey's Mississippians. Who would win the race of the reserves?

Hancock had the same equation in mind as he rode down the rear of the ridge to see what reserves were available. He met Sedgwick riding up the hill to find him. Sedgwick's aide-de-camp recorded the meeting.

I was at Sedgwick's side when Hancock arrived with the colors of the army commander behind him. This great command had passed 'Uncle John' by once

---

[29]* Longstreet to Senator Wigfall, letter, 3rd July 1866, The Wigfall Papers, Georgia State Archives, Atlanta.

again, but he showed no sign of any disappointment. Instead he was there to lend his every effort as a loyal subordinate. He was a great man, and I would have served him unto death, but I must admit that Hancock was magnificent as he rode up on his big bay, radiating power in absolute control of the situation. 'Well, John,' he said, 'I see you have things in hand,' he said as he reached out to take Sedgwick's hand. They rode off a little ways with Hancock speaking with great animation and pointing up over the ridge to the left. As they rode back, I heard Hancock saying, 'You know what to do, John.' [30]

Already Wright's 1st Division and Wheaton's 3rd Division were up. From the Taneytown Road east, the rear of the ridge was packed with 9000 men wearing the Greek Cross, most of them moved in as the Confederate artillery fire had slackened. That assembly had not been without some loss. Lieutenant Rhodes and the 2nd Rhode Island had endured the Confederate cannonade at some cost. 'It is said that this fire continued for about two hours, but I have no idea of the time, and we could only cover ourselves the best we could behind the rocks and trees. About 30 men of our Brigade was killed or wounded by this fire. Soon the Rebel yell was heard.' [31]

3:50 PM, the Angle

About twenty yards in front of Webb's position near the Angle a great mass of Confederates stood rooted to the ground. They were firing steadily but could not advance. These were the men of Kemper, Garnett, and Archer – Virginians, Tennesseans, and Alabamians, brigades in name only by now, for a brigade assumes a command structure carefully woven by leaders from squads to companies through Regiments to a single commander. All of this was gone. The flags were still kept in the air, but all organization had evaporated, leaving only a single dense mass of men maybe twenty or thirty deep.

With men thus placed the natural prejudice in favor of living tended to take over. Physically, there was no barrier to prevent any front-rank man from rushing ahead. But, as Civil War soldiers noted, there seemed to be in such a situation an imaginary line beyond which no man could advance and live. Psychologically, by mass reaction, the soldiers seemed caught between discipline and courage on the one hand, and prudence on the other. They would stand their ground and fire, but they would be hard to get moving again. [32]

A few men of action were about to set things in motion. Colonel Wheelock

---

[30]* Charles Whittier, *Sedgwick of Gettysburg* (D. Appleton, New York, 1880) p.314.

[31] Elisha Hunt Rhodes, *All For the Union: The Civil War Diary of Elisha Hunt Rhodes*, ed. Robert Hunt Rhodes (Orion Press, New York, 1985) p.116.

[32] Stewart, op.cit. p.210.

Veazey's 16th Vermont had just come in from the skirmish line and was reforming behind the 13th Vermont. These regiments and the 14th Vermont formed Stannard's 3rd 'Paper Collar' Brigade on the left flank of Gibbon's Division. Kemper's Brigade had already passed by the front of the Vermonters, who had given the enemy the first taste of steady rifle fire, leaving their front littered with more bodies. Kemper's regiments continued to edge northward, now parallel with the II Corps front, bringing them past first Harrow's then Hall's Brigades, which poured more deadly musketry into them. In front of Hall was a patch of rough, bushy ground with sizeable rocks that proved both an obstacle and a shelter. Kemper's men naturally shied away from crossing it, but, at the same time, many of them found it offered their first real shelter. Men peeled off to take up positions from which they could finally fire back at the enemy. Then, for the first time, Gibbon's men felt the sting of Confederate musketry. But the natural drift northward was pushed along by Kemper's shout, pointing at Cowan's Battery, that 'There are the guns, boys, go for them!' – and the flags continued to edge north, dragging most of the men with them.[33] By now Kemper's Brigade had lost almost all organization as the clumps of men following the battle-flags melted into Garnett's clumps of men following their own battle-flags, just as the canister was raking both. The battle ended then for Kemper. Still on horseback, he was an irresistible target and was knocked off his horse with a terrible wound.

It was then that Hancock arrived at Stannard's side. The same thought had occurred to both men at the same time – flank them! The 13th and 16th wheeled out at right angles to the stone wall and opened a destructive fire on the right of Kemper's Brigade. Veazey described it:

> As we advanced in that charge the enemy were in great masses, without much order, and were rushing rapidly upon the lines to our right, and regardless of the exposure of their right flank ... the left of my regiment extended well around their flank... Our regiments fired a few volleys as they moved forward under the combined movement on the enemy's flank and rear ... those great masses of men seemed to disappear in a moment.

The steady fire of the Vermonters was such a destructive shock that the nerve of the men on Kemper's right was shattered. The ground 'was literally covered with dead and wounded men.' Hundreds more immediately surrendered and were hurriedly passed to the rear. Stannard could spare no guards and needed none, so eager were the prisoners to get out of harm's way.[34]

Veazey's regiment suddenly had another enemy appear on the scene. San-

[33] Mayo, op.cit.
[34] Wheelock Veazey to G.G. Benedict, 11th July 1864, Vermont Historical Society.

ders' Brigade was belatedly quick-timing in to cover Kemper's right. Stannard at this time ordered Veazey to return to the brigade front along the stone wall. Veazey, like Sawyer on the other flank, decided he was here to fight and moved off to the left at right angles to Sanders' Alabamians and Floridians. On the way he met Stannard, who gave him permission to attack. 'Upon the order the men cheered' and ran forward 'without firing a shot and quickly struck the rebel flank.' Sanders' men had descended into the safety of a bushy swale which protected them from fire from the front.[35] But the fire came from the flank, and so murderously that they collapsed and fled to the rear, leaving over 200 dead, wounded, and captured on the field.

At the Angle itself, three men broke the trembling balance at the same time. Gibbon now ordered his second line, the 72nd and 106th Pennsylvania, up behind the 71st along the stone wall. Behind the Confederate mass, still on his prancing bloodied stallion, Pickett could see the almost 500 men of this second line moving forward. His optimism of minutes ago had disappeared as he realized that his forward brigades had suffered so greatly and in such a small space of time. Kemper's right had been smashed, and now Dick Garnett's men were stopped dead in front of the stone wall, along which the Yankees were blazing away, dropping his men by scores. To his beloved, he would later write of that moment:

Your soldier boy wanted more than anything to flee that carnage straight to your arms and never again risk our life together. But you would never have wanted me if I had done that when so many other noble Southern women were losing sons and husbands who stood their ground. Old Peter needed me then, just as he passed the flag to me at the wall on Chapultepec Hill so many years ago.[36]

He looked back to see Armistead's brigade of almost 2000 men coming up fast. He turned to his single surviving aide, Captain Bright. 'Ride, John, ride to General Longstreet. Tell him I can take this position, but I cannot hold it. He must come up with support.' Bright rode off, and Pickett rode forward. 'Come on, Boys! Come, on! Over the wall. Home is over the wall!'

Pickett spurred his horse through the press and broke out into the deadly space marked with a barrier of his dead and wounded. Every eye was drawn to the man and horse shooting forward to sudden death. His polished sword and the gold embroidery of his uniform and cap glinted. No one could hear him above the roar, but instantly the Confederate mass knew that the invisible line

---

[35] Veazey, ibid.
[36]* Pickett to Sallie Corbell, letter, 18th August 1863, The Pickett Papers, Virginia State Archives, Richmond.

holding it back had dissolved. Garnett emerged from the line a split second later to confirm this. The paean of the Rebel Yell rang out, and the mass surged forward, the battle-flags densely arrayed in front. Along the stone wall near the Angle, the 71st Pennsylvania flinched; their dead and wounded already lay thick along the stone wall, and now they turned and fled. Cushing died then by his guns, a bullet through the mouth spinning the already twice-wounded hero to the ground. His battery first-sergeant, the feisty blond-bearded German, Frederick Fuger, stood by the guns, now shorn of their crews, to pull the lanyards one last time. Double canister spewed into the oncoming, howling mob, tearing Garnett off his black horse to be lost among the heaps of slain. Yet his men kept coming, firing as they did so.

Pickett dashed ahead and leapt the stone wall. His horse reared near the guns, and for a moment, just as at Chapultepec so many years ago, he was the first and only man to break the enemy's line. In that one moment, come what may, imperishable glory settled its raiment over George Pickett. 'Come on, Boys!' he shouted as he waved to his men, 'They're on the run, they're on the run!' The Rebel yell screeched higher and higher as the Virginians, Tennesseans, and Alabamians went over the wall in their hundreds.

Things had just gone smash for the Union position on the Angle. Webb watched helplessly as the 71st fled, unstoppable. Then the Irishmen of the 69th further down the wall, with their colors of Emerald Green, recoiled as the Confederate mass came up to the wall, firing. But they only moved back as far as the shelter of the Copse of Trees and Cowan's guns. At that moment Gibbon was shot in the back as he rode up to exhort a cowering reserve unit into action, and was led wounded from the field. Webb rushed up to the 72nd and 106th and ordered them forward, but they did not budge. He was new to his command, and the men may not all have recognized him. He would admit later that he was wrong not to have issued the command through their colonel. He even tried to wrestle the color from its bearer, who would neither let go nor go forward. Now they were dropping in twos and threes as the Confederates were forming a thick firing line on this side of the stone wall. Like Pickett's men just a short while ago they too were held back by an invisible wall. Haskell rode up just then, in time to rally some of the men of the 71st behind the 72nd. Seeing Webb trying to drag the 72nd forward, he tried to push from behind, even crowding them with his horse but to no avail. Help was needed, but there was no senior man left to set it in motion. Haskell rode off to see what a first lieutenant could do.

To the left, Pettigrew rode to the front as his old brigade came up even with Cushing's guns. His North Carolinians were badly thinned by the canister pouring from the twelve guns along Hays' line and the concentrated rifle-fire that hung a fire-spitting pall over the stone wall ahead. The situation was plainly out of control. All he had left of his four brigades were his own North

Carolinians. Archer's Brigade had melted into Pickett's first line, while Davis' Brigade behind was coming up in line with Armistead, it seemed. Then he looked to his right to see the wondrous sight of Pickett leaping the stone wall all alone, and thought to himself, 'It will be alright now.'[37]

The impending disaster was only too real to Colonel Arthur Devereux of the 19th Massachusetts and Colonel James Mallon of the 42nd 'Tammany' New York, Hall's Brigade, whose regiments were standing a hundred yards or so behind and to the left of the Copse of Trees. Devereux was struggling with his desire to get into the fight and his hesitancy to move without orders. His initiative got the upper hand, and he said to Mallon, 'We must move.' Just then he saw Hancock riding up, and, running to him, waved him down. 'See, general. They have broken through; the colors are coming over the stone wall; let me go in there!'

So quickly had Hancock reined up that his horse had reared, but he had taken in everything in a glance and said quickly, 'Go in there pretty God-damned quick!' Devereux shouted the orders and the barely 200 men of the shrunken regiments – 'New England's sturdy courage and Ireland's fiery valor' – surged forward, determined to throw the enemy back.[38] They met them in the Copse of Trees, the Irishmen in the lead and the Baystaters behind. The fighting was already hand-to-hand, with the Irishmen of the 69th savagely fighting the Virginians for every foot of ground. But the Virginians smelled victory, and stabbed and bludgeoned their way forward with bayonets and rifle butts, leaving every square foot of the copse's floor covered with the dead and writhing wounded.

Amazingly, Pickett still sat his horse waving his sword as his men blazed away at Webb's thin line. He was drunk with battle-joy now that he could smell the enemy about to break. Around him were a forest of Virginia's battle-flags and a mass of almost a thousand men who had come over the wall. Many of them had broken into the trees, from which arose the awful sounds of men at each other's throats. The rest were firing steadily at the line in his front. They were just a solid mass of men, every shred of regimental coherence gone, but they fought, and the blue line in front thinned and wavered with each passing second. From his vantage point atop his horse, Pickett saw there was nothing behind that one line, and from the direction he had come he saw old Lo Armistead leading his brigade up to the wall, and behind Armistead even more bayonets shimmered in waves. Old Peter would be there. And they were cracking! The Yankees were cracking! He saw the general in front of the Yankee line in front go down

---

[37]* James J. Pettigrew, *In the Service of the Southern Confederacy* (Hall and Sledge, Weldon, North Carolina, 1885) p.413.

[38] Stewart, op.cit. p.220.

and the color-bearer next to him too. Then the whole line fell apart and fled to the rear. The way was open.

As Webb fell, Haskell was galloping down the line to the left. He pulled his horse up sharply in front of Colonel Norman Hall, who asked immediately, 'How is it going?'

'Well, but Webb is hotly pressed and must have your support, or he will be overpowered – Can you assist him?'

'Yes.'

'You cannot be too quick.'

'I will move my brigade at once.'

In moments Hall's three remaining regiments were rushing rapidly to the right. Haskell looked in vain for Colonel Harrow as well, but decided his regiments would do nicely in his place. On his own authority he ordered each of them to the right.[39] And they went, and quickly too, drawn eagerly to the fighting. Few men wearing the White Trefoil stinted of eager courage that day. But on the battlefield, time is the great goddess who measures out the courage, and she was slipping away. Pickett's gallant horse had finally collapsed from too many wounds, but its master was still untouched, and the forest of battle-flags followed him forward. Among the trees, Devereux's and Mallon's men had died hard with the men of the 69th; the last handful of them surrendered as the Virginians picked up their green colors to add to their own of red and blue. Only Cowan's Battery and the 59th Pennsylvania were left of Webb's line. Hunt, still astride Bill, was towering above Cowan's guns as the last of his gunners dropped by their pieces. Directly across from them the Confederates had hidden as much as they could behind the low stone wall to protect themselves from the canister, and between blasts had been cutting down the gunners. They had waited for the last blast to rush the guns before the few remaining Redlegs could reload. Cowan 'saw a Confederate officer not more than 20 feet away. I heard him yell, "take the gun," referring to one of my guns.' Cowan called for double canister. Private McElroy shouted above the roar, 'Captain, this is our last round!' Cowan shouted back, 'I know it, Jake,' only to see him go down with three bullets in the face. Just after ramming home the last round Private Gates fell across the trail of his gun, shot through the legs. Cowan recalled that 'I ordered, "fire," and all five blew the line to pieces with double canister. The officer was gone.' But more Virginians kept coming over the bodies of the fallen. Cowan tried to pull his guns back by prolonge ropes, but the enemy was upon them. Hunt, now on Cowan's left front, had pulled out his pistol and was firing point-blank into them, yelling 'See 'em! See 'em!' Bill staggered and collapsed, pinning Hunt under him.[40]

---

[39] Haskell, op.cit.

[40] Cowan to Bachelder, 26th August 1866, Bachelder Papers, vol. I, pp.282–3; and Stewart, op.cit. p.222.

Cowan's battery died hard, but died all the same. Cowan fell too, shot through the shoulder, as the last of his gunners were cut down or fled. Rebels helped Hunt out from under his dead horse almost gently, and an officer gallantly offered his hand.

'Too late, too late,' screamed the evidence of Haskell's own eyes as he rode back towards the Angle with Hall's and Harrow's reinforcements. 'Webb's noble band had fallen and the guns were lost; the brave Rebels were coming up the crest in a ragged but thick mass from Cowan's Battery to Arnold's guns on the end of Hays' line. We could only throw ourselves in their path, one last effort to stem the Rebel tide.' [41] Arnold's left section were pivoted to its left to throw double canister into them at fifty yards, smearing a wide gouge three men deep and fifteen men across. The other section was firing at Pettigrew's North Carolinians to its front. Pickett fell at last, riddled with canister balls, and with his fall men found their courage drained away for the last time; the invisible line formed again across their path, even though hands reached across it to drag Pickett's bleeding body out of harm's way. A half-dozen men carried him back toward the stone wall and there met Armistead, climbing over it at the head of his brigade. Armistead spared only a brief glance at Pickett as he stood on the wall, the 53rd Virginia behind him, then looked over the heads of the halted survivors of Garnett's and Archer's Brigades to the Federals coun-terattacking to the right. To his left, Davis' regiments were coming up in fairly good order too. But directly ahead, the way was open all the way to the crest – and beyond, just over the crest, was home. Then waving his sword and the hat that had slipped down to the hilt, he shouted to his men, 'Boys, remember Pickett! Boys, give them the cold steel!' [42] They too had seen the body carried gently by so many men, its round head dripping with ringlets and knew instantly who it was. A cheer shot down the ranks, turning into the most ferocious Rebel yell Armistead could ever remember hearing.

Armistead was too good a soldier not to know that the main chance of the war had fallen into his hands. His brigade had suffered comparatively little from the artillery in its march across the valley, except for those awful guns on the 'mountain'. One damned shell had failed to explode and had bounced down a line, killing or wounding thirty men. Still, he had started the march with over 2000 men and still had most of them at hand, and, more importantly, in good order. His regiments were still holding together. The 53rd, his battalion of direction, was in the center, with the 38th and 57th on the left and the 9th an 14th on the right. He stopped to dress them on the other side of the wall and then ordered them forward at the double-quick. The clumps of men in front opened quickly to let his through. Canister hit them from the left, but the gaps

---

[41]* Haskell to Bachelder, November 1867, Bachelder Papers, vol.III, p.97.

[42] Martin, op.cit.

closed up quickly. On his left, Davis' Brigade was pushing through Pettigrew's men to close with the enemy as well, but there the Yankees were still strongly posted behind a stone wall, and four men deep at least.

His immediate problem was the counterattack on the right, coming towards the captured battery and the woods. He ordered the 9th and 14th to change front by right oblique while he took the remaining three regiments, perhaps a thousand men by now, forward to the crest. They had not gone far when he heard a thunderous volley from the right. The Union counterattack which had come on in a hurried, formless mass had been rocked back by the steady 9th and 14th. It was that same volley heard by Longstreet as he jumped his horse over the stone wall. Garnett's and Archer's exhausted survivors were standing around, vacant-eyed, as the few surviving officers tried to gather them under their flags, not one of which had been lost. But they seemed so many and the men assembling under them so few. Colonel Mayo came up to him and saluted. 'It appears, General, that I am the senior officer of Garnett's Brigade.'

Longstreet looked down on him and extended his hand. 'Your men have done well, Colonel. Now assemble them behind the wall in case they are needed again.' Mayo winced, but saluted again as Longstreet wasted no more time on conversation. Micah Jenkins strode by and stopped long enough to enthusiastically shake his hand as well. 'South Carolina salutes gallant Virginia, sir!' Then he was off as his strong brigade passed quickly over the wall. Mayo turned to watch the South Carolinians advance. To the south on their flank he could see Corse's fellow Virginians as well. A great day for Virginia, he thought, but he could summon no joy, only grief at the sight of the skeleton of his regiment and the imagined faces of all the widows and orphans. He turned in the direction of the stone wall at the sound of horses and wheels to see Colonel Alexander riding up with a dozen guns in train behind him. Alexander called out to the survivors, 'Here, men, help us knock some holes through these stones so we can go through.' None of the infantry moved as the gunners frantically began heaving stones and rails aside. Mayo stared, and it finally hit home that he was in command. 'Alright, boys, help the artillery! Virginia is still in this fight!'

4:00 PM, Spangler's Woods

As Pickett had leapt the stone wall, Longstreet's aide had galloped up to Lee at his vantage point on the edge of Spangler's Woods. He gasped out Longstreet's request to release Wright, Mahone, and Posey. The aide waited, but Lee's attention seemed to be elsewhere. In fact, the man realized, he had never seen Lee look so bad. He waited, then ventured, 'General Lee?' But Lee was not hearing him. His heart was pounding so hard that he felt it was going to burst from his chest. Then a giant hammer struck him there. The aide saw a startled look come over his face. His eyes rolled back to expose the whites, he sagged forward, and just slid off Traveler into the grass.

Colonel Marshall and Longstreet's aide were at his side in seconds. Marshall was shocked at Lee's corpse-like pallor and the cold, clammy feel of his hands, and shouted for a doctor. Marshall quickly unbuttoned Lee's coat and vest and noticed that his shirt was drenched as if he had been soaked to the skin in the rain. His breathing was shallow and labored. The colonel ordered him carried to the shade of the trees a few yards away. In minutes a doctor arrived and knelt down to examine Lee. Awake but almost incoherent, Lee was only able to say, in a weak voice, 'I have terrible pain.' The precise nature of his illness still eluded doctors in the 1860s, but they had been able to treat the symptoms with some success for over a hundred years. 'General Lee,' said the young doctor softly, 'I will give you something for your pain.' His black servant was standing by with his medical bag. The man had been with the doctor, and his father before him, long enough to have absorbed a great deal of practical medical knowledge. Before the doctor could ask, he produced a glass syringe and began to fill it with morphine. The doctor was so used to this he did not even take notice but quickly administered the narcotic. Next, the doctor and his servant began applying rotating tourniquets to his arms and legs to slow down the circulation. Again it was empirical experience they were working from. The right side of the heart continued to receive blood from the limbs and pump it out rapidly. From the right side of the heart it would go through the lungs and then through the left side of the heart, but that side was damaged and could not perform efficiently. The result was that blood quickly congested the lungs. Rotating the tourniquet from one limb to the other was then a means of slowing the blood to the right side of the heart so as to lessen the demands on the wounded left. Empirically-based or not, it worked.

As the morphine began to take effect, the doctor ordered up an ambulance. The driver was almost trembling at the thought of his passenger. He could not have been more nervous had they told him he was carrying Baby Jesus. An orderly took the bit of one of the horses to guide the team at a slow walk to avoid even the slightest unevenness of the ground, to spare Lee as much as possible from the agony of a ride in the springless vehicle.

Colonel Marshall and most of the rest of the staff accompanied the ambulance on its way to Lee's headquarters at the Seminary. Their duties lay forgotten after their pillar of iron had fallen. Only Lieutenant Colonel Walter Taylor, Lee's efficient Assistant Adjutant General, the man who came closest to being Lee's chief of staff, remained. Taylor stared at the ambulance until it was masked by the trees, stood thoughtfully for a minute, and then turned to Longstreet's aide, who had been standing around helplessly all the time. 'Well, lieutenant, I guess you had better inform General Longstreet that he now commands the Army of Northern Virginia. God help him.'

CHAPTER 14

3rd July 1863
'My men, follow me!'

4:00 PM, the crest of Cemetery Ridge

Hall's and Harrow's Brigades had lost all formation. Even the regiments merged together as the men rushed forward to come to grips with the enemy. This was II Corps at its best. No officers were needed to tell the men to fight. They fought on in small bands that grew and shrunk as the fight lashed back and forth. Again and again they closed the small deadly space separating them from the 9th and 14th Virginia. But the fire of the Virginians was so heavy that each wave receded leaving more blue-clad bodies in the grass. The smoke was so thick that they failed to see that Kemper's men, who had clustered for safety in front of the rough ground, had now come forward on either side of the rocks and bushes. Behind them were the unbroken ranks of 'Bulldog' Corse's Brigade. For Kemper's men it was eerie to climb over the undefended wall; they had seen the defenders all pull out to the right and disappear into the powder smoke.

Only Rogers' two 10-pounder Parrotts continued to defend the ridge here. Then one gun exploded through the inexperience of its volunteer infantry crewmen. It flipped over and crushed one man. Another was dead and five wounded. Minutes ago the front here had been defended by most of a division; now there was only Rogers' remaining gun. He ordered double canister at forty yards. Corporal Walter Brogan pulled the last lanyard, to send the shotgun blast into the enemy.

> The enemy swept over all obstacles and around our pieces, and for the first time ... in the history of Battery B, the hands of the foe were laid upon its guns ... Sergeant Darveau fired his revolver at the foe as they came on, and when an officer planted his colors on a gun, exclaiming, 'This is our gun', Sergeant Darveau seized the trail hand-spike, and struck him full across the forehead, as I blasted him with my revolver, killing him on the spot ... Darveau fell instantly, riddled with bullets.[1]

---

[1] David Schultz, *'Double Canister At Ten Yards': The Federal Artillery and the Repulse of Pickett's Charge* (Rank and File Publications, Redondo Beach, California, 1995) p.58.

Corse's regiments swept forward to align themselves with Armistead. He wheeled the 15th and 17th Virginia on his left to strike the enemy still resisting behind the Copse of Trees. They fired into the backs of Hall's and Harrow's men, bringing them down in droves. Caught in front and rear, they finally panicked. Scores of pairs of hands went up as others fought on or fled by their open right flank over the crest. The White Trefoil had finally fought its last, and none had done so more tenaciously. In motion now, both Virginia brigades advanced to the crest, the Rebel yell sent keening before them.

That is what Lieutenant Rhodes and the 2nd Rhode Island had heard as they stood waiting in ranks at the base of the reverse slope. The commands to move forward ran down the division front, with three brigades in line, each two lines deep. Brigadier General Frank Wheaton rode past with his staff, and soon his 4700 men were on the move up the slope. Brigadier General Horatio Wright's 4200-man 1st Division came forward further south at the same time. Behind Wheaton rode 'Uncle John' for a while, his VI Corps flag bearing the Greek Cross extended in a sudden breeze. Then he was gone, off to the south.

As they ascended the slope, the men on Wheaton's right saw Hancock race past them and then slant up the slope. He rode up behind Hays' Division to a scene of mounting confusion. Arnold's Battery had fired its last canister at the North Carolinians of Pettigrew's and Davis' Brigades, coming up the slope at them in the same sort of disorganized mob as Garnett's and Archer's Brigades had become. Armistead's men had come so close on their left that they were able to enfilade the battery, dropping so many of the artillery crews that the guns fell silent. Smyth's Brigade on the stone wall was refusing its flank to Armistead, which relieved pressure on the North Carolinians, who surged forward with a yell. It looked as if Hays' Division, which had seemed so strongly posted, was about to be pressured out. As Hancock rode up he passed Carroll's small brigade, barely the size of a strong regiment, in reserve. 'Colonel, go in there right now, and don't come back alive if you fail!' Carroll had been standing there his arms folded in growing agitation as II Corps' center had collapsed. Now he broke into a delighted grin and drew his sword. Stepping forward, he shouted down the brigade line, 'At the double-quick, march!'

Hays galloped up to Hancock as he was waving Carroll's men forward. 'General, we can flank them. Robinson and I can flank them. I can swing Willard's Brigade onto their flank as Robinson strikes the enemy in front of the hill.'

Hancock asked sharply, 'Are they up to it after yesterday?'

'I will lead them myself!'

'Then, by God, do it!' Hancock almost shouted.[2] Hays sped off and Hancock rode ahead to catch up with Carroll's attack. It hit at the Angle, where Arnold's

---

[2]* Alexander Hays, *My Service in the War* (Hubbard, Philadelphia, 1880) p.249.

guns sat surrounded by their dead crews. The North Carolinians were swarming over the wall and the guns as Smyth attempted to form a new line at right angles to the wall. Armistead's flank regiment, the 38th Virginia, had already passed that point. Carroll's men gave a cheer, dropped point on their bayonets and charged into the North Carolinians milling around the guns and wall. A ragged volley pitched a few of them into the ground. The rest closed as the enemy tried to get out of the way but were prevented by their own crowded ranks and the wall itself.

Hancock rode up to the wrecked Leister House to watch the enemy brigade on the left make for the crest. His eye went to the man out front with his hat impaled on his sword. His throat caught. Was it Lo? Lo Armistead? The memories of that last meeting in California, the goodbye party, flooded back.

Hancock's staff had again caught up with him. Now one of them said, 'Look, General, back by the trees.' Hancock followed his finger to the edge of the copse. A group of officers on horseback stood there, a color-bearer among them. Almost simultaneously they turned their attention in Hancock's direction. Hancock looked through his glasses. He said out loud, more to himself, 'Well, I'll be damned – Longstreet.' He rode the big bay a few yards ahead of his staff, took off his hat in a flourish and salute. The big bearded man near the copse rode forward a bit and waved his hat as well. 'Hah!' said Hancock, out loud this time. 'Longstreet, by God! Gentlemen, you have seen a great general today. Never forget it.'[3]

'Don't they ever run out of reserves?'

4:15 PM, the Copse of Trees

Longstreet's glasses were just as good as Hancock's, but his comments more laconic, despite the chivalrous return of his salute. 'Hancock, huh.' There was business at hand. A forest of colors was coming up the reverse slope of the ridge on a collision course with Armistead and Corse's Brigades. He almost grunted in irritation to Sorrel, 'Don't they ever run out of reserves, Moxley?' He had just scanned the valley behind him to see if the three brigades he had asked for were on their way – but nothing. Three thousand men would make a big difference right now, he thought. Alexander's dozen guns were the last Confederates to cross the valley, and they were trailing behind the Virginia brigades or deploying on the flanks to counter enfilade fire and discourage any more flank attacks.

Without waiting for an answer from Sorrel, he spurred forward between Jenkins' regiments to find their young commander. Jenkins was standing in front of his old 5th South Carolina. His youth shone in his face and in every graceful movement of his body. Longstreet thought briefly, as he rode up, that he was just like Pelham, Lee's brilliant young gunner, killed unexpectedly in March. What had Lee said of him? 'It is glorious to see such courage in one so young!'[4] Then a shadow crossed his mind. He shook it off and looked down into Jenkins' upturned face. His eyes were dancing with a cold blue fire more terrible than the fiercest heat. He paused, then reached over to take Jenkins' by the shoulder. 'General, Armistead is about to catch hell any minute now,' and as if on cue, the front exploded in deafening volleys as the Virginians and Wheaton's brigades closed on each other along a 500-yard front. The thunder of the exchange blotted out his voice. He leaned over to almost yell into Jenkins' ear. 'Listen, son, you are my last reserve. If you don't break 'em . . .' He could not finish. It was too painfully obvious.

But Jenkins just smiled and said, 'South Carolina will do her duty, General!' Then he drew up his sword in a handsome salute. 'Well, General, it were well it were done quickly.'[5] Longstreet nodded, and Jenkins rode up to the brigade, called his regiments to attention, and walked over to the commander of the 5th South Carolina, his old friend, Colonel Asbury Coward. 'Old man, we are in for it today . . . Your regiment is the Battalion of Direction. Tell your men that South Carolina is looking for every man to do his duty to her this day.'[6] He waited a moment for Coward to exhort his men, then shouted his favorite command again: 'Follow me, my men, follow me!' They were in columns of regiments now, three deep, and he aimed them at a gap that was opening between Armistead and Corse as the latter edged to the right to avoid being overlapped by Wheaton's longer front. He raced ahead of them to inspect the gap, then turned to wave them forward with his sword.

Smoke filled the gap, drifting from the continuous firing on the crest of the ridge. The South Carolinians marched forward past Longstreet, cheering and waving their hats. The 5th on the left and the 1st on the right were the first to enter the gap and disappear into the smoke. Waiting across the firing line was Wheaton's 2nd Brigade and Lieutenant Rhodes. It was impossible to see anything in all the smoke that hung heavy in the air, not even the 10th Massachusetts, the 2nd Rhode Island's brother regiment on the left. Behind, in the second Union line, were the 10th and 37th Massachusetts. Rhodes' twenty-two men of Company B were as solid as the granite of home. Eleven more had fallen at Chancellorsville in an action that had saved the corps. But the smoke magnified fear by letting in only the terrible din of the musketry to either flank.

---

[4] Major John Pelham (1838–63), the Alabama *beau ideal* of the Confederacy; Mark M. Boatner III, *The Civil War Dictionary* (David McKay Co. Inc., New York, 1959) p.630.

[5]* Longstreet, *From Manassas to Gettysburg* (J.B. Lippincott, Philadelphia, 1896) p.435.

[6] Natalie Jenkins Bond and Osman Latrobe Coward, eds., *The South Carolinians: Colonel Asbury Coward's Memoirs* (Vantage Press, New York, 1968) p.134.

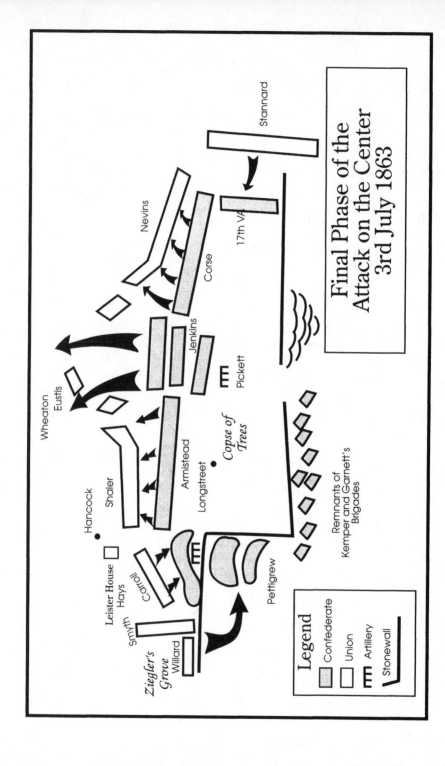

Final Phase of the
Attack on the Center
3rd July 1863

Legend

Confederate
Union
Artillery
Stonewall

Only here and there did the black clouds tear slightly apart to reveal some glimpse of the fighting, only to quickly close up again. Bullets came through the smoke, dropping men here and there, until the front ranks had been closed up dozens of times along the brigade front. Then a small eddy of breeze parted the smoke ahead just enough to reveal the silvery hedge of bayonets and red battle-flags. 'Fire! Fire!' Hundreds of rifles came to the ready and discharged in one ear-splitting crack of thunder. The Rhode Island men heard a groan and screams above the noise, above the clatter of their own ramrods frantically ramming balls down the barrels of their rifles – then through the smoke came the shouted commands, then the rattle of hundreds of muskets raised to firing position. They steeled themselves, and one wag pronounced, 'Lord, make us thankful for what we are about to receive.' 'Fire!' Another crash. Now Rhode Island and Massachusetts felt the sting, tumbling men into the grass amid the cries and shrieks of the wounded.

Longstreet waited by the Copse of Trees, watching his last reserve go into action. Jenkins' last regiments disappeared through the smoky gap. All along the firing front all he could see were the backs of his regiments half-wreathed in gray wisps of smoke. They were leaking a constant stream of men stumbling to the rear clutching wounds. A few crawled back through the ranks. Longstreet saw hardly a whole man use the ruse of helping a wounded comrade to the rear to escape danger. One of those who staggered back was an older senior officer clutching a shoulder blotted with blood. Major Sorrel exclaimed, 'Why, that is General Armistead!' Several men from the staff ran to him and helped him to the shade of the trees where a dressing station had been set up amid the carpet of bodies.

Longstreet dismounted and came over to him. Armistead looked up as the doctor cut away his coat, and said, 'We'll break them, Peter! We'll break them.' He struggled to reach into his pocket and finally pulled out a handful of dried corn. He held it up. 'Men that can live on this, can do anything!' Then he fell back, breathing hard as the overworked doctor ordered a man to hold him down better. Longstreet had seen the same sort of light in young Jenkins' face only minutes ago.

Lieutenant Rhodes had lost another five men in less than five minutes, but the rest just kept firing into the smoke. The wounded lay where they fell or dragged themselves back out of the line. Strangely, he could hear above all the noise a fine tenor voice calling out, 'Keep it hot, my men. Keep it hot!'

To the left, unbeknownst to anyone, the hammering had assumed the ultimate symbolism. The 1st South Carolina and the 10th Massachusetts were shooting death and hatred into each other at a gruesome rate. Their dead and wounded formed low walls of tortured flesh where the front ranks had been. South Carolina and Massachusetts, the two implacable poles of the war, each obdurate, and unforgiving, were in mortal combat on this greatest field of the nation's strife. They were pouring out all their fury and anger at each other, soaking the ground with their blood as if it were an altar to their passions. Even the air became a party to their madness and stirred itself to rip away the clouds of anonymous smoke. For a moment the firing slackened on both sides as they looked across the deadly space at the skeletons of each other's regiments. But the passion had only paused to feed itself anew as both sides pushed in new regiments to the front. Lieutenant Rhodes stumbled back with the seven survivors of his company as the 37th and 7th Massachusetts's moved to the front, and the crash of musketry resumed. Rhodes heard once again, faintly, as he moved back, 'Keep it hot, my men. Keep it hot!'

Along the entire line, Longstreet's three brigades remained locked with Wheaton's three. On the right, the fight did not even seesaw but remained a stationary killing machine. There Stannard was extending his brigade again, hoping to repeat his performance against Kemper. But Corse was quicker and refused the 17th Virginia. Pettigrew's two jumbled brigades were fighting at close range, often hand-to-hand with Carroll's men along the stone wall. Alexander squeezed a battery into the Angle near the Leister House and was throwing canister into Carroll's lines.

Again Longstreet looked back toward Seminary Ridge and saw nothing. Time was slipping away. Even if they started now across the valley, time was against them. The only forward movement was a single horseman approaching the stone wall. Then, out of the woods on the ridge, fresh battle-lines appeared and advanced, bayonets glittering in the early afternoon sun. The horseman had cleared the stone wall and rode up to him. It was the aide he had sent to Lee. Longstreet cracked one of his rare smiles so relieved was he to see the success of his mission. But as the lieutenant explained, the smile fell from his face. He could hear the exclamations of shock and hurt from his staff. Though they had taken Longstreet's side in his arguments with Lee, they had kept it tightly within his official family, but even they were unconscious believers in Lee, the right hand of God and savior of the Confederacy. The young man went on to explain that when Taylor had sent him on his way, he was halfway back across the valley before he realized that General Longstreet needed those three brigades even more now that he was the army commander, and he did not have to ask permission either. On his own he had ridden to Wilcox to inform him that it was the order of the General Commanding that his division come forward. Wilcox had been stunned to learn what had happened to Lee. His men had heard even faster as the word had spread through Spangler's Woods from the walking wounded and stragglers who had taken shelter there. It had taken longer than usual to get them moving; everyone seemed to be in a daze, from colonels to privates. Not Lee. There was no army without Lee. The end of the world had come.

Longstreet felt the weight of the world crash down upon his shoulders. Now there was no-one to hide behind if things went bad, if his advice were not taken or his efforts failed. It was all his. But character is everything, or was in these more manly times. He squared his shoulders and barked at his staff, 'Gentlemen, pay attention. We still have a battle to win. Grieve later. Work now!' He turned again to look at the advancing brigades, and pulled out his watch. It read 4:15. Wilcox's brigades were coming straight across the valley. There would be only a little artillery to slow him. Hurry, hurry! Maybe twenty minutes if he was lucky. They had to hold on to the enemy and tear at him for another twenty minutes. He glanced back at the continuous stream of wounded. Even twenty minutes seemed too long.

4:30 PM, Ziegler's Grove

Hays had ridden out in front of Willard's old brigade and explained what he wanted to do. He praised their action of yesterday and goaded their pride; he asked, 'Are you up to it today?' They shouted back an angry, 'Yes!' He gave the command to advance, and they climbed over the stone wall and ran rather than marched in a wheel around to the right through the orchard. Pettigrew's brigades were so mixed and packed up by then from struggling against Carroll that they could not have refused a flank to ward off Hays' advance if they had wanted to. The men on the edge of the mass saw it coming. Some turned to fire, others tried to run, but most were simply trapped by the crush of men against the stone wall on their right. The volley boomed, and a groan rose from Pettigrew's men as hundreds on the edge of the mass fell. Another volley, and the mass began to panic, frantic to get out of the way. The rear unravelled and began fleeing back across the valley. Those pushed up against the stone wall spilled over to run between Cushing's silent guns and the Copse of Trees, jumping over the stone wall and through Mayo's men positioned behind.

Robinson was in motion at the same time, his object to strike the flank of Rodes' Division to relieve the pressure on Howard. It was easier than he thought. Rodes' and Lane's brigades were staggering from the bloodletting they had endured in attacking from Long Lane through Osborn's massed guns and throwing themselves fruitlessly against Howard's suddenly stubborn Germans. Hundreds of unhurt men had slunk back across the fields to the safety of the sunken road. The morale of the rest quivered like an over-full water glass in which only the static pressure along the rim kept it from overflowing. Robinson's Division was only a shadow of itself after two days of hard fighting, but these I Corps men were made of stern stuff. They looked it too, as they double-quicked out at right angles to the enemy held at bay at the base of the hill. Robinson halted them, ordered them to face right, and fire. One volley was all it took for the water glass to spill over. The Confederate right-hand regiments broke first, making for the rear, then those of the center and left. In minutes thousands of men were in flight back to the sunken road. Howard was cheering harder than any of his men, and got even more excited as he ordered his own thinned ranks to charge racing down the hill with them.

4:20 PM, the center of Cemetery Ridge

As Sedgwick rode along their front in the center of the ridge the Greek Cross on the Corps flag was clearly visible to the men. Sedgwick stopped momentarily to speak to Doubleday, Crawford, and Birney, and then rode back down the line. Each general turned quickly to pass out his orders to his subordinates and they to theirs until the company commanders were shouting their commands. The men had been watching the great contest to their left and right for an hour-and-a-half in growing states of excitement and anxiety. They had watched the great Southern host march in its pride and power across the valley, and not one man failed to see that the war, the destiny of the nation, and the sum of all the sacrifice and blood that came before, were now trembling in the balance. Now they cheered, not the idle noise ordered for some passing great man, but a spontaneous explosion of released tension. Down the slope they came, quickly, eagerly, great serried lines of regiments, most winnowed by two terrible days of battle, their colors now thick along the line and the Stars and Stripes like dashes of clean color above the dusty, dark blue ranks. Behind them, with Sedgwick himself in the lead, was a second great wave of his 1st and 2nd Divisions, another 7000 men and the last batteries from the Artillery Reserve.

Colonel Humphreys' heart sank as his men in the Plum Run swale began to shout and point to the left at the blue wave pouring off the ridge. For the survivors of Barksdale's Brigade, the spirit could take no more. The shock among McLaws' other brigades was equally unnerving. The swale was already full of their dead, and more were spread up the slope where charge after charge against McGilvery's guns had been beaten back. They had killed as well at that short distance. Their rifle fire had dropped scores of gunners by their pieces. Now the Redlegs cheered wildly as the attack went in on their right. Below them the swale emptied in a heartbeat as McLaws' thousands made for the safety of Alexander's guns on the Emmitsburg Road. McGilvery redirected his pieces to that new target. The enemy guns had become mute almost as soon as their infantry had advanced. McGilvery suspected they were out of everything but canister, and he wanted to make sure they would be able to use as little of that as possible. Hazlett and his gunners on Little Round Top watched the scene below in open-mouthed amazement before he too realized what the guns must do. Their fire was immediately directed at the Confederate guns.

Along the Emmitsburg Road, the Confederate gunners waited in shocked silence as the enemy masses came down the slope straight towards their left and the army's center on Seminary Ridge. Their pieces were already loaded with canister, but it was useless until they came within range. Helpless, they stood

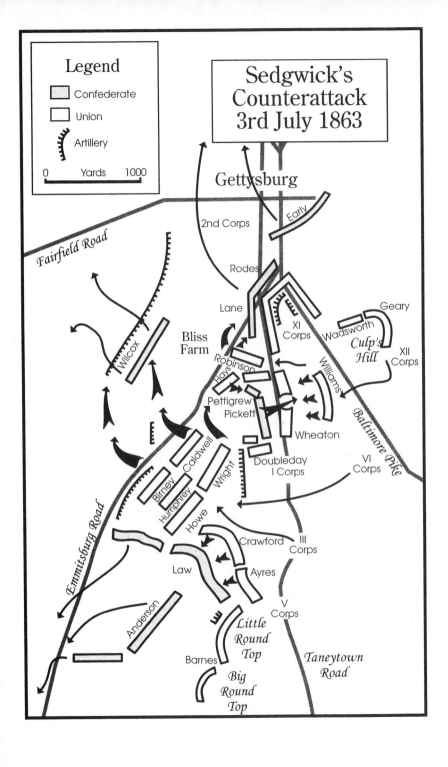

by their guns as round shot and shell converged on their gun line and the limbers and caissons behind them.

4:30 PM, the Copse of Trees

Longstreet could not see any of this. The smoke from the great struggle to his front had drifted around the flanks and blotted out whatever was happening there. What he could see were Pettigrew's men panicking. He rode into them shouting for them to rally and face about. 'Hold on, men, hold on! Supports are on the way!' Many did, wanting only to be taken in hand and assured they had not been put in the forefront of the battle and abandoned like another old soldier, Uriah the Hittite. 'Damn!' he shouted, 'Wilcox, hurry, for God's sakes, hurry!' Across the valley, Wilcox's brigades were barely a third of the way along. He called out to Colonel Mayo, who came over the stone wall to him. 'Colonel, form your men and bring them back here. I may need one last effort from them.' Looking at the stunned expression on Mayo's face, he said a bit more softly, 'I am asking a great deal, Colonel, but everything may depend upon it.' Leaving Mayo in shock, he rode back towards the firing line where the last two of Jenkins' regiments, the Palmetto Sharpshooters and the 6th South Carolina, waited to go into action. His last reserve – two regiments – and Jenkins' there in the middle of the line, dueling with the enemy center. His right fist tightened as his arm hung down his side, his left hand still lightly holding the reins of his horse. His self-possession in battle was legendary – so perhaps it was only Major Sorrel who saw the fist tighten and understood the strain. In an even voice, Longstreet said, 'If Jenkins punches through, they will break. It all depends on Jenkins.'[7]

Jenkins, the South Carolinian Mars, was on foot now, his splendid horse brought down early in the attack. If anything, he was even more animated with that icy fire that let him burn but still see everything with a cool, clear detachment. Above the havoc he could admire the enemy, tough as nails, as stubborn as his own South Carolinians, and not to be budged in this slugging match. Already his brigade was consuming itself like a blue flame. Time was running out. He ran behind the firing line, telling his colonels, 'We're going in with the bayonet.'[8]

The Massachusetts men heard the shouts across the firing line: 'Bayonets!' They had little time to prepare, whipping out their own bayonets without orders. Firing ceased, replaced with a clatter of bayonets being twisted and locked into place. Then again that voice: 'My men! Follow me!' – a shout, the Rebel yell, and through the powder smoke they came, running with leveled

---

[7]* Sorrel to Bachelder, 11th April 1872, Bachelder Papers, vol.4, p.727.
[8]* J.M. White, *Reminiscences of the Sixth South Carolina Volunteers* (B. F. Publishing Co., Richmond, Virginia, 1899), p.128.

bayonets, absorbing a ragged volley. Their screaming ran ahead of them across the thirty smoke-wreathed yards, magnifying the fears of the Massachusetts men. There was an instinctive backing away. Contrary to popular belief, men rarely stand to receive a bayonet charge if they cannot scare the charging side off first. And there was no scare in South Carolina. The Baystaters had finally flinched. Every man wanted to get out of the way of the sharp steel, a herd decision that instantly dissolved all sense of cohesion. They were wavering when the South Carolinians crashed into them, howling and thrusting like devils or madmen. The Massachusetts men broke and fled into the regiments behind, which were disorganized as well. The 112 men left in the 2nd Rhode Island tried to stand but were pushed aside by the mob. Then the enemy was upon them as well. Lieutenant Rhodes and his handful of Company B men stood in a knot, like a rock in a raging torrent, as the enemy swept around them. He glanced up and down the rear of the division to see the neighboring regiments begin to waver too as the enemy poured through. Racing at the head of them was a finely dressed young officer, sword in one hand and the captured colors of the 37th Massachusetts in the other.

Longstreet seized the moment when a runner from Jenkins came to tell him that the brigade was going in with the bayonet. He and his staff rode behind the firing line, urging the Virginia regiments to follow the South Carolinians with the bayonet. The shouting in the center as Jenkins went in was followed to the right and left by shouts, 'Bayonet! Bayonet!' The invisible line that had been forming in front of them evaporated as the battle-joy surged down the line, bursting out in the Rebel yell. 'Forward! Forward!' The enemy firing lines in front of them seemed to be dissolving. Longstreet rode through the evaporating powder smoke to see the whole enemy division reeling back, its center already broken by the Carolinians.

Near the Leister House, Hancock watched Wheaton's Division go. Around him his staff groaned and cursed, but he remained calm. His eyes looked over the fighting to the dark columns approaching at the double-quick over the Baltimore Pike and across the fields. It was Williams' Division, over 4000 strong, come down off Culp's Hill to the summons of Meade's last command.

By now Longstreet had seen them too. Right there, he knew it was over.

Epilogue

Longstreet surrendered his sword to Hancock that afternoon at the Copse of Trees. He had tried to pull his brigades back across the valley, but it was filled with Sedgwick's huge column. Alexander's guns had been badly smashed up before the column swept over them. Wilcox had had the good sense to withdraw his brigades back into the woods and beyond. Sedgwick had swept over the ridge after them into the enemy's disorganized rear, filled with wounded, stragglers, and trains, all now suddenly set in terrified motion. For Sergeant Sullivan in the Gettysburg railroad depot cupola, it was glorious. His guards had disappeared as they heard

> the Northern cheer. We knew that the rebs were scooped, and the old Army of the Potomac was victorious. There were ten or fifteen of us in the observatory, and they were wild with joy, some cried, others shook hands, and all joined in [the] best cheer we could up. I forgot about my wound, and was very forcibly reminded of it when I went to shout as I had to sit down to keep from falling. The other wounded down below joined in the cheer.

The men were as happy as 'if the paymaster had come into camp.' [1]

With the center gone, only the fragments of the Army of Northern Virginia on the wings survived to fly off in opposite directions. Ironically it was Ewell, the most ineffectual senior officer on the field, who saved even a part of the army. He pulled out the remnants of his corps, Early's, and what he could of Rodes' Division, by the Chambersburg Pike. Along the way, they were joined by the two cavalry brigades that had duelled ineffectually with Gregg's blue cavalry on the northern flank. They formed the rearguard. They also picked up Beverly Robertson's Cavalry Brigade – 1200 men who had sat out the battle because Robertson had again managed to stay safely out of the way. Ewell arrested him on sight. The crucible of the catastrophe somehow burned away his indecision. He conducted a model withdrawal, bringing over 10,000 men safely home to Virginia, all that was left of the seemingly invincible host that Lee had brought north. He was also to win the last laurels of Southern arms

---

[1] William J.K. Beaudot and Lance J. Herdegen, eds., *An Irishman in the Iron Brigade: The Civil War Memoirs of James P. Sullivan, Sergt., Company K, 6th Wisconsin Volunteers* (Fordham University Press, New York, 1993) p.101.

when he turned his command on Gregg's pursuing cavalry division and nearly destroyed it.

The survivors of Anderson's, Law's, and McLaws' Divisions tried to escape south-east down the Emmitsburg Road, covered by the two cavalry brigades on the flank. Buford and Kilpatrick's cavalry pursued ruthlessly in a running battle with the Confederate rearguard cavalry. They closed the trap when the fugitives were stopped by Wesley Merritt's Reserve Brigade near the Maryland border, taking 11,000 prisoners. Other fugitives from the army's broken center were also fleeing towards the safety of the Catoctin Mountains, just over the state line.

The Army of Northern Virginia had been irretrievably broken at Gettysburg. Even Ewell's remnant was not enough to rebuild upon, even if the Confederacy had enough time. It did not. Four days after the battle, the Army of the Potomac was re-crossing its pontoon bridges at Edward's Ferry, the bridges that had carried it out of Virginia in pursuit of Lee ten days earlier. Now the world had changed. Hancock was still mounted on the big light bay he had been given to ride along the stone wall. He cantered the horse across the bridge to the Virginia side and halted by the road to take the salute of the first corps to cross. He took off his hat as the White Trefoil fluttered by, its ranks now so much thinner than ten short days before. The troops cheered him as they marched by, some shouting 'Gettysburg, Gettysburg!' and others, 'On to Richmond! To Richmond!' He glanced southward. Yes, the way was clear at last.[2]

Meade was recovering from his wounds at Washington, wreathed in honors as Hancock led the army south. And Lee –

On that late afternoon, the seven miles of road to Fairfield had been jammed with wagons, ambulances, caissons, and guns. Only the concentration of Federal cavalry on the flanks saved the Confederate center from being run down. One of the ambulances carried a special patient – Robert E. Lee. Major Marshall had made the decision to remove Lee. The doctors pleaded for him not to be moved, but Marshall was loathe to let him be captured. Unconsciously he was weighing in those seconds Lee's mortal life against his immortal glory. Mattresses were hurriedly thrown into the back of the ambulance, and Lee's headquarters physician volunteered to ride with him. His small cavalry escort

[2]* Woodrow Wilson, *The Presidency of Winfield Scott Hancock 1868–1872* (Longmans and Green, New York, 1905) p.vi. As a Democrat, Wilson found much to admire in the Hancock presidency, not the least of which was his continuation of Lincoln's policy of reconciliation and rapid reintegration of the defeated South. Ironically it was Lincoln's very generosity that spelled the defeat of his party in the 1868 elections, as the South solidly lined up behind Hancock. The Republicans were back with their own war hero from the Western Theater in the 1872 election, which saw the victory of 'The Great Reconciliation Ticket' – Ulysses S. Grant and his vice-president, James Longstreet.

waited nearby while Lee was placed on a stretcher by careful hands and carried
to the ambulance. Around them was a scene of utter chaos. The roads and fields
were full of men who were no longer an army. Yet around Lee's tent, as he was
carried to the wagon, was a circle of orderlies, cooks, and guards as calm as on a
garrison Sunday. Every head was bare. Many of the men openly cried, an
admission of insurmountable grief in a society that worshipped manly fortitude.
They reached out to touch the stretcher or the blanket over him, murmuring
their goodbyes.

At a word from the doctor that Lee was ready, Marshall mounted his horse
and gave the command to move out. The cavalry escort shot ahead, but one
horseman carrying the headquarters colors, a red pennant with 'A.N.V.' in
black letters, rode alongside the ambulance.

The escort used their sabers and horse pistols on more than one occasion to
clear the road for the ambulance, but even amid the stink of a rout, the name of
Lee brought the men around. At the intersection of the Cashtown Road, they
found 'Grumble' Jones and his brigade. Jones was frantically trying to find out
what had happened, as Colonel Marshall rode up to him and explained. Jones
was stunned for a moment, then came out of it swearing that if Marshall could
get Lee home through the mountains, he would stay and hold the road open for
the rest of the army. 'But take a company of my "Bloody Sixth" along with you,
Marshall. You will need someone to strong-arm your way through.' Without
waiting for a reply, he turned to Colonel Flournoy and put Lee's safety into his
hands. He then ordered the 11th Virginia to close the road long enough for
Lee's ambulance and escort to move quickly ahead.

In Fairfield the ambulance stopped at the Lutheran Church used as a field
hospital. The doctor jumped out and ran inside to beg for any morphine they
might have. The trip through the mountains would be long and difficult, and
before long the dose keeping Lee's pain under control would wear off. The word
spread immediately that it was Lee in the ambulance outside, and the doorway
was quickly filled with the walking wounded, Confederates and Yankees alike,
talking in hushed voices. The doctor ran out, distressed at the failure of his
search, and the ambulance and escort moved out.

Somewhere hours later on the leafy mountain road to Waynesboro, the little
column was ambushed. A volley from the woods emptied saddles and threw the
ambulance driver from his seat. With a shout a hundred Yankee cavalrymen
swept out of the trees with saber and pistol. The road became a shambles of
rearing horses, shouting men, gunfire, the ring of blade on blade. Captain
Dahlgren was in the middle of the melee on the right, exchanging saber blows
with a trooper in gray. He beat down the man's guard and drove the saber
under his arm; the man's horse leaped forward, carrying him off.

As two Union troopers rode up to seize the bridles of the lead pair in the
ambulance team, Tom Faulkner's mount leapt forward like a shot, crashing

into another enemy who was trying to climb into the ambulance. The man fell under the hooves of Tom's horse with a shriek. Faulkner did not even pause, but kept his eyes on the two men at the head of the team. One was dead, shot through the forehead, before he noticed the Virginian horseman was even upon him. The other tried to raise his saber but was off-balanced by trying to hold on to the team, and fell backward over the rump of his own horse as Faulkner fired twice more.

Faulkner's brothers had raced up behind him, and kept a Union squad off the ambulance in a swirl of sabers as, without pausing, he stood up on his saddle and jumped onto the ambulance seat, grabbing the reins. He could see how the enemy had momentarily drifted away from the road just ahead. Major Marshall rode up to him, sword drawn, shouting, 'Get it out! For God's sake!' There was just a chance.

Then the lead horse in the team reared, shot in the chest, and fell kicking in the traces, driving the other animals into a panic. Faulkner shouted in rage. Dahlgren, meanwhile, had taken the scene in quickly. The fight had shrunk to a desperate circle around the ambulance, and he could see that many of the defenders were well-dressed officers in fine gray uniforms and braid. His eyes widened to see the red pennant waving above the ambulance. 'Cease fire! Cease fire!' he shouted. The noise died away, both sides staring hard at each other, waiting for someone to take charge. Clearly the Confederates were surrounded and not likely to get out.

Dahlgren walked his horse up to the senior officer, and saluted with his bloody saber. 'Captain Ulric Dahlgren, of General Meade's staff. You are my prisoner, Major.'

Everything rebelled in Marshall at this last humiliation, everything but duty. In a moment he had mastered himself and returned the salute. 'Captain, I have the honor to be the Aide-de-Camp to General Robert E. Lee, Commander of the Army of Northern Virginia.' He briefly studied this young man, who appeared in every aspect to be a gentlemen, and was quietly relieved. 'I am, of course, your prisoner, Captain, but I must inform you, that today I am the least of your prisoners.' Dahlgren looked puzzled. 'You have captured Robert E. Lee as well.' [3]

---

[3]* Ulric Dahlgren, *The Capture of Robert E. Lee* (D. Appleton, New York, 1868), p. 186.

Battles and controversies

All great battles generate great controversies. Given the high stakes represented by these battles and the play of chance, character, and competence, this is inevitable. It holds true from Kadesh to Desert Storm. Waterloo is probably the most well-worn of all in this regard, and the Normandy Campaign is another more recent example, which draws a response not only from historians but among survivors of the action. Gettysburg was such a battle. Few would argue that it was one of history's decisive battle, or that it vies with Waterloo in the power of the controversies that continue to swirl around it. Both battles share the aura of national epics. Interest in them is tireless, much as the *Iliad* enthralled the Greeks for centuries and continues to enthral their modern descendants, as well as their cultural heirs now broadcast around the world.

It is especially the controversies that prick and tease the imagination. 'What if?' is the endlessly-argued question. Gettysburg is particularly rich in these dramas. The battle was not only one on which trembled the fate of American civilization, but much of world history as well. Had the Confederacy triumphed, it is highly unlikely that any of the fragments of the old Union would have been able to decisively intervene in the great struggles for freedom in the next century.

The controversies surrounding Gettysburg are particularly tantalising. They often reflect a sudden departure from the past behavior and experiences of both armies. The Army of Northern Virginia had rolled from victory to victory because of superior generalship, the high levels of ability and initiative, and the overall combativeness of officers and men at all levels. If ever there was an army that marched to the sound of the guns it was Lee's. But at Gettysburg, everything seemed to go wrong. Lee was not at his best and had not had time to adjust to a new command style required by different personalities. Initiative and co-operation among subordinates was not at its previous high levels. Chance also seemed to be against the Army of Northern Virginia, as Shelby Foote has observed: 'Even the Stars in their courses seemed to conspire against Lee.' Stars, perhaps not, but certainly the Army of the Potomac did its best to thwart Lee, and for once everything seemed to come together to produce a winning Union team. Under new, competent, and rational leadership by General Meade, the Army was handled well, really for the first time. The high quality of officers and men which had been masked by their leadership was now able to come to the fore. However, the immense disparity of the armies after Chancellorsville meant that the general lowering of the capabilities of Lee's army and the raising of that of Meade's probably brought them much to the same overall level of effectiveness.

It was on the knife's edge of this unstable balance that the opportunity for alternative events was so possible. The scope for a slight shift in even a few of these wobbly situations was enormous. I explored the consequences of such a scenario in *Disaster at D-Day* (Greenhill, 1994). In that account of the Normandy Campaign, a few small, highly plausible changes ricocheted through the campaign, altering events exponentially so that the outcome was the opposite of what really occurred. The unstable situations in the Gettysburg Campaign were, in many ways, more delicate and numerous because both sides were so evenly matched. This book has been an attempt to rationally explore what changes might have occurred and then track their geometric rate of change in the situation, producing in the end a different outcome.

The first of these controversies was the one surrounding Stuart's arrival at the close of the second day of the battle. By 30th June, Lee had become so concerned about Stuart's absence that he directed Early to try and make contact with him. Early returned from York and heard the sound of the fighting around Hanover between Stuart and Kilpatrick but did not investigate. Had he done so, Stuart might have arrived much earlier and been able to influence the second day of fighting.

This, in turn, could have influenced probably the greatest single controversy of the battle – the tension between Lee and Longstreet on the nature of the campaign: was the strategic offensive to be coupled with the tactical offensive or tactical defensive? This issue began to smoulder at around five o'clock in the evening on 1st July, when Longstreet arrived on the field. This took the form of Longstreet's insistence, at that point, that Meade should be maneuvered out of position rather than directly assaulted. Lee, on the other hand, felt he had no choice but to defeat Meade on the field of Gettysburg because, without Stuart as the eyes of the army, he did not feel confident about the risk such maneuver would entail. With Stuart available a day earlier and able to conduct the reconnaissance that would push back the surrounding operational darkness, Lee may well have looked upon Longstreet's proposal more favorably. Had he done so, the nature of the battle on the second day would have changed dramatically.

A third controversy revolves around the poorly co-ordinated and understrength attack on the third day. The changes in the second day's fighting would have influenced the perceptions of the requirements for the third day's operations. In this case, Longstreet's recognition that his plan of the second day had failed leads to his enthusiastic support for Lee's plan for a much larger frontal assault on the third day. And that idea came from Lee's recognition that the poorly co-ordinated and piecemeal attacks had dissipated their strength. A single, massive attack across the valley from Gettysburg to Little Round Top would prevent Meade form rushing reserves to any one spot when every spot was equally threatened at the same time. Longstreet's recognition of the change wrought upon tactics by the killing power of modern weapons is tempered by his conclusion that this attack might well succeed if it is properly organized, supported, and conducted – and he is the man to do it. Of course, this would also redeem his failure on the second day. Success would have been worth the horrendous cost if it was to be the stroke that looked as if it would end the war.

At the same time, Lee's commitment to an attack by over 30,000 men puts the army at great risk should the attack fail. The risk would have come from the threat of a strong Union counter-stroke. Meade apparently was not the man to seize such an opportunity when the enemy recoiled. Someone like Hancock, who had an instinctive feel for the main chance, was far more likely to have attempted such a counter-stroke and done it well! That missed opportunity, I believe, was the greatest 'What if?' of Gettysburg.

For the briefest of moments, Nike extended the victory wreath to the Army of the Potomac, and then it was gone. It was not the offer of a defensive victory but a total one, the greatest of rarities on a Civil War battlefield. A bold counter-attack into the broken and exhausted center of Lee's army had an excellent chance of shattering it completely. The wings at the ends of a long arc would have been driven in opposite directions to be crushed one at a time. The path to Richmond would have been open. The Confederacy could not have replaced the Army of Northern Virginia, and without that mighty host, the South could not have sustained the war. The country would surely have been spared the great bloodletting and destruction of the final two years of conflict. With the wells of bitterness not sunk so deep, national reconciliation may well have been far easier, and the lingering ghosts of the struggle allowed to rest.

A note on the Footnotes

As the reader will have realized – hopefully – there are a number of fictional footnotes in the story. These are denoted by an asterisk placed after the footnote number. The purpose of fictionalising footnotes is to give the reader a sense of a thoroughly integrated alternate history that would have generated its own literature. For example, if the Civil War ends in 1863 as the reader may assume by the end of the book, then a title for a primary source such as Longstreet's *From Manassas to Appomattox* (J.B. Lippincott, Philadelphia, 1896) may seem wildly out of place. After all, the surrender at Appomattox occurred two years later, in 1865. Had the war ended shortly after Gettysburg, Longstreet might well have written *From Manassas to Gettysburg* instead. Other works cited are by those figures who survived the Gettysburg Campaign, such as Ulric Dahlgren. In order to create a forum for the post-war discussion and argument of issues, I have created a fictitious journal, rather than ascribe such contributions to actual historical journals such as the *Southern Historical Society Papers (SHSP)*. I have entitled it *The Military Annals of the Confederacy (MAC)*.